# WORLD WAR II

WEST
SIDE
PUBLISHING

# CONTENTS

✯ ✯ ✯

# INTRODUCTION

✮ ✮ ✮

**Armchair Reader™:** *World War II* has been a labor of love for us at the Armchair Reader editorial offices. Many of us have had a longtime fascination with this brief but epic interlude in human history. The conflict left marks that will never fade.

We wanted to present the greatest variety of topics possible. We didn't ignore the battles, bombings, and politics of the time, but we made a special point to focus on the personalities, reveal the intriguing and often overlooked details of the war, and bring to light some of the little-known human stories.

Here are some of the riveting tales you'll find inside:

- Survivors' accounts of the London Blitz
- Russia's most ruthless hero
- *Kamikaze* terror
- The Port Chicago mutiny
- Hitler's women
- And much, much more

Once you get into **Armchair Reader™:** *World War II,* you'll find it hard to put down. You need not start at the beginning, either—we designed the book to be enjoyed no matter where you open it.

*Allen Orso*

Allen Orso
Publisher

P.S. If you have thoughts, questions, or ideas concerning this book, or if you would like more information about our other West Side Publishing titles, please contact us at **www.armchairreader.com.**

# IMPORTED NAZIS GET LITTLE TRACTION: THE BRIEF LIFE OF THE GERMAN-AMERICAN BUND

*Hitler's feeble attempt to launch Nazism in the United States was a dud that did more harm than good for Germany's cause.*

When Adolf Hitler became Chancellor of the German Reich in 1933, he wanted to remain friendly, or at least neutral, with the United States, lest it become a major obstacle to his plans for conquest. To further that cause, Hitler's deputy Rudolf Hess directed a Nazi operative named Fritz Spanknöbel to consolidate various U.S.-based Nazi splinter groups into the Friends of New Germany (FNG). Its membership reached about 10,000 people at its peak, mainly German nationals and recently naturalized German-Americans. Its primary base was in New York City, and it had outposts in other large cities.

The FNG spent the next several years railing against Jews and Communists. New York's Jewish community responded with boycotts of nearby German-owned shops, and a Jewish congressman began investigating this new organization. Even in the established German-American community, the FNG gained few followers and scrambled to make ends meet during the Depression. In March 1936, hoping to reach a broader base, Berlin installed Fritz Kuhn, a naturalized U.S. citizen, as head of the renamed German-American Bund. Kuhn learned where he stood in the Nazi hierarchy when he attended the 1936 Berlin Olympics and barely managed to meet Hitler. Undaunted, Kuhn promptly returned home and announced that Hitler had named him "America's *Führer.*"

As war clouds darkened over Europe, Kuhn's Bund raised its profile with events and inflated assertions. Rumors circulated that the Bund had hundred of thousands of fanatical members, when in fact it hadn't grown much since the FNG days. During the summers of 1936–39, Bundists and sympathizers gathered at Camp Siegfried on Long Island to camp, drink beer, sing Nazi anthems, and raise money for Germany.

Yet all was not well with the Bund. Hans Dieckhoff, the German Ambassador to the United States, complained to Berlin that Kuhn was "stupid, noisy and absurd"—and doing more harm than good. The ambassador's complaints were grounded in his understanding of Americans. In American culture, immigrants were expected to shut up, learn English, fly the Stars and Stripes, work hard, and adopt American moral standards. Kuhn was loud, spoke terrible English, flew the Nazi flag, spent his days preaching racial antipathy, drank a lot, and openly consorted with a variety of single and married women. Berlin ordered Kuhn to cease using Nazi symbols and accepting non-U.S. citizens; Kuhn ignored the mandates.

The Bund's most visible moment came in February 1939 when it held a massive rally in Madison Square Garden. Nazi and U.S. flags hung from the walls along with a huge portrait of George Washington. At one point during Kuhn's oration, an enraged Jewish plumber tried to storm the stage and was wrestled down by Bund security men, but most attendees had come to *"Heil"* rather than heckle. Newsreel footage of the event shocked America. Many Americans had seen films of huge Nazi rallies set in Germany—but never before in New York.

Far from sparking a surge of American Fascism, the Garden rally ignited legal troubles that would soon destroy the German-American Bund. Manhattan District Attorney Thomas Dewey began investigating Kuhn and his Bund, and by May 1939 had sufficient evidence to indict Kuhn for grand larceny and forgery. In the meantime, the state government unleashed another devastating weapon by revoking Camp Siegfried's liquor license. By the time Kuhn entered New York's Sing Sing prison in December 1939, war had broken out in Europe and Camp Siegfried was an empty memory.

When the military draft began in 1940, the remnant Bund encouraged its members to evade conscription. The FBI had watched the Bund all throughout the thirties, and now had clear evidence of illegal activity. After August 1940, alien residents had to register at the nearest U.S. Post Office, including 315,000 German nationals from whose ranks most Bundists had come. With Germany's declaration of war on the United States shortly after Pearl Harbor, the U.S. government outlawed the Bund and locked up most of its current and former members, 10,905 in all. Kuhn's naturalization was revoked in prison. After the war he was deported to the new Federal Republic of Germany to stand trial for wartime Nazi activities. A broken man who never saw himself as a wrongdoer, Fritz Kuhn died December 14, 1951.

What did the Bund accomplish? For the Nazis, it mostly caused setbacks. It did prompt loyal German-Americans and resident German nationals to demonstrate their loyalty and raise money for the German war effort. But it also helped convince the FBI to arrest and intern every Nazi sympathizer who might work against Allied interests. Its vocal presence in New York City helped raise awareness of the Nazis' true feelings toward Jews. And its final decline lowered Nazi prestige in American eyes. The Nazi seed in the United States, sown on the New York City pavement, bore no fruit worth harvesting.

✯　　✯　　✯

- *The United States hadn't quite heard the last of Camp Siegfried. During the war, a few German saboteurs landed by U-boat on the New England coast. They were rounded up quickly, before causing any damage. It was discovered that the men had previously participated in events at Camp Siegfried.*

✯　　✯　　✯

- *Maginot Line duty was a cozy existence for the troops. It included housing, miniature railways to transport ammo and supplies, air-conditioning and heating, and even theaters, hot showers, and chapels.*

# THE *URITSKY*

*The huge* Kido Butai, *or Japanese Attack Force, steamed across the Pacific to attack Pearl Harbor. One ship saw the fleet before it reached Hawaii, but the U.S. military was never notified.*

In late 1941, the *Uritsky,* a medium-size Russian transport ship, waited while desperately needed American-built M2 medium tanks were loaded aboard. On November 28, the *Uritsky* departed on its vital mission for Vladivostok, Russia.

The Soviets knew the Japanese fleet was maneuvering in the North Pacific, and reportedly notified the Japanese of the route *Uritsky* intended to travel. They made it clear that Russia would declare war if the Japanese fleet sank *Uritsky.* However, they also promised they wouldn't report any activity they may see.

Admiral Chuichi Nagumo, commander of the Japanese fleet, had previously ordered any vessel flying a foreign flag to be sunk; *Uritsky's* crew knew their trip carried a high risk.

As the sun rose on December 5, the skipper of the *Uritsky* found he had sailed into the thick of aircraft carriers and escorts of the Japanese task force preparing to attack Pearl Harbor. The warships trained their guns on the lone transport.

A Russian crewman or two may have smiled and waved; otherwise, the *Uritsky* steamed on past the flotilla without a peep. Even many miles out of range of the *Kido Butai,* the transport kept its telegraph key locked down.

The *Uritsy's* crew said nothing of its encounter with the Japanese fleet. Some believe the Soviets stayed quiet to avoid another confrontation with Japan, as the nations had recently signed a treaty. Others have speculated that Russia expected to benefit from the United States entering the war, and thus stayed quiet to ensure America would have no choice but to join the escalating conflict.

# Fast Facts

- In August 1942, Admiral Karl Dönitz, commander of the Kriegsmarine U-boat arm, made a colossal political mistake. In search of easier sinkings, he sent a U-boat squadron to the coast of Brazil—a nation friendly to the Allies but still officially neutral. The U-boats sank five Brazilian ships, just off Bahia, in one day. While these were not the first U-boat sinkings of Brazilian vessels, they were the most brazen. Crowds rioted in Rio de Janeiro, venting rage on Nazi flags and German-owned businesses. On August 22, 1942, Brazil declared war on the Axis.

- Eighteen-year-old Private Guy Gabaldon learned enough street Japanese growing up in Los Angeles to be conversant in the language. With that skill, he put his life at great risk to talk to 1,500 Japanese soldiers and civilians surrendering to him on Saipan. He was awarded the Navy Cross and put in line for the Medal of Honor.

- On September 12, 1942, a U-boat sunk Laconia, a British liner traveling near Ascension Island in the South Atlantic. To the horror of the U-boat crew, some 1,500 Italian POWs were among the victims.

- As Washington closed its books for the 1943 fiscal year, it was revealed that 93 percent of the federal budget was allocated to national defense spending.

- In World War I, Germany had owned a deep-water navy that rivaled Britain's, but much of it had been interned by the Allies and scuttled by German crews.

- Lieutenant Colonel Lewis "Chesty" Puller was the definition of an "Old Breed" Marine. The first time he saw a demonstration of the flamethrower, Puller asked: "Where do you put the bayonet on the damned thing?"

- During one phase of the battle for Iwo Jima, U.S. forces expended 10,000 gallons of flamethrower fuel every day.

# "THIS . . . IS LONDON!"
# OLD-SCHOOL EMBEDDED
# REPORTING

*Edward R. Murrow and William Shirer, the CBS News broadcasting team, took separate European beats, and created the lasting standard for live broadcast journalism during World War II.*

When the first AM radio broadcast aired in 1906, forward-thinking listeners knew that the new medium would transform lives. By 1922, 600 radio stations were operating in the United States, and that number continued to increase as more households bought receivers. For the most part, radio shows were programmed, featuring music, sporting events, stories, news updates, and weather. The medium had seemed to reach a plateau in the 1930s, until a pioneer named Edward R. Murrow revolutionized radio journalism.

## THE NEW VOICE OF RADIO

Murrow grew up in a small town in Washington state and attended Washington State College, majoring in speech. He moved to New York after graduation, and in 1935 began planning radio broadcasts for CBS (Columbia Broadcasting System).

In 1937, Murrow got a big break: CBS needed a new European director in London, and he got the job. With tensions in Europe growing by the day (Nazi Germany had reoccupied the Rhineland, and Britain and France were trying to preserve European peace), CBS would need a voice from the European continent, to report on daily life and local culture. Hearing that seasoned European hand William Shirer was seeking work, Murrow made his pitch over dinner. While talking, the men arrived at the question, "Why report news after the fact? Why not report it from the scene?" Their thinking brought a whole new dimension to radio journalism.

In 1938, Murrow almost missed his chance for a stellar live broadcast. Just before Hitler's troops moved in to annex Austria, Murrow and Shirer were covering a series of children's choirs throughout eastern and central Europe. Murrow chartered a plane and arrived in Vienna to broadcast the *Anschlüss*.

## RADIO NEWS GETS A NEW FORMAT

Realizing the power of live broadcasts, CBS chief executive Bill Paley ordered his staff to broadcast for a half hour live each night. Murrow and Shirer were thrilled, and the news was fresh and authentic.

The new format, daily news broadcasts from multiple locations with analysis and commentary to follow, would outlast the war. CBS had set the broadcasting standard. As the situation across the world intensified, ears perked up. You couldn't easily get the *New York Times* on a Dakota wheat farm, but your whole family could hear history unfold on your farmhouse radio—and Ed Murrow's team would help you understand what you heard.

The coverage was raw and authentic. Murrow broadcasted from London rooftops during the Blitz with bomb explosions in the background: "This...is London!" One observer noted that although Blitz newsreel footage was in black and white, "Ed's radio reports were in color." He went on bombing raids over Germany, recording them for later broadcast. The CBS news staff expanded to include many talented reporters, nicknamed "Murrow's Boys," all characterized by descriptive skill, intelligence, and guts.

Murrow chose his words carefully and revealed emotion in his broadcasts. One of his most powerful moments on the air came as the U.S. Army liberated the Buchenwald concentration camp:

"Murder had been done at Buchenwald. God alone knows how many men and boys have died there during the last 12 years. Thursday, I was told that there were more than 20,000 in the camp. There had been as many as 60,000. Where are they now?

"I pray you to believe what I have said about Buchenwald. I have reported what I saw and heard, but only part of it. For most of it, I have no words. If I have offended you by this rather mild account of Buchenwald, I'm not in the least sorry."

After the war, the partnership of Paley, Murrow, and Shirer would break up over various disputes, notably Paley's postwar commitment to television. Murrow left CBS in 1961 and died in 1965 of lung cancer. Paley remained a towering figure among media executives until his passing in 1990. As for William Shirer, he gained particular fame for broadcasting from Berlin into autumn 1940, bringing Americans a powerfully honest perspective from Nazi Germany. Later he would write best-selling books based upon his experiences, notably *The Rise and Fall of the Third Reich*. Shirer died in 1993.

☆　☆　☆

- *During Hitler's early years, Murrow spent much of his time helping German scholars—Jewish and non-Jewish—escape persecution and find positions at U.S. universities.*

☆　☆　☆

- *Murrow didn't merely embellish his resumé to get hired at CBS; it was composed of out-and-out lies. He changed his major, added five years to his age, and awarded himself a Master's degree from Stanford.*

☆　☆　☆

- *The clincher for Murrow in hiring Shirer was that Murrow's chief rival hack at CBS New York, Paul White, couldn't stand the sound of Shirer's voice. Deciding that anyone Paul White hated had to be all right, Murrow offered Shirer the job on the spot.*

☆　☆　☆

- *One of "Murrow's Boys" was Mary Marvin Breckenridge, CBS's first female newscaster.*

☆　☆　☆

- *The original title of* Mein Kampf (My Struggle) *was* Four Years of Struggle Against Lies, Stupidity, and Cowardice.

# FROM LUCK AND LIGHT TO DOOM AND BLIGHT: THE SWASTIKA'S JOURNEY

*The simple, mesmerizing elegance of the swastika lends itself to curves, serifs, and any other artistic touch one might add. If not for the Nazis, one might call it beautiful.*

The hooked cross we know as the swastika is an ancient symbol recurring throughout history in so many contexts that it's impossible to pinpoint its origin in a single era or region. The term "swastika" is derived from the Sanskrit words *su* and *asti,* meaning "it is well" or "well-being." Hindus and Buddhists have long associated the symbol with good fortune, long life, and success. When ancient Troy was rediscovered, artifacts in its ruins bore the swastika, common in Greek culture for many centuries as the *tetraskele.* Several Native American peoples across the Americas have used it, either for decoration or to symbolize the four directions. The Ashanti, Africans in what became Ghana, marked golden weights with the swastika. The ancient Norse—a source of much cultural inspiration to the Nazis—carved swastikas in stone as the whirling might of will symbolized by the sun.

Circa 1920, most people in Europe knew the swastika as a good-luck sign. It was a pleasant touch added to artwork or design. In America, the symbol adorned poker chips, children's books, and board games. Adolf Hitler's infant Nazi Party adopted the swastika in 1920. Within 15 years it went from the symbol of a few radicals to the emblem of a cataclysmic mass movement. Why did Hitler choose it?

In 1920, a Party dentist brought Hitler a sample flag in red, white, and black depicting the swastika. Hitler made some careful modifications, and the swastika was adopted to symbolize the Nazi Party. Hitler briefly mentions what the symbol meant to him in *Mein Kampf:*

## Swastikas on Display Today

*Yuma, Arizona, United States.* Americans decorated the Laguna Diversion Dam with swastikas in the early 1900s; it may have been a nod to Native American traditions, or perhaps an architect thought it looked neat. Though vandalized, the swastikas remain visible at this writing.

*Dar-es-Salaam, Tanzania.* Some buildings are decorated with repeated swastikas, most likely due to centuries of Hindu influence on this ancient Indian Ocean island port.

*Lantau Island, Hong Kong, China.* A large Buddha statue displayed here bears a swastika on its breastbone. Swastikas remain a common ornament on Buddhas throughout the world, especially in Asia.

*Swastika, Ontario, Canada.* Founded in 1908, this northern mining town sits near the Québec boundary. It was named for the Swastika Gold Mine at a time when the swastika was just a good-luck symbol. One place the swastika *isn't* on display: The modern Federal Republic of Germany. Flying a swastika flag in Germany is a serious crime. Even World War II computer games marketed in Germany may not depict it.

"Not only because it incorporated those revered colours expressive of our homage to the glorious past and which once brought so much honour to the German nation, but this symbol was also an eloquent expression of the will behind the movement. We National Socialists regarded our flag as being the embodiment of our party programme. The red expressed the social thought underlying the movement. White the national thought. And the swastika signified the mission allotted to us—the struggle for the victory of Aryan mankind and at the same time the triumph of the ideal of creative work which is in itself and always will be anti-Semitic."

The national flag that so prominently represented Germany during Word War II was adopted on September 15, 1935, and variations were adapted for government and military organizations.

The Nazis tarnished the ancient symbol; it has become synonymous with hatred. But in other countries, the swastika is a religious and cultural symbol still used in festivals and ceremonies.

# THE NORDEN BOMBSIGHT

*Civilian populations in some areas may have been spared during the war due to the tinkering of a humble engineer.*

In 1920, Dutch immigrant Carl Norden began working on an advanced bombsight for the U.S. Navy. Two years later, he partnered with Theodore Barth, and during the next four years the team designed and built a bombsight from locations in both the United States and Switzerland. The firm incorporated in 1928 and finished a revolutionary bombsight the same year. Its key feature was a timing mechanism that indicated when the bombardier should release his payload.

Norden demonstrated his bombsight's capabilities in 1931 to senior Navy personnel, who were duly impressed and placed a contract for 40 sights. The Army Air Corps also placed an order. In 1935, the Air Corps tested the new bombsights, which had been installed on B-10 bombers: By the end of testing, bombardiers were able to drop 50 percent of their bombs within just 75 feet of their targets.

## HOW DID IT WORK?

The Norden bombsight was a complex piece of equipment consisting of an analog computer, gyros, levels, mirrors, electric motors, and a small telescope. The final version, the Mark XV, comprised more than 2,000 individual components.

Approximately 30 to 45 minutes before reaching the target, the bombardier would run through a series of precise, carefully predetermined functions to prepare the bombsight for use. He would input altitude, airspeed, wind speed, and the angle of drift into the bombsight's computer, which then calculated both the trajectory of the bombs and the exact time the payload should be released.

Antiaircraft fire and weather conditions severely decreased the accuracy of the bombsight. To help counter these adverse conditions, Norden had a hand (Minneapolis-Honeywell was also involved) in the invention of an automatic pilot, which worked in conjunction with the sight. The autopilot helped reduce turbulence and overcontrol by anxious pilots, which increased the accuracy of the sight.

The actual bombing run began when the airplane reached a point specified at the preflight briefing. The bombardier then ran through a series of final steps that began with aligning the vertical and horizontal cross hairs on the target and ended with the bomber's auto-pilot engaging and the bombs dropping.

## THE BOMBSIGHT BECOMES A MUST-HAVE

Norden's factory had prewar production capabilities of about 800 bombsights per month. After the Japanese attack on Pearl Harbor, Norden factories began producing some 2,000 units per month. By the fall of 1945, more than 43,000 sights had been manufactured.

Norden was paid just $250 for his bombsight. In the spirit of patriotism typical of the times, he sold the rights to his invention to the U.S. government for just one dollar more. Norden was satisfied with the fact that his invention enabled the military to more accurately strike targets, thus minimizing the collateral damage done to civilian populations.

✯  ✯  ✯

- *Despite the bombsight's secret classification, the* Luftwaffe *obtained plans for the device two years before Germany invaded Poland. In 1937, a Norden employee received $3,000 from the Germans for stolen plans. The employee was eventually caught and jailed for 18 years.*

✯  ✯  ✯

- *The last wartime use of the sight occurred during the Vietnam War, when members of Observation Squadron 67 used the sight to help them drop sensors on the typically well-connected Ho Chi Minh trail.*

# SIR OSWALD MOSLEY AND THE BRITISH UNION OF FASCISTS

*Selected as the "Twentieth Century's Worst Briton" by the BBC, Oswald Mosley was a fiery orator and man of genius who could not be deterred from promoting his Fascist political platform.*

Oswald Mosley was a shining star of Britain's political arena: Born in 1896 into Anglo-Irish wealth, an international fencing champion, an injured veteran of the First World War, and the youngest sitting member of Parliament (elected at age 22), he quickly gained a reputation as a powerful public orator whose extemporaneous speeches (he refused to use notes) espoused an isolationist, pro-England, pro-tariff platform. He was reputed to be an arrogant man unafraid of controversy and dedicated to bold, swift action.

Soon after Mosley's election to Parliament, he resigned from the Conservative Party in protest of its violent repression of Irish Nationalism. The young baronet served out his remaining term as an Independent. He then joined Labour in 1924, but left that party as well when his friend, Ramsay MacDonald, the newly elected Prime Minister, gave Mosley the lowly post of Chancellor of the Duchy of Lancaster. As Chancellor, Mosley helped the Lord Privy Seal address the county's enormous unemployment woes and developed a series of radical proposals that called for high tariffs, industrial nationalization, and a wide-sweeping program of public works similar to what FDR would institute in the United States with the New Deal. When it became obvious that none of his proposals would pass Parliament, Mosley resigned from the government and founded the short-lived New Party.

In 1930, Fascism was on the rise in Spain, Germany, and Italy. Angry and disillusioned by his recent political defeat, Mosley traveled to Italy and observed Mussolini's government firsthand. Inspired by what he saw, Mosley returned to England in 1932 and founded the British Union of Fascists (BUF); an organization that drew 40,000 members and whose rallies were a lightning rod for protests and violence. Mosley soon organized what was intended to be a security force: Known as "the blackshirts," they usually caused most of the violence they were supposed to prevent. In October 1936, a BUF march disintegrated into street fighting sparked by clashes between police protecting the marchers and protestors who had traveled from all over England.

Mosley was convinced that England had too many problems of its own to become involved in a European war. As war with Germany became increasingly probable, the BUF backed candidates on the noninvolvement platform of "Mind Britain's Business." Mosley even went so far as to blame an international Jewish economic conspiracy for starting the war. On several occasions he was nearly assaulted in the street by angry British citizens.

After England entered the war, Mosley and his wife were imprisoned under the emergency Defense Regulations. In truth, Mosley's internment was more of a vacation than a punishment. He and his wife lived together in a small cottage on the grounds of Holloway prison; during his three years of confinement, Mosley passed the time by researching classical civilizations. He was released for medical reasons in 1943.

After the war, Mosley's supporters urged him to return to politics, and he organized the Union Movement. Mosley watched closely as England and Europe began to recover from the war, and he began calling for an all-encompassing European nation that would be in a much stronger position in a world increasingly dominated by the United States and the Soviet Union. Disorder and violence reigned at the Union Movement's meetings, and Mosley, still convinced that his vision was true, relocated to France. Upon his departure he famously said, "You don't clear up a dungheap from underneath it."

Oswald Mosley lived to be an old man. He continued to advocate for a united Europe throughout his life and anticipated the political wars of the latter twentieth century. Commenting on the nature of the new generation of wars he saw coming, he said, "It will then certainly be found that to win a war which is basically a war of ideas it is necessary first to have ideas."

To some he was a clear-headed visionary who predicted the European Union, the war on terrorism, and the postmodern international economy; to others he was an embarrassment. If nothing else can be said of Oswald Mosley, he was most certainly a man who lived by his ideas, however unpopular.

☆  ☆  ☆

- *Oswald Mosley's personal life was no less colorful than his political career. His first wife was Lady Cynthia Curzon, the daughter of the former Viceroy of India. Many people, including Cynthia's father, suspected that Mosley married into the prominent family for political advancement. Mosley was conspicuously unfaithful to his wife; a trend that continued his entire life. During his marriage to Cynthia, Mosley had affairs with both her sister and stepmother. When Cynthia died, Mosley married his mistress, Diana Mitford, also the daughter of a prominent and wealthy family. Diana was an admirer of Nazi Germany and claimed that Hitler had "mesmeric eyes." Oswald and Diana were married at a small ceremony in Germany that was attended by Joseph Goebbels and Adolf Hitler.*

☆  ☆  ☆

- *British wit P.G. Wodehouse lampooned Mosley in one of his Jeeves/Bertie Wooster novels,* The Code of the Woosters. *In Wodehouse's take on privilege and political posturing, Mosley became the demagogue Sir Roderick Spode, founder of the Fascist "Black Shorts."*

☆  ☆  ☆

- *After the liberation and war's end, France resumed use of the Maginot Line. Only when France developed a nuclear deterrent was it finally decommissioned. Much of it is now a tourist attraction.*

# THE MAGINOT LINE: WINNING THE PREVIOUS WAR

*France built the Maginot Line in order to win another World War I. Unfortunately for the French, Germany did not plan to refight World War I.*

Which illustrious general said,
"The side which stays within its fortifications is beaten"?

Answer: Napoleon Bonaparte, Emperor of France

To understand why France built the Maginot Line, review the French World War I experience: France hosted nearly the entire Western Front, with six million soldiers killed, wounded, or captured. French generals concluded that modern defense was stronger than modern offense. "Next time," reasoned French generals, "we will inflict rather than suffer those losses."

From 1930 on, France spent vast sums blanketing its German and Luxembourg frontiers with a network of steel and concrete fortifications. A much lesser version extended along the Belgian frontier to the English Channel. People named it the Maginot Line for the French Minister of Defense who spearheaded it, André Maginot.

## A DEFENSIVE MASTERPIECE

The Line was no modern Great Wall, but a series of mutually supportive fortifications. Let's tour a section to get a clear image.

Picture a verdant hill topped by an armored observation post, studded with concrete bunkers and steel turrets, flanked by lesser forts and pillboxes. Interlocking fields of fire take excellent defensive advantage of all terrain. In places the concrete is ten feet thick. Out front are tank traps and wire. In the distance to each side you can see another hill with similar defenses; interval casemates lie between. Indoors, several stories of tunnels connect the various bastions like the roots of a gigantic tree. Ammunition elevators and railways move ammo to the guns and the wounded to a modern sickbay.

One thousand men defend this clean, modern fort complex, called an *ouvrage*. No more gas attacks; no more muddy, filthy trenches. Artillery can (and would, in one case) shell it all day without effect. The Maginot Line contained 44 large *ouvrages*, 58 small *ouvrages*, and 360 interval casemates.

## A HUGE BLOW TO FRANCE

German generals saw no reason to assail the Line: A quick and violent strike through the Netherlands and Belgium would enable Germany's mobile advance guard to bite deep into France north of the *ouvrages*, aided by close air support. The infantry, using standard tactics, would follow to occupy, consolidate, and control.

The strategy worked to perfection. On May 10, 1940, Germany tore into the Low Countries, quickly breaking into France well north of the *ouvrages* at Sedan. A minor German covering force tied down the 36 divisions defending the Line. Forty-six days later France surrendered.

All the Maginot Line did was encourage the Germans to find an easier place to invade.

🌟　　🌟　　🌟

- *Perhaps it was a mercy that Maginot himself did not live to see what became of his defensive line and his nation. He died in 1932, of typhoid caused by contaminated oysters.*

🌟　　🌟　　🌟

- *Germany did attack the Maginot Line during the French Campaign, but only halfheartedly, to make sure significant forces stayed holed up in the* ouvrages.

🌟　　🌟　　🌟

- *Mushroom farms now occupy portions of the line.*

# Timeline

## 1931
Japan invades Manchuria in Northern China, establishing a protectorate region it will rename Manzhouguo

## 1932
**November 8**
Franklin Delano Roosevelt is elected the 32nd U.S. president

## 1933
**January 30**
Adolf Hitler becomes chancellor of Germany

**March 20**
Heinrich Himmler establishes the Dachau concentration camp for political prisoners

**April 1**
Hitler orders a boycott of Jewish-owned businesses

**July 14**
All political parties except the Nazi party are outlawed in Germany

## 1934
**June 30**
At least 77 and perhaps as many as 400 people are killed during the "Night of the Long Knives," a purge ordered by the Nazi party to secure Hitler's position

**August**
Hitler officially becomes Der Führer, a combination of chancellor and president

## 1935
**August 31**
Roosevelt signs the U.S. Neutrality Act

**September**
The Nazi party adopts the swastika for its national flag

## 1937
**December**
Japanese troops pillage the Chinese Nationalist capital, Nanking, murdering 250,000 civilians in what would later be known as the Rape of Nanking

## 1938
**March 12**
The Anschlüss (annexation) of Austria; many Austrians welcome the German soldiers

**November 9–10**
Nazi troops engage in Kristallnacht ("Night of the Broken Glass"), a night of terror against Germany's Jewish population. More than 1,000 shops and synagogues are destroyed, 20,000 Jews are arrested, and nearly 40 are killed

## 1939
**August 2**
Albert Einstein writes to President Roosevelt informing him that scientists have discovered how to create a nuclear chain reaction

**August 23**
Germany and Russia sign the Molotov-Ribbentrop Pact, also known as the German-Soviet Non-aggression Pact

**September 1**
Germany invades Poland, occupies Gdansk (also known as Danzig)

Soviets and Japanese clash on Manchuria/Outer Mongolia border

# THE SUPER WEAPON THAT FIRED SOUND

*One of the most important weapons of World War II never fired a shot and was helpless if attacked—but it brought down hundreds of enemy aircraft and saved thousands of lives.*

The Radio Detection and Ranging device, or radar for short, was developed independently by researchers in eight nations, beginning nearly four decades before World War II. The technology used sound waves to create an echo that would bounce off metal objects such as ships. When the echo returned to the sending unit, it could be analyzed to determine the distance—and to a lesser extent, the size—of the target.

## RADAR DEVELOPMENTS

By the late 1930s, the major belligerents began crash programs to develop the technology for naval- and air-defense purposes. The U.S. Naval Research Laboratory, the British Meteorological Office, and the German *Kriegsmarine* had developed a series of workable sets by the time hostilities broke out in Europe.

As an island, Britain was protected by the sea and an impressive navy, but its vulnerability to air attacks meant it had much to gain from developing radar. In the late 1930s, it developed a rudimentary radar network called Chain Home. While the technology was merely adequate, the devices could be rushed into production in time to help defend the Home Isles against the *Luftwaffe* in the summer of 1940. That same year, two British researchers at the University of Birmingham developed the cavity magnetron, a device that allowed radar operators to use higher-frequency sound waves that could be focused more tightly. Britain shipped the prototype in secrecy to the United States, where researchers at Massachusetts Institute of Technology (MIT) developed production models for an improved radar system.

The Soviet Union had one ship-based radar device, the *Redut-K* system, in place by 1940. For its radar needs, the USSR relied heavily upon Lend-Lease sets from the United States and Britain.

Neither Germany nor Japan elected to keep pace with the Allies' radar development. Although Germany's Freya system was more sophisticated than the early Chain Home units fielded by Great Britain, Germany had only eight operational units in the field at the outbreak of the war. Further, Freya technology did not accurately determine altitude. The *Kriegsmarine* received several Freya systems in 1937, and in 1942, after the conquest of France and the Low Countries, the Third Reich established the Kammhuber Line, a chain of radar installations running from Denmark to central France. These stations helped the Germans defend against RAF attacks, but by 1942 British air planners could overwhelm the flak and air interception potential of the Kammhuber Line by concentrating bomber formations.

Japanese radar lagged well behind advances in the United States and Europe. Early in the war, the Japanese also created a small number of reasonably effective naval-radar sets. They relied on some captured devices, including a British model taken after the fall of Singapore and two American devices found when the army overran the Philippines.

## RADAR EVOLVES

Ships were equipped with radar to spot enemy craft (and periscopes) at night. De Havilland Mosquito fighter-bombers and Bristol Beaufighter fighters, among others, were fitted with miniature radar sets: These allowed the fighters to locate *Luftwaffe* bombers at night or in bad weather. Even artillery shells were equipped with tiny radar systems known as proximity fuses, which were especially useful in antiaircraft roles.

As radar became more sophisticated, air forces began using countermeasures, such as chaff (metal strips that reflected radar waves). On radar devices, chaff looked the same as a formation of enemy planes. Raiders would drop the metal strips to divert interceptor resources from their planned targets and protect their planes.

# THE PHONY RAID THAT STARTED THE WAR

*If one man could be said to have started World War II, some historians believe it would be Alfred Helmut Naujocks, an SS officer who led a fake attack on a German radio station outside the city of Gleiwitz on the Polish border.*

Under the command of Nazi security chief Reinhard Heydrich, Alfred Naujocks served in the *Sicherheitsdienst* (SD), the intelligence service of the SS. He played a role in several Nazi espionage actions in the 1930s, including the smuggling of explosives to pro-German militants in Slovakia in March 1939. The explosives were used to create "incidents" in the days preceding Germany's occupation of Czechoslovakia.

## OPERATION HIMMLER

The night before Germany invaded Poland, Germans staged numerous attacks along the Polish-German border. Part of Operation Himmler, the attack on a radio station near Gleiwitz, Poland, received the most attention.

On the night of August 31, 1939, Naujocks led a dozen SS troopers dressed in Polish uniforms to the Gleiwitz radio tower. There they waited for the delivery of the *Konserve,* or "canned goods," the Nazi code word for expendable prisoners. SS agents delivered 12 or 13 condemned criminals, including Franciszek Honiok, a German dissenter who had sympathized with the Poles. The prisoner had been given a lethal injection before reaching the site and was dressed in a Polish uniform. The SS troopers posed his body and shot several bullets into him.

Then, Naujocks and his team of SS men stormed the tower, surprising the staff, who knew nothing about the attack. Speaking Polish, members of the assault team shouted anti-German statements on the air, broadcast a message calling on Poles to attack Germans, and fired several shots into the ceiling before leaving.

Radio stations across Germany announced that police were repelling an attack by Polish troops at Gleiwitz. The next morning, German authorities at Gleiwitz showed the inmates' bodies to journalists and foreign diplomats as proof of the incident. The German Army was already roaring into Poland as Hitler declared before the Reichstag in Berlin, "This night for the first time Polish regular soldiers fired on our own territory. Since 5:45 A.M. we have been returning fire, and from now on bombs will be met with bombs."

## THE GLEIWITZ INCIDENT REVEALED

In October 1944, Naujocks deserted Germany and surrendered to American forces. Appearing as a witness at the Nuremberg trials after the war, he told the story of what happened at Gleiwitz. He later became a businessman in Hamburg and is alleged to have been one of the organizers of Odessa, a secret organization of Nazi veterans that helped former SS officers wanted for war crimes escape to South America. Naujocks is believed to have died, a free man, in 1960.

✯　✯　✯

- *The Nazis were not alone in using fake attacks to justify invasions. In 1931, the Mukden Incident occurred when Japanese officers blew up a section of a Manchurian railroad, blaming Chinese dissidents and providing an excuse for the annexation of Manchuria. In 1939, the Russian town of Mainila on the Finnish border was shelled by heavy artillery. The Soviets blamed Finland. Documents released after the fall of the Soviet Union proved that the Red Army had shelled the town to justify Stalin's invasion of Finland four days later.*

✯　✯　✯

- *Italy went to great lengths to shield its antiquities from wartime damage: Statues were surrounded by sandbags; monuments were shelled in masonry and sandbagged scaffolding.*

# THE GESTAPO: INSTRUMENT OF TERROR

*The Gestapo terrorized German citizens into cowering obedience and cast a fearfully oppressive shadow over Occupied Europe.*

The Gestapo was a state-sanctioned instrument of terror, perhaps rivaled in history only by the Soviet Union's NKVD and KGB secret-police organizations. Its sole purpose was to eliminate enemies of the Nazi state, both real and imagined, and intimidate ordinary citizens into unquestioned obedience.

The Gestapo was the most nefarious of the many bureaus within the SS. At its height in 1944, the Gestapo counted 30,000 to 40,000 members, and as many as 160,000 informants and spies throughout Germany and the occupied territories.

## FORMED BY GÖRING, SHAPED BY HIMMLER AND HEYDRICH

The Gestapo was created by Hermann Göring in 1933 after he assumed control of the Prussian state police. Göring purged the force of its Nazi opponents and reconstituted it into the *Geheimes Staatspolizei* ("Secret State Police"). Supposedly, its infamous acronym was invented by a postal official who needed a name that fit on a regulation-size rubber stamp.

While Göring was creating the Gestapo, Heinrich Himmler, head of the SS, was bringing the rest of Germany's police forces under his sway. Himmler, who formed the SS as the elite security arm of the Nazi party, coveted the Gestapo and entered into a power struggle with Göring for its control. It wasn't much of a fight. Göring, who had his sights set on running the armed forces, willingly ceded leadership of the Gestapo to Himmler in 1934.

Afterward, Himmler and his toady Reinhard Heydrich began shaping the Nazi police state. The SS was reorganized into two branches—the uniformed *Waffen*-SS (armed SS), and the Main

Office of Reich Security, the intelligence and security branch, headed by Heydrich, which included the Gestapo.

Himmler also worked to secure the unlimited power of arrest and detention that was to become the crux of the Gestapo's control. He persuaded Hitler to decree in 1933 that anyone could be taken into "protective custody" and held indefinitely on suspicion of anti-Nazi activities. Himmler used this pretext to arrest thousands of politicians, Jews, journalists, academics, and other "enemies of the state." To hold them all, he established the concentration camps that came to symbolize Gestapo tyranny. The Gestapo's arbitrary power was formalized in 1936 with the passing of the Gestapo Act which declared, "Neither the instructions nor the affairs of the Gestapo will be open to review by the administrative courts." This freed the Gestapo to act above the law without any regard to legal or judicial process.

## SUBDUING THE POPULACE

The Gestapo wielded its power with impunity, and threats of arbitrary arrest, detention, or summary execution became its tool for subduing the German population. The Gestapo's extensive network of informants kept tabs on everything everyone said and did. The average citizen didn't know who the informants were—they could be neighbors, the local shopkeeper, coworkers, even children. As such, people lived as self-censoring automatons who carefully avoided any activity that could be construed as "subversive."

People feared the Gestapo. Nobody wanted to get the dreaded middle-of-the-night knock on the door from Gestapo officers clad in their menacing black uniforms, or tap on the shoulder while on the street from agents garbed in long black leather trench coats and snap-brim fedoras. People shuddered when they received a letter telling them to report to the local Gestapo headquarters.

Those in custody were subjected to sadistic interrogations that included repeated near drownings in tubs of ice water or electric shocks via wires attached to hands, feet, and genitalia. Sometimes prisoners had their wrists tied behind their back and were hung by the arms until their shoulders dislocated. Beatings with nightsticks and whips were common, as were burnings with matches or soldering irons. Pedestrians strolling outside the Gestapo prison in Berlin cringed when they heard screaming coming from inside.

## PACIFYING THE CONQUERED; PERSECUTING THE JEWS

The Gestapo employed the same intimidation tactics in the occupied territories to eliminate resistance to German rule. Under the auspices of Hitler's Night and Fog Decree, the Gestapo arbitrarily whisked suspects away in the middle of the night. These people were often never seen again, and families would never learn of their loved ones' fates.

The Gestapo was also responsible for the persecution and, eventually, extermination of the Jews. The Gestapo's Race and Resettlement Office (RSHA) Section IV B4 managed all matters relating to Jewish affairs, evacuation, and dispossession of German citizenship rights. The department was headed by Adolf Eichmann, the uber-bureaucrat who managed the logistics of the "Final Solution" with devastating efficiency.

## INGLORIOUS END FOR GESTAPO LEADERS

The Gestapo's insidious reign came to an end with the inglorious destruction of Hitler's Third Reich. The various leaders of the Gestapo met a similar fate.

Hermann Göring surrendered to the Americans on May 8, 1945 and was tried at Nuremburg—a right of which Gestapo victims were deprived. He was convicted and sentenced to death, but cheated the hangman by committing suicide in his cell on October 15, 1946. Heinrich Himmler surrendered to the British two weeks after Göring and committed suicide while in custody on May 23, 1945. Reinhard Heydrich was assassinated by Czech partisans in May 1942; the Gestapo avenged his death with the annihilation of the Czech village of Lidice. Heydrich's successor and the Gestapo's last leader, Heinrich Müller, cocooned with Hitler in the *Führerbunker.* He fled the bunker on April 30, 1945, and was never seen again. He remains the only senior Nazi figure not captured or confirmed dead.

# LIFE AMID THE FALLING BOMBS: SURVIVAL STORIES FROM THE BLITZ

*Nighttime air raids. Crowded bomb shelters. Burned-out houses. Loved ones killed. That was everyday life for Britons during the Blitz.*

The Blitz, Germany's terror-bombing campaign against Britain in 1940-41, was a horrifying experience. More than 43,000 civilians died during the bombing; one million homes were destroyed or damaged.

The Blitz shook Britons to their very core. They were scared and depressed; their homes and neighborhoods lay in ruins. But their spirit was never broken. Somehow, they found a way to get through it all and show Hitler that the best he could throw at them wasn't good enough.

To mark the 60th anniversary of the end of World War II, the BBC invited Britons to relive their wartime experiences for a unique online archive titled *WW2 People's War.* Included among the archive's 47,000 colorful recollections are thousands of firsthand accounts from those who survived the Blitz. They depict both perilously close calls and the indomitable fortitude that enabled the British people to persevere. Here are some excerpts.

## DENIS GARDNER, PECKHAM, SOUTHEAST LONDON
### BBC article ID A4104343

[I was] not quite 14 when the Blitz started in 1940...[The woman who owned the paper shop] did not have an Anderson shelter in the back garden, but the hallway of the house had been reinforced to make a shelter. She had said if a raid started during the time I was delivering the papers I was to make my way back to the shop and take shelter [there]. On the morning of 15th October the siren sounded, so I finished the deliveries in the street I was in, and then

I started to make my way back to the shop. On the way I could see German aircraft in the sky and the see bombs leaving the planes. It was fascinating. There were other people around all staring at the sky. I carried on cycling [to] the shop... The next thing I remember was being put in an ambulance and being taken to St. Giles Hospital, Camberwell. A bomb had hit a house as I was cycling past. I had cuts on the forehead and back of the head. Also my wrist was cut and my arm was injured. They told me afterwards that my greatest concern was whether my bike was O.K... I did not go back to delivering papers any more. I was now the local hero....

## PETER ADDIS, PORTSMOUTH
*BBC article ID A2097236*

In the summer of 1940 I was 16... At school we all cheered when the Air Raid Siren [sounded], it meant we could play around in a very interesting shelter and skip the lesson. Our teacher said that one day we might stop praying for air raids... Then came the time when silly boys stopped praying for air raids. It was a January night 1941. The bombing started at dusk and the first bombs put out all the lights. Continuous incendiary bombs set whole streets alight... I was not thrilled anymore, I was scared... Daylight came and the raid finished... Then we went home. But it was gone. All that was left was a small square of rubble... It was a bitter blow to my parents, not only was it their home but also their shop and means of livelihood... We walked out of town, carrying a small bag [that] held all the important family documents... We travelled up to Maidenhead to relatives... our arrival was a complete surprise [but] we were given a great welcome... The next night we went over to Marlow and met more family, all evacuated from London, they took us to the local pub, where there was an impromptu dance. My mum and dad were dancing less than 48 hours after losing everything.

## DORIS FISHER, ILFORD, ESSEX
*BBC article ID BBC article ID A2124316*

I was 24 years old when overnight my life changed forever. A so-called Doodlebug [V-1 flying bomb] landed on my home, destroying everything that I owned and uprooting the Anderson Shelter in which I had taken refuge with my dog, Trixie. Blind, deaf and with multiple injuries I was taken to the nearest emergency centre. Trixie was dead, mercifully still curled around as though asleep. At the emergency centre I was transferred to a plastic surgery unit in Hill End Hospital, St Albans where a medical team not only saved my life but my very reason for I had horrific facial injuries...Plastic surgery cannot be hurried and as the weeks in that ward turned into months, it became my second home and the other patients around me a surragate [sic] family. There was Kitty in the next bed to me who had been in a bus when a bomb exploded nearby and shattered the glass causing her to lose an eye amongst other injuries. There was the young housewife who had been blinded but cared only that the baby she carried inside her still stirred. We all shared each others' joys and sorrows, forming a bond of sympathy when a husband or boyfriend failed to turn up at visiting time, unable to cope with the altered appearance of their partner. [But] there was laughter when I threatened to shoot the first cow I saw when leaving hospital. Having had my fractured jaw in clamps for weeks...and been on a daily diet of milk, Horlicks or Ovaltine through a straw.

## ERIC BOWKER, SALFORD, LANCASHIRE
*BBC article ID A2066933*

December 1940, nine years old... We had a lovely time with Uncle Bill, Auntie Elsie and their three daughters, time for going home. [Auntie Maggie and I] got on the bus just as it was going dusk... Then the sirens sounded... we proceeded at snails pace until we eventually arrived at Trafford Bar....

Maggie took my hand, the night sky was alive and loud with shell burst and the distinctive drone of German aeroplanes. We got to a street shelter an air raid warden...popped out from behind the blast wall "You can't come in here its [sic] full" then he popped back in. Maggie found our way to Trafford Bridge, a policeman, stationed in the middle of the road, "Sorry love I can't let you cross here, there's an unexploded bomb on the other side." My brave courageous Auntie Maggie, all four foot four of her, was not beaten yet... Passing the coal yard we crossed Robert Hall Street, then just a few doors down and knocking on the front door we were admitted by Gladys, Maggie's younger sister...Moments after our arrival a great explosion rent the air...A parachute bomb...obliterated the coal yard that we had walked by not more than five minutes ago. With the cold grey dawn came the wail of the all clear. Maggie and I began our long walk home...Then at the start of Mulgrave Street [we saw] devastation, piles of rubble, the heavy rescue squad digging for survivors, blanket covered stretchers. Told that we could not pass, Maggie explained "We live at the end of this street on the corner of Montague and Edith Street"... [There was] a great gaping hole in the roof of our house, windows and frames blown out, a blackened remnant of curtain hanging forlornly from a downstairs window... Our front door hung open, the acrid rotten smell of burning was everywhere. Mam, Dad and Vera were in, what was left, of the living room, "Are you all right," from everybody. Bone tired, blackened, our home a shambles. We were alive. Thank God.

I think lots of ordinary civilian folk deserved medals in that war. Including my Auntie Maggie.

☆   ☆   ☆

- *The Blitz created dangerous morale problems in Britain. To galvanize the people, Churchill lied and said that a German invasion might be imminent. The fib worked, and the British rallied.*

☆   ☆   ☆

- *Nearly 180 Londoners died during a raid on March 3, 1943—but not from bombs. A woman tripped entering an underground station; the crowd rushing for cover crushed her and many others, suffocating them.*

# Timeline

## 1939

**September 3**
SS *Athenia*, a British passenger ship, is sunk in the North Atlantic by German submarine U-30; Battle of the Atlantic begins

**September 17**
Soviet Union invades eastern Poland

**September 18**
Members of the Polish Cipher Bureau escape with two ENIGMA machines; they arrive in Paris on October 1

**September 25**
Warsaw is bombed into submission by the Luftwaffe; the city surrenders on September 27

**September 29**
Japanese reach outskirts of Changsha in Hunan Province

**October 2–6**
Heavy fighting occurs around Changsha, China

**October 11**
Soviet Union presents territorial demands to Finland

**October 19**
Germans establish first Jewish ghetto in Lublin, Poland

**October 27**
U.S. Senate passes an amendment to the Neutrality Act allowing the sales of arms to besieged allies, so long as they are not transported by American ships

**November 1**
Germany annexes Danzig and the Polish Corridor

**November 4**
Warsaw's Jews are herded into a ghetto

**November 15**
Japanese land on the coast of Kwangsi Province; they will take Nanning and Kwangsi, China, nine days later

**November 30**
Soviets invade Finland's Karelian Isthmus, bomb Helsinki; the Winter War begins

**December**
Chinese counterattack from Mongolian border to southern China.

**December 1**
Chiang Kai-shek elected Head of Chinese National Government.

**December 13–17**
Battle of River Plate (off Uruguay); German battleship *Graf Spee* scuttled in Montevideo harbor

**December 24**
Pope Pius XII makes a Christmas Eve appeal for peace

**December 30**
Finns annihilate Soviet 163rd Division near Suomussalmi, Finland

## 1940

**January 8**
Finns destroy Soviet 44th Division near Suomussalmi, Finland

**January 22**
Japanese take Xioshan, China

**January 25**
Japanese defeat Chinese counterattack at Nanning

**August 9**
British troops abandon Shanghai

# U.S. ARMY AIR CORPS AND NAVY HIT BACK: THE DOOLITTLE RAID ON TOKYO

*On April 18, 1942, the U.S. Army and Navy teamed up to launch a surprise attack on the Japanese mainland. With low casualties for both sides, the raid was a success for the Allies, striking a desperately needed blow to Japanese morale.*

After Pearl Harbor, the Allies received one dire news report after another from the Pacific. The Japanese were eagerly advancing through Malaya, the Philippines, the Netherlands East Indies, and Burma. President Franklin D. Roosevelt needed to lift Allied morale, and reasoned the best way to do so would be to strike back at the heart of Japan. In January 1942, a submariner is said to have suggested the way: Perhaps army bombers could take off from navy carriers to reach Japanese targets? A successful attack would dent Japan's invincible aura even if every bomber was lost—which was quite possible.

U.S. leaders decided to try it. Only one U.S. Army bomber, the medium-size B-25B Mitchell, could probably take off from a carrier—but it couldn't land there; there simply wasn't enough room. The navy would have to hoist the bombers aboard, and because of fuel constraints, the surviving raiders would have to land in China—much of which was occupied by Japan. Many feared it would be a suicide mission.

## THE RAIDERS ASSEMBLE

An Air Corps officer approached the B-25B-equipped 17th Bombardment Group requesting volunteers for a "classified mission involving tremendous risk." The volunteers (unmarried men were preferred) were transferred to Eglin Field in the Florida panhandle, their aircraft flew separately.

The B-25Bs showed up in Florida with a new look. Ball turrets beneath the bombers had been removed, the holes covered with sheet metal. Black-painted broomsticks sprouted from the Mitchells' tails to simulate tail guns. A big rubber fuel bag filled the tail gunner's access space. The bomb bays carried a combination of incendiary and high-explosive bombs. Each bomber's radio was gone, as were the secret Norden bombsights; in place of these were jury-rigged sliding gauges made from scrap aluminum. The alterations halved the B-25B's defensive weaponry but doubled its range and let it carry a reasonable bomb payload.

The men were surprised to learn their instructors were from the navy. They trained on a secluded Eglin airstrip marked with a line well short of its end; pilots needed to be airborne before reaching the line. After takeoff, the crews practiced flying as low as possible—a favorite pastime, for bomber pilots had few opportunities for aerobatic shenanigans, unlike the envied fighter pilots. As the crews practiced, mechanics fussed and fretted over fixing leaks in the extra fuel tanks. Though it didn't take much intuition to guess that they'd be flying from a navy carrier, none of the trainees yet knew the mission's target, much less who would command it.

On March 3, the volunteers packed into Eglin's operations office to learn their objective. There stood the world-famous Lieutenant Colonel James H. Doolittle—now they knew the mission was even more important than they'd imagined. They were ordered not to speculate aloud about the mission. If any outsider did so, and the men failed to report it, the entire mission might be suicidal. Lastly, Doolittle offered everyone another chance to quit without stigma. In the case of family men, he practically ordered them to quit. No one dropped out—a tribute both to their personal daring and Doolittle's leadership and prestige.

## DESTINATION: JAPAN

By April 2, 1942, the last of 16 B-25Bs was winched onto the USS *Hornet's* flight deck. Once outbound from San Francisco, Navy Captain Mitscher told his crew just what the army aircrews intended to do. The sailors honored the army guests with their warmest hospitality, giving them the most comfortable bunks and offering many gestures of aid and respect. Naval aviators picked up the thread of training, helping the army pilots understand the difficulties involved in flying a medium bomber off the end of a heaving platform in the face of seaspray. Despite intensive training at Eglin, the army pilots had never taken off from a carrier. At Pearl Harbor, Task Force 16 (TF 16) assembled in full: Two carriers were escorted by cruisers and destroyers. If they met a Japanese battle fleet, carrier USS *Enterprise* could provide air cover while *Hornet* hurried to ready its own fighters.

The past few months had been grim for the Allies. Singapore had fallen two months earlier. Rommel was pressing the Allies hard in North Africa. Japan held the oil-rich Netherlands East Indies and was bombing Australia. Germany's panzers were slashing across the Soviet Ukraine. The day after TF 16 left Hawaii, U.S. and Filipino prisoners began the Bataan Death March. Good news was sorely overdue.

Early naval-aviation pioneers, the Japanese had considered the possibility of a carrier-based attack. However, Japanese commanders believed that U.S. carriers would not launch air strikes without fighter cover, meaning an approach within about 200 miles of Japan. They screened their home waters with vigilant air and surface patrols.

Doolittle anticipated Japan would have patrols in place. He planned to launch the bombers about 500 miles offshore without fighter cover. If Japanese aircraft chased the raiders, they would end up over China rather than discovering the carrier force.

## DOOLITTLE'S RAIDERS TAKE TO THE SKY

Early April 18, some 700 miles from shore, navy lookouts spotted Japanese patrol vessels. One radioed a warning before the escorts' gunfire could silence it.

It was now or never.

The bridge announced: "Army pilots, man your planes!" Heavy seas pitched foam over the decks as *Hornet* turned into the wind east of Tokyo. Sixteen bombers took off, formed single file just above the waves, and made for the Imperial capital. The Navy task force turned for home, their job done.

With better coordination, Japanese defenses might have butchered the bombers short of their targets. As matters stood, the Japanese Army and Navy barely spoke to one another, and each was responsible for a portion of the air defense. Japan's best pilots and planes fought at the front, leaving mostly old planes and green pilots in Japan. With Doolittle's raiders fast approaching, fighter pilots scrambled to attack. But the raiders prevailed, downing several Japanese fighters. One B-25B was forced to abort its run; the other 15 splattered the Tokyo area with explosives and firebombs. All 16 ran for Asia.

So far, so good. But could the Doolittle Raiders reach friendly territory?

Due to leaky tanks and the early mission start, all 16 aircraft were low on fuel. One reached Vladivostok in Soviet territory, where its crew remained confined until 1943. The rest came down, mostly by parachute, on China's soil and coastal waters. One crewman died in a mountain landing and two died swimming to shore. Two crews fell into Japanese captivity; four of these eight men survived the war. Cheered by news of the raid, many Chinese took great risks to help the other 64 scattered aviators reassemble.

## GOOD NEWS AT LAST!

The Allies rejoiced, especially President Roosevelt. Doolittle, expecting court-martial for losing all his airplanes, instead received the stars of a brigadier general and the Medal of Honor. The bombing did minor physical damage, but it delivered a stinging insult to Japan's overconfident leaders. The commander of Tokyo's air defenses atoned by commiting suicide. Propaganda aside, Japanese civilians began to privately question the certainty of victory. Their leaders now realized how near the northern front was to their home soil. The Japanese shifted their strategic focus to the North Pacific, especially the Aleutian Islands and Midway Island.

# Fast Facts

- The early hope was to land the B-25B bombers in the USSR after the raid, giving them to the Soviets as Lend-Lease war materiel. Stalin rejected this proposal because he wasn't yet at war with Japan, nor could he afford to be.

- The USS Nashville fired 924 six-inch shells over half an hour before finally sinking the IJN Nitto Maru, a converted fishing boat. After the mission Nashville was sent back to the United States for further training.

- To take off from a carrier deck, B-25B pilots had to apply full throttle with their brakes on, then release those brakes. The technique is similar to that used by drag racers.

- The Imperial Palace was an obvious target (and a helpful navigation aid), but Doolittle nixed an attack on the structure out of fear it would galvanize the Japanese will, much as German attacks on Buckingham Palace had put steel into the British populace. Nevertheless, if they saw they would be shot down in Japan, several of the pilots had decided to ram their bombers into the Palace rather than be taken alive

- The Japanese did heed the picket boat's last message, but calculated that no attack would be feasible for at least a day. The immediate launch accounted for the tardy, ineffective antiaircraft and air interception response opposing Doolittle.

- The Chinese people paid an awful price for helping the raiders escape. Generalissimo Chiang Kai-Shek estimated that 250,000 Chinese civilians died in reprisals.

- The full bomb payload of the entire Doolittle Raid would have fit in two B-29s with room to spare.

- The U.S. Army Air Corps B-29 Superfortress used high-tech electric coordination equipment so that a gunner could fire several powered gun turrets in concert at an enemy.

# THE PUNJABI AMBUSH
# AT THE BATTLE OF
# HONG KONG

*On December 8, 1941—mere hours after the attack on Pearl Harbor—Japanese planes roared out of the sky to attack the British garrison on Hong Kong. Churchill knew that the colony would eventually be lost, but insisted, "There must be no thought of surrender."*

## HONG KONG MUST BE DEFENDED

The task of defending Hong Kong fell to Major General Christopher M. Maltby, who was well aware that the battle would likely end with the Japanese capturing the colony. Still, every day he could hold out would help the Allied cause, and he was determined to do his duty. He commanded a force of 10,000 men, among them Canadians, Scots, and Punjabis.

Maltby was familiar with the Punjabi, and they were no strangers to the British Army. He had served in India for 30 years. Indians had served in the British military for the better part of a hundred and fought for the East India Company for years before that. They had proved their mettle, and their actions in the defense of Hong Kong would earn them a reputation for ferocity.

## A MOMENT OF TRIUMPH

The primary Punjabi battalion in Hong Kong was the 2nd Battalion, 14th Punjab Regiment, and they performed notably on the first day of the battle. The Japanese were advancing swiftly, and the British attempted to slow them down by destroying roads and bridges while retreating. At about 6:30 in the evening, a platoon of Punjabis guarded a demolition squad in the village of Tai Po. Concealing themselves in the stalls and doorways of the open-air market, they watched as their enemy came right down the road. The Japanese had not scouted the village and they walked straight into town, dragging artillery and driving pack mules with them. "I don't believe it," remarked one officer. "You'd think they were on a victory march through Trafalgar Square." The Punjabis waited until the Japanese were sufficiently close before unleashing a hail of bullets, resulting in 50 quick casualties. The Japanese survivors fled without firing a shot; the Punjabis asked permission to fix bayonets and run them down, but the request was denied.

The 14th Punjab Regiment proved vicious in other instances of the fight for Hong Kong. On hearing a rumor that another British unit had unceremoniously fled an encounter, they vowed to compensate for such shameful conduct, and reports indicate their success—as well as their ruthlessness—in dealing with the enemy. In one occurrence, a platoon from the 14th Punjab Regiment refused to evacuate, even as their position was being overrun, waiting until civilians had been ferried away before jumping on the last boat and fighting their way to safety. Another incident found a platoon desperate to give British sappers time to destroy a bridge. The Punjab soldiers opened fire on a Japanese force that was attacking from behind a wall of human shields, leaving no survivors.

Hong Kong had been expected to hold out for three months. It fell in less than three weeks, surrendering on Christmas Day. But although the siege was brief, it would have been even shorter had it not been for the valor of the Punjabi defenders.

☆　　☆　　☆

- *Hitler had boasted that his troops would meet the British anywhere they might land. During a commando raid in Norway, one plucky British officer located a telegraph shack and sent Hitler a telegram saying, "Where are your troops?"*

☆　　☆　　☆

- *Japan's brilliant Admiral Yamamoto Isoroku, who had studied at Harvard and the U.S. Naval War College prior to the war, made his aides play poker. He believed it would sharpen their ability to deceive and surprise their enemies.*

## 1940

**February 3**
Japanese and Chinese clash at Wuyuan on the Mongolian border and at Xioshan in China

**February 12**
Germans and Soviets sign a trade agreement

**February 28**
British ULTRA team breaks German ENIGMA code for the first time

**February 28–29**
Soviets overrun Finnish defenses in Karelia, Finland

**March 1**
U.S. Undersecretary of State Sumner Welles meets with Hitler, offers to mediate peace talks

**March 8**
Soviets take Viipuri, Finland

**March 12**
Finland and the Soviet Union sign a treaty ending the Winter War

Japanese launch an offensive in southern China

**March 28**
Britain and France agree to not act independently in establishing treaties with any third nation

**March 30**
Japan sets up puppet Chinese government under Wang Ching-wei in Nanking, China

**April 1**
Chinese retake Wuyuan, China, after ambushing some 3,000 Japanese troops

**April 3**
Soviet secret police murder more than 22,000 Polish prisoners in the Katyn Forest Massacre; the Russian government will deny culpability until 1989

**April 9**
Germany invades Denmark and Norway; Denmark surrenders

**April 15–18**
British troops land in Norway

**April 17**
Japan launches offensive in Shansi Province

**April 21–30**
Germans advance steadily on all fronts in Norway; British troops will evacuate southern Norway on April 26

**April 29**
Japanese begin bomber offensive against Chungking, the Nationalist Chinese capital

**April 30**
Germans establish Jewish ghetto in Lódź, Poland

**May 1**
Japanese begin an offensive along the upper Yangtze River

**May 10**
Germany invades the Netherlands, Belgium, Luxembourg, and France

Churchill succeeds Chamberlain as British prime minister

**May 15**
The Netherlands capitulate to Germany

**May 19**
Chinese defeated at Battle of Yichang

# ROOSEVELT'S ROAD TO WAR

*From 1935 to 1941, America awoke from a decades-long spell of isolationism to the reality that it was part of the world, and the world was in flames—whether the United States wanted war or not.*

## FROM GREAT WAR TO GREAT DEPRESSION

Ever since the Senate voted down the League of Nations Treaty in 1919, U.S. foreign policy was based on avoiding the kind of foreign entanglements that had cost America thousands of lives in World War I. For America, the 1920s were all about prosperity, Prohibition, and the creation of fabulous wealth, while the early '30s were consumed with a struggle against the Great Depression.

## A WEB OF ISOLATION

As tensions mounted in Europe and Japan invaded Manchuria, Congress began penning legislation that would keep America from another Great War entanglement. In 1935, Congress passed the first of its prewar Neutrality Acts, temporarily banning arms shipments to any nation at war.

When Mussolini's Fascist Italy announced plans to invade Ethiopia, President Franklin D. Roosevelt signed the act and urged citizens to clamp a "moral embargo" upon Italy, the aggressor. The public refused to go along, though, and commercial exports to Italy increased as Italian tanks clattered through the African desert.

With the outbreak of civil war in Spain in 1936, Roosevelt urged U.S. arms manufacturers to impose a "moral embargo" of non-interference with Fascist and Nationalist factions, but again his pleas were ignored. One U.S. company managed to obtain an export license to sell bomber parts to the rebels—a sale that FDR opposed as unpatriotic, but not illegal.

In 1937, Congress passed legislation making the 1935 Neutrality

Act permanent. The 1937 Act also provided that, at the president's discretion, goods other than war materiel could be traded with belligerents so long as they were paid for in cash and carried on their own ships—to avoid the repayment mess the United States found itself in after World War I.

Although the public and Congress wanted no part in any European war, Roosevelt saw the rising empires of Germany and Japan as twin threats to U.S. interests.

## TURNING POINTS

Hitler's 1938 annexation of Czechoslovakia's Sudetenland and 1939 occupation of the rest of Czechoslovakia pushed Roosevelt even closer to the anti-German coalition, He began pressing for changes to the Neutrality Acts to allow aid to the European democracies. By midyear, the public opinion on military exports to France and Britain was evenly divided, but Congressional opposition persisted; FDR had to await a further shift in public opinion before he could act.

It was not long before the Nazis handed Roosevelt the tools he needed to support Britain and France publicly. On September 3, two days after Hitler's panzers rolled into Poland, German submarines sank the British liner *Athena,* killing 28 Americans. By the end of September, nearly two thirds of Americans approved of material support to the Allies, and on November 4, 1939, Roosevelt signed legislation allowing arms sales to belligerents on a "cash-and-carry" basis.

## LIFELINE TO A FRIEND

In the spring of 1940, as Britain ran desperately short of war materiel, Prime Minister Winston Churchill appealed to FDR, his unofficial ally, for help. In September, the Roosevelt administration entered into a swap agreement with Britain, trading more than 50 outdated destroyers for 99-year leases on territories that would be used as naval bases in the Caribbean and Newfoundland.

The War Department allocated large stocks of supplies to England and its allies, but the biggest obstacle was Britain's acute shortage of cash. On December 17, after securing an unprecedented third term as president, FDR proposed the Lend-Lease program, under which Britain would receive military aid in return for joint actions supporting creation of a liberalized postwar international economy. The president explained his policy in terms every voter could understand, likening England's anti-Nazi struggle to a neighbor whose house was on fire. "What do I do in such a crisis?" the president asked at a news conference. "I don't say, 'Neighbor, my garden hose cost me $15; you have to pay me $15 for it.' I don't want $15—I want my garden hose back after the fire is over." The following March, Congress passed the Lend-Lease Act, authorizing the president to sell, lease, lend, "or otherwise dispose of" military equipment the president deemed vital to the defense of the nation.

## THE FINAL COUNTDOWN

In early 1941, Hitler's invasion of Yugoslavia spurred Roosevelt to accelerate material aid to the Allies. In late March, Congress approved a $7 billion Lend-Lease appropriation, and on April 9, U.S. forces occupied Greenland to extend the security zone of convoys carrying supplies to England. A day later, the U.S. destroyer USS *Niblack* fired depth charges on a German U-boat, and by the summer of 1941, the United States was in a state of undeclared naval war against Germany.

After Germany's surprise invasion of the Soviet Union on June 22, FDR sent two emissaries to Moscow to negotiate Lend-Lease shipments. In August, FDR met with Churchill and his staff aboard the battleship Prince of Wales, where the two leaders reaffirmed their liberal war aims in what became known as the Atlantic Charter. Two months later, Congress approved $1 billion in Lend-Lease aid to Stalin, and before the war's end, the U.S. would send some $50 billion in material aid to Britain, the Soviet Union, and their allies.

Japan's surprise attack on Pearl Harbor on December 7, as well as Hitler's declaration of war on the United States three days later, sealed the fates of many nations. The long journey from isolationism to war was over, and the world would never be the same.

# *MEIN KAMPF*

*Dictated to Rudolph Hess in Landsberg Prison in 1924,* Mein Kampf *gave the world a look at the philosophies of Adolf Hitler. His own words clearly demonstrate his positions without the need for much elaboration. In hindsight, its content is chilling.*

The first edition of *Mein Kampf,* or *My Struggle,* was issued in 1925. It sold well enough to make Hitler a millionaire—and also a tax cheat, as he failed to report his income to the government. After he became chancellor, his debt was forgiven, and Germany bought millions of copies to give as official presents to all couples getting married. In the book, Hitler goes on at length about a wide range of topics, including his life story, architecture, and the proper dress for a young man, but the core of the book revolves around his views on race and the state.

## THE STATE AND RACIAL PURITY

Hitler describes the proper role of the state as existing to uphold the status of the race. He believes racial purity is the "center of all life," and the state must give its citizens the freedom to achieve it "based on the victorious sword of a master people, putting the world into the service of a higher culture." That culture, of course, is Aryan. The Aryan, in Hitler's view, rightly "subjected the lower beings" just as he made use of "various suitable beasts which he knew how to tame." The state should go on to defend the purity of the Aryan race by teaching the sickly that it is "a crime" to pass on their weakness, and even establishing racial commissions to approve individual reproductive rights if necessary.

## THE PEOPLE

Despite passages about the nobility of the German worker, average citizens are generally portrayed in a less-than-flattering light. Hitler reasons that speeches must be tailored to elicit an audience response, and "terror and force" should win out over logic. The truth should be avoided, since it "might bring out something favorable for the opponent." But avoidance of the truth is no matter, since the people "will more easily fall victim to a big lie than to a small one." In some sense, convincing the people is nothing more than a necessary evil, since "sooner will a camel pass through a needle's eye than a great man be 'discovered' by an election." But once in charge, a leader's job is "consolidating the attention of the people against a single adversary" and "make different opponents appear as if they belonged to one category." For Hitler, the single adversary was obvious.

## THE JEWS

Perhaps no topic is revisited as frequently in *Mein Kampf* as is the subject of the Jews. Jews are referred to as parasites, bastards, apes, vampires, or simply "the personification of the devil." Jews, Hitler writes, were "without any true culture, and especially without any culture of [their] own," but rather wormed their way into and subverted other societies. Hitler associates the Jews with most major problems. He claims they control the press, the trade unions, and the banks. Syphilis is a "Jewish disease" which has spread to young Germans: The Jewish propensity to value the intellect leads to the "emergence of sexual ideas" at too young an age. The Jew represents "the counterpart to the Aryan"—in other words, the opposite of all that is good. He is a "force which always wants evil." In a passage near the end of the book, Hitler ominously foreshadows the policy that would ensure his future infamy as the murderer of millions. Speaking of Germany in World War I, he laments that if "twelve or fifteen thousand of these Hebrew corruptors of the people had been held under poison gas . . . the sacrifice of millions at the front would not have been in vain."

Hitler's rise to power and the subsequent events of the war place the book in an odd position. Its contents have value as a resource to document how one man could do so much harm; however, the danger also exists that the material could be used for inspiration to future generations of tyrants and supremacists. As a result, *Mein Kampf* was banned in a number of countries following the war. The copyright to the work is owned by the state of Bavaria, which tries to restrict the publication of new editions to this day.

# WAKE ISLAND:
# ALAMO OF THE PACIFIC

*On December 11, 1941, the Marines on the beaches of Wake Island witnessed an imposing sight: the approach of three cruisers, six destroyers, and two troop transports, all flying the ensign of the invincible Empire of Japan. Pearl Harbor had been smashed, the Philippines was under invasion, and the largest British warships in the area had been sent to the bottom by Japanese bombers. Now, the Marines knew, it was their turn.*

Wake Island is a three-island coral atoll some 2,300 miles southwest of Hawaii, part of a chain of defensive U.S. bases that ran from Hawaii to the Philippines. Home to an airstrip, 523 Marines and sailors, and another 1,200 civilian contractors, Wake Island was a perfect staging area for raids against the Japanese Mandate Islands, which included the critical Marshall and Marianas island chains.

## THROWING BACK THE INVADERS

Flushed with smashing successes throughout the Pacific, the unbeaten Japanese Navy decided to capture Wake and rid itself of a potential aerial threat. Because Wake and its connected islands, Peale and Wilkes islands, possessed few natural defenses and only a dozen F4F Wildcat fighters, the Japanese high command was confident that a relatively small invasion force, preceded by its vaunted tactical bomber service, would get the job done quickly and easily.

But they neglected to plan for the determination and skill of the defending Marines. Although the bombing campaign on December 8th killed scores of Marines and reduced the Wildcat squadron from 12 to 4 flyable planes, on December 11, when the Japanese flotilla appeared on the horizon, Marine gunners were waiting for them. After enduring a savage shelling from the light cruisers and destroyers that escorted a 450-man Special Naval Landing Force detachment, the Marines waited until the transports were close in, then let loose with their coastal batteries. On Peacock Point, at the southern tip of Wake Island, gunners scored four hits on the cruiser *Yubari*, flagship of Rear Admiral Sadamichi Kajioka, and minor hits on several other ships. Their counterparts on Peale Island wasted no time in sending the destroyer *Hayate* to the bottom, while lucky strafing runs from the Wildcats managed to detonate a rack of depth charges at the stern of the destroyer *Kisaragi*, putting her out of action for good.

With his force reeling from the violent, unexpected resistance, Rear Admiral Kajioka postponed the invasion to wait for reinforcements, and the cheering men on Wake Island became the only island defenders to throw back an amphibious invasion—a feat all the more impressive because the garrison started the war with only enough personnel to man about half the island's defense guns.

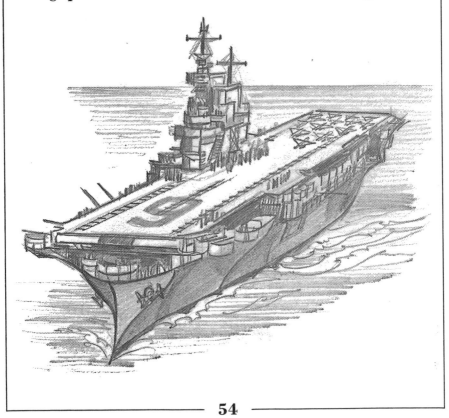

## AN ISLAND ALONE

But the ordeal was not over. While naval commanders in Hawaii made plans to relieve the island, they fretted over scarce resources. The U.S. Navy had few aircraft carriers and virtually no battleships to defend the Pacific Ocean, and naval commanders were wary of sending their precious flattops into a potential trap. The Navy dispatched the seaplane tender *Tangier* to Wake carrying batteries from the 4th Marine Defense Battalion, supplies, and ammunition. Shortly afterwards, it ordered the carrier *Saratoga* and the slow-sailing Task Force 14 to escort the relief effort. The carrier *Lexington* was sent belatedly to support Task Force 14, but the relief effort dispatched December 15 was too little, too late.

The Japanese enjoyed the crucial advantage of air bases within striking distance of Wake Island, and land- and sea-based bombers pounded the defenders daily after December 11, knocking out two of four Wildcats and repeatedly demolishing unsalvageable fighters rolled into the open as decoys. The last two Wildcats were brought down by fighters from the heavy carriers *Soryu* and *Hiryu* on December 22. With news of the two carriers in the vicinity, U.S. fleet commanders changed the *Tangier's* orders from reinforcement to evacuation. But on December 23, with the task force still about 430 miles from Wake, a thousand-man battalion of Japanese soldiers stormed the island before daybreak. Seventy defending Marines on Wilkes Island delayed the landing there, but the defenders of Wake Island were overwhelmed. Before midday on December 23, Wake was in Japanese hands.

The loss of Wake Island was a bitter blow to the U.S. Navy, which had suffered a string of disasters since December 7. But in the dark days of December 1941, Navy planners decided that their only line of defense—their few precious carriers plying the Pacific's waters—could not be risked for the island.

The U.S. never attempted to retake Wake Island. Vengeance would have to wait until the Battle of Midway the following June. Meanwhile, Wake remained in Japanese hands until September 1945, nearly a month after Japan's surrender.

# THE SOVIET LOGISTICS MIRACLE

*With the German* Blitzkrieg *hastily conquering Soviet land, the Russians embarked on a bold evacuation to salvage war production industries. It turned out to be one of the most amazing feats of logistics the world has even seen.*

## INVASION

In the early morning of June 22, 1941, three million German troops stormed into Soviet territory across a 4,000-mile front, marking the beginning of Operation Barbarossa. Riga and Minsk fell to the invaders within days as the Germans struck toward the center of Soviet industry. By the following day, Joseph Stalin had ordered the first industrial evacuations of tank factories, which had to be moved out of the way of the enemy advance. By June 24, the Soviets had formed a Council for Evacuation, and it began identifying key factories that would head east, to the Urals and even far-off Siberia, out of reach of both the German air and ground forces.

But there had been little planning for the massive undertaking. The possibility of evacuation had been discussed before the war, but there was no cohesive strategy for relocating Soviet production. In contrast, the Germans had extensive plans for such an eventuality despite their doubt that they would ever be subject to invasion. Given this lack of foresight on the Soviets' part, the entire operation became an exercise in improvisation, and there were some inevitable missteps along the way. Some resources were captured by the enemy, and some factories had to be relocated twice, not moving far enough from the front the first time.

## HEADING EAST

The Council made the necessary decisions, and Soviet industry got on the move. Entire factories were disassembled and sent east at an average rate of 165,000 trailer loads per month. Then they were reassembled and began production immediately. Faced with the ridiculous edict to accomplish relocation and yet not fall behind in production, Soviet workers performed nothing short of miracles. Disassembled factories arrived in the undeveloped regions of the interior and were reassembled by exhausted employees in the worst weather conditions possible. Workers at a munitions factory rebuilt a foundry that had originally taken two years to build in a mere 28 days; another plant went from reassembly to operating at full capacity in two weeks.

The Soviets adopted a scorched-earth policy toward factories that couldn't be moved in time, opting to raze them rather than let them fall into German hands.

The factory laborers traveled with the machinery, or at least about 30 to 40 percent did; the rest were called into the army to fight off the Germans. The remaining laborers arrived and were expected to start work immediately despite inadequate housing and food. Many workers were given seeds and sent out to cultivate the land around the new factories after having worked a full shift in the plant. Women and adolescents often picked up the slack for missing employees. The displaced workers also had a disruptive impact on the areas they settled; Uzbekistan alone had to absorb two million additional people. The influx of people and technology produced miniature industrial revolutions in some of the less developed, more remote areas of the country.

## BETTER THAN EVER

The relocation succeeded in spectacular fashion. The Soviets relocated 1,523 industrial concerns, including the bulk of the production facilities used for certain war-related industries such as chemistry, engineering, and metallurgy. By 1943, overall production was four times what it had been in 1941, and the German threat to Soviet industry was long over. The impact of the evacuation effort on the overall war would be hard to overestimate; Soviet General Georgi Zhukov believed that the workers were "smelting victory side by side with the soldiers at the front," and after the war he offered the opinion that the evacuation had been as significant as the battles fought by the troops.

# Fast Facts

- In 1939, the German Fl 282 Kolibri Hummingbird was the first helicopter produced and put into operational service.

- Before the war, Japanese pilots were selected at age 14 from the best academic and most physically fit students. Their five-year training program was the most arduous in the world.

- During their invasion of the Philippines, the Japanese were suitably impressed by the bravery of American pilot Lieutenant Russell M. Church—they gave him a military funeral.

- When the Japanese attacked Pearl Harbor, many U.S. politicians and military officers had to be paged over the public-address system at Griffith Field, where the Washington Redskins were playing the Philadelphia Eagles. Similar messages were heard at New York's Polo Grounds, where the football Giants faced off against the Brooklyn Dodgers.

- When Robert W. Malloy, a rookie FBI agent stationed in Honolulu, finally made contact with J. Edgar Hoover in New York on December 7, 1941, he held the phone out the window so the director could hear the bombs exploding.

- Japanese pilots attacking Pearl Harbor had studied tourist postcards (provided by spy Takeoyoshi Yoshikawa) to learn where ships were normally positioned in the harbor.

- Knowing that America would enter the war after the attack on Pearl Harbor, Winston Churchill said he went to bed that night and "slept the sleep of the saved and thankful."

- Winston Churchill's before-breakfast beverage of choice: Scotch. With breakfast, he enjoyed white wine.

- It wasn't easy to become an Air Corps pilot. In addition to strict physical standards, the candidate had to pass a tough entrance exam. On a lark, the president of MIT (the prestigious Massachusetts Institute of Technology) took the exam—and failed.

# STELLA GOLDSCHLAG: THE BLONDE POISON

*From August 1943 through the end of the war, a strikingly
beautiful young blonde Jewish woman walked freely through the
streets of Berlin. Unlike her fellow Jews, she had no fear of being
discovered by the Nazis. They were already well aware of her
presence. In fact, she worked for them.*

Being Jewish in prewar Berlin was at best barely tolerable. Constant threats, physical harassment, and official speeches made
it clear that German society had turned against them. The easi-
est targets were refugees from Eastern Europe. They had been
driven to Germany by Czarist purges at the turn of the century,
had never assimilated into the city's culture, and were easily identified by their attire and language. But there were others, including
self-described Germans of Jewish Origin, patriotic families that
proudly traced their German heritage back centuries. They looked
down on their Eastern cousins almost as much as their gentile
neighbors did, and took great pains to distance themselves from
their brethren.

Stella Goldschlag was the daughter of one such family. About
20 years old, already with a reputation as being a bit wilder than
other girls her age, she commanded the attention of all the young
men around her. She was not just attractive, but beautiful in a way
that conformed to so-called Aryan standards: Her blue eyes and
blonde hair made her the very picture of the German ideal. Stella's
father couldn't believe that the new measures being enacted
against Jews would ever apply to families such as his. Like many
German Jews, he considered himself a valuable German citizen.
By 1940, however, Stella's father could no longer deny reality, and
tried to emigrate to America, Palestine, Santo Domingo—anywhere. His applications met with no better success than those of
tens of thousands of other Jews. The time to go into hiding had
come.

## CAPTURING A U-BOAT

Stella and her family became U-boats, as Jews living submerged beneath visible Berlin society called themselves. It was a harsh existence, defined by a constant fear of capture, but about 1,400 of these courageous individuals managed to survive the war undetected. However, U-boats couldn't survive in complete isolation. They needed some resources, primarily ration books for food and identity papers in case they were stopped on the street. A veritable industry of forgery sprung up, with the difference between life and death hinging on the skill of the artist producing the documents.

Stella's papers looked authentic, and she managed to survive for a time. Her luck ran out on July 2, 1943 with a disastrous lunchtime visit to a café, considered a safe activity because of the large number of people such locations drew. As she sat at her table, Stella happened to smile at a friend, a plump woman named Inge Lustigo. The brief recognition was enough, and Gestapo operatives rushed in to seize Stella. Her acquaintance turned out to be a *Greifer*, a Jew employed by the Nazis to root out other Jews in hiding. *Greifers*, or catchers, were rewarded with a cash prize for every Jew turned in, but more importantly, they were exempt from being sent to the death camps—at least while they remained useful.

With typical subtlety, the Gestapo took Stella to a basement and beat her for days, until her bones were almost broken. Her torturers demanded to know the location of the forger of her papers. Stella didn't have the answer they wanted, but she did manage to escape and return to her family. She was rearrested in less than 12 hours, and this time the Gestapo found her parents as well.

The Goldschlags were placed in a collection camp. Stella's questioning began again, but this time the Gestapo had new leverage: Her mother and father had been put on the list to be sent to Auschwitz. Stella still didn't have the information they wanted, but quickly realized the semblance of cooperation could mean a reprieve for her family. She pretended to know where her forger might be found, and guided the authorities in their search. Stella's treatment improved, and she liked the change.

The Gestapo would only be stalled for so long, and Stella knew it. She could not deliver the source of her forged documents, but she could deliver other Jews. She had been a U-boat, had extensive prewar social contacts in the Jewish community, and a presence that caused men to lower their defenses. She put all her resources to effective use. Each capture bought a delay in her parents' date with the death camps—at least until February 1944, when they were put on the trains despite Stella's service.

## THE "TIGRESS"

Her parents' departure might have been the end of Stella's cooperation with the Nazis, but that was not the case. Acquaintances of the time report that she enjoyed her special status and served her masters faithfully, even with zeal. She seemed to hate Jews more than the Nazis themselves; whereas they viewed Jews as less than human, Stella took their existence as a personal affront. Stella roamed Berlin at will, armed with papers from the Gestapo asserting that she was working for them in the matter of "Jewish affairs," and often paired with a former boyfriend who she personally recruited to the *Greifer* ranks.

Keeping no schedule other than her own, Stella frequented locations known to be visited by Jews, accompanied by a Nazi squad waiting to pounce when she made a catch. She would often net more than one victim at a time, once arresting an entire family in a theater lobby, and on another occasion using her body to block a revolving door as Jews tried desperately to get past her while the Gestapo descended upon them. She even stooped to lying in wait at funerals of deceased Germans who had been married to Jews. She developed a reputation as being heartless, at one point telling a captured former friend, "You'll get out of here all right...as a corpse!"

Word spread quickly among the Jews of Berlin that a "Blonde Ghost" or "Blonde Poison" was among them, and they circulated a picture of her amongst themselves as a warning. The remaining resistance groups attempted to assassinate her, and at one point delivered to her a message bearing a sentence of death, the verdict to be "executed at the end of the war."

## AFTERMATH

No such execution was to take place, however. After the war, Stella, pregnant by an unknown man, was captured by the Soviets and sentenced to ten years in prison. Characteristically, she developed a reputation among the prisoners for cooperating with her Soviet guards. Stella underwent a second German trial at which spectators waited in line for hours, heckled her during the trial, and tried to assault her during a break in the proceedings. Her daughter was taken from her. Living in Israel, Stella's daughter grew to hate her mother and occasionally fantasized about matricide. After her legal difficulties were settled, Stella spent the rest of her life in relative obscurity, claiming the Jewish witnesses at her trial had hated her because she was blonde and pretty.

Adolf Eichmann had claimed that getting Jews to work against other Jews was "the very cornerstone" of the Nazis' Jewish policy. While far from the being only collaborator, Stella Goldschlag assured her place in infamy: Her acts of betrayal condemned as many as 2,300 of her fellow Jews to concentration camps. Even among the dubious society of the catchers themselves, she stood out; according to one former *Greifer* colleague, Stella had been the very embodiment of their profession.

✯　✯　✯

- *In 1939, Stella studied fashion drawing, and earned income as a nude model for art students.*

✯　✯　✯

- *Peter Wyden, whose biography of Stella was published in 1992, had been a classmate of Stella. He lost touch with her after 1937, when he and his family were lucky enough to obtain visas that took them to the United States. In the 1980s, Wyden began to research Stella's story.*

# THE STRANGE FLIGHT OF RUDOLF HESS

*On May 10, 1941, Deputy* Führer *of the Third Reich Rudolf Hess flew a Messerschmitt Bf-110 long-range fighter to Scotland, presumably to negotiate peace with Britain. But he wasn't acting on Hitler's orders. In fact, everyone seemed confused by the mission, including Hess himself.*

Reichsminister Rudolf Hess was an early lieutenant of Hitler's and had helped him create *Mein Kampf* in Landsberg Prison. In 1941, Hess flew to Britain without authorization, hoping to broker an Anglo-German peace; he left his wife and son behind in Germany, perhaps expecting to return.

From the moment his parachute caught the Scottish air until his asphyxiation in Spandau Prison at age 93, Hess's life was shrouded in secrets, hidden files, conspiracy theories, and wild claims. The British and German governments both seemed shocked by Hess's bizarre flight. Given his actions in prison, many believed he'd lost his mind.

### Was either side really surprised by Hess's flight?

Perhaps not. Hess had spent four months preparing for the flight, which would have been impossible in the Nazi police state without Hitler's assent. The most surprised person was Hess, who expected dignitary treatment (however discreet) followed by a quick return home. Instead he found himself taken prisoner by a Scottish farmer.

### What did Hess offer in the peace proposals?

Hess claimed that Germany would let Britain be, provided it didn't interfere with German interests in Europe, which meant Germany had no intention of giving up the land it had taken. Most likely, the Nazis wanted to negotiate peace with Britain so they wouldn't have to fight a two-front war—Germany hadn't yet invaded the Soviet Union, but it was preparing to do so.

However, Churchill knew that Hitler had a history of breaking agreements. Should Hitler defeat the Soviets, the British could logically expect him to turn on them. Churchill ordered that Hess be imprisoned for the duration of the war.

*So Hess waited out the war as a prisoner in Britain. How did he handle it?*

Hess acted depressed and paranoid. He attempted suicide and claimed there were drugs in his food and drink (he made others taste them before he would eat). Some believed he was mentally unstable, others thought he may have been putting on an act since at times he seemed lucid. Some of his postwar letters while imprisoned in Spandau boasted of duping his captors into thinking him insane—but such boasts do not prove him sane.

*Was he drugged, and if so, under what circumstances?*

Early in his British captivity, Hess described symptoms that resemble being given sodium pentothal, sometimes called truth serum. In hopes of learning about Nazi plans, his captors may have dosed him with this. Even so, Hess's guards treated him quite kindly.

*The Nuremberg court sentenced Hess to life in prison. Did his sanity come into question at the trial?*

Hess had long been an eccentric, fussy hypochondriac. The Nuremberg psychiatrists pronounced him sane enough for trial, which does not necessarily mean normal. He often appeared uncomprehending or apathetic. Some thought he was faking.

*He then became "Prisoner #7" in Spandau. What do the years of confinement reveal about him?*

Hess acted as he had in British captivity, only he seemed more paranoid, depressed, and withdrawn. He annoyed the other prisoners, wouldn't cooperate with staff, and refused to seek release or even see his family for many years. From 1966 until his death in 1987, Hess was Spandau's only inmate.

*Not wanting out of jail, and not wanting to see family—isn't that insane?*

Hess had lucid times all his life, even in his feeble final years touched with senility, but those grew progressively rarer. No one knew for sure whether he'd crossed the threshold to insanity, whether faking insanity became his norm, or whether he drifted back and forth between moments of sanity and insanity.

*When and how did he die?*

Hess died on August 17, 1987, at age 93. Officially, he hanged himself with electric cord. Dissenters argue that he was too feeble to hang himself, that there were signs of struggle, that his suicide note looks fake, and that his second autopsy suggests manual strangulation.

*Wouldn't that merit a big investigation?*

Spandau was in the British sector of what was then West Berlin. An inter-Allied commission consisting of France, the United States, Britain, and the Soviet Union operated the prison. They did not apply a high standard of forensic investigation. Soon after Hess's death, Spandau was razed, every brick ground to powder and the rubble dumped in the North Sea.

*Does that ending suggest a cover-up?*

Not necessarily. Hess's death meant closure of a prison, a four-power Cold War diplomatic issue, and a major expense for the West German government. For 21 years, Spandau had no purpose but to house a single ancient Nazi. At 93, likely close to a natural death, he seemed to have killed himself.

*What of the theories of his death in a plane crash and replacement by a double?*

A British flying boat did crash under odd circumstances (i.e., a flying boat crashed on land) in Scotland on August 25, 1942, 15 months after Hess's Bf-110 flight. Some allege Hess was aboard the second flight, and a double had replaced him in the Bf-110. Major questions regarding the prisoner included loss of lifelong habits and knowledge, as well as major discrepancies, including the prisoner's lack of a major chest scar Hess received during World War II. Yet Hess's wife and son believed him genuine. Their view is not easily dismissed. Also, photos of Hess at Spandau look quite like elderly versions of earlier photos of him. Hess had a distinct look, with brambly eyebrows and a square jaw.

### What has infused this case with such levels of suspicion?

Britain has kept documents related to Hess and his imprisonment carefully guarded.

### Will we ever know more?

In 2017, more British archives are slated for declassification. That doesn't mean they'll be intact. Some information is on permanent loan to the Royal Archives, where only the monarch's direct order can reveal it. This permanent loan raises suspicion that the lent files might humiliate the House of Windsor, which may be why many of them remained secret.

&#10066;  &#10066;  &#10066;

- *Hess bailed out not because he couldn't land his aircraft—he was an experienced pilot even before the war—but because it was dark and he had lost his bearings. Even so, had he shown more sense, he wouldn't have been in that predicament.*

&#10066;  &#10066;  &#10066;

- *Rudolf Hess, Hitler's deputy, should not be confused with Rudolf Höss (often spelled Hoess), SS officer and Auschwitz executioner. The latter was hanged for his wartime exploits.*

&#10066;  &#10066;  &#10066;

- *When Hess landed, he was face-to-face with Scottish farmer David McLean. He introduced himself as Captain Alfred Horn. Farmer McLean called the authorities, of course, to whom Hess soon revealed his true identity.*

# IL DUCE'S REIGN OF ERRORS

*During World War I, Italian Prime Minister Giovanni Giolitti
remarked that the generals he had to deal with were the products
of a country where the stupidest sons, black sheep, and halfwits
had been sent into military careers. Their successors in World War
II were a similar embarrassment, made worse by the vanity and
obtuseness of Benito Mussolini.*

Often making irresponsible decisions, Mussolini was an adept
political bully who had a thin grasp of military matters. He played
his own game of favorites in the military, often promoting less than
competent new officers who were loyal Fascists. Some historians
speculate that Mussolini had an inferiority complex in dealing with
his generals, whom he often played off one another in a strategy
of "divide and rule." He was hampered by his continual rivalry
with King Victor Emanuel III, who maintained a jealous relationship with the military: The professional officer class was loyal to
the King, not *Il Duce*. The Italian military command resembled
a comic opera of mutual distrust, clique rivalries, and personal
feuds.

Despite his shallowness in military affairs, Mussolini believed that
preserving his power required supervising the military personally.
In 1926 he made himself minister of the marines, the navy, and
the air force, and remained so until 1943. His frequent contradic-
tory decisions led to administrative paralysis, making intelligent
coordination of the armed forces nearly impossible.

Mussolini was impressed with large numbers rather than quality of troops and armaments, and on paper, the Italian military
looked impressive. But infantry divisions were largely made up of
conscripts and reserve troops from the peasantry, who were badly
equipped and poorly trained. Their few tanks were inferior to any
armor the Allies fielded.

*Il Duce*'s dilettantism would be his downfall, as World War II quickly turned bad for Italy. Three months after declaring war on the Allies, Mussolini ordered the invasion of British-controlled Egypt in September 1940. The misadventure would end five months later with Commonwealth troops having nearly routed the Italians from Libya, capturing 130,000 POWs while suffering less than 2,000 casualties of their own.

Not content with an offensive in North Africa, *Il Duce* also invaded Albania in October 1940. After a few victories, the Italian drive stalled and soon faced a Greek counter-offensive. Despite having more troops, the Italians were again nearly routed. Disastrous defeats in the Balkans and North Africa were staved off only by Hitler's interventions, diversions that hampered Germany's war on the Eastern Front (the Nazi invasion of the Balkans delayed Hitler's invasion of the Soviet Union by six crucial weeks).

After little consultation with his generals, Mussolini insisted on sending an Italian expeditionary force to join the Germans on their march to Moscow. A year and a half later, the entire Italian Eighth Army was destroyed outside Stalingrad. Simultaneously hundreds of thousands of Italian troops surrendered to British and American forces in North Africa.

With the Allied occupation of Sicily, King Victor Emmanuel III joined his generals in ending *Il Duce*'s reign of errors. Following a meeting of the Fascist Grand Council on July 25, 1943, the king called Mussolini to his palace and stripped the dictator of his power.

Rescued from his imprisonment a few days later by German paratroopers, Mussolini was installed by Hitler as the ruler of the Italian Social Republic, a Fascist puppet state set up in northern Italy to support the German occupation. On April 28, 1945, Mussolini and his mistress, Clara Petacci, were shot by Italian partisans and hung by their heels at a street market in Milan. Mussolini's corpse was subsequently shot with arrows and guns, and beaten with fists and objects. Once the people had taken their vengeance, *Il Duce* was cut down, his battered face literally unrecognizable.

# CIVILIAN CASUALTIES AT PEARL HARBOR

*While the largest loss of life at Pearl Harbor on December 7, 1941, occurred when the forward magazine on the battleship USS Arizona exploded, a forgotten fact about the "Day of Infamy" is that at least 48 civilians also lost their lives.*

The Japanese attack on U.S. naval forces at Pearl Harbor began at 7:53 A.M. Hawaiian time, December 7, 1941. By 9:00 radio stations throughout the island urged civilians to "get off the roads and stay off...don't block traffic...stay at home."

Friendly fire was a major cause of American casualties. Thirty-two civilians were killed in the city of Honolulu. The largest group was killed on the corner of Kukui Street and Nuuanu Avenue. Jitsuo Hirasaki, his three children, and their cousin all died when an anti-aircraft shell exploded on top of their family-run restaurant. Seven restaurant patrons also died.

The second largest loss of civilian life came at the intersection of Judd and Iholena streets. Joseph Adams, his son, John, Joseph's brother-in-law Joseph McCabe, Sr., and McCabe's nephew David Kahookele had just attended Catholic Mass and were on their way home when they heard a radio announcement asking all shipyard workers to report for work. The men were killed en route to Pearl Harbor when an antiaircraft shell hit their car. Twelve-year-old Matilda Faufata was killed by shrapnel from the explosion while standing in her front doorway.

On Kamanaiki Street in north Honolulu a family of four was killed in their house by an exploding shell. Sisters Barbara and Gertrude Ornellas were killed by shrapnel: Gertrude was standing on the front porch and Barbara was in her bedroom. The girls' uncle, Peter Lopes, and family member Frank Ohashi also lost their lives.

Hayako Ohta, her three-month-old daughter Janet, and the baby's aunt Kiyoko died when a shell hit their building on the corner of King and McCully Streets.

Patrick Chong and his seven-month-old daughter Eunice Wilson were killed when a shell exploded near their house on Leilehua Lane. Nineteen-year-old Edward Kondo died in the same area, while several of his family members were wounded.

Torao Migita, a private with D Company, 298th Infantry Regiment stationed at Schofield Barracks, was the only Japanese-American serviceman to die on December 7. Migita was on a weekend pass when he was killed in downtown Honolulu.

Ten civilians died in various rural locations on Oahu including Wahiawa, Waipahu, Pearl City, Red Hill, Ewa, John Rodger Airport, and the Kaheohe Bay Naval Air Station.

The greatest loss of civilian life outside of Honolulu occurred at Hickam Air Force Base. Three members of the Honolulu Fire Department, Captain John Carreira, Thomas Macy, and Harry Pang, were killed when a Japanese bomb exploded in the hanger where they were fighting fires. Two other civilians died at Hickam.

Despite the fact Japanese planes strafed targets after dropping their payload, only one civilian was killed in this manner. Daniel LaVerne, a defense worker at Red Hill, died late on December 10 after being hit by bullets from a Japanese plane.

According to the 1940 census, 160,000 Hawaiian residents were of Japanese descent. A large mix of Korean, Chinese, and Filipino descendents also called the islands home. While official estimates of civilians killed on December 7 ranges from a low of 48 to a high of 68, the great majority of those killed were of Asian-Pacific descent. Just as the young men of America's military had their lives taken from them that fateful Sunday morning, so too did a group of largely forgotten Hawaiian civilians.

# LIGHTNING STRIKES FROM ON HIGH

*The most successful American fighter was the P-38 Lightning. The single-seat, twin-engine craft and its skilled pilots compiled an astonishing ten-to-one kill ratio against Japanese opponents.*

The P-38 was designed by Clarence "Kelly" Johnson and his team of Lockheed engineers, the nucleus of the legendary "Skunk Works" shop. The prototype cost $134,284. NASA's predecessor, the National Advisory Committee for Aeronautics, performed the wind-tunnel tests. In 1939, during a publicity stunt, the P-38 broke the cross-continental flight record with a time of seven hours, two minutes. Although the test pilot crashed on landing, the Army Air Force had already contracted Lockheed for 66 P-38s.

## HIGH MARKS FOR THE LIGHTNING

The plane set many other performance marks. Its two turbo-charged V-1710 engines propelled the craft at 413 mph, a speed unmatched until the jet-powered P-80 Shooting Star entered service in 1944. Its range—1,100 miles—was tops for any U.S. fighter. Moreover, the P-38 could climb to 40,000 feet, and it zoomed up far faster than hostile planes. The twin engines made it more durable than the single-engine P-51 Mustang fighter.

Advanced features led to unmatched versatility. The P-38 could double as a bomber and carry 4,000 pounds of munitions, almost as much as a B-17. Equipped with two torpedoes, it had the potential to attack large ships, although it never did so in combat. Outfitted with radar, it served as a nighttime reconnaissance plane. But most impressive was its firepower. You may have seen archival footage of U.S. fighters strafing and blowing up Japanese ships; in all likelihood the footage was shot by camera-equipped P-38s, firing four .50-caliber machine guns and a 20-mm cannon.

# A TOP SECRET TASK

The P-38's strengths played to its most famous mission, the killing of Yamamoto Isoroku, Commander in Chief of the Japanese Combined Fleet and mastermind of the Pearl Harbor attack. In April 1943, naval intelligence intercepted plans for Yamamoto's airborne arrival at Ballale Airfield off Bourgainville in the Solomon Islands.

A U.S. ambush force arrived at its destination at 9:34 A.M., exactly as the punctual Yamamoto's entourage appeared, with its two Mitsubishi "Betty" bombers and six Zeroes flying cover. Four attacking P-38s sent the admiral's bomber crashing into the jungle. All but one P-38 returned safely to base. U.S. newspapers published a cover story stating that an Allied coast watcher had spotted Yamamoto, leading the Japanese to believe their communications were still secure.

## MINOR SETBACKS

Still, the P-38 had its problems. Earlier models had a terrifying tendency to freeze up during dives. Because the engines were off to the side, they provided no warmth to the cockpit, which was freezing cold during bomber support runs over Germany. Because the P-38 was so fast, pilots could not open the canopy in flight, so they kept the canopy shut, and sweltered in the tropical Pacific.

## LIGHTNING ACES

The Lightning's best pilots overcame the obstacles. One was Major Thomas "Tommy" McGuire, credited with 38 kills, 7 in one battle alone. He scored the second most kills ever among American pilots. The top American ace of all time was Major Richard "Dick" Bong, with 40 kills, and like McGuire, a winner of the Congressional Medal of Honor. Bong once buzzed the San Francisco area on a P-38 training flight, knocking the clothes off a woman's laundry line. His enraged commander ordered, "Monday morning you check this address out in Oakland, and if the woman has any washing to be hung out on the line, you do it for her!"

But fun and games were few for such aces. The physical forces of an all-out air fight would literally warp the metal of their planes. But the exertions were worth it. Said Sakai, the Japanese ace, "The P-38 ... destroyed the morale of the Zero fighter pilot."

# POISON FOR YOUNG MINDS: NAZI EDUCATIONAL LITERATURE

*The methods and materials used to instill Nazi virtues of strength and purity in German children led to cultural disaster.*

Though it lasted only 12 years, the German Reich was supposed to last a thousand. Early in his political career Hitler argued that in order to survive and prosper, future generations of Nazis would need to maintain a single-minded dedication to purity and strength. As such, the Nazis imbued all areas of public education with their party's ideology. These lessons took several forms:

## Children's Stories
One of the more widespread lessons taught to young children was a story called "The Poison Mushroom." A mother and her son are picking mushrooms in the forest, and the boy finds some poisonous mushrooms. The mother compares the dangerous mushrooms to the dangers of a certain kind of people. The boy rightly concludes that she is speaking of the Jews. The mother is proud of her son and exhorts him to learn to identify Jews in all their dangerous guises. The story was part of a collection published by Julius Streicher, who was executed as a war criminal in 1946. Repugnant yet alluring art by "Fips" (Philip Rupprecht, a *Der Stürmer* staffer) is the capper.

## Primers
Nazi elementary books used simple illustrations and stories of children. Many of the stories include veneration for military parades and weapons. They also portray Hitler as a great man who is kind to children who bring him gifts. In one story, a boy named Karl attends a Hitler Youth rally. He wants to march with his older brother, but is too young. After the march, a race for young children takes place. Karl wins and receives a sausage and a pretzel, which he promptly eats.

## Geography

Geography lessons stressed the concept of *Lebensraum* ("living space"), which Nazis proclaimed would provide the German people with land and resources that had been stolen from them after the Great War. Texts emphasize not only the need for this territory, but also the Germans' historical right to it. They mention Germany's cultural and historical influence on the countries surrounding it, as well as its geographic disadvantages, such as the ease with which the country was blockaded during World War I.

## Biology

In German textbooks, biology was synonymous with racial purity and strength. Girls were given rigorous instruction in the selection of a suitable mate and the proper method of nurturing the next generation of Germans. Women's magazines often ran articles advising mothers to raise strong, physically active children who eschewed the classroom for the playing field. The articles advised parents to be stern with their children since "only he who has learned to obey can lead."

## Mathematics

Even the discipline traditionally least susceptible to cultural bias, mathematics, was tainted by Nazi influence. For instance, word problems asked students to calculate the amount of money wasted on handicapped citizens and the amount of ammunition a plane could carry over a certain distance to bomb an ethnic slum.

☆ ☆ ☆

- *A 1937 Nazi pamphlet for teachers,* The Jewish Question in Education, *quotes "Munich scientist Dr. Escherich," who relates a hare-brained tale of guards at a thriving termite colony who fall for the seductive charms of "foreign insects" of a different "race." In short order, "the foreigners had murdered the queen," and destroyed the colony. The pamphlet suggests that schoolteachers encourage students to draw a parallel between this astonishing natural event and predatory Jews who threaten the Aryan gene pool.*

## Fast Facts

- Beginning in the fall of 1942, each American family was limited to three gallons of gasoline per week and two new pairs of shoes per year.

- During the Second World War, 43,000 Americans were conscientious objectors, refusing to serve in combat. Of these, 37,000 agreed to serve in noncombat roles, and the remaining 6,000 were jailed.

- The gold leaf of the Massachusetts State Capitol dome on Beacon Hill in Boston was painted black to thwart enemy planes during the war.

- The famous comedy duo of Abbott and Costello donated their profits from a 1942 cross-country tour to the U.S. government to build a bomber. They raised about $89 million.

- The term "allotment Annie" referred to women who married American servicemen about to be deployed overseas in order to collect the allotted $50-per-week allowance—and perhaps the $10,000 life-insurance policy accorded each man.

- At the height of the war, the Office of Price Administration (OPA) printed as many as three billion ration stamps per month.

- Former Congressmen Maury Maverick, head of the Smaller War Plants Division, coined the term "gobbledygook" for the overwhelming proliferation of bureaucratic jargon engendered by the war.

- Virtually no photographs showing only dead American soldiers were published until nearly two years after the end of the war.

- The American B-24 Liberator, which went into service in 1943, had an unprecedented 18-hour flight time and succeeded in closing the North Atlantic submarine surveillance gap.

- By 1944, the U.S. government had 3.8 million employees, up from 1 million in 1939.

# DORIE MILLER:
# AN UNLIKELY HERO

*Doris "Dorie" Miller, so named because his mom's midwife had
expected a girl, stood that early December 1941 morning on the
deck of the USS West Virginia. Trained as a cook, no one would
have thought he'd emerge from Pearl Harbor as a hero.*

## DECEMBER 7, 1941

Twenty-year-old "Dorie" Miller joined the navy in September
1939. He enrolled at the recruiting post in his hometown of Waco,
Texas, after taking a ride in the back of the bus with a group of
other black recruits. Blacks in the navy were then restricted to
kitchen duty. So when he enrolled, Miller became a mess attendant, eventually working his way up to ship's cook.

On an otherwise sleepy Sunday, Miller watched as an array of
aircraft drew near. Two sections of the squadron dove toward the
harbor and the airfield at adjacent Ford Island. Alongside his ship,
the *West Virginia,* was the battleship *Tenneesee.* Along the quays
forward were the *Maryland* and the *Oklahoma,* and to the stern
was the *Arizona.* One of Miller's duties was to collect officers'
laundry on Sunday mornings, so unlike most of the crew he was on
duty. Although barred from a combat post because of his race, he
had proved himself a fighter—he was the *West Virginia's* heavy-
weight boxing champ.

It was odd, Miller thought, that aircraft were training so close to
a naval and air base. Then four of the planes dove toward Ford
Island. Suddenly, the airport's hangar and a clutch of Devastor dive
bombers on the runways exploded in flames. Miller later recalled,
"I found myself an unwilling occupant of a front-row seat from
which to witness the proceedings."

Miller watched another group of planes, rising suns on their wings,
veer down toward the *West Virginia,* and drop five 18-inch-wide
torpedoes into the waves. Within seconds the ship shuddered

and heaved from massive explosions. Soon after, Japanese planes dropped two armor-piercing bombs into the battleship, sparking massive fires.

The ship's communications officer pressed Miller into action—the captain was bleeding badly and had to be moved. Miller and the officer made a nightmarish journey through the dark, smoke-filled corridors of the vessel. En route Miller felt a gigantic explosion—not from the *West Virginia,* as it turned out, but from the nearby USS *Arizona,* which had blown up, taking the lives of 1,177 men. Employing his strength as a boxer and an ex-high-school fullback, Miller helped hoist the gravely injured captain to the forecastle, and later to the bridge.

Back on deck, Miller saw the ship was listing; water poured over the side. Just ahead, Miller could see the now-capsized hull of the *Oklahoma.* He pulled wounded sailors on the main deck to the relative safety of the quarterdeck. Miller and Lieutenant Commander Frederic White then turned to a half-dozen survivors bobbing in the fiery, oily waters alongside their battleship. He and White tossed out ropes, hauled the sailors aboard, and then collapsed from exhaustion. However, the force of 181 Japanese aircraft continued their bombing and strafing runs.

Miller and White rushed to a pair of Browning .50-caliber antiaircraft machine guns. Even as a cook, Miller had been trained for combat, but not specifically in the use of antiaircraft guns. He put his training in gear. "The sky seemed filled with diving planes and the black bursts of exploding antiaircraft shells," he remembered. He tracked a swooping Japanese plane through the gun sight, his thumbs squeezing the firing levers. Smoke billowed out of the aircraft. Seconds later, it crashed, throwing up a great plume of water from the embattled harbor.

"It wasn't hard," Miller stated. "I just pulled the trigger and she worked fine. I had watched the others with these guns. I guess I fired her for about 15 minutes." As the attackers tried to finish off the U.S. Pacific Fleet, Miller and a few other gunners battled back defiantly. Finally, the *West Virginia* settled into the shallow harbor, with 130 of its 1,541-man crew killed. Miller and other survivors swung over by rope to the waiting *Tennessee.*

## STATESIDE RECOGNITION

Word spread back to the mainland about Miller's Pearl Harbor heroism. The *Pittsburgh Courier,* a prominent black newspaper, campaigned to have the sailor decorated. And in May 1942, Admiral Chester W. Nimitz, commander of the Pacific Fleet, stood on the aircraft carrier USS *Enterprise* and personally awarded Miller the Navy Cross, the service's third-highest decoration. Said Nimitz: "This marks the first time in this conflict that such high tribute has been made in the Pacific Fleet to a member of his race and I'm sure that the future will see others similarly honored for brave acts." Capitalizing on Miller's fame, the navy sent him stateside on a war-bonds tour, with stops in his hometown of Waco and in Dallas, and at Chicago's Great Lakes Naval Training Center, which had begun training blacks for positions more responsible than mess attendant.

## DORIE RETURNS TO SERVICE

One more war mission awaited Miller. He was onboard the escort carrier USS *Liscome Bay,* whose planes supported the bloody but successful November 1943 invasion of Tarawa atoll. As the invasion fleet was readying to leave the area, the Japanese submarine I-175 struck the carrier. Its torpedo ignited the magazine and practically tore off the vessel's stern where Miller was manning an antiaircraft gun. He was most likely killed instantly (though not officially presumed dead until a year and a day later). Three hundred seventy-three of his fellow 646 crewmen were also killed.

Miller's courage against the enemy and against the racial codes of the day had great effect. In February 1944 the Navy commissioned its first black officers, and in 1948 President Truman formally integrated all branches of the U.S. armed services. A final legacy of Miller's was the commissioning in 1973 of the *Knox*-class frigate the USS *Miller,* named in his honor. The *Miller* saw service in the Persian Gulf, Black Sea, and elsewhere.

# THE DEATH OF HITLER'S DREADNOUGHT

*From the time she set out on her first mission in May 1941, the German battleship* Bismarck *inspired fear in the North Atlantic. Fortunately for the Allies, her reign was brief—albeit violent.*

## THE TERROR OF THE SEAS

Realizing that Germany's *Kriegsmarine* could not hope to defeat Britain's Royal Navy in a ship-to-ship engagement, the Third Reich built the battleship *Bismarck* as a heavy commerce raider. She boasted eight 15-inch guns mounted on four massive turrets and could speed along at 32 knots in calm waters. Broad enough to ride out treacherous North Atlantic swells, *Bismarck* could out-fight any ship that got in her way.

Commissioned in August 1940, *Bismarck* did not sail until May 19, 1941, when she weighed anchor in company with the heavy cruiser *Prinz Eugen*. The two ships were the core of Operation *Rheinübung* ("Rhine Exercise"), the Reich's plan to destroy Allied shipping, draw British battleships away from the Mediterranean, and temporarily cut Britain's lifeline to America.

Heading across the Norwegian Sea to the Denmark Strait, *Bismarck*'s commander, Admiral Günther Lütjens, hoped to break out into the open waters of the Atlantic and prey upon Allied convoys. Because the Royal Navy could eventually organize enough battleships to send him to the bottom, Lütjens knew that success would depend on evading the watchful eyes of British planes and vessels.

## SINK THE *BISMARCK!*

From the time Britain's cryptologists got wind of *Bismarck*'s departure, the RAF and Royal Navy worked overtime tracking the German threat. RAF bombers narrowly missed her at anchor, and two heavy cruisers patrolling the Denmark Strait, the *Suffolk* and *Norfolk*, were driven off by *Bismarck*'s massive, long-range guns.

On May 24, *Prinz Eugen* picked up the hydrophone signal of two large ships heading toward the Denmark Strait. Closing in, Admiral Lütjens engaged the British battleship *Prince of Wales* and her consort, the battle cruiser *Hood*. At about nine miles out, the British ships turned to bring their broadsides to bear against the Germans. But before they could range their targets, *Bismarck's* gunners managed to drop a 15-inch shell onto the *Hood* from about nine miles away, plunging through her decks and setting fire to her magazines. *Hood* exploded amidships, broke in two, and sank within three minutes, taking all but 3 of her more than 1,420 crewmen to their deaths. *Prince of Wales*, hit seven or eight times during the 10- to 15-minute battle, pulled away under a smoke screen, all but one of her heavy guns out of action.

The Battle of the Denmark Strait was a resounding victory for the *Kriegsmarine's* sailors, but they paid a price: *Bismarck's* forward fuel tanks had been hit, the forward radar was smashed, and she had to reduce speed to 20 knots to conserve fuel. Worst of all, the Royal Navy knew exactly where the German squadron was; they would undoubtedly be back—and in greater numbers. Weighing his options, Admiral Lütjens decided to cross the Atlantic and head for St. Nazaire, a friendly French port in which he could safely repair his ship.

The Royal Navy gave top priority to sinking the *Bismarck*. With the ship still in their sights, a squadron of "Swordfish" torpedo bomber planes attacked the *Bismarck* shortly after the *Hood's* sinking, but they did little damage. The savvy Admiral Lütjens managed to evade

his pursuers for nearly two days, sailing to within 700 miles of the French coast. Then a reconnaissance plane spotted the flagship, and before long, the aircraft carrier *Ark Royal*, the battle cruiser *Renown*, and the cruiser *Sheffield* managed to corner the wounded tiger before she could reach French waters.

*Ark Royal* launched a squadron of Swordfish against the German dreadnought, scoring one lucky hit that jammed *Bismarck's* rudder, leaving her helpless. By May 27, the British battleships *King George V* and *Rodney* closed in for the kill. Lütjens knew what was to come. He radioed headquarters that his position was untenable; he would fight to the last shell.

*Bismarck's* final battle began just before 9:00 A.M. on May 27, just nine days after leaving port. *Rodney, King George V,* and two heavy cruisers, *Norfolk* and *Dorsetshire*, fired some 2,876 shells at their prey, blowing apart *Bismarck's* upper structure and killing most of her senior officers. About an hour later, the *Dorsetshire* ranged for attack. To avoid a mass drowning, the *Bismarck's* executive officer ordered the crew to scuttle and abandon ship. Less than two hours from the initial salvos, *Bismarck* slipped beneath the waves, taking more than 2,100 sailors to the bottom.

## HITLER'S GREY GHOST

The legend of the *Bismarck* persisted long after her death, through stories and films such as *Sink the Bismarck!* (1960) and a 2002 James Cameron documentary on her final resting place.

There was also a popular, 1960 Johnny Horton tune that reminded radio listeners of the most dangerous battle cruiser to sail the oceans:

*The* Bismarck *was the fastest ship that ever sailed the seas.*

*On her decks were guns as big as steers and shells as big as trees . . .*

The tune ends with a musical tribute to the Royal Navy's gallant sailors and their bloody work:

*We found the mighty* Bismarck

*And then we cut her down.*

# Timeline

## 1940

**May 20**
Chinese counterattack in Shansi Province

A concentration camp begins operating in Oświecim, Poland, known as Auschwitz in German

**May 26–June 3**
Allied troops evacuated from Dunkirk to Britain

**June 5**
Germans begin offensive in southern France

**June 7**
Norwegian leadership flees the country and establishes a government-in-exile in London

**June 10**
Italy declares war on Britain and France, Canada declares war on Italy; South Africa, Australia, and New Zealand will join Canada the following day

**June 12**
Japanese take Yichang, China

**June 14**
German forces occupy Paris

**June 20**
France allows Japanese military missions into Indochina

**June 22**
France surrenders to Germany

**June 24**
France surrenders to Italy

France closes Indochina frontiers

**June 28**
Britain recognizes General Charles de Gaulle as leader of Free French forces

**July 1**
U-boat "Happy Time" begins in the Atlantic

French government relocates to Vichy

**July 2**
Japanese take Lungchou, China

**July 3**
British Navy sinks French warships at Mers El Kebir, Algeria, and commandeers French ships in British ports to prevent them from falling to the Germans

**July 10**
Battle of Britain begins with a Luftwaffe raid on docks in Cardiff and Swansea

**July 11**
Henri Pétain becomes head of France's Vichy government

**July 16**
Japanese Cabinet resigns; Prince Konoye becomes premier, Hideki Tojo becomes war minister

**July 18**
Britain acquiesces to Japan's demand that the Burma Road be closed to shipments of war materiel, cutting off aid to China

**July 19**
Roosevelt signs the Naval Expansion Act, providing a 70 percent increase in the size of the U.S. Navy

**August 3**
Italy invades British Somaliland from Ethiopia

# MAVERICKS WITH WINGS: THE FLYING TIGERS

*The ragtag group of volunteer pilots and outdated planes may not have seemed impressive at first, but the Flying Tigers earned a legendary reputation for defending the Burma Road.*

In 1937, Captain Claire L. Chennault of the U.S. Army Air Corps was 44 years old and suffering from partial deafness. He had served in the First World War, had spent time as the Chief of Pursuit Training, leading the development of combat tactics, and had been part of the three-man Air Corps' precision flying team, "Three Men on a Flying Trapeze," but he was fed up with military bureaucracy. He had argued frequently with his superiors. Chennault retired from the Air Tactical School in 1937, and after receiving an offer from Madame Chiang, wife of Generalissimo Chiang Kai-shek, to train China's fledgling air force, he moved to China.

The Chinese pilots considered instruction demeaning, and Chennault watched helplessly as the nation's air force was reduced to almost nothing by the superior Japanese pilots. During this time, however, Chennault was able to observe the Japanese pilots' tactics firsthand, and he amassed a collection of training manuals and aircraft specs from downed enemy planes.

In 1940, he returned to the United States with the intention of recruiting American pilots and planes to form a volunteer air force, paid by the Chinese but ostensibly operating under the aegis of the Central Aircraft Manufacturing Company (CAMCO, an American company that also assembled planes in China). Despite the protests of numerous military officials, President Roosevelt gave the plan his approval. The company soon recruited 300 men (100 pilots and 200 ground crew) to form the core of the American Volunteer Group (AVG) in China. The pilots traveled on the Dutch ship Jaigersfontaine, and carried passports that listed occupations as diverse as metalworker, teacher, and farmer.

## BIRTH OF THE TIGERS

Once in China, the group occupied an old British air base, and Chennault began relentlessly drilling his men on the geography of their new home and the flying tactics employed by the Japanese pilots. Chennault managed to procure 100 Curtiss P-40B Tomahawk fighters—ill-equipped for combat, these planes lacked gun sights, bomb racks, and provisions for attaching auxiliary fuel tanks. Nevertheless, the intrepid ground crews learned how to fashion crude ring-and-post gun sights for the planes and improvised using spare parts and scrap metal to make up for their other deficiencies. Though slower and heavier than the Japanese fighters, the P-40Bs were tough and could dive much faster than the lighter enemy craft. Chennault taught his pilots how to use these traits to their advantage.

Soon after arriving in China, some of the pilots noticed a magazine illustration of a P-40 in North Africa emblazoned with a grinning shark face on its nose. It made an impression, and soon all of the AVG planes were painted with the characteristic fierce smiles. Walt Disney Studios designed many of the U.S. squadron logos, including a winged tiger flying through a victory "V," and the group quickly earned the nickname the "Flying Tigers."

In case they were shot down in friendly territory, each pilot was issued a silk blood chit scarf with the free China flag, which read: "This foreign person has come to China to help in the war effort. Soldiers and civilians, one and all, should rescue, protect, and provide him medical care." Some of the pilots sewed the chits on the back of their flight jackets, others simply stuffed them in their pockets.

## THE TIGERS PROVE THEIR METTLE

The only supply route to interior China without access to China's ports in the fall of 1941 was the tortuous Burma Road. Beginning at the Burmese port of Rangoon, supplies were transported to Lashio in northern Burma and finally carried over the 717-mile road to Kunming in Southwest China. At the behest of the British defenders of Rangoon, Chennault sent one of his three AVG squadrons to Rangoon. On December 25, 1941, the AVG shot down 23 Japanese planes in their first and biggest single-day victory. On January 23, the Japanese launched an all-out attack on the city, losing 21 more planes to AVG. In 10 weeks of intense aerial battles over Rangoon, the Flying Tigers shot down 217 enemy aircraft with the loss of only 4 American pilots and 16 aircraft. The British pilots barely broke even against the Japanese, while the Americans established a 15–1 kill ratio.

## THE LEGEND LIVES ON

During the war, the AVG shot down 286 enemy aircraft and kept the port of Rangoon open for two and a half crucial months, saving China from collapse. Moreover, its victories provided a much-needed morale boost for Chinese and Americans in the darkest days of the war.

Winston Churchill praised the efforts of the AVG in defending Rangoon. "The victories of these Americans over the rice paddies of Burma," he wrote, "are comparable in character, if not in scope, with those won by the RAF over the hop fields of Kent in the Battle of Britain."

The AVG disbanded on July 4, 1942, and was absorbed into the U.S. Army Air Force. By that time, many of the original pilots had returned to their respective services; the techniques they had learned from Chennault spread quickly through the American squadrons. Many of the war's top aces saw their first combat as Tigers, including Tex Hill, Charlie Bond, John Petach, and Gregory "Pappy" Boyington, who went on to form the Black Sheep squadron.

# THE ARYAN "SPRING OF LIFE"

*Seeking to ensure a steady influx of "racially pure" children into society, the Reich established the* Lebensborn *program, which provided care for mothers who gave birth out of wedlock— provided they were Aryan.*

Heinrich Himmler, commander of the dreaded *Schutzstaffel* (SS), officially unveiled the *Lebensborn* ("Spring of Life") program on December 12, 1935. Located in Munich, the registered society sought to support members of the SS and their offspring. In fact, the program encouraged the men to reproduce even if they were not married: The core objective was to carry on their bloodline.

Himmler decreed the minimum offspring expected of a member of the SS was four boys. His rationale was that "a nation which has an average of four sons per family can venture a war; if two of them die, two transplant the name. The leadership of a nation having one son or two sons per family will have to be fainthearted at any decision because they will have to tell themselves, 'We cannot afford it.'"

## PROMOTING RACIAL PURITY

Declining birth rates and a high abortion rate contributed to *Lebensborn's* creation. One of the main goals of the program was to provide "racially pure" unwed mothers the opportunity to give birth to their children in secret and without scrutiny.

To be accepted for care at *Lebensborn* facilities, the mother had to prove that the father of her child was "racially approved." Many of the fathers were reported to be men of the SS, and as such fulfilled that requirement.

Himmler encouraged unwed SS officers to marry the mothers of their children. If the SS officer was already married, the society encouraged the mother to keep the child and provided a wide range of assistance programs to help her raise the child, including grocery coupons and better apartments with subsidized rent.

The first *Lebensborn* home opened in 1936 in the small village of Steinhoring, outside of Munich. Other maternity homes soon cropped up across Germany, often located in refurbished villas, ski chalets, or hotels. The society also operated homes outside of Germany's borders, opening the first facilities in occupied Norway in 1941. Later it established maternity homes in Austria, Belgium, Denmark, France, Luxembourg, and the Netherlands.

## WHAT BECAME OF THE PROGRAM?

Some 15,000 to 20,000 children were born in *Lebensborn*-run homes in Germany and Norway. While *Lebensborn* wards operated in other countries, the number of children born there is not known.

Most *Lebensborn* documents were destroyed at the war's end. When Nazi forces were driven from an occupied country, *Lebensborn* facilities were quickly closed, and all related documents were transferred back to the original home outside Munich. When American forces entered Steinhoring in May 1945, SS officers fled the area and either burned or dumped the documents in the Isar River.

Several former administrators of the *Lebensborn* program were charged after the war with kidnapping children in occupied countries. Unknown thousands of children were reportedly taken by force from their homes in Poland, the Ukraine, and the Baltic countries and resettled with German families. The defendants were found not guilty.

After the war, rumors persisted that the *Lebensborn* program was nothing more than a breeding program for Nazis. However, when scholars searched through captured *Lebensborn* documents at the U.S. National Archives, they found no such evidence.

In 2005, the *Lebensspuren* ("Traces of Life") society was formed to help children of the *Lebensborn* program. Many of these children grew up without knowing their real parents. The society was formed to act as a support network and help survivors trace their genealogy.

# Fast Facts

- In the 1930s, British negotiators had given up the right to use Irish ports in wartime. Churchill bemoaned this decision—launching escort ships from Cork or Galway would have added hundreds of miles to their range. He even hinted that Britain would consider invading the Republic from Northern Ireland—the Six Counties whose British control many Irish still resented. The day after Pearl Harbor, Churchill sent Taoiseach (Prime Minister) Eamon de Valera a simple message: "Now is your chance. Now or never! A nation once again. I will meet you wherever you wish." However, de Valera never replied to the message.

- Poland was the first to discover the underlying clues to the German ENIGMA encryption machine. In 1939 the Polish handed the ball off to the British; it then became the ULTRA project. While Polish arms performed valiantly in Europe, this handsome present may have been Poland's greatest gift to Allied victory.

- In August 1942 Admiral Karl Dönitz, commander of the Kriegsmarine U-boat arm, made a colossal political mistake. In search of easier sinkings, he sent a U-boat squadron to the coast of Brazil—a nation friendly to the Allies but still officially neutral. The U-boats sank five Brazilian ships, just off Bahia, in one day. While these were not the first U-boat sinkings of Brazilian vessels, they were the most brazen. Crowds rioted in Rio de Janeiro, venting rage on Nazi flags and German-owned businesses. On August 22, 1942, Brazil declared war on the Axis.

- A U.S. draftee had to be at least 5 feet tall and weigh 105 pounds; he also had to have at least 12 teeth. The two most common physical attributes that led to a draftee being rejected were flat feet and venereal disease.

- In January 1942, the bodies of sailors from merchant ships torpedoed by German submarines began washing up on Florida's beaches.

# BEASTS OF BURDEN

*Although World War II is well-known for its tanks, airplanes, and advanced communications, both sides were surprisingly reliant on old-fashioned horses and mules to keep their armies provisioned and on the move.*

## HORSES IN THE GERMAN ARMY

Despite the German Army's reputation for panzer assaults, only 1 out of 6 of its 300 divisions were armored or mechanized. A German infantry division had a striking low-tech component: Typically there was one horse for every three of its men. The proportion of horses was even greater for mountain and light divisions. And the use of horses grew as Allied bombers destroyed Germany's industrial plants for manufacturing tanks and for refining petroleum. Meanwhile, the extensive horse farms of Prussia and Pomerania lay untouched, their production strong until overrun by Soviet armies in 1945.

Horses were especially vital for the German and Russian armies on the Eastern Front. The region's vast expanses, primitive highways, and extremes of weather put enormous strains on mechanized transport. Horses were often better suited than trucks for traversing the endless steppes or for slogging through muddy or snow-covered roads.

Contrary to general belief, the German juggernaut that invaded the Soviet Union was surprisingly low-tech—at least 750,000 horses supported it. They demanded 16,350 tons of feed daily, according to the Eisenhower Institute. Much of the grain to sustain them was taken at gunpoint from Russian peasants, adding to the horrific losses of civilians under the occupation.

The animals themselves suffered staggering losses. According to the Imperial War Museum, the Soviets used 21 million horses in the war; 14 million perished between June 1941 and May 1945. The Germans lost 6.7 million horses in the East. When surrounded at Stalingrad, starving German soldiers ate 26,000 of them.

## RELYING ON MULES IN BURMA

U.S. General Joseph "Vinegar Joe" Stilwell faced the seemingly impossible task of conquering the Japanese-occupied land in Burma. He desperately needed to get supplies to China's hard-pressed armies. His force, "Merrill's Marauders," commanded by General Frank Merrill, had to retreat, and then advance, across hundreds of miles of jungle, mountains, and swift-flowing streams. With mechanical equipment scarce and hard to maintain under the tropical conditions, mules proved essential to the enterprise.

During their 1942 retreat along the Chaunggyi River in Burma, many in the ragtag force keeled over from heatstroke. Then-Major Merrill succumbed to a heart attack. To survive, the soldiers had to rely on unusual means of transport. Forestry Service officers from Great Britain commandeered 60 native men to haul equipment. Stilwell requisitioned a mule team from China that had crossed his path. He limited his exhausted men to carrying ten pounds of gear and put everything else on the mules, including the sick and injured men who could no longer walk. Stilwell's soldiers survived, barely escaping a pursuing force of Japanese cavalry.

"Mule skinners" and "muleteers," as the animals' drivers were called, learned the peculiar habits of their animals. Their charges hated bodies of water, making river crossings difficult, and hated elephants even more. This was a problem in Burma, where pachy-derms had long been used to carry cargo. And, being mules, the creatures were stubborn: Their refusal to leave corrals and rest spots nearly allowed the pursuing Japanese to catch up.

In the 1944 Galahad offensive to seize Burma's strategic Myitkyina airfield, the Marauders had to march over the bamboo thickets of the Kumon mountain range, crossing one winding river some 56 times. They had to cut out steps through the passes for the mules. Some animals slipped off mud-covered passages to their deaths. Half the 3,000 humans in the force were felled by exhaus-tion or disease—or from kicks by the ornery beasts. "For weeks we had more casualties from mules than from Japs," remembered Lieutenant Don Thrapp.

Each rifle company in the expedition was assigned 42 mules. The medics got a dozen mules, mostly to evacuate wounded. The animals, which weigh about half a ton, can carry about 200 pounds of equipment. Mortars and heavy machine guns required four mules each to haul. Other animals were obtained from Chinese troops, who captured tiny Japanese ponies and traded them to the Americans for cigarettes, flashlights, or other items. In 1944–45, the British followed the Americans' lead, employing 7,000 horses and 24,000 mules in Burma, along with elephants that cleared jungle paths.

Feedstuff for the animals was dropped from C-47s in 80-pound bags onto designated fields. "Occasionally a plane load of grain would get mixed up with parachuted loads," recalled Thrapp. Such cargoes, accelerating downward for a thousand feet, sometimes would hit unsuspecting soldiers, killing them.

## PHASING OUT THE BEASTS

Yet, World War II remained the first mostly mechanized war. The year before Pearl Harbor, the U.S. Army still had a pair of regiments with horse-drawn artillery, as well as two cavalry divisions and several regiments with combined motor and horse transport. However, horses found few uses outside of patrolling the coasts for U-boats. The last U.S. cavalry unit to see action was the 26th Cavalry Regiment, the Philippine Scouts. In March 1942, at the besieged Manila Bay bastion of Corregidor, its 250 horses and 48 mules were slaughtered to supply food for the starving U.S. and Filipino defenders.

In 1943, only four new horses were brought into service. After the war, the Army's horse-breeding program was transferred to the Department of Agriculture.

Still, in at least one future conflict, the beasts of burden continued to serve. During the Korean War, a mule captured from the Chinese Army, with brand ID 08KO, turned out to be one that the U.S. had given the Chinese during the Second World War.

# "VINEGAR JOE" BATTLES THE JAPANESE—AND HIS ALLIES

*U.S. General Joseph Stilwell was adamant in his efforts to fight the Japanese in the Indo-Burma-China Theater. His cantankerous personality and disagreements with other officers earned him the nickname "Vinegar Joe."*

A West Point graduate who won a Distinguished Service Medal for his service in France during World War I, Stilwell served three tours in China in the 1930s and became fluent in the language. He was rated the best corps commander in the U.S. Army in 1940, and when war broke out, he initially was chosen to head the Allied invasion of North Africa. Because of his experience in China, however, Stilwell was sent back to Asia to ward off the Japanese.

Stilwell arrived in Burma during the Japanese offensive and personally marched U.S. forces by foot from their overrun positions. Wearing an old campaign hat, GI shoes, and no insignia of rank, he presented himself as the "soldiers' general" and captured the imagination of an American public in need of a hero. However, his bluntly honest assessment of the situation—the Japanese had just cut off all land and sea routes that Allies had been using to resupply forces in China—foreshadowed the frustration that would continue to mark his command. He undertook resupplying China through air cargo lifts that flew over "The Hump" of the Himalayas, and began training two Chinese divisions in India.

The India-Burma-China Theater remained a low priority for supplies and troops, and Stilwell struggled to spur his allies into action. Generalissimo Chiang Kai-shek, commander of Chinese Nationalist forces, was more concerned with fighting his Chinese Communist foes in a looming civil war. Chiang hoarded his Lend-Lease supplies rather than using them to fight the Japanese, and often issued orders contradicting Stilwell's attempts to engage the enemy. Infuriated by what he considered Chiang's corruption and incompetence, Stilwell filed reports to Washington offering his assessments and tried to have Lend-Lease aid cut off to China. He also feuded with General Claire Chennault, commander of American air forces in China, who sided with Chiang and also made his own large demands for supplies.

To break the political deadlock, in 1943 Stilwell was given charge of the new Southeast Asia Command under British Vice Admiral Mountbatten. Although he did lead British and Chinese troops in taking territory to shorten supply routes to China, the offensive took heavy casualties. Among Allied troops, some doubted his competence after units such as the British Chindits and "Merrill's Marauders" were nearly wiped out. When Japanese forces overran Chinese air bases in 1944, General Chennault blamed Stilwell for the losses. However, earlier on, Stilwell had advocated delaying Allied air offenses in the theater until forward bases could be fortified by infantry—advice that Chennault refused.

After three years of struggle with recalcitrant and corrupt allies, horrendous supply problems, and some of the most difficult geography in the world, in October 1944 Stilwell was unceremoniously relieved of his command. Historian Barbara Tuchman wrote that Stilwell was removed to placate Chiang and his powerful backer, the "China Lobby" in Washington. "Vinegar Joe" had undermined his own position with his harsh assessments and inability to get along with allies, subordinate officers, and other American commanders in the theater. Always a professional, however, he refused to criticize the decision or his detractors. Before the war ended, he was given command of the U.S. 10th Army during the battle for Okinawa and later served as U.S. 6th Army Commander.

Stilwell died of cancer on October 12, 1946, at the Presidio of San Francisco, still on active duty. His service in the Far East would have profound impact during the postwar years. After reading Stilwell's assessments of Chiang, President Harry Truman pronounced the Nationalists "all a bunch of damn thieves!" and cut support to the regime, precipitating their downfall and the victory of the Chinese Communists.

# Timeline

## 1940

**August 13**
"Eagle Day" in Battle of Britain: The Luftwaffe bombs British fighter airfields and aircraft factories

**August 20**
Chinese Communists launch "Hundred Regiments" offensive, attacking Japanese-held railways in northern China

**August 23–24**
The Luftwaffe bombs London—though oil facilities east of the city are targeted, London proper sustains most of the damage

**August 25**
First RAF bombing raid on Berlin

**August 29**
Vichy France cedes bases in Tonkin (Indochina) to Japan

**September 3**
The United States agrees to give destroyers to Britain in exchange for bases

**September 7**
The London Blitz begins

**September 13**
Italy invades Egypt from Libya

**September 15**
Massive German bombing raids on English cities: climax of Battle of Britain

**September 17**
Hitler indefinitely postpones Operation SEALION, the invasion of Britain

**September 22**
Japanese invade Indochina

**September 27**
Germany, Italy, and Japan sign Tripartite Pact, an economic and military alliance that will form the Axis

**October 1**
Japanese occupy Weihaiwei, China

**October 17–20**
U-boats sink 32 ships in 2 Allied convoys

**October 18**
In defiance of Japan, Britain reopens the Burma Road

**October 23**
Franco meets with Hitler in Spain; refuses to join Axis

**October 28**
Against Hitler's wishes, Italy invades Greece

**October 28–29**
Chinese retake Lungchou and Nanning; Japanese troops retreat to Indochina

**October 29**
United States holds first-ever peacetime military draft

**November 1**
Jews are forbidden to leave the Warsaw ghetto

**November 5**
Franklin D. Roosevelt elected to third presidential term

**November 11**
British carrier planes sink three Italian battleships at Taranto, Italy

**November 14**
Most of Coventry, Britain, including its stunning cathedral, is destroyed in a Luftwaffe raid on the city; the Night Blitz begins

# ROMMEL'S WAY

*Led by "Desert Fox" Erwin Rommel, Germany's Afrika Korps
nearly took the Suez Canal. Was it leadership? Tactics?
Luck? Enemy bungling? All of the above? How on earth
did Rommel do it?*

German General (later Field Marshal) Erwin Rommel fought for
Africa's Mediterranean coast from 1941 to 1943. He took over a
disintegrated Italian position in western Libya, stormed all the way
to Egypt, was forced to retreat to his starting point, and rebounded
again to within 60 miles of Alexandria—the gateway to the Suez
Canal. In the end, even with his forces caught in Anglo-American
pliers, he fended off his enemies in Tunisia for months.

## CONDITIONS IN AFRICA

Rommel's achievements were impressive given his circumstances:

- The German Army was low on supplies near Tripoli, a problem
  that grew worse every mile his men advanced from that main
  base.

- The German panzers in Africa were adequate, but rarely
  superior.

- Rommel's men came to Africa unschooled in desert warfare.

- His Italian allies interfered, and disappointed him in battle.

- British code breaking enabled the Allies to read Rommel's
  reports to and directives from Germany. (But Rommel had
  access to decoded British messages.)

In the end, it took a devastating blow followed by a crushing pincer movement to run Rommel and his *Afrika Korps* out of Africa.

The Allied divisions in Africa proved tough adversaries for the
*Afrika Korps*. Among the esteemed units were the Coldstream
Guards, the 9th Australian Division, the Long-Range Desert

Group, the Royal Gurkha Rifles, General Freyberg's New Zealanders, Klopper's dour South Africans, the Free Frenchmen of Bir Hacheim, and the Seaforth Highlanders—all of whom were proven warriors. The Allied forces generally had enough food, water, and fuel. They had air superiority. While some of their gear was unreliable, in the desert nothing was terribly reliable for anyone. While their commanders made mistakes, so did Rommel; in any event, their leaders were battle-tested career military men with guts of iron. And unlike Rommel's superiors, Churchill told his leaders to be aggressive—to march to the sound of their guns.

## ROMMEL'S RULES

The *Afrika Korps'* special élan emanated from its famous chieftain. Rommel's policies embedded themselves in his soldiers' minds. Soon his officers and men did things his way by reflex. If not, Rommel found out, and someone was sorry.

One of his rules taught itself by necessity: Don't waste. Rommel would not squander supplies or equipment, nor did his men. They couldn't afford to, for the *Afrika Korps* lived in a state of chronic scarcity. Getting Axis supplies past British-held Malta was like climbing a razor-wire fence: He who succeeds also bleeds. If his officers asked Rommel for more supplies, he would order them—without sarcasm—to steal from the Allies, who had plenty. Often they would.

Like most outstanding commanders, Rommel knew that soldiers will nearly always obey two commands: "Do as I do!" and "Follow me!" *Afrika Korps* troopers knew that Rommel might show up anywhere. He piloted his own reconnaissance plane over enemy territory. In one famous incident, he dropped a weighted note to his troops telling them to get moving or he would come down there. If Rommel's vehicle got stuck, Rommel would help push it free. He ate what his men ate; he took time to thank his troops for work well done. He set the example and expected his officers to follow.

Rommel stressed independence and flexibility. To understand why, it helps to grasp the low troop density of the theater. Virtually the whole campaign was fought along or near a single key road stretching over 1,000 miles, with an average of five to eight effective divisions on both sides until the end in Tunisia. (For comparison, the Russian front had hundreds of divisions. The day it was attacked in 1940, even the Royal Dutch Army had ten divisions.) This meant a scattered battlefield with units spread widely apart in open desert, requiring junior officers to act independently and with initiative. In far-flung desert warfare, his units reorganized themselves as situations developed. Rommel's standing order was "In the absence of orders, go find something and kill it." They usually did.

Near the end, with his forces pushed back in Tunisia, Rommel's health forced him back to Germany. Hitler refused Rommel permission to return to Tunisia and fight on with his troops, but the leader's spirit survived in them. As they prepared to surrender to the Allies, some of his last *Afrika Korps* troopers sent Germany a radio message worth remembering:

"Ammunition expended. Weapons and equipment destroyed. Obedient to its orders, the *Afrika Korps* has fought until it can fight no more. The German *Afrika Korps* will rise again! *Heia Safari!*"

Had they done any less, they might well have worried that Rommel himself would come to their POW camps under a flag of truce to give them a piece of his formidable mind.

✫ ✫ ✫

- *"Heia Safari!" translated as "Drive Onward!" was the Swahili-based motto and battle cry of the Deutsche Afrika Korps. The force changed names several times, but we remember it best by its most famous one.*

✫ ✫ ✫

- *The North African campaign might have been one of the most decent of the war, if any warfare can be called decent. The SS and Gestapo were absent from the theater, and with them the brutal fanaticism that often left a trail of atrocities. Many units would reach unofficial understandings when they outnumbered their foes, agreeing not to shoot without warning. Both sides were generally quite chivalrous to prisoners of war.*

# MIDWAY: SHATTERING THE EMPEROR'S SWORD

*Across miles of rolling oceans, the world's two mightiest fleets were about to wage the greatest aircraft carrier battle of all time. At stake: command of the Pacific Ocean.*

The epic contest began as a fight over a tiny coral atoll called Midway, some 1,000 miles northwest of America's naval base at Pearl Harbor. Japanese naval commanders, stung by the carrier-based Doolittle Raid on Tokyo in April 1942, hoped to draw the American flattops out of the vast emptiness of the Pacific Ocean and into a decisive battle, where they could be destroyed once and for all. To force the Americans to battle, Admiral Yamamoto Isoroku, commander of the Japanese Combined Fleet, decided to attack the island of Midway. If successful, in one stroke Yamamoto would rid the Pacific of an irksome U.S. air outpost—the "unsinkable carrier," it was called—and pose a serious threat to the Hawaiian Islands.

Yamamoto's tactical plan was simple: A carrier force would blast the island's air defenses, a battleship fleet under his personal command would reduce the coastal defenses to rubble, and a landing force would capture the real estate. With luck, the attack would also draw the U.S. carrier fleet into the open, where Japan's superior forces would send it to the bottom.

## OPPOSING FORCES

In late May 1942, Japan ruled the seas. For his assault on Midway, Yamamoto would call upon four huge aircraft carriers under Vice Admiral Nagumo Chuichi: the *Kaga, Akagi, Soryu,* and *Hiryu.* Yamamoto would miss two other carriers damaged at the Battle of the Coral Sea that same month, but with a fighting force that included several battleships, 2 light carriers, 16 cruisers, and more than 70 destroyers, Yamamoto believed he had little to fear.

The U.S. Pacific Fleet, commanded by Admiral Chester W. Nimitz, could only muster two carriers, the *Enterprise* and the *Hornet.* A third carrier, the *Yorktown,* had been seriously damaged at the Battle of the Coral Sea. As Nimitz was planning his next moves, *Yorktown* was back at Pearl Harbor, where 1,300 dockyard workers labored around the clock to get her back into service.

But Japanese fleet strength, impressive as it was, was largely offset by America's super-secret trump card: American code breakers had cracked the naval ciphers that the Japanese government believed to be impregnable. From radio intercepts, Admiral Nimitz learned of Yamamoto's plans for Midway, and Nimitz was determined to ambush Yamamoto as he pounced on America's tiny outpost.

Nimitz combined the *Enterprise* and *Hornet* carrier group with Task Force 17, a cruiser group reinforced with the timely arrival of the *Yorktown,* which had managed to slip her cables at Pearl Harbor on May 30. He threw out a protective submarine screen around Midway, and his carriers kept search planes circling in all directions, looking for an enemy lurking in the dark Pacific waters.

## HAMMERING THE "UNSINKABLE CARRIER"

The first contact with Nagumo's carrier fleet came around 5:30 A.M. on the morning of June 4, when a PBY reconnaissance plane based at Midway reported contact with a hostile carrier force. Base commanders at Midway scrambled their light bombers, and soon Nimitz knew the location of his foe. The contest for Midway was on.

Admiral Nagumo's four carriers launched 108 bombers and escorting fighters to devastate Midway's defenses, unaware of Nimitz's fleet just 215 miles away. U.S. Navy, Army, and Marine bombers from Midway took off to attack the Japanese fleet while fighters scrambled to take out the incoming Japanese bombers. The Marine warbirds waged a bitter fight against the agile A6M Zero fighters, but the attackers drove the Marines off with heavy losses, and soon bombs began falling on Midway. The Japanese effort was not wholly successful, however; circling over the island's air facilities, the Japanese attack commander radioed back to his carrier group that another air strike would be needed to put the island's facilities out of commission. Admiral Nagumo accordingly ordered his second-wave squadrons to remove their torpedoes and refit with bombs to finish off Midway's defenses.

While Midway was being plastered, the plucky U.S. submarine *Nautilus* stuck up her periscope in the middle of the Japanese formation. She let loose a torpedo, missing her target. She attracted unwanted attention for the next hour or so by the destroyer *Arashii,* which circled the sub's last position while the carrier fleet steamed away. This seemingly inconsequential skirmish would make a huge difference later on.

As U.S. bombing runs from Midway were ending in disappointment for the Americans, a Japanese scout pilot spotted *Yorktown's* flotilla and alerted his superiors. But his vague report did not fully communicate to Nagumo that a carrier group was heading his way. Nagumo had been in the middle of rearming his planes for a second bombing run against Midway, which he still considered the main threat, but after some delay he learned that the American surface ships included aircraft carriers. He ordered his planes to remove their bombs and again refitted his squadrons with torpedoes for an attack on the U.S. carrier force. Nagumo expected he was about to secure the eastern limits of the Empire of Japan.

## GOING FOR THE KILL

While Midway's airmen were being cut apart by Japanese fighters, Nimitz's task force launched three squadrons of torpedo bombers and five squadrons of dive-bombers, with their usual cordon of escorting fighters. The first wave of TBD-1 Devastator torpedo bombers from the *Hornet* ran into a swarm of Zeros, and the entire U.S. squadron was shot down. Two more torpedo squadrons attempted to get through to the Japanese carriers, with similar results.

As the Devastators were being gunned down by the deadly accurate Zero pilots, three squadrons of SBD-3 Dauntless dive-bombers from the *Enterprise* and *Yorktown* arrived high overhead, having searched for enemy ships without luck until two squadrons from the *Enterprise* picked up the wake of the destroyer *Arashii*, which was speeding back to join her carrier group after her run-in with the submarine *Nautilus*. In a stroke of luck, the three American dive-bomber squadrons arrived high over the Japanese carrier group.

The Japanese carriers had just turned into the wind to launch their bombers when they saw dive-bombers screaming out of the sky from two directions. The Japanese carriers were at their most vulnerable—their fighter escorts were engaged at low altitude, their flight decks were stacked with bombs and fuel, their planes were aligned on deck wingtip to wingtip. High explosive bombs rained down, setting fire to the decks and starting chain reactions as stored ordnance exploded and fuel burned out of control. Within minutes, the carriers *Kaga, Soryu,* and *Akagi,* Admiral Nagumo's flagship, were out of action with fires raging across their decks: All three would lie at the bottom of the Pacific by the next morning.

Nagumo's fourth carrier, *Hiryu,* steamed ahead of the other ships, striking back furiously at the American attackers. She managed to get 36 Type 99 Val dive-bombers and ten Kate torpedo planes off her decks around 11:00 A.M., sending them toward *Yorktown.* U.S. interceptors, Navy F4F Wildcats, shot down most of the Vals, but seven made their way to the *Yorktown* and three scored hits. A second wave of bombers put two torpedoes in her side, and she began to list. Her commander ordered the veteran ship abandoned, but she refused to die; the legendary carrier did not sink for another two days, and only then after a Japanese submarine put a third torpedo into her hull.

Although she had put *Yorktown* out of action, *Hiryu* would not live to see her victory. Dive-bombers from the *Enterprise* put four bombs along her flight deck, and fires soon gutted the hangar deck and engine rooms. The carrier's admiral and captain ordered the crew to abandon the doomed ship, and both commanders committed suicide. Japanese ships put a torpedo into her hull to keep her out of American hands, and she went down at 9:00 A.M. the next morning.

## THE RISING SUN BEGINS TO SET

The Battle of Midway profoundly shifted the balance of power in the Pacific. Japan lost 3,400 sailors and experienced carrier pilots, an admiral, three carrier captains, and two heavy cruisers. Most critically, four of Japan's precious carriers had been sent to the bottom, giving the U.S. the edge in naval airpower.

The war's great carrier battle also enabled the United States to take the strategic initiative and shattered Japanese plans for a defensive perimeter close to United States territory. For the rest of the war, Japan would remain on the defensive, while the United States, with its huge industrial might, would dictate the tempo of the struggle.

✯   ✯   ✯

• *Japanese battleships' gun shells contained dye to help gunners adjust their fire by the colored splashes.*

✯   ✯   ✯

• *Before the start of World War II, General Joseph Stilwell was nicknamed "Uncle Joe" for the concern he showed for average American GIs.*

✯   ✯   ✯

• *Many of the U.S. aircraft that launched from Midway Island were outmoded F2A-3 Buffalos—chubby, alarmingly slow fighters that flyers dubbed "Flying Coffins."*

# THE RISE AND FALL
# OF THE *LUFTWAFFE*

*It screamed out of the Polish sky, rained destruction upon
London, and smashed tanks along the Russian steppes. But by the
last year of the war,* Reichmarschall *Hermann Göring's dreaded*
Luftwaffe *had become a beast in its death throes, slain by the
overwhelming industrial might of the United States, Great Britain,
and the Soviet Union.*

The arm that gave the *Blitzkrieg* its devastating reach began as a
covert project before Hitler came to power. The Treaty of Versailles, signed at the end of World War I, forbade Germany from
fielding an air force. To evade the Versailles restrictions, the Weimar Republic developed training programs for ostensibly civilian
pilots, often at Dutch or Soviet bases. As Germany's land power
grew and the Third Reich no longer feared the threat of an invasion to enforce Versailles restrictions, the German government
began contracting with manufacturing concerns such as Junkers,
*Bayerische Flugzeugwerke* (Bavarian Aircraft), and Heinkel to
build a new generation of warplanes.

By 1936, when the Spanish Civil War broke out, the Nazi government sent pilots to Spain to undergo real combat testing under the
name "Condor Legion," fighting on the side of General Francisco
Franco's Fascists. Hitler's smuggled crews put the famous Messerschmitt Bf-109 fighter and the Junkers JU-87 Stuka bomber
through their paces. They flew terror-bombing raids on Republican strongholds such as Guernica, which later became the subject
of Pablo Picasso's famous painting of the same name.

By September 1939, when World War II broke out, Göring's *Luftwaffe* ruled the skies. The Stuka became the symbol of the *Blitzkrieg,* while the Bf-109 fighter dominated the air from the English
Channel to the Soviet border. Consistent with the *Blitzkrieg*
nature of German fighting, heavy, long-range strategic bomber

development was given a backseat to medium bombers such as the Heinkel HE-111 and the JU-88, which carried payloads of about 2,500 pounds of bombs.

In the summer of 1940, Hitler assigned the *Luftwaffe* its most ambitious operation to date—the destruction of the British will to resist. Göring assured his master that the *Luftwaffe* was up to the task, but the Battle of Britain handed his beloved air service its first major defeat. By asking vulnerable dive-bombers and slow medium bombers to enter skies swarming with hostile Spitfire and Hurricane fighters (and tipped off by radar installations), Hitler's eagles found a task beyond their ability.

After Hitler's invasion of Russia in 1941, the Eastern Front demonstrated in more dramatic terms the limits of German airpower. Horrendous weather grounded much of the *Wehrmacht*'s vaunted close air support, and the vast scale of fighting in the East—1,280 combat planes were committed to the invasion effort—drained the *Luftwaffe* of its most talented fliers.

By the end of 1942, the tide had begun to turn against Hitler's aces. Allied bombing had begun to affect supplies of fuel, engine oil, and parts needed for aircraft manufacture, and plants producing warplanes came under attack. British and American bombers began penetrating Göring's protective fighter screen in greater numbers, and the balance of airpower decisively turned against the men flying the swastika.

To make up for the disparity in numbers, Göring's engineers upgraded existing airframes with improvements such as heavier armament. The Stuka was fitted with a 37-mm under-wing cannon to combat tanks, the JU-88 fighter-bomber was accessorized with night-fighting radar, and the Bf-109 fighter was upgraded with a more powerful engine and heavier guns. From 1941 on, German designers were able to mass-produce a few superior new models, such as the Focke-Wulf 190 ground attack plane, but with increasing numbers of Allied P-38 Lightning and Yak-9 fighters appearing on both fronts after 1943, Germany's obsolete engines and airframes could not keep up.

To remedy the imbalance, the Reich looked for technological innovations. In mid-1944 it developed the first operational jet fighter, the Messerschmitt-262, which could outrun anything in the Allied inventory. But by then German factories could not produce the fast, high-flying Me-262 in the numbers needed to overcome their opponents in the air war. An even swifter rocket plane, the *Komet*, barely progressed beyond prototypes.

The Allies, whose production facilities were safely beyond the reach of German bombers, responded with improved models of their own, such as the upgraded Spitfire and Soviet La-7 fighters. When American P-51 Mustangs were able to escort bombers into the Reich's heartland, the *Luftwaffe* was doomed. One by one, aircraft engine plants, parts factories, and fuel refineries were shut down as Göring's men struggled to guard a shrinking pool of irreplaceable assets.

By early 1945, the *Luftwaffe* was a small (though still dangerous) shell of its former self. Antiaircraft crews knocked down four times as many Allied planes as the once-proud airmen, who could do little more than protect the skies above Prussia to buy time for their comrades to surrender to the west. Many pilots flew into captivity, their planes impounded. After the war, Göring, the once-cocky *Luftwaffe* chief, committed suicide in a Nuremberg jail cell, his swastika-emblazoned eagles grounded for all time.

✯　✯　✯

- Reichsmarschall *Hermann Göring had also been appointed Reich Hunt Master and Chief Forester; he took pains to preserve endangered raptor species of Germany.*

✯　✯　✯

- *Germany placed dozens of "rescue floats" in the English Channel to help* Luftwaffe *pilots who'd bailed from their aircraft. Each station provided food, shelter, and a first aid kit to tide the airmen over until rescue.*

# THE WOMEN IN HITLER'S LIFE

*Adolf Hitler's personality stands in the shadows of his historic legacy—much as he expected most women to stand in his own shadow. But since Hitler generally found women nonthreatening and more loyal than men, women saw parts of Adolf Hitler's inner self that few men ever did.*

## HIS MOTHER KLARA

The first woman in Hitler's world, of course, gave him life. Klara Hitler (née Pölzl) was the young wife of a much older husband when she brought "Adi" into the world on April 20, 1889. But their home would always be tinted with mourning, for Adi and his little sister Paula were the only two of Klara's six babies to survive to adulthood. Small wonder Klara spoiled her only surviving son, especially after his father died when Adi was only 13.

Hitler was devoted to his mother and revered her memory all his life. He was about 19 when she died from breast cancer— Adolf had spent months by her side caring for Klara as her condition worsened. Her loss severed a crucial strand binding him to humanity.

## HIS SISTER PAULA

With Paula, Adolf had friendly relations but little in common. After their mother's death, Adolf moved to Vienna and lost contact with his sister until the early 1920s. He did, however, assign her his share of the orphan's pension from the state. Beyond that, Paula and Adolf were in only sporadic contact for many years as their paths in life diverged.

## HIS HALF SISTER ANGELA AND HER DAUGHTER GELI

By 1928, Adolf Hitler was a bachelor nearing 40 and chieftain of a rising political party. He lived in a rented house in Bavaria. His half sister Angela Raubal (*née* Hitler, long since widowed) came to run the household, bringing her daughters Geli and Friedl. At about 20 years old, Geli Raubal was lovely, charming, and flirtatious—and Adolf fell hard for her. The fact that Geli was his niece and young enough to be his daughter did not seem to have bothered him; he behaved more like a jealous boyfriend than an uncle, restricting her from social and creative activities. Any time she showed interest in other men, as saucy Geli often did, her uncle went into a rage. After a bitter argument with Adolf one fall day in 1931, Geli was found dead with a bullet through her heart, an apparent suicide. Hitler was so distraught he considered following suit. His brief and stormy relationship with Geli brought his controlling nature and fierce jealous streak to the fore.

## EVA BRAUN

Even while Hitler was getting angry with Geli over her independent behavior, he had begun seeing Eva Braun, a receptionist/assistant in the shop of Hitler's official photographer. This would be his last and most enduring romance—but it was only on his terms. Hitler made Germany his first priority, often neglecting Eva. In the early years, when he had not yet consolidated his power, she was a well-kept secret and grew so lonely she tried twice to commit suicide. Later, their relationship became better known, but he resisted marriage until the Third Reich was beyond saving; she became Hitler's bride mere hours before the two of them committed suicide on April 30, 1945. Eva was presumably everything Hitler wanted in a lover: German, beautiful, much younger, loyally devoted to him, disinterested in politics, and content with mundane pastimes. He treated her tenderly enough, at least when he spared time for her.

## HIS SECRETARY TRAUDL JUNGE

In the professional sphere, Hitler mostly encountered women as secretaries. One secretary who shared her recollections was Traudl Junge (*née* Humps), who served Hitler until the last days in the bunker. Traudl described Hitler as a self-deprecating, considerate boss who tried hard to put her at ease. When her young husband died in combat at the front, Hitler took time out from the war to console her. The wives of Hitler's lieutenants also found him compassionate and charming at most times: He always asked about their children, and if they were along, he would talk to the boys and girls themselves.

## LENI RIEFENSTAHL

Hitler knew one woman who was nobody's stenographer: Leni Riefenstahl. Riefenstahl was already well-known in cinema as an actress when Hitler first asked her to produce a documentary. Lacking confidence, she initially delegated the project to a subordinate. Hitler found out, yet wasn't angry or harsh, simply persuasive as only Hitler could be. Riefenstahl reconsidered and poured herself into making the film. When Hitler suggested some changes to the film to placate certain politicians who felt slighted, she angrily refused, citing artistic principles. Not even his chilling reply "Are you forgetting whom you're talking to?" could bend her will. Hitler gave in, and Leni Riefenstahl did it her way. The result was her vision of the 1934 Nazi Party Congress in Nuremberg. *Triumph Des Willens* ("Triumph of the Will") has become one of the best-known examples of propaganda in film history.

☆ ☆ ☆

- *Hitler did not like cut flowers. He likened it to "being surrounded by corpses."*

☆ ☆ ☆

- *When Rommel first landed in Libya, in order to awe and galvanize Italian watchers in Tripoli, he used an ancient trick. His parading tanks circled, then moved out of sight, then paraded again, appearing to be a much larger force than was actually the case. Shortly thereafter, when he installed Italian divisions in their first defensive positions at Sirte, Rommel augmented them with wood and canvas fake tanks mounted on Volkswagens—a tactic to make the British hesitate. To the officer he appointed to command this "Cardboard Division," he joked, "I won't mind if you lose one or two."*

# *Fast Facts*

- In the latter half of his life, Hitler was a strict vegetarian—that is, if one considers sugar a vegetable. He put seven spoonfuls of it into every cup of tea, and he had a great appetite for pastries and chocolates.

- Children always charmed Hitler—yet he never seriously contemplated having any of his own.

- When he was a child, young Adolf was a hellraiser who once let a bunch of cockroaches loose in class.

- Before Hitler was a militaristic dictator, he was a draft dodger. He went to Germany partly to escape service in the Austro-Hungarian Army, under a regime he despised. Since he volunteered for the German Army immediately after World War I broke out, it certainly wasn't because he was afraid to fight.

- Hitler was way ahead of his time on tobacco. He forbade it in the Wolfsschanze command post at Rastenburg when he was present, lectured his guests on how it could damage their health, and pushed Eva Braun to quit.

- Eva Braun was quite talented with the camera. She is not in most color photos and films of Hitler's leisure life because she took many of them herself.

- Cosmetics turned Hitler off, because they came from animal by-products—but he didn't forbid Eva Braun to wear them.

- Hitler was a very wealthy man due to sales of Mein Kampf, which was a necessary social accessory in virtually every German office and household.

- Hitler suffered from meteorism (excessive intestinal gas), but there is no record of anyone having teased him about it.

- His favorite movie was King Kong.

- Rienzi, by Wagner, was Hitler's favorite opera. Wagner himself saw the opera as an embarrassment.

# LIEUTENANT VERNON BAKER AND THE BUFFALO SOLDIERS

*Of the almost one million black Americans who were either drafted or voluntarily enlisted in the U.S. Army during World War II, only one all-black Army division experienced infantry combat in Europe—the 92nd Infantry Division.*

Most black American soldiers during the war were relegated to duty as cooks, clerks, and other positions in rear-echelon units. The military, like much of American society at the time, was segregated. But after years of pressure from the black community, in 1941 the U.S. federal government relented and rescinded official policy that had excluded African-Americans from combat duty.

## BRING BACK THE BUFFALO SOLDIERS

Under the new policy, the 92nd Infantry Division was reactivated in October 1942. (The original 92nd Infantry Division was activated in October 1917. The all-black unit was sent overseas in July 1918 and saw action in the Meuse-Argonne Offensive, one of the last big military battles of World War I.)

The 92nd Infantry Division of World War II was a segregated unit composed of mostly Southern black enlisted men and junior officers under the exclusive command of white senior officers. Most of the enlisted men in the unit were uneducated and could neither read nor write.

The men of the 92nd maintained a proud tradition started by members of their World War I unit—they retained the buffalo as their divisional insignia. (Native Americans originated the "buffalo soldiers" term in 1866, in reference to the 9th and 10th black U.S. cavalry regiments.) The design featured a black buffalo in silhouette against an olive background. The 92nd kept a buffalo as its mascot and even named its newsletter after the animal.

The unit was sent overseas, disembarking in Naples, Italy, on July 30, 1944. Shortly after coming ashore, members of the 92nd first experienced combat when they faced off against German Field Marshal Albert Kesselring's troops at the infamous Gothic Line—a series of fortifications across the northern part of the Italian peninsula. One component of the 92nd, the 370th Regimental Combat Team, had its first taste of combat in September 1944 near the Arno River. By midmonth, the all-black regiment had managed to drive the defenders to the base of the Apennines mountain range.

## VALOR IN ACTION: LIEUTENANT VERNON BAKER

Vernon Joseph Baker was born in Cheyenne, Wyoming, on December 17, 1919. Tired of being what he called a "servant," Baker quit his job as a railroad porter and enlisted in the Army on June 26, 1941. He was later assigned to the 370th Regimental Combat Team.

On April 5 and 6, 1945, Lieutenant Baker led his weapons platoon, as well as three rifle platoons, in an attack on a German stronghold at Castle Aghinolfi near Viareggio, Italy. During the patrol, Baker managed to kill nine Germans single-handedly and destroy three machine-gun positions, an observation post, and a dugout. The following evening Baker led an advance patrol through minefields.

During the engagement, Baker claimed his white company commander abandoned him. When he returned to regimental headquarters to deliver the dogtags of the 19 men killed during the patrol, Baker later recounted being "chewed out by the regimental commander Colonel Sherman himself, because I wasn't wearing a steel helmet."

Lieutenant Vernon Baker was originally passed over for a Medal of Honor. He was awarded the Distinguished Service Cross for his actions. However, a 1992 study commissioned by the U.S. Army discovered "systematic racial discrimination in the criteria for awarding medals" during the war. The study recommended several African-American recipients of the Distinguished Service Cross, including Baker, be upgraded to the Medal of Honor. He received the highest military award from President Bill Clinton in a ceremony held at the White House on January 13, 1997. Of the seven African-Americans so honored at the ceremony, Baker was the only living recipient.

## RECOGNITION FOR SERVICE

The 370th fought German and Italian units throughout the Serchio River Valley in Tuscany and finished the war in the Ligurian city of Genoa. During the Italian campaign, 2,848 soldiers of the Buffalo Division lost their lives. These gallant African-American soldiers captured or helped capture some 24,000 enemy soldiers and, in return for their gallant conduct on the battlefield, received more than 12,000 decorations and citations.

Segregation in the military ended officially on July 26, 1948, when President Harry Truman issued Executive Order 9981. The order declared "that there shall be equality of treatment and opportunity for all persons in the armed services without regard to race, color, religion, or national origin."

---

## The "Tuskegee Airmen" Take to the Skies

One of the first groups of African-Americans to see action in World War II were the "Tuskegee Airmen." In June 1943, pilots from the 332nd Fighter Group conducted a dive-bombing mission against German units on the Italian island of Pantelleria. Battling the *Luftwaffe* throughout the war, the 332nd racked up an impressive record. They flew more than 15,000 sorties, often escorting bombers to their targets. In all, they downed 109 *Luftwaffe* planes.

# Timeline

## 1940

**November 14**
Greek counterattack drives Italians into Albania

**November 29**
Plans for Operation Barbarossa, the Nazi invasion of the Soviet Union, are finalized

**November 30**
Japan signs treaty with Chinese puppet government in Nanking

**December 9**
British begin Western Desert offensive in Egypt

**December 23**
Chiang Kai-shek disassociates himself from the Chinese Communist Party

**December 25**
With Italian bombers threatening, the town of Bethlehem is blacked out

**December 27**
Massive Luftwaffe incendiary raid on London

**December 29**
Roosevelt declares that the United States must be the "arsenal of the democracies"

## 1941

**January 5**
Chinese Nationalist and Communist forces clash

**January 10**
Greeks take Klisura, Albania

**January 16**
First Luftwaffe attack on Malta

French and Thai forces clash in Indochina

**January 19**
British forces invade Eritrea in East Africa

**January 22**
British take Tobruk, Libya

**January 25**
Japanese launch offensive in China's Honan Province

**January 31**
Japanese impose an armistice on Thai-French conflict

**February 1–14**
German battleship Hipper sinks seven ships in the Atlantic

**February 2**
Japanese capture Wucheng in Honan Province

**February 7**
At the Battle of Beda Fomm in Libya, British take Agedabia

Thailand and Vichy France negotiate a peace settlement in Tokyo

**February 11**
British invade Italian Somaliland from Kenya

**February 12**
Germany's Afrika Korps arrives in Tripoli, Libya, to aid the floundering Italian Army in North Africa; General Erwin Rommel is tapped for command of the Korps

**March 1**
Bulgarian King Boris is coerced into accepting Hitler's terms and joins the Axis; German troops occupy Sofia, Bulgaria

# THE MOST DECORATED UNIT

*From internment camps to combat in Italy, the men of the 442nd "Go for Broke" regiment of mostly Japanese-Americans proved themselves tenacious and loyal soldiers.*

When the Japanese attacked Pearl Harbor, future U.S. Senator Daniel Inouye, a Japanese-American high school student on Oahu, raced on his bicycle to help out at a first-aid station. An elderly Japanese man grabbed the handlebars of his bike, asking the 17-year-old Inouye, "Who did it? Was it the Germans? It must have been the Germans."

"I shook my head, unable to speak," recalled Inouye, a second-generation American, or *Nisei*. The Japanese-Americans "had worked so hard. They had wanted so desperately to be accepted, to be good Americans. Now, in a few cataclysmic minutes, it was all undone."

## UPROOTED AFTER PEARL HARBOR

For months, rumors flew around Hawaii that Japanese-Americans had sabotaged power plants and cut a giant arrow in the mountains pointing at Pearl Harbor. There were, in fact, some Japanese-American spies. One ring in Honolulu monitored U.S. warships entering and leaving Pearl Harbor. The West Coast Tachibana ring collected data on weapon factories, dams, and army and navy bases. But, after the attack on Pearl Harbor, roundups on the Hawaiian Islands of 1,800 first-generation *Issei* extended to businessmen, judo instructors, and Japanese language teachers. Every Buddhist monk, whose religion was linked to Japan, was taken into custody.

On the mainland, 110,000 Japanese-American residents, mostly from Washington, Oregon, and California, were ordered into internment camps. All Americans of Japanese descent were suspended from military service.

In Hawaii, however, 40 percent of the population was Japanese-American, and internment would have wrecked the economy. The small Hawaiian National Guard, largely *Nisei* in composition, was a different matter. The commander of the U.S. Army in Hawaii, General Delos Emmons, didn't trust them. He recommended sending the Guard's 298th and 299th Infantry Regiments to the mainland for reorganization. In June 1942, they shipped out.

## UNCERTAIN LOYALTIES

"When we landed in Oakland on June 12," recalled the 298th's Raymond Nosaka, "everyone thought we were prisoners." The Hawaiian regiments were formed into the 100th Infantry Battalion. Their ranks swelled in February 1943 when President Roosevelt rescinded the ban on Japanese-Americans in the military. He pronounced: "The principle on which this country was founded and by which it has always been governed is that Americanism is a matter of the mind and heart; Americanism is not, and never was, a matter of race or ancestry."

Still, prospective GIs were handed a loyalty questionnaire. Question 28 asked, "Will you . . . forswear any form of allegiance or obedience to the Japanese emperor, or any other foreign government, power, or organization?" Question 27 asked, "Are you willing to serve in the armed forces of the United States on combat duty, wherever ordered?" About a quarter of *Nisei* men, especially those with families interned on the mainland, answered "No" or didn't answer. Eventually, about 3,000 Japanese-Americans from Hawaii and 800 from the States joined for service.

Ronald Oba of the 100th Battalion was 17 when a Honolulu policeman spoke to his high school, telling the students, "You must volunteer, to prove your loyalty." Oba recalled, "I didn't take kindly to his words, because I was born an American . . . I didn't need to prove my loyalty." But Oba volunteered for the army for patriotism's sake. "My country needed me," he said.

## TRAINING THE 100TH INFANTRY BATTALION

Combat training began at Camp McCoy, Wisconsin, continuing with more drills at Camp Shelby, Mississippi. There, remembered

Oba, "Our superiors wouldn't let us off the trains until after dark, to allay the fears of Americans who hadn't seen Japanese before." He added, "[The] next morning, a newspaper headline read, 'Japs Invade Hattisburg.'"

Every officer, from company commander up, was white. Protestant chaplains took the place of Buddhist monks. There were also tensions at first between enlistees from the mainland (known as "katonks"—from the sound of a coconut falling on a head) and those from Hawaii (nicknamed "buddhaheads"—from Japanese-English slang, "buta," or "pig-headed").

Some recruits were sent to Camp Savage, Minnesota, for training as translators and interrogators of Japanese POWs. Others went to a secret training program at Cat Island, Mississippi, to act as "guinea pigs" for military Doberman pinschers and German shepherds. The army was attempting to train guard dogs to recognize the scent of Japanese soldiers. But "officials realized," said Nosaka, "that Japanese blood doesn't smell any different than American blood."

## ACTION IN ITALY

As Japanese-Americans were barred from fighting in the Pacific, the 100th fought in North Africa, Italy, and France. It formed part of the 34th, then later the 36th Division, of the U.S. 7th Army.

In Italy, the men saw heavy action at Monte Cassino, the bombed-out Benedictine monastery that blocked the way to Rome. The fighting there in early 1944 helped the 100th earn its nicknames, "the Purple Heart Battalion" and "the little iron men." In January, in an attack along the flooded Rapido River, the battalion faced the crack German 1st Parachute Division; of three assaulting American companies of 187 men, 173 were casualties. The next month, the battalion fought halfway to the monastery, but had to retreat when the units on its flanks couldn't keep up. One platoon lost 35 men out of 40. From an initial strength of 1,300, the 100th was reduced to 521 effectives.

In another Italian battle near San Terenzo, now-Second Lieutenant Inouye won a Distinguished Service Cross. "With complete

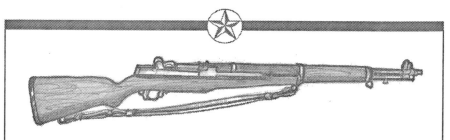

disregard for his personal safety," reads his citation, Inouye "crawled up the treacherous slope to within five yards of the nearest machine gun and hurled two grenades, destroying the emplacement... Although wounded by a sniper's bullet, he continued to engage other hostile positions at close range until an exploding grenade shattered his right arm. Despite the intense pain, he refused evacuation and continued to direct his platoon." Inouye lost his right arm; in 2000, his award was upgraded to the Medal of Honor.

## "GO FOR BROKE!"

The 100th Battalion merged into the 442nd Regiment in June 1944, and in August joined the invasion of southern France. The unit's motto was "Go for Broke." Its most memorable action occurred that October in the frigid, thickly forested Vosges Mountains near the German border. The *Wehrmacht* had cut off 211 men of the 141st Regiment, "the Lost Battalion," on a ridge and surrounded the approach with mines, tanks, machine guns, and mortars. The U.S. commander for the region told the 442nd, "There's a battalion about to die up there and we've got to reach them."

For many terrible days the regiment attacked the ridge. "We were charging uphill all the time," recalled 442nd veteran Henry Arao. The Germans "were just sitting waiting for us with machine guns. They had the hills loaded with mines. If you walked in the wrong spot, you'd get your leg blown off." Stung by frostbite and trench foot, soldiers cut their boots off of their swollen feet and slept in the snow. "The daytime sun doesn't penetrate there; it's dark as hell," recalled the 442nd's Tom Goto.

But "the worst was the tree bursts," Goto said. Mortar shells burst in the forest canopy, showering down burning splinters. "You can hear it whistling before it comes down, but by then it's too late," he added. Arao's squad leader was killed by mortar fire; only 4 of the unit's 17 soldiers got out in one piece.

Surrounded for six days, the San Antonio-based Lost Battalion, nicknamed "the Alamo Regiment," was losing hope. One of its sergeants, Bill Hull, remembered, "I thought I was going to die." So "I kept shooting, not worrying about saving my ammunition. Then suddenly there was a lot of noise behind me...when I turned to look I saw this little Japanese-American soldier jumping into the dugout."

After four days, the 442nd had broken through, but at horrific cost. At the start, the outfit had 2,943 men. But its casualties were at least 800, with more than 200 killed or missing.

The Purple Heart Battalion had a full strength of just 4,500 men. Yet in three years of combat, as men funneled in and out, it received 9,486 Purple Hearts and 18,142 decorations for bravery. These included 4,000 Bronze Stars with 1,200 Oak Leaf Clusters, more than 500 Silver Stars, 52 Distinguished Service Crosses, and 20 Medals of Honor. Seven hundred and forty-seven men were killed or MIA. In proportion to its size, it was the most highly decorated unit in the annals of the U.S. military.

The 442nd's Stanley Akita became "struck by the fact that other American units...wanted soldiers of the 442nd next to them in combat." Akita recalled the samurai role models he enthusiastically admired as a child. He noted, "We were taught from a very early age not to shame the family name, or embarrass the family by being a coward."

☆ ☆ ☆

- *The date of Rommel's counterattack to thwart the early phase of Operation Crusader, Auchinleck's counterattack that drove Rommel back to his start line, was grimly ironic: November 23, Totensonntag ("Sunday of the Dead") on the German calendar. The holiday honored Germany's World War I veterans. Rarely had it been celebrated in such fashion.*

# THE REAL RIVER KWAI

*For most people, the "bridge on the river Kwai" conjures memories of the Oscar-winning movie about British prisoners of war made to build a bridge in Japanese-occupied Southeast Asia. They might recall the film's compliant British commander, the firm-but-fair Japanese leader, the daring commando raid on the bridge. Yet in most respects, the movie got it wrong. In fact, the prison camp there was part of a system that resulted in some of Japan's worst war crimes.*

## BUILDING THE "DEATH RAILWAY"

The Khwae Yai, or Kwai, river bridge was part of a massive construction project, the Thailand–Burma Railway, to supply Japanese troops fighting in Burma (now Myanmar) and support an invasion of British India. The Allies were blocking Japanese freighters from sailing around the Malaysian Peninsula, and Tokyo needed a land-based route to transport 3,000 tons of supplies daily.

From September 1942 to October 1943, 61,000 Allied POWs and more than 200,000 native laborers constructed more than 600 bridges and laid track through deep mountain passes and thick jungle along the 257-mile line. The railway, built from track and other materials looted from Malaysian and Indonesian railroads, stretched from terminals near Bangkok to the Burmese coast. Decades earlier, British surveyors had deemed such a project almost impossible, requiring a minimum of five years to complete. The Japanese succeeded in 16 months—due to the ruthless use of forced labor for the "Death Railway."

The nickname was apt. Of the 61,000 POWs, about 16,000 died. Of those, 6,318 were British, 4,377 American, 2,815 Australian, and 2,490 Dutch. The death rate was higher among the native conscripts, mostly Thais, along with Burmese and Chinese—perhaps 100,000 perished. They endured brutal treatment; were poorly fed; and suffered from beriberi, dysentery, and other tropical diseases. Work shifts lasted 12 to 18 hours. Laborers at the mountainous "Hellfire Pass" were forced to lug 110-pound sacks of rice and share the burden of 600-pound buckets of concrete.

## THE NIGHTMARE OF THE KHWAE YAI RIVER

One of the major spans constructed along the route was Bridge 277, the concrete-and-steel Khwae Yai bridge, immortalized in *The Bridge On the River Kwai*. It was built by British POWs at the nearby prison work camp of Tha Maa Kham, or Tamarkan, in Thailand. The 1,200-foot-long construction was composed of 11 arches laid atop pylons painstakingly pulled and then pounded into the riverbed. A POW who survived described the toil:

"[The] Jap standing on the riverbank [shouted] through a megaphone the required rhythm . . . You pulled in unison, you let go in unison. *'Ichi, ni, san, si, ichi, ni, san, si'* . . . Hour after hour, day in, day out, from dawn to dusk. On returning to camp it was often difficult to raise the spoon to eat the slop issued to us. Your arms protested in pain, often preventing you from snatching some precious sleep. And yet, come dawn you repeated the misery of the previous day."

In the movie, the bridge is made of wood, but only a temporary span at Khwae Yai was made of that material. The movie also falsely portrays Tamarkan's real-life senior officer, British Lieutenant Colonel Philip Toosey, played in the movie by Alec Guinness as Lieutenant Colonel Nicholson. The real Philip Toosey refused to kowtow to the Japanese, but tried to foil them and protect his men. Under his charge, the POWs poured inferior concrete for the bridge and collected white ants to eat wooden constructions. Toosey complained about his men's mistreatment (although he was beaten for doing so), helped several prisoners escape, and contacted a daring Thai merchant, Boonpong Sirivejjabhandu, to smuggle in medicine and food. Refusing special treatment, he had all officers reside and eat with the enlisted men; his own weight dropped from 175 to 105 pounds during internment. Toosey was later knighted and made a brigadier general.

The film's portrait of Toosey enraged ex-POWs. Indeed, the movie was based on a Pierre Boulle novel *Le Pont de la Rivière Kwai*, which was based on the author's memory of French, not British, collaborationists.

There was no mistaking the kind of prison life later described by former POW Fred Seiker. Ordered up-country from Tamarkan to work on railway embankments, he recalled:

"You carried a basket from the digging area to the top of the embankment, emptied it, and down again to be filled for your next trip up the hill...The slopes of the embankments consisted of loose earth...very tiring on thigh muscles and painful, often resulting in crippling cramp. You just had to stop...Whenever this occurred the Japs were on you with their heavy sticks, and beat the living daylights out of you."

Caught snatching a container of fruit at another camp, Seiker was tied to a tree with barbed wire, beaten, left overnight, and told, falsely, he was scheduled for execution.

The dangers of disease surpassed the perils of work. Tropical ulcers disfigured limbs, sometimes requiring amputation—without anesthesia. Cholera, transmitted by contaminated water and through mud, was prevalent in the rainy season. During monsoons, recalled POW Rod Allanson, "We slept on boards within inches of black slimy mud...We would return from the railway covered in mud and extremely tired...We would go out to work each day stepping over the bodies of dead Tamils, and trudge four miles through more mud to the railway." In some camps, cholera killed almost all the native workers.

With barbed wire, the Japanese quarantined cholera-afflicted camps, ordering the corpses burned. During epidemics, inmates piled bodies around the clock onto smoking pyres. "It was particularly macabre...during nighttime," remembered a POW. "Bodies would suddenly sit up, or an arm or legs extend jerkily."

Camp doctors held "sick parades" late into the night to count the number of ill, trying to convince guards to give the afflicted days off from work. To survive, men resorted to ingenuity and tricks. Short of intravenous tubes, orderlies cut up stethoscopes to make drips. One overworked physician drew on his experience to later devise medical breakthroughs: After the war, Dr. James "Frank" Pantridge, a camp doctor, codeveloped cardiopulmonary resuscitation (CPR) and invented the portable defibrillator.

The savagery of camp life ended suddenly with war's end, as fleeing Japanese left the sick and malnourished inmates for rescue by Red Cross trains steaming up the railway the prisoners had built. After war crimes trials, more than 200 Japanese involved in the Death Railway were hanged.

As for the critical Khwae Yai bridge, it was destroyed, not by commandos, as in the movie, but by bombs. Allied flyers attacked the bridge eight times. In April 1945, U.S. pilots flying just above it hit the bulls-eye with four 1,000-pound bombs, destroying two spans, rendering the bridge impassable.

The destroyed sections were rebuilt by Japan as war reparations to Thailand. The bridge, and a lengthy section of the railway, are in use today—along with museums commemorating the tens of thousands lying in mass graves nearby.

✯　✯　✯

- *The bridge crosses the Mae Khlung River, not the Kwai. Writer Pierre Boulle—who didn't visit the bridge before writing his novel—knew a rail line ran parallel to the Kwai, and assumed that it crossed that river at some point.*

✯　✯　✯

- *In order to encourage tourism after the 1957 release of the blockbuster film,* The Bridge On the River Kwai, *the enterprising Thai government gave the Mae Khlung a new name: Kwai Yai.*

✯　✯　✯

- *Today, passenger trains cross the famed span three times daily, though many visitors prefer to travel by rickshaw.*

# JAPAN'S DOCTOR MENGELE: DOCTOR ISHII SHIRO AND UNIT 731

*Not only did Japanese scientists test their weapons on captives, Japan used them on a large scale against civilian populations. After the war, rather than bring the guilty to justice, the United States sold the guilty parties immunity from prosecution in return for their data.*

Dr. Ishii Shiro became the father of Imperial Japan's biological warfare and medical experimentation program. Though Japan had signed the 1925 Geneva Protocol, an agreement to not use biological weapons in war, it made little difference to Dr. Ishii. He recognized the danger of developing these weapons and wanted Japan to be on the cutting edge should they become necessary.

Like other ultranationalistic Japanese of his time, he considered other races less valuable than the Japanese. During the 1920s, Japan occupied Korea and was extending its influence into Manchuria and China, securing the resources (especially iron) Japanese industry needed for growth. Ishii figured he could use these conquered lands to benefit his research, and he cultivated influential supporters among the hawkish faction that was leading Japan toward militarism. When Japan invaded Manchuria in 1931 and transformed it into the puppet state of Manchukuo, Ishii hastened to obtain authority and funding to establish a medical and bio-weapon experimental facility.

The first facility opened at Harbin, but others soon followed at Beiyinhe, Pingfan (home of the actual Unit 731), Changchun, Hailar, Songo, Nanking, and other locations. After the Japanese invaded China proper in 1937, new centers followed the Japanese Army's progress. Each location received a numeric designation: Unit 100, Unit 731, Unit 1644, and so forth. Experimental subjects included political dissidents, captured guerrillas, other POWs, and even some average people scooped up by the *Kempatai* (secret police) as necessary. They included men, women, and children. Each facility contained cells to confine test subjects, lab and sample storage facilities, animal cages, and a crematorium. Researchers referred to the subjects as *maruta* ("logs").

## IN THE NAME OF "RESEARCH"

Researchers tested various means of spreading infection on thousands of *maruta*. The diseases read like a list of medieval horrors: glanders (respiratory lesions), visceral anthrax, typhoid, typhus, gas gangrene, smallpox, dysentery, bubonic plague, cholera, tuberculosis, syphilis, diphtheria, whooping cough, tularemia, scarlet fever, encephalitis, yellow fever, meningitis, Korean hemorrhagic fever, hepatitis, and more. During or after the tests, researchers dissected the *maruta,* often alive and always without anesthesia, to see if they could learn anything else. They removed samples and organs for preservation and then incinerated the remains.

Dr. Ishii's testing program went well beyond bioweapons. Researchers subjected *maruta* to phosgene, mustard gas, hydrogen cyanide, electricity, freezing, blood draining, amputation and reattachment, and radiation.

Once Ishii's organization had designed the weapons, the Japanese Army used them against both military and civilian targets. (Some claim these were merely field tests; others contend they were full-on biological attacks.) Aircraft dropped porcelain plague bombs, usually carrying multitudes of infected fleas. Men distributed disease-tainted food, released sick mice and rats, and contaminated wells. The full death toll is difficult to estimate, but it likely exceeds 50,000 and may be ten times that number.

## RECORDS AT THE EXPENSE OF JUSTICE

Ishii's organization tried to obliterate the evidence of their programs, but advancing Soviet troops captured some of the facilities and scientists in Manchuria. Their trial transcripts provided damning evidence about the scope of the program. After the Japanese surrender, U.S. officers interviewed former members of Unit 731. Fearing what might happen if the research fell into Soviet hands,

General Douglas MacArthur struck a secret, diabolical bargain with the bioweapons researchers. He ordered the scientists to turn over their research, and in return, stated that they would not be prosecuted. Safe from legal retribution, many Unit 731 researchers went on to very high positions in Japanese government and corporate circles after the war. Dr. Ishii Shiro died in 1959 in his native Japan, a free man.

☆　　☆　　☆

• *Despite popular perceptions created by admittedly atrocious World War II POW handling, Japan did not have a history of cruelty to captives. From the Sino-Japanese War of the 1890s through World War I, Japanese POW treatment was exemplary.*

☆　　☆　　☆

• *Not all of Dr. Ishii's research was devoted to bioweapons. He developed a water filter for soldiers in the field and demonstrated his invention before skeptics in a very graphic way. In full view of the audience, he urinated into a glass. Then he poured his fresh urine into his filter—and chugged the result.*

☆　　☆　　☆

• *Dr. Ken Alibek, the former Soviet bioweapons researcher, alleges that the Soviet Union unleashed a desperate biological attack on German troops before Stalingrad in 1942. The alleged agent was tularemia (rabbit fever), generally classed as an incapacitant among bioweapons. Alibek's contention has never been corroborated, but there was a documented and particularly virulent outbreak of tularemia in the Don/Volga region in late 1942.*

☆　　☆　　☆

• *Unit 731 wasn't a mystery to every American POW: Rebellious prisoners were routinely threatened with relocation to the facility.*

# HITLER'S VALKYRIE MAIDEN

*Named Unity because her parents hoped that World War I,
which had just begun, would end peacefully, she was also given
the middle name Valkyrie, after the Norse maidens of war.
Unity Valkyrie Mitford's life would prove as unusual
as her name.*

Unity Valkyrie Mitford, a tall, beautiful English woman who
became part of Hitler's inner circle, was one of six daughters of
David Bertram Ogilvy Freeman-Mitford, the eccentric Second
Baron Redesdale and noted Fascist sympathizer. Collectively
called the Mitford Sisters, the siblings were notorious for their
wealthy lifestyles and controversial political bents, which took
wildly divergent paths. Two of the sisters married nephews of
prime ministers. Sister Diana left her wealthy husband for British
Fascist leader Sir Oswald Mosley, while sister Jessica eloped with a
young Communist and served in the Spanish Civil War.

In 1932, Diana introduced Nazism to her younger sister Unity,
who quickly became enamored of Hitler. Unity persuaded her parents to send her to Munich for a year abroad. Through her German tutor, she learned of a local restaurant where Hitler dined and
managed to meet the Führer. Joined by Diana, the two Mitford
sisters soon counted Goebbels, Himmler, and Göring among their
acquaintances. Hitler called them "perfect specimens of Aryan
womanhood," garnering the sisters outraged coverage in the British press.

Calling her "more Nazi than the Nazis," British intelligence noted
that Unity once gave the "Hitler salute" to the British Consul
General in Munich and addressed Nazi rallies wearing a black
shirt. Besides her personal charms, the Nazis may have seen her as
a possible conduit to sympathizers in Great Britian, though her sister Jessica later noted that Hitler failed to understand their father's

lack of political influence.

Unity despaired as war loomed, saying she would rather die than see either Germany or Britain destroyed. She was in Germany on the day war was declared, and she sent a farewell letter to Hitler, then tried to kill herself with a pistol. The shot to her head didn't kill her, but it left her an invalid. Despite his preoccupation with the invasion of Poland, Hitler called the hospital several times to check on her condition and visited her before she was sent back to England.

Unity Mitford died in 1948 of meningitis, caused by the cerebral swelling around the bullet still lodged in her brain. After her marriage to Mosley, Diana became one of the most hated women in Britain and, along with her husband, was imprisoned by the British government for the duration of the war. Sister Jessica later moved to the United States, joined the civil rights movement, and became a noted investigative journalist. As the Duchess of Devonshire, sister Deborah turned her aristocrat husband's home of Chatsworth into one of Britain's most successful stately mansions, while sister Nancy had a longstanding relationship with French statesman Gaston Palewski and became one of the best selling novelists of her day.

☆   ☆   ☆

- *Unity Mitford was conceived in a cabin in Northern Ontario, Canada, outside the town of Swastika, where her father was speculating on a gold mine.*

☆   ☆   ☆

- *Unity's nephew, Jonathon Guinness, speculated that his aunt became enamored of Hitler and Nazism because of her intensely visual nature, which was sparked by startling propaganda images of the Party's enormous, stage-managed rallies at Nuremberg. To the day of her death, Mitford kept her Nazi armband, and lay in a bedroom filled with photos of her beloved Hitler.*

# "PAPPY" BOYINGTON AND HIS BLACK SHEEP

*The men of VMF-214 had a reputation as the black sheep of the U.S. Air Corps. However, the tactics and skill of the pilots and their commanding officer, "Pappy" Boyington, made them heroes.*

It was August 4, 1941, and Marine Corps aviator Gregory Boyington had reached rock bottom. Stationed in Pensacola, Florida, he was broke, his wife and children had left him, and his reputation for brawling and drinking had eliminated his chances of promotion despite his talent as a pilot.

That night in Florida, he knew that a representative of the Central Air Manufacturing Company was in a nearby hotel recruiting pilots for a volunteer mission in China. Tired of the Marines and lured by the promise of money, Boyington stopped at the bar for a few drinks and signed up.

He trained with the American Volunteer Group (AVG) in China, also known as the Flying Tigers. Led by Claire L. Chennault, the notorious group learned tactics to combat Japan's best pilots. Boyington remained a drinker and brawler, but with six kills, he earned a reputation as a formidable combat pilot as well. However, Chennault had a maverick personality, and his views frequently clashed with Boyington, who eventually left the AVG and rejoined the Marine Corps. He was recommissioned as a major and sent to New Caledonia in the South Pacific, where he mastered one of the service's newest planes, the bent-wing F4U Corsair.

While on convalescence following a leg injury, Boyington learned that the Marines badly needed to form new Corsair squadrons, and he organized an ad hoc unit comprising pilots and Corsairs dispersed by other units. The pilots' levels of experience ranged from combat veterans with several air-to-air victories, to new replacement pilots from the United States. Many of the pilots that Boyington pooled to form VMF-214 were known as misfits with reputations for discipline problems. The group quickly earned the nickname "the Black Sheep." Boyington once famously quipped, "Just name a hero and I'll prove he's a bum." A discipline problem himself, Boyington understood these pilots and trained them using tactics he'd learned as a Flying Tiger. It worked—in 84 days the Black Sheep destroyed or damaged 197 enemy planes.

His men called their leader "Gramps" because, though only in his early thirties, Boyington was ten years older than most of them. The press dubbed him "Pappy," and the name stuck as his reputation grew. Between August and September 1943, Pappy had added 22 confirmed kills and was on his way to eclipsing Eddie Rickenbacker's World War I record of 26 downed planes.

On January 3, 1944, however, Boyington was shot down and believed to be dead. In fact, he was taken prisoner by the Japanese, who, knowing his identity, tortured him and refused to report his status to the International Committee of the Red Cross. His fate was not known until 18 months later, when Boyington emerged from a POW camp. Though the numbers are disputed by some historians, Boyington is officially credited with 28 kills, making him the leading Marine ace of the war. He was awarded the Medal of Honor.

☆    ☆    ☆

- *Pappy Boyington published his popular autobiography* Baa, Baa Black Sheep *in 1958. Full of self-reflective passages, the book has since been criticized for factual inconsistencies. Nevertheless, it inspired a popular television series of the same name that aired from 1976 to 1978 and starred Robert Conrad as Boyington. Many members of the Black Sheep felt betrayed by the show's overstated portrayal of the unit as a group of hard-drinking, misbehaving rebels. Boyington, however, was proud of the show, and worked on it as a consultant.*

# BLITZKRIEG

*"Man schlugen jemand mit der Faust und
nicht mit gespreizten Fingern."*
*("One hits somebody with his fist and not with fingers spread.")*

—German tactician General Hans Guderian
describing the basic concept of Blitzkrieg warfare

The static trench warfare of World War I led to the deaths of
approximately ten million soldiers. Frontal attacks over hundreds
of yards, through open tracts of "no man's land" strewn with
barbed wire, offered defending soldiers easy targets that were
gunned down en masse. The appalling loss of life during the Great
War caused many military strategists to rethink how war was
waged.

## THE THEORY BEHIND *BLITZKRIEG*

The evolution of German military doctrine began in the years
following World War I. However, the new German Army was
severely limited in size and scope by restrictions placed on Germany by the Treaty of Versailles. To circumvent the treaty's conditions, General Hans von Seeckt signed a secret military alliance
with the Russians, which allowed the Germans to test new weapons systems and tactics at Russian military sites.

Prussian-born Heinz Guderian was instrumental in developing
new armored-warfare tactics. Fluent in both English and French,
he studied the theories advocated by military tacticians in Britain
and France. As the head of the Inspectorate of Transport Troops,
Guderian and his colleagues developed and tested new mechanized warfare strategies.

Guderian advocated the elements of what would later be called
*Blitzkrieg* in his book *Achtung—Panzer!* He believed an armored
attack along a narrow front supported by airpower would have the
best chances of success. In October 1937, Guderian wrote, "We
believe that by attacking with tanks we can achieve a higher rate

of movement than has been hitherto obtainable and . . . that we can keep moving once a breakthrough has been made."

The main elements of Guderian's new theory included

- Deploying a large number of tanks.

- Utilizing motorized infantry that could move rapidly in conjunction with tanks.

- Coordinating air force attacks against the enemy front line and rear echelon with a focus on airfields, transportation links, and communication centers.

- Using self-propelled artillery.

- Establishing radio communication between frontline units and command centers to ensure the proper coordination between army and air force units.

- Surprising the enemy. Germany never openly declared war before invading any country during the war.

The development of panzer divisions in combination with the new tactics enhanced the early successes of the German Army. Each panzer division was a self-contained unit consisting of tanks, mechanized infantry, self-propelled artillery, engineers, and antitank, antiaircraft, reconnaissance, and service personnel.

## PUTTING *BLITZKRIEG* TACTICS TO THE TEST

The first test of Germany's new military strategy occurred during the Spanish Civil War of 1936–39. Attacks by German tanks, fighter planes, and dive bombers were coordinated. Guderian later remarked the use of tanks in Spain was executed on too small a scale to make an accurate assessment of their effectiveness.

Hitler's desire to expand the territorial boundaries of the Third Reich forced his commanders into battle before they were fully provisioned for the *Blitzkrieg*-style assault they had hoped for. Only six newly formed panzer divisions were ready for battle when the Germans crossed the frontier into Poland in September 1939. The war in Poland was fought with predominantly unmotorized

Following World War I, British tactician Major General J.F.C. Fuller advocated using tanks in concentrated numbers. During World War I, Fuller planned the British tank offensive at Cambrai, an attack along a narrow five-mile front using a combined force of tanks, infantry, airpower, and cavalry that drove the Germans back eight kilometers in some areas. While the Germans later recovered most of the lost territory, the battle proved the tanks' worth in a coordinated attack and laid the groundwork for tactics that would be employed in the Second World War.

infantry and artillery. The panzer divisions that took part in the Polish invasion played, for the most part, a supplementary role to the conventional infantry divisions.

The real test for Guderian's new tactics came with the invasions of the Low Countries and France on May 10, 1940. Guderian's XIX Panzer Corps raced across France and captured the port cities of Boulogne and Calais on May 25 and 26. Dejected elements of the British Expeditionary Force and French Army were evacuated from Dunkirk beginning on May 26. General Erwin Rommel's 7th Panzer Division sped through France, reaching the English Channel on June 10. Nine days later he captured the vital port city of Cherbourg. Paris was occupied by June 14, and on June 25 the French capitulated to the Germans.

*Blitzkrieg* tactics proved successful beyond all expectations when the Germans invaded Russia in June 1941. Within six months the German juggernaut had reached the outskirts of the capital city, Moscow. Unfortunately for the Germans, winter conditions, a calamitous lack of steady supplies, and inept leadership on the part of Hitler (who had dismissed some top generals and ignored the implications of a Russian counteroffensive), spelled the eventual defeat of the invading forces.

As a testament to Guderian's foresight, Allied commanders, including General George S. Patton, adapted Germany's mechanized tactics for their own use. *Blitzkrieg*-like elements have even found their way into more recent conflicts, including the American military's Operation Desert Storm.

# MINOR ATTACKS, MAJOR ALARM

*Pinprick attacks by the Japanese and Germans against the North American mainland heightened fears in the United States and Canada of an Axis invasion of the home front.*

Steven Spielberg's 1979 film release was a quirky comedy called *1941*, which parodies hysterical Californians preparing frantically for a Japanese invasion after the attack on Pearl Harbor. The film features enthusiastic coast watchers keeping vigil for Japanese ships and planes and, in its climactic scene, a gung ho American fighter pilot taking on imagined Japanese zeros during an illusory air raid on Los Angeles.

Looking back, it's easy to poke fun at home-front fears of a Japanese invasion of the United States. But in the aftermath of Pearl Harbor and Germany's declaration of war on the United States, it seemed as if World War II was landing right on North America's doorstep.

The Japanese shelled and bombed areas along the Pacific coast and landed troops in Alaska. German submarines massacred Allied ships all along the Atlantic coast. For many Americans and Canadians, still in shock from Pearl Harbor and dismayed by unchecked Axis victories in Asia, Europe, and Africa, these unnerving strikes at their home turf made a mainland invasion seem a very real possibility.

While the threat posed by German submarines was serious, *direct* attacks on the continental mainland were minor, isolated, and ineffective. Though it is clear that there was never any real danger of an enemy landing, at that time invasion fears were not unreasonable.

However, in keeping with the spirit of *1941*, here is a tongue-in-cheek look at the attacks that heightened invasion fears among many North Americans.

# THE JAPANESE ASSAULT ON CALIFORNIA—
## FEBRUARY 23–24, 1942

During a radio address by President Roosevelt just one week after the president told a newspaper reporter that the United States was vulnerable to enemy attack, the Axis took its first strike at mainland North America.

A Japanese submarine, I-17, surfaced one mile off the shore near Santa Barbara, California, and took aim at the nearby Ellwood oil refinery. The sub lobbed 12 to 15 shells in 20 minutes but caused little damage. Most shells landed harmlessly in the foothills of the Santa Ynez mountains. A witness to the attack later stated that the attack failed because "[the Japanese] shooting wasn't very good."

Fearing civilian panic, government censors ordered the media not to report the attack. But Californians were already jittery. The night after the Ellwood refinery attack, U.S. Army antiaircraft gunners around Los Angeles fought a pitched battle against phantom Japanese planes they believed to be terrorizing the California skies. They fired at least 1,400 rounds at what was later officially determined to be a lost weather balloon. The Battle of Los Angeles, as it was sardonically called, would later be spoofed in the memorable closing scene of Spielberg's *1941*.

After Pearl Harbor, U.S. defense planners established a network of coast watchers all along the Pacific coast. These were mainly civilians who were trained as plane spotters and armed with binoculars and radios. Integrated into the Los Angeles Defense Information Center, they became a vital part of the coastal defense infrastructure and stood ready to sound the alarm in the event of a Japanese invasion. Their greatest achievement, however, may have been the prevention of another Battle of Los Angeles.

## CANADA FEELS JAPAN'S WRATH—
## JUNE 20, 1942

Days after Japanese marines occupied the Alaskan islands of Attu and Kiska, 34,000 Canadian troops in British Columbia braced themselves for an invasion of Canada's Pacific coast. It was good planning. Soon after the occupation, the Japanese submarine

I-26 shelled a lighthouse and wireless station at Estevan Point on Vancouver Island. The attack caused no damage as Japanese gunners missed everything in sight. Clearly, the presence of so many edgy Canadian soldiers unnerved the Japanese to the point where they couldn't even shoot straight.

Never again would the Japanese attempt such a brazen assault on the Great White North, and the Estevan Point attack would mark the only time during the war that enemy shells would fall on Canadian soil.

## OREGON UNDER ATTACK—JUNE 21, 1942

One day after their invasion of Canada was repelled, the Japanese tried their luck in Oregon. Submarine I-25 sneaked up and fired 17 shells at the U.S. Army Coast Artillery Station at Fort Stevens. The attack was the first and only shelling of an American military installation on the U.S. mainland.

The barrage caused little damage, but lots of confusion. "I opened the door of my room and stood there in my drawers cussing at the guys to shut up," First Sergeant Lawrence Rude later said. "Some nut yells back that the Japs are shooting at us and then tore out of the barracks. It was a real madhouse."

Army personnel quickly regained their composure and aimed their guns—but failed to fire a shot at the sub, erroneously determining that it was out of range. The station commander later explained that fire was withheld to avoid giving the Japanese the precise location of the American defenses.

The Japanese missed all the military installations, but scored a direct hit on a nearby baseball diamond—thus striking a symbolic blow to the great American pastime.

## OREGON UNDER ATTACK, PART 2—SEPTEMBER 1942

Only barely recovered from the Fort Stevens attack, Oregon again faced the brunt of Japanese aggression. This time it was from the air, in what would be the first and only military aerial attack against the U.S. mainland. On September 9, 1942, a Japanese seaplane catapulted from submarine I-25 and dropped an incendiary bomb on the forest near the town of Brookings. The intent was to cause a massive forest fire that would divert U.S. manpower and resources away from the war front and trigger panic among civilians.

The bomb caused a small fire, which was extinguished quickly by two forest service lookouts who spotted the rising smoke. Undaunted by the failure of this first attack, the Japanese bombed the forests a second and final time on September 29, only to be thwarted by unusually wet weather.

Government censors tried futilely to keep the attacks out of the newspapers. State defense officials later used the news to raise awareness about the possibility of enemy attacks. Oregon state coordinator Jerrold Owen even predicted that the bombings were "a forerunner of what may be expected in the future." To avoid spreading panic, however, Owen confidently reassured the public that thousands of Oregonians were trained to respond effectively to such attacks.

## THE GERMAN BLITZ OF NEWFOUNDLAND— SEPTEMBER AND NOVEMBER 1942

Tiny Bell Island, located off the eastern coast of Newfoundland near St. John's, twice came under German attack in 1942. Both times German U-boats targeted Allied merchant ships docked at the island while being loaded with iron ore.

On September 5, the German sub U-513 torpedoed and sunk two iron ore carriers. On November 2, U-518, en route to the Quebec coast to drop off a German spy, made a side trip to Bell Island and sunk two more carriers. An attack on a third ship missed, however, and the errant torpedo exploded into the island's loading pier. This totally unintentional strike against the Bell Island pier would mark the only direct German attack on North American territory during the war.

Canada can't lay claim to being the only North American country to suffer a direct homeland hit from the Germans. At the time of the attack, Newfoundland was still a British possession and wouldn't become a Canadian province until 1949.

# The U-boat Invasion of the Atlantic Seaboard

The German U-boat campaign along the Atlantic seaboard began in January 1942 with a probe into American waters by five long-range subs. Code-named Operation *Paukenschlag* ("Drumbeat"), the five subs sank 25 ships in 23 days before heading home in February.

Buoyed by the success of Drumbeat, long-range and shorter-range German subs, refueled at sea by supply subs dubbed "milk cows," prowled American waters. German submariners gleefully proclaimed the campaign the "Second Happy Time."

It must have seemed as if the entire German U-boat fleet was parked off the coast waiting in prey. In actuality, fewer than 20 subs were active along the Atlantic seaboard at any given time.

When the campaign started, the U.S. Navy lacked the ships, planes, weapons, and tactics required to defend coastal shipping, thus enabling U-boats to hide below the surface during the day and emerge undetected at night. U-boats also preyed on inexperienced merchant-ship crews that sailed with their lights on, broke radio silence, or were lured into danger by deceptive German naval signals.

American authorities failed to implement basic precautions such as coastline blackouts and changing ship routes. Ships silhouetted at night by city lights became sitting ducks.

Most importantly, the U.S. Navy was inexplicably loath to implement escorted convoys along the Atlantic coast, despite the fact that the British had proven the system effective in fending off U-boats. Navy officials contended that escorted convoys offered more targets and left harbors unprotected. Instead they employed their few combat ships to hunt patrols—which the Germans easily evaded.

By April, with the number of shipping losses almost too much to bear, the navy finally relented and adopted the convoy system. Given more ships and planes, the system evolved into a standard operation by May and became an interlocking system extending from Halifax down to South America by July 1942.

U-boats left American coastal waters by the end of July in favor of richer killing grounds off Brazil and along the Arctic coast of Russia. The threat to the Atlantic seaboard was gone, but not before more than 2.5 million tons of Allied shipping had been sent to the ocean floor.

# ACTION IN THE FAR NORTH ATLANTIC

*During the dark days of 1942, newspapers were directed each week to print the false headline, "Two medium-sized Allied ships sunk in the Atlantic," when the Allies were losing 33 vessels weekly. The convoys making the Arctic run to the Soviet ports of Murmansk and Archangel were among the hidden casualties.*

The perilous route across the north Atlantic began in Iceland, then from September 1942 in Scotland's Loch Ewe. It wound northeastward past the North Cape (the northern tip of Norway), near Hammerfest, and through the Barents Sea and the White Sea to Murmansk in the Soviet Union. In warmer months, the route continued to Archangel, whose port was icebound in winter.

## DANGERS OF THE ARCTIC WEATHER

The route varied by season. In winter, ice sheets extending from the North Pole expanded, forcing convoys closer to occupied Norway and to marauding German bombers. In summer, the ice sheets shrank, and convoys sailed farther north. The downside was the never-setting Arctic sun, which made ships visible to U-boats around the clock. Convoys were constantly threatened by German submarines; warplanes that could drop aerial bombs, torpedoes, or mines; and the formidable German surface fleet, which included swift-moving "commerce raider" battleships like the *Tirpitz,* with its 15-inch guns.

The conditions for sailors en route to Murmansk or Archangel were the worst of the maritime war. Except during the short summer, heavy seas brought sleet and snow. Sailors on watch strained to spot icebergs through the mists of long Arctic nights.

"Engines broke down under the strain of keeping formation in rough weather," wrote naval historian Samuel Eliot Morison. "Heavy vehicles broke loose from their deck lashings and crushed men...The destroyers and corvettes had to crash through high seas, their exposed bridges drenched with spray that often froze."

Thick fog made it hard to keep convoys together, although it helped cloak freighters from prowling U-boat "wolf packs." Force-12 gales carried 80-knot gusts—the wind chill brought frostbite to exposed skin. With thick mittens, those on deck carefully grasped railings: Being tossed overboard meant hypothermia in minutes. The steward of the SS *Will Rogers* said of the voyages, "I'd sure like to go any place else—just any place at all!"

## PROTECTING AGAINST WOLF PACKS

As elsewhere in the Atlantic, the Arctic transports formed convoys for protection against U-boats. Freighters and Liberty ships with the most valuable cargo were placed in the middle of the formation. Disadvantages of convoys were the time it took to assemble ships and the reduced travel speed: Once underway, the fastest cutter had to travel at the speed of the slowest trawler. A typical convoy might move at 7 knots, while a U-boat sped along the surface at 17 knots, 7 knots submerged. The tardiness of convoys contrasted with the big troop-carrying passenger ships like the *Queen Mary,* which skimmed across the Atlantic at nearly 29 knots, outrunning any stalking submarine. The fastest escort ships were put on the convoy's periphery and raced about from point to point.

Wolf packs would congregate within 15 miles or so of the expected path of a convoy. Attacks often took place at night to mask the submarines from Allied planes and surface fire. U-boats would suddenly surface in the middle of a convoy, close to the merchants and far from the protecting destroyers. They would attack in waves from different directions, attempting to sink anything they could.

Recalled engine crewman John Bunker, "The wild clanging of the bells called all hands to battle stations. Men off watch tumbled out of bunks and grabbed helmets, life jackets, and extra clothing for the wintry blasts...The steward mustered his cooks, and they broke out bandages, splints, and anesthetics."

Sailors on oil tankers knew their ships would likely explode if torpedoed, killing everyone aboard. Men on iron-ore ships knew their boats would sink rapidly, so they slept on the freezing decks to permit a rapid evacuation.

From August 1941 to May 1945, according to the U.S. Naval Historical Center, 78 convoys totaling 1,400 merchant ships ran the Arctic gauntlet. Losses were heaviest in 1942, during the height of the U-boats' success in the north Atlantic, with 63 ships sunk, according to the U.S. Merchant Marine.

## THE TRAGEDY OF PQ17

The convoy that suffered the most, dubbed PQ17, came under attack in July 1942 above the Arctic Circle. PQ17 consisted of more than 30 merchant ships and an oil tanker. Escorts included four cruisers, eight destroyers, submarines, minesweepers, anti-aircraft ships, and ten corvettes. The flotilla was further backed up by the battleships HMS *Duke of York* and USS *Washington,* which traveled parallel to the convoy, 200 miles away.

When Allied intelligence learned that the powerful *Tirpitz,* pocket battleship *Admiral Scheer,* and heavy cruiser *Admiral Hipper* had left the port of Trondheim, First Sea Lord Dudley Pound assumed they were intercepting PQ17. Although it became clear the warships were merely switching ports, Pound ordered the escorts to back off and the convoy's freighters to scatter. "Scatter fanwise," read the order. "Proceed to destination at utmost speed." At the time, Pound was under extreme stress from a brain tumor as well as a thinly stretched Royal Navy.

Meanwhile, a U-boat and three BV 138 flying boats tracked the convoy. From July 4 to July 10, submarines and the *Luftwaffe* ripped up the lightly defended transports, which were stuck 700 miles from safe haven. Land-based bombers and torpedo planes made more than 200 sorties. U-255 alone sank five ships, including one on the return journey from Murmansk. In all, 153 mariners and armed guard members died. The Germans captured at least 37 survivors, some of whom had floated for weeks on open lifeboats and lost limbs to frostbite. Twenty-four ships were lost. Sent to the bottom were 430 tanks, 3,500 vehicles, and 200 aircraft—about 250,000 tons of shipping in all.

After the incident, Churchill remarked, "PQ17 was one of the most melancholy episodes of the war." Despite bitter protests from the Soviets, then embattled at Stalingrad, the next convoy was postponed, and the ones thereafter suspended until the shorter, safer days of winter.

## U-BOAT KILLS UPSTAGE THE GERMAN SURFACE FLEET

The Germans had less success when sending their surface ships out to attack. Fearing an invasion of Norway, Hitler and the *Kriegsmarine* were wary of losing major assets in convoy assaults. In December 1942, in the Battle of the Barents Sea, British cruisers and destroyers protecting convoy JW51B drove off the pocket battleship *Lützow* and the *Admiral Hipper.* The following December, the battleship HMS *Duke of York* and supporting cruisers and destroyers guarding the 19-ship convoy JW55B sank the battleship *Scharnhorst.* After the Barents Sea fight, an enraged Hitler fired his naval commander-in-chief, *Großadmiral* Erich Raeder, and ordered the scuttling of all capital ships, including the *Tirpitz* and *Scharnhost,* for U-boat scrap, until dissuaded by Raeder's successor, Admiral Karl Dönitz.

## MUCH-NEEDED AID REACHES RUSSIA

Murmansk was the most frequent endpoint for frazzled convoy

crews. Yet it wasn't the cheeriest place for shore leave. The commodore of a British convoy described Murmansk as a "bombed city filled with black ghosts moving in the twilight over the snow in deathly silence, broken only by tinny music broadcast by the State." After surviving the arduous journey, ship mascots were sometimes stolen by stevedores unloading the cargo: Dogs and cats were a source of meat for the famished wartime families.

Still, the Russians were grateful for the badly needed supplies. Moscow bestowed 177 citations on U.S. sailors for "valor and courage" in "aiding the delivery to northern ports." The merchant marines beat the elements.

After a disastrous 1942, the fortunes of the Arctic convoys dramatically improved as the U-boat threat in the Atlantic decreased. The threat from the *Tirpitz* ended in November 1944 when British Lancaster bombers sunk it. Drained by losses in other fronts, the *Luftwaffe* decreased its attacks. Ultra intelligence on U-boat movements allowed planners to provide convoys with appropriate escorts.

Through the Murmansk and Archangel run, convoys supplied the Soviet Union with 15,000 aircraft, 7,000 tanks, 350,000 tons of explosives—and 15,000,000 pairs of boots, the latter especially prized during the harsh winters.

☆　　☆　　☆

- *Of all the service branches, the Merchant Marine suffered the proportionally greatest casualties—more than the U.S. Army or Marine Corps. Of 215,000 U.S. Merchant Marine personnel, 9,300 perished in combat, about 1 in 25; 11,000 were wounded. According to the U.S. Merchant Marine, 1,554 merchant ships were sunk, 733 of them more than 1,000 gross tons.*

☆　　☆　　☆

- *Boise City, Oklahoma, was inadvertently bombed on July 5, 1943, when a B-17 pilot mistook the lights on the town square for his training target.*

# Fast Facts

- Some confuse the 1943 Warsaw Ghetto Uprising with the 1944 Warsaw Rising. The 1944 Rising included Jews, of course (including some survivors of the 1943 uprising, now fighting with the Armia Krajowa), but was actually a far larger rebellion dominated by non-Jews.

- How large were the ghetto forces? Reputable historians disagree, but the usual estimates range between 750 and 1,500. Some who did not train with ŻOB or ŻZW fought alongside them.

- Ghetto dwellers especially loathed the Jewish Police, who helped round up deportees. Jews who served the Nazis as police were "rewarded" by being sent to Treblinka in the final shipment, when they were of no further use to the Nazis.

- Stroop gloated over the annihilation of the ghetto and took particular glee in dynamiting the ruins of the ghetto synagogue after the fighting. On September 8, 1951, the Polish People's Republic hanged Jürgen Stroop for war crimes.

- Even after the primary action was over, a few Jews somehow managed to survive in the ghetto ruins. Jewish prisoners clearing the rubble found the last survivor on December 13, 1943: a girl, badly burned and near death. For reasons that remain obscure, the Gestapo gave her medical care until she recovered her health—then took her back to the ruins and shot her.

- SS ranks paralleled those of the regular Heer, but their names translate to rather grandiose titles. An SS senior private was a Sturmmann ("stormtrooper"). A second lieutenant was an Untersturmführer ("junior storm leader"). A colonel was a Standartenführer ("regiment leader"). Any man who rose to the rank of SS sergeant or higher had the term Führer in his rank.

- Nazi propaganda minister Joseph Goebbels believed so strongly in the power of patriotic music that each of Germany's troops was issued a patriotic songbook as part of their standard kit.

# GESTAPO OF THE RISING SUN

*A late-night knock on the door was often the first warning. Inside, inhabitants huddled together as a small group of armed, uniformed men burst in. Rounding up those unfortunates whose names appeared on their lists, they would carry off their victims, who were often never heard from again.*

The visitors were the dreaded *kempeitai*.

By the war's outbreak, Japan's closed society was ruled by the Japanese secret police, whose best-known element was the *kempeitai*, or Japanese military police. The *kempeitai* performed military, civilian, and foreign espionage functions, much like the German Gestapo and Soviet NKVD. The security force was established in 1881 during the Meiji Restoration. As with other totalitarian governments, the *kempeitai* were powerfully connected at the top levels of Japanese government; one of their alumni, Tojo Hideki, became Japan's prime minister—a virtual dictator—during the war.

Within their military jurisdictions, the *kempeitai* acted as military police, taking orders from the local field or garrison commander. Massacres of prisoners in occupied areas (such as in the days following the capitulation of Singapore) were often carried out under the supervision of the *kempeitai*. Local *kempeitai* in China procured human subjects for biological experiments, and a small number of captured Doolittle Raid airmen were tortured and executed at the *kempeitai's* headquarters in Tokyo.

At home in Japan, the *kempeitai* worked to coordinate propaganda efforts, stamp out subversive ideas, and root out spies in their midst, such as the incredibly effective spy ring run by Richard Sorge, an affiliate of the German embassy in Tokyo. (Sorge's ring, to the *kempeitai's* embarrassment, was actually exposed by local Tokyo police.) Japan's Peace Preservation Law, passed in 1925, gave the *kempeitai* a nearly open license to arrest, detain, and even execute Communists, pacifists, and any Japanese citizen suspected of disloyalty to the state or the Emperor.

# HERO NATION: THE RESCUE OF DENMARK'S JEWS

*At the height of the Holocaust, the people of Denmark banded together to rescue their fellow citizens from deportation to Nazi death camps.*

The Holocaust was one of the darkest chapters, not only of World War II, but in all of human history. Out of this darkness, however, there emerged a few shining examples of human kindness and compassion triumphing over evil and hatred.

One such example was the combined effort of the people of Denmark to save the country's Jewish community from destruction by the Nazis. It was a remarkable feat of collective courage that unfolded at a time when the systematic extermination of Europe's Jews was reaching its murderous peak.

## A LENIENT OCCUPATION

Germany invaded Denmark (along with Norway) on April 9, 1940. The Danes, facing impossible odds, surrendered the same day after putting up token resistance. Though defeated, the Danes had two factors working in their favor that initially prevented their subjugation by the Germans. The first was Germany's desire to secure Denmark's economic cooperation. The second was Hitler's ideological belief that the Danes were closely related to the German "race" and should be treated accordingly. As a result, the Germans imposed a relatively lenient occupation that allowed the Danes to remain nominally independent.

Under this arrangement, Denmark's royal family remained in the country, and Danish parliamentary and government organizations, including the police force and army, continued to function as before. German authority was represented through the traditional diplomatic channels of the German Foreign Office, whereas other parts of occupied Europe were directly ruled by the German

# A Few Who Saved Many

During the war, many individuals acted compassionately to save Jews from extermination by the Nazis, risking and in many instances paying for their actions with their own freedom or lives. Here are four individuals, all of whom have been declared Righteous Among the Nations by Yad Vashem (the Holocaust remembrance authority), whose courage and moral fortitude saved thousands of Jews from the horrors of the gas chambers.

### Raoul Wallenberg

Wallenberg was a Swedish diplomat stationed in Budapest who saved more than 100,000 Hungarian Jews from July to December 1944. He designed, issued, and personally distributed some 4,500 "protective passports" that gave Jewish holders perceived safe passage to Sweden under the protection of the Swedish Crown. Wallenberg issued at least another 12,000 passports. When acting personally, he often handed the passports to Jews aboard trains awaiting deportation and convinced authorities they were to be released under his protection. He also established havens for Jews in Budapest homes, dubbed "Swedish houses" because they flew the Swedish flag and were declared Swedish territory. Finally, he used diplomatic and moral pressure to prevent the liquidation of the Jewish ghettos in Budapest. On January 17, 1945, Wallenberg was arrested by Soviet agents and never seen again. In 2000, the Russians admitted his wrongful imprisonment and reported that he died in captivity in 1947, a claim that many still doubt.

### Yvonne Nèvejean

Nèvejean headed the *Oeuvre Nationale de l'Enfance* (ONE), a Belgian agency supervising children's homes. Funded by underground Jewish organizations and the Belgian government-in-exile, Nèvejean rescued more than 4,000 Jewish children by providing them with new identities, ration cards, and places of permanent refuge in private homes and institutions. She also arranged for the

military or the SS. Any interference by German agencies in Danish internal affairs, including those pertaining to Denmark's Jews, was prohibited.

Although now a conquered people, the Danes, including approximately 7,700 Danish Jews, continued living pretty much as they had before the German invasion.

release of a group of children taken by the Gestapo to an internment camp to be readied for deportation. Children rescued by Nèvejean became known as "Yvonne's children."

### Sugihara (Sempo) Chiune

Sugihara was the Japanese consul general in Kovno at the time of the Soviet invasion of Lithuania. When the Soviets ordered all foreign delegations out of Kovno in July 1940, Sugihara asked for a 20-day extension and, in defiance of explicit orders from the Japanese Foreign Ministry, issued transit visas to Polish and Lithuanian Jews seeking to escape both the Nazis and the Soviets. Through August 1940, he and his wife, Yukiko, worked day and night signing papers for Jews waiting in long lines around the Japanese consulate building. In a race against time, he provided lifesaving documents for more than 6,000 "Sugihara Survivors," signing papers and shoving them through the train window even as he was leaving Kovno. "I should follow my conscience," he said at the time. "I cannot allow these people to die, people who had come to me for help with death staring them in the eyes."

### Oskar Schindler

Immortalized in the film *Schindler's List,* Schindler was a German businessman and Nazi Party member who entertained and bribed German Army and SS officials in Poland to obtain contracts and Jewish labor for an enamel kitchenware factory in Krakow he had taken over from a Jewish firm. Awakened to the fact by his Jewish accountant that work in his factory meant survival for Jews, Schindler hired more Jews than he needed, convincing SS officials with bribes that he needed their "essential" skills. In all, he saved more than 1,300 "Schindlerjuden" by employing them in his various factories. When Nazis who elected to ignore Schindler's "arrangement" put scores of Schindler workers onto a train headed for Auschwitz, Oskar came up with additional bribes, and had the workers released into his custody. "If you saw a dog going to be crushed under a car," he said later of his actions, "wouldn't you help him?"

## THE GERMANS LOWER THE BOOM

By 1942, however, as the demands of the war began to press down hard on Germany, the Germans began to ratchet up pressure on the Danes. Germany began extracting greater economic concessions from the Danish government, which in turn led to rationing, inflation, and shortages.

Resentful of the hardships caused by these concessions, the Danes grew increasingly restive under German rule. Facing a less acquiescent Danish nation, the Germans moved in October 1942 to implement a more stringent occupation administration. German authority in Denmark was transferred from the Foreign Office to the military and the SS. The German crackdown in Denmark had begun.

The new administration continued to impose harsh economic demands on the Danes. At the same time, the SS was embarking on the Final Solution and the mass deportation of Jews from occupied Western Europe to the death camps in Poland. They began pressing Danish authorities to take similar actions against local Jews.

In response, and encouraged by tide-turning defeats of the German military at Stalingrad and in North Africa, the Danes began a campaign of open resistance in 1943 that spread and intensified as the year progressed. Initial nonviolent tactics, such as printing underground newspapers, gave way to widespread labor strikes in the summer and the formation of an armed Danish resistance movement that sabotaged factories, rail lines, and German military installations.

German attempts to quell the resistance were stymied by the Danish government's refusal to force an end to the strikes and introduce the death penalty for acts of sabotage. The Germans also grew increasingly frustrated with the government's continuing protection of local Jews. By August, the Germans had had enough, and declared a state of emergency. The Danish parliament was disbanded, and all civil liberties were suspended. The darkness of Nazi rule had descended on Denmark.

Most ominously, the imposition of emergency rule presented the Germans with the opportunity to settle the score with Denmark's Jews.

## UNITED AGAINST ANTI-SEMITISM

Anti-Semitism, especially the virulent strain espoused by the Nazis, had failed to take root in Denmark as it had in most other European countries at the time. Political, economic, and social emancipation had been granted to Danish Jews in 1849, and by the outbreak of World War II, the tiny Jewish community was fully integrated and assimilated into Danish society.

This acceptance of Jews, declares writer Harold Flender, was a product of a Danish tradition of democracy that rejected any form of racism. Holocaust historian Leni Yahil echoes this sentiment. She cites the special character and moral stature of the Danes, in particular their collective love of democracy and freedom, as the driving forces behind Denmark's resistance to Nazi attempts to implement the kind of destructive, anti-Jewish measures adopted in other parts of occupied Europe.

This shared love of freedom kept the Danes remarkably united under the strains of German occupation. Other occupied countries were plagued by internal factionalism that the Germans often exploited to their advantage. Factionalism also played into the hands of the SS, which relied heavily on local anti-Semitic collaborators to aid in the roundup and deportation of Jews to extermination camps in Eastern Europe. The complicity of local groups in many nations other than Denmark was a crucial factor in the ability of the SS to implement the Final Solution to such devastating effect.

Denmark's population, however, maintained the prevailing sentiment that an attack against one Dane was an attack against all Danes—and the Danes made it clear to the Germans that Danish Jews were included in this sense of national oneness. In short, non-Jews in Denmark considered the fate of local Jews to be their fate as well.

## THE SS IS THWARTED; A COMMUNITY IS SAVED

This sense of communal fate manifested itself in an extraordinary way in September 1943, when Danish authorities were tipped by a sympathetic German shipping official of the SS plans to round up local Jews on October 1. Coinciding with the overall suppression of civil liberties by the Germans, the SS plot to move against the Jews further reinforced the Danish idea of oneness. Acting virtually on reflex, the Danish people mobilized to rescue the Jews.

Danish officials worked with the Danish resistance and ordinary civilians to move Jews to safe locations near the coast for evacuation to neutral Sweden. Flotillas of fishing boats were organized to smuggle the Jews out of Denmark, evading German patrol boats while making the treacherous sea voyage to Sweden under the cover of darkness.

Within three weeks, 7,200 members of Denmark's Jewish community had been safely evacuated. Only 475 Danish Jews were captured and deported by the Germans. The people of Denmark had successfully carried out one of the largest single acts of collective resistance against the Germans during the war.

The Danes subsequently turned their vigilance to those Jews who had been caught. Danish authorities pressured the German government to send the captives to the "model" concentration camp at Theresienstadt, Czechoslovakia, instead of the death camps. The Danish Red Cross made visits to Theresienstadt (stage-managed by the Nazis) to monitor the well-being of the Danish Jews, while Danish civilians sent packages of clothing, food, and vitamins to help them survive their ordeal.

Through this support, all but 51 of the captured Danish Jews survived the war and returned to Denmark. Upon returning, they found that their homes, gardens, personal belongings, and even their pets had been cared for by their neighbors in their absence.

For their heroism, the Holocaust remembrance authority, Yad Vashem, recognized "the Danish people" who participated in the rescue of the Danish Jews as Righteous Among the Nations, an honorary title bestowed upon non-Jews who risked their lives to save Jews from extermination by the Nazis.

☆　☆　☆

- *Not all SS units cringed before Hitler. As the German forces battled to hold onto Hungary, the* Leibstandarte *(Hitler's bodyguard regiment) launched an unsuccessful attack on Soviet forces. Hitler threw a fit and ordered them to remove their Gothic-script "Adolf Hitler" cuffbands as a penalty for failure. After six years of brutal fighting and heavy casualties, the hard-bitten SS troopers had no patience for their* Führer's *disrespect. A number of them removed their medals, placed them in a latrine bucket, and sent them to Hitler.*

# "*JUDEN HABEN WAFFEN!*"
# THE 1943 WARSAW GHETTO UPRISING

*In April 1943, German forces moved into Warsaw for the final liquidation of the Jewish Ghetto. This is the story of the Jews who vowed to fight and die rather than face deportation to death camps.*

Warsaw's Jews numbered some 400,000 in 1941, when the German occupiers sealed them into a two-square-mile ghetto. Conditions were so poor that about 10 percent of those confined died each year. When the deportations began in July 1942, some decided to go out like lions.

## ORGANIZING THE RESISTANCE IN WARSAW

The Jews hoped to get weapons from the Polish *Armia Krajowa* (AK, or "Home Army"). David Appelbojm's right-leaning *Żydowski Zwiazek Wojskowy* (ŻZW, "Jewish Fighting Union") received moderate support from the AK. Commanded by Mordechai Anielewicz, a Zionist activist in his early twenties, the *Żydowska Organizacja Bojowa* (ŻOB, "Jewish Fighting Organization") became the larger of the two ghetto forces. However, the AK hesitated to arm it, distrusting the ŻOB's left-leaning politics. From mid-1942 to April 1943, both Jewish organizations geared up to resist, keeping independent command structures but cooperating in defense planning.

The first deportation wave ended in September 1942, leaving only about 60,000 Jews in the ghetto. In October, ŻOB carried out its first reprisal, executing the deputy commander of the hated, Nazi-compliant Jewish Police. Another Nazi puppet met the same fate. The Nazis paid little heed; each deputy lost was one less Jew.

Another mass deportation began January 18, 1943, but lasted only four days. As SS men and Ukrainian militias began rousting Jews, a ŻOB detachment assaulted the intruders with pistols and clubs, killing several and driving the rest back. The ambush infused the sad ghetto remnant with hope: Resistance may not repel the Germans, but it might buy time for the Jews trapped in the ghetto.

On the last day of the January deportation, German troops with Latvian and Ukrainian auxiliaries slaughtered at least a thousand Jews in reprisal. ŻOB and ŻZW could only watch—and swear revenge.

## THE STANDOFF

Furious, *Reichsführer*-SS Heinrich Himmler demanded the eradication of the Warsaw Ghetto. The evening before Passover 1943, the ghetto's Jews learned that a Nazi invasion was imminent. As most readied for their final Passover seders, they also readied their weapons and assumed defensive positions. The Jews had two key advantages: They could use the urban landscape defensively and knew that surrender equaled death. Die they might, but it would be a fighting death. By now, all 1,500-odd ŻOB and ŻZW fighters had pistols, improvised grenades, or Molotov cocktails, plus a few rifles and submachine guns.

Early in the morning of April 19, 1943, some 2,000 men under the command of SS-*Oberführer* (senior colonel) Ferdinand von Sammern-Frankenegg invaded the ghetto. The force was a patchwork of SS men, regular soldiers, Slavic auxiliaries and concentration-camp guards.

As one Nazi column advanced, Jews opened fire using rifles and pistols. Men and women flung grenades and Molotov cocktails, setting an SS tank on fire. The column dissolved in confusion, then fled. Another column met a similar fate. *"Juden haben Waffen!"* ("The Jews are armed!") screamed one wounded German as he lay in the street.

Few Jews had ever heard Nazis cry out in terror or panic. The SS troops were accustomed to bullying and intimidating Jews; being shot at by armed Jews was an entirely new experience, and one not to their liking.

The first day was a Jewish tactical victory, though at the painful cost of ŻZW commander Appelbojm's life. SS-*Brigadeführer* (general) Jürgen Stroop, a dedicated and ruthless Nazi, reorganized the troops for new incursions. Their advance was slow and painful. Armed Jews fought back, turning every building into a potential ambush point.

Outside the ghetto, AK leaders debated whether and how to help—but they did little. Most AK assistance came from a few men who acted independently by smuggling in munitions and fighting alongside the Jews.

Jews who surrendered were shot or shipped to concentration camps. Stroop's men used artillery, demolition charges, poison gas, and flamethrowers to blast and burn the ghetto to the ground, building by building. ŻOB commander Anielewicz's final command post was Mila 18 (18 Mila Street), where his forces held out until May 8. He and most of his men committed suicide to avoid being captured.

The fighting finally came to an end on May 16, 1943. Few survived the uprising—some ŻZW fighters escaped through the sewers with help from the AK. Fewer still survived the war.

Viewed as a battle, the Warsaw Ghetto Uprising was small, but in emotional and cultural terms, it was a watershed for the Jewish people.

☆　　☆　　☆

- *The SS emblem of doubled S (known as "sig" during the SS's reign) runes, which look much like twin lightning bolts, traces its lineage back to the rune* sowilo *of the Elder Futhark, an ancient Germanic script known from Roman times. Back then it symbolized the sun, but was reinterpreted by the poet, nationalist idealogue, and mystic Guido von List to symbolize the concept of* Sieg *("victory"), thus the primary SS association before and during World War II. Two S-runes overlaid at a 90-degree angle form a swastika. Design variants of the pagan SS rune symbolized such things as the sun, family and communal spirit, prosperity, faith, death, self-sacrifice, and zeal. One, the* Wolfsangel, *supposedly allowed the wearer to ward off wolves.*

# THE DOGS OF WAR

*Even "man's best friend" was drafted into military service during the war. The four-legged soldiers protected their two-legged comrades. In fact, no patrol led by a war dog was ever ambushed or fired upon without warning.*

The use of dogs in war was not new. In ancient times, Romans and Gauls drove packs of semi-wild dogs onto battlefields to attack and terrify their enemies. During the Great War, both sides used them as watchdogs and light beasts of burden, among other duties. Then between 1939 and 1945, dogs became sophisticated, highly trained assistants to their masters in uniform. Using their endurance, speed, and extraordinary senses of hearing and smell, they saved many lives during combat.

## CANINE GUARDS, SCOUTS, AND SOLDIERS

Germany had the largest prewar canine program of any of the belligerents and trained as many as 200,000 dogs. Each concentration camp had an SS dog unit and the animals were trained to attack prisoners, instilling fear. Other canines were trained as patrols or scouts and used in combat. The SS valued dogs, particularly German Shepherds, because they were fast, intelligent, low to the ground, and, with proper training, almost fearless. The *Wehrmacht* used dogs on all fronts, and even provided some 25,000 dogs to its Japanese allies to use in China.

On the Eastern Front, the Soviet Union conscripted breeds like the reliable Samoyed, a hardy Siberian sled dog, to pull light equipment and litters bearing wounded men. Eventually, the Soviet Army formed 168 canine units from a variety of breeds and developed specialized guard breeds such as the Black Russian Terrier at its Red Star Kennels outside Moscow. Some of the Red Star's less-fortunate graduates also included "suicide dogs," conditioned to locate food underneath tanks while carrying backpacks loaded with high explosives.

To the west, Britain and France also recruited dogs for auxiliary duty. In May 1940, as the *Wehrmacht* swept across France, nearly 200 dogs were among the host evacuated from Dunkirk across the English Channel.

## DOGS FOR DEFENSE—TRAINING CANINES IN THE UNITED STATES

In the United States, patriotic members of the American Kennel Club started an organization called "Dogs for Defense" and called on citizens to donate dogs to the war effort. The War Department began inducting dogs as service animals in March 1942, assigning them to the Quartermaster Corps. During the war, the U.S. Army, Marines and Coast Guard trained more than 10,000 German Shepherds, Doberman Pinschers, Belgian Sheep Dogs, and other "acceptable" breeds for what became popularly known as the "K-9 Corps."

U.S. services trained their dogs at several special camps, including one established on Cat Island near Gulfport, Mississippi. The eight- to twelve-week training course went well beyond teaching Private Rover to "sit," "come," and "stay" on command; dogs acclimated to the sounds and smells of battle, practiced riding in military vehicles, and even learned to wear gas masks.

On front lines and in the rear, U.S. war dogs were assigned a variety of duties, depending on their breed, training, and personality. More than 9,000 dogs pulled sentry and reconnaissance duty. They were especially effective in detecting enemy soldiers hiding in foliage or sneaking up on a camp. About 150 dogs were specially trained for messenger duty, running dispatches under fire between the front lines and military headquarters. Others were assigned to the Medical Corps and performed outstanding service locating wounded GIs. Still others, known as "M-Dogs," were tasked with sniffing out enemy land mines.

Army war dogs proved particularly effective in the Pacific Theater, where dense eye-level vegetation obscured enemy soldiers from the average GI. In an age before infrared sensors and satellite reconnaissance, a dog's senses of sight, smell, and sound were the best tools a foot soldier had for picking out an enemy hiding in the bushes. In just one of many instances, the Quartermaster Department reported that during the marine landings on Bougainville Island in November 1943, "D-Day dogs" ran messages, pointed out snipers in trees, and sniffed out dug-in Japanese defenders at ranges of over 100 yards, giving the marines time to find cover before enemy guns opened fire.

## CANINE HEROES

GIs learned to value their dogs, and several valiant animals were awarded company citations for heroism. A few dogs even earned combat medals such as the Purple Heart before the War Department changed its policy to restrict combat awards to humans. One famous German Shepherd named Chips faithfully served the 3rd Infantry Division in every major European and African operation. He wore eight battle stars bestowed by his company's men. In one instance while fighting in Sicily, Chips broke away from his handler and attacked an enemy pillbox by himself, mauling one enemy soldier and forcing the machine-gun crew to surrender.

At war's end, the dogs, like their human companions, were repatriated to civilian life. The War Department reconditioned the four-legged warriors to view humans as their best friends, and thoroughly tested them for docility before returning them to their original owners.

☆    ☆    ☆

- *In 1993, Disney produced a television movie about Chips called* Chips the War Dog.

☆    ☆    ☆

- *In recognition of his service, Chips was awarded the Distinguished Service Cross, Silver Star, and Purple Heart, but all were later revoked when the War Department decided animals shouldn't receive medals.*

# Timeline

## 1941

**March 11**
Roosevelt signs the Lend-Lease Act

France cedes parts of Laos and Cambodia to Thailand

**March 15–25**
Chinese repulse Japanese offensive near Nanchang in Honan Province

**March 24**
Rommel takes El Agheila, Libya

**March 28**
Japanese troops are defeated in Battle of Shangkao in Honan Province

Plutonium-239, a uranium isotope that will prove critical in developing nuclear weapons, is discovered by a team of American physicists

**March 30**
Rommel launches offensive in Cyrenaica (East Libya)

**April 3–4**
The U.S. Navy establishes convoy protection in the North Atlantic to help defend supply ships from U-boats

**April 4**
Rommel takes Benghazi, Libya

**April 6**
Germany invades Yugoslavia and Greece

**April 11**
Roosevelt extends Pan-American security zone in Atlantic

Rommel takes Bardia; siege of Tobruk begins

**April 12**
U.S. troops occupy Greenland

**April 20**
Greece surrenders to the Axis

**April 21**
Japanese occupy Foochow, China

**April 26**
Rommel's Afrika Korps advances, forcing the Allies out of Libya and into Egypt

**April 27**
German troops raise the swastika flag over the Acropolis in Athens

The United States, Britain, and the Netherlands discuss defense plans for Singapore

**May**
SS *Reichsführer* Heinrich Himmler decrees that writing one's name, counting to 500, and obedience to Germans is all the education needed for the non-German population of the Reich

Ho Chi Minh forms Viet Minh in French Indochina

**May 1**
Australian forces repulse German attack on Tobruk

**May 7**
Stalin is named Soviet premier

Japanese launch offensive in Shansi Province

**May 9**
Thailand and Vichy France sign peace treaty

**May 10**
In a bizarre incident, third-ranking Nazi Rudolf Hess flies to Scotland and parachutes into British custody, claiming he is there to negotiate peace with Britain

# PEARL HARBOR II: THE IMPROBABLE BOAT PLANE RAID THAT BROKE RECORDS

*On March 4, 1942, the Japanese public heard news of a second air attack on Pearl Harbor. Supposedly quoting a broadcast from Los Angeles, radio and newspaper reports claimed that considerable damage was done to military installations, with the deaths of 30 sailors and civilians. Propaganda aside, two seaplanes did reach Pearl Harbor for a second encounter in 1942.*

After December 7, 1941, the Japanese Imperial Navy searched for new ways to tie down U.S. forces defending the Hawaiian Islands. A bombing raid was planned using new H8K Emily flying boats to cross the Pacific. Code-named Operation K (K was the Japanese code signature for Hawaii), the plan called for two planes to fly from the Marshall Islands to a rendezvous with Japanese refueling submarines at French Frigate Shoals, an atoll halfway between Midway and Hawaii. Relying on a full moon for visibility, each Emily would carry four 550-pound bombs, with the intended target of navy docks at Pearl Harbor. A second raid was to follow a few days later.

Lieutenant Hisao Hashizume, an expert seaplane pilot proficient in open-ocean navigation, was chosen as commander. Taking off from the Marshalls on the night of March 3, the two boat planes met two submarines at French Frigate Shoals without incident and completed the dangerous operation of refueling at sea. Closing in on Hawaii on the early morning of March 4, Lieutenant Hashizume was unaware that U.S. radar stations on the islands had already spotted them as potential bogies. Flying at 15,000 feet, cloud cover had obscured the raiders' visibility by 80 percent.

At Pearl Harbor, air-raid alarms were sounded and fighters scrambled to intercept the planes. With the lighthouse at Kaena Point his only visible reference point, Lieutenant Hashizume made his best guess and dropped his bombs on the slopes of Mount Tantalus; the second plane dropped its payload into the ocean at the entrance to Pearl Harbor. U.S. fighter pilots, radar operators, and ground controllers failed to find the Japanese aircraft as they banked toward the west on their flight back to the Marshall Islands. Taking 35 hours and covering 4,750 miles of the Pacific Ocean, the raid was the longest air mission flown by any nation in the war and proved the feasibility of using submarines to extend the range of seaplanes. The second raid was canceled because a delay meant inadequate moonlight for visibility. After its defeat at Midway, the Imperial Navy never considered launching a similar raid.

In the end, Operation K proved much more valuable to the United States. The raid demonstrated the need for airborne radar and fighter pilots trained in night interception, which proved devastating to Japanese fliers in the final years of the war.

☆   ☆   ☆

- *There were very few SS women. Membership was officially closed to them, but a few were admitted to the* Waffen-SS *and many served as SS auxiliaries, predominantly as concentration-camp guards and wardens. Some racked up their own records of death camp infamy.*

☆   ☆   ☆

- *Nazi propaganda minister Joseph Goebbels long dreamed of overseeing a mammoth historical film to be called* Kolberg, *an account of a 19th-century Prussian town that resisted occupation by an invading force sent by Napoleon.* Kolberg *began production in 1943, budgeted at the equivalent of $2.1 million. Worse, it pulled 200,000 soldiers from the crumbling Eastern Front for use as extras. By the time* Kolberg *opened in January 1945, Allied boming had incinerated or flattened many German theaters. Audiences were sparse.*

# QUEEN OF THE STALINGRAD SKIES

*The most feared fighter pilot over Stalingrad was a woman. Lily Litvak, the "White Rose of Stalingrad," terrorized German pilots and helped inspire a nation to a monumental victory.*

In the Ukraine city of Krasy Luch, there stands a tall marble monument with 12 gold stars ascending its column, capped with a large, striking bust of a woman crowned in an aviator's cap and glasses.

The monument is dedicated to Lily Litvak, the celebrated Soviet fighter ace who struck fear into German pilots in the skies over Stalingrad. The 12 gold stars on her monument commemorate the 12 solo and 3 shared kills she recorded in her brief but illustrious career.

## A DEADLY FLOWER

Litvak was affectionately called the "White Rose of Stalingrad" for the white lily (which was mistaken for a rose) painted on each side of the cockpit of her Yak-1 fighter plane. Her skill and tenacity as a fighter pilot became so well-known that German pilots would allegedly peel away when they saw the white flowers coming.

A licensed flying instructor by her 18th birthday, Litvak volunteered for an aviation unit after Germany invaded the Soviet Union, but she was rejected because of her lack of flying time. After embellishing her experience, she joined the famed all-female 586th Fighter Regiment, where she honed her fighter-pilot skills.

Initially, Litvak faced more of a challenge from chauvinistic attitudes than from enemy pilots. When she transferred to an all-male air unit at Stalingrad in September 1942, her commander refused to let her fly.

After continual pleading, she was finally given a plane and quickly made believers of her male comrades after scoring her first two kills on her second combat mission.

## A TIMELY INSPIRATION FOR A BELEAGUERED NATION

For the next 11 months, the stunning beauty with golden blonde hair and captivating gray eyes outwitted and outfought German pilots, who often couldn't believe that they had been shot down by a woman. A German fighter ace who was shot down by Litvak refused to believe that he had been bested by a woman until they were introduced, and she herself described to him minute details of their dogfight that only the two of them could have known.

Through the course of 168 combat missions, Litvak was shot down two or three times, once sustaining serious injury to her legs. She bounced back each time with a more determined will to fight that was further hardened following the death of her fighter-pilot husband. Her luck finally ran out on August 1, 1943, when eight German fighters ganged against her and sent her crashing to her death 17 days shy of her 22nd birthday.

Although her remains weren't found until 1979, Litvak's heroics in the skies over Stalingrad were never forgotten by the Soviet people. Her bravery and achievements provided a timely inspiration to a nation facing defeat and desperate for something from which it could draw hope. In recognition of her contribution to her nation's monumental victory, Litvak was posthumously awarded its highest honor, the Hero of the Soviet Union, in 1990.

☆　☆　☆

- *The Soviet Yak-1 fighter plane favored by Lily Litvak evolved into the Yak-9, one of the best and most feared fighters of the war. Large-scale production of the Yak-9 was underway at the time of Litvak's death, and the plane played a decisive role in the 1943–44 Soviet defense of the besieged city of Stalingrad. A superb handler that excelled at low altitudes, the Yak-9 helped put an end to* Luftwaffe *air superiority in the East.*

# GOING TO WAR IN STYLE

*Millions of Allied troops got to experience something they likely wouldn't have as ordinary civilians—an ocean voyage on a luxury passenger liner.*

During World War II, scores of luxury passenger liners were pressed into service as troop-transport ships. Symbols of grandeur, privilege, and national prestige, these magnificent vessels were stripped of their finery, refitted, repainted, and recommissioned into decidedly more utilitarian craft that were indispensable to the Allied war effort.

The first large-scale troop transport involving luxury passenger ships left Halifax on December 10, 1939. Five camouflaged luxury liners—*Empress of Britain, Duchess of Bedford, Monarch of Bermuda, Aquitania,* and *Empress of Australia*—carried 7,400 soldiers of the Canadian Army 1st Division for deployment in Britain.

By war's end, millions of Allied soldiers sailed aboard converted ocean liners to and from North America, Europe, Africa, Asia, and Australia. Here are looks at some of the more notable luxury ships that carried them to war in style.

## QUEEN MARY

The jewel of the Cunard-White Star Line fleet, the *Queen Mary* stood alone among the classic ocean liners of its era, both as a peacetime luxury liner and as a wartime troopship.

It began its wartime service in May 1940. Painted gray while laid up in New York and fitted as a troopship in Sydney, the *Queen Mary* initially transported Australian troops to Scotland and Africa. In mid-1943, it was transferred to service in the Atlantic Ocean.

The *Queen Mary* was fast—at the outbreak of the war it was the undisputed holder of the shipping industry's Blue Riband award for the fastest trans-Atlantic liner. With a cruising speed of 28.5 knots, it often sailed unescorted, as German subs could not catch or keep up with it. The *Queen Mary* was also huge. It was eventually fitted for a capacity of 15,000 troops—equivalent to a whole division—and in July 1943, it established the still-standing record for the most people on a single voyage when it set sail with 16,683 soldiers and crew on board.

In all, the *Queen Mary* sailed 569,429 miles and carried a total of 765,429 military personnel during the war, surviving both a collision with a British light cruiser and a $250,000 bounty placed by Adolf Hitler. It returned to civilian service in 1946, but not before making 11 voyages bringing war brides to the United States and Canada.

## AMERICA (USS WEST POINT)

The queen of the United States Line fleet, the *America* was launched on August 31, 1939, and entered into service in 1940. Within a year, the 33,560-ton liner was commissioned as an AP (armored personnel) ship by the U.S. Navy, renamed the USS *West Point,* and in only 11 days, refitted and put into service as the navy's largest troopship.

Nicknamed the "Gray Ghost" because of its wartime, dull gray makeover, the *West Point* could carry up to 8,175 troops at average speeds of approximately 25 knots. Through the course of the war, it would log distances equivalent to 16 circumnavigations of the globe while enduring several perilous encounters with the enemy. Off of Singapore in January 1942, Japanese bombers attacked the *West Point* and came within 50 yards of scoring a direct hit. The ship also faced air attacks in the Red Sea, off Australia, and at Port Suez, and close calls with submarines, including one that fired torpedoes across its bow off Brazil.

The *West Point* was decommissioned in early 1946 after having transported more than 350,000 troops to ports of call all around the world.

## MANHATTAN (USS WAKEFIELD)

Another ship of the United States Line fleet, the *Manhattan* was chartered by the U.S. government in 1940 to bring American citizens home from warring Europe. It was later commissioned by the U.S. Navy in May 1941 for use as a troop carrier and renamed the USS *Wakefield.*

Capable of carrying up to 6,000 passengers, the *Wakefield* often traveled as a "lone wolf," unescorted and fast enough to outrace German subs. Despite this, the *Wakefield* had a rough go of it early in its commission. It was traveling with the *West Point* off Singapore when alert Japanese bombers attacked the *Wakefield,* scoring a direct hit that resulted in five fatalities. In September 1942, the *Wakefield* caught fire in the North Atlantic and was towed while still burning to Halifax, where it was almost capsized by a torrential storm.

The *Wakefield* was eventually repaired and recommissioned in February 1944 to continue serving as a troop transport. It finished out the war sailing primarily in the Atlantic, carrying 217,237 troops and passengers before being decommissioned in June 1946. Unlike the *Queen Mary* and the *America,* however, the *Wakefield* never returned to its former glory as a luxury liner. It remained in the navy's possession, in reserve and out of commission, until released in 1959 and scrapped five years later.

☆   ☆   ☆

- *On the night of December 12, 1939, in chill seas off the coast of Liverpool, the 20,000-ton British liner* Samaria, *which had been refitted for troop transport, cut unnoticed through a convoy of five other liners that had been tapped for troop duty. The* Samaria's *presence might have gone undetected if the ship had not struck the radio masts of the convoy's escort ship, HMS* Furious.

☆   ☆   ☆

- *In 1942, plans were afoot for the Royal Navy to convert the* Queen Mary *and the* Queen Elizabeth *into aircraft carriers. The idea was abandoned when the ships' greater value as troop transports became obvious.*

# HITLER'S HYDRA: THE MANY HEADS OF THE SS

*Corporation, private army, political police force, jailer, church, and imperial guard—the double-S runes of the SS stood for them all.*

*Leibstandarte SS Adolf Hitler. Das Reich. Hitlerjugend. Totenkopf. Florian Geyer. Handschar.* Dirlewanger-all were names of *Waffen-SS* ("armed SS") divisions. Some were fierce and elite; some followed the fighting divisions to oppress villagers. Indeed, they perpetrated most of the deeds attributed to them. However, the *Schutzstaffel* (SS) was more than elite panzer divisions with blonde troopers, black uniforms, and fierce reputations; it went far beyond sadistic concentration-camp guards and brutal reprisals.

## FORMATIONS OF THE SS

Founded in 1925 as Hitler's bodyguard assembly, the SS began its 20-year existence subordinate to the much larger *Sturmabteilung* (SA), the early Nazi Party's main paramilitary arm. Heinrich Himmler joined the SS in 1925 and by 1929 was *Reichsführer*-SS, commander of its thousand members. After the Nazis took power in 1933, SS membership ballooned to over 200,000. In the 1934 "Night of the Long Knives," the SS helped remove key SA leaders, paving its own way to supplant the SA as the mailed fist of Nazism.

Before 1934 was out, the SS underwent its first restructuring. Himmler divided it into three commands: the *Allgemeine*-SS ("General SS," essentially the SS bureaucracy), SS-*Verfügungstruppe* ("SS *Special Assignment* Troops," the early *Waffen*-SS), and the SS-*Totenkopfverbände* ("SS Death's Head Formation," concentration-camp guards). All were uniformed, primarily in black, with special ranks that generally corresponded to military ranks. By oath of membership, every SS man (and a few women) owed all loyalty to Adolf Hitler through the Nazi Party and the *Reichsführer*-SS, Heinrich Himmler.

# DUTIES OF THE SS

SS corporate activities were born of the concentration camps, the first being Dachau in 1933. Camps cost money to operate, yet offered a source of labor. Inmates were used to produce products or services, turning imprisonment into a profit-generating system. In addition to subjecting them to slave labor, SS guards confiscated prisoners' valuables, which were later sold, or used to manufacture consumer goods and even weapons. The SS became more of a moneymaking operation with each passing day.

Policing and intelligence were early SS functions, taking the forms of the notorious *Sicherheitsdienst* ("Security Service" or SS-SD) and *Geheime Staatspolizei* ("Secret State Police," the feared Gestapo). At first, a ruthless and flamboyant Reich intelligence official named Reinhard Heydrich (nicknamed "the Hangman") headed both organizations. After Heydrich's assassination in 1942, Ernst Kaltenbrunner (nicknamed "the Gorilla") took command of the SD, while the efficient career policeman Heinrich Müller became head of Gestapo.

The larger and more diverse the SS became, the more the divisions duplicated each other's efforts. The SS-SD and Gestapo, both busily rooting out domestic and foreign enemies of the Nazi state, trod on each other's toes. The *Waffen*-SS, which barely amounted to a couple of divisions during the invasion of France, expanded to become an army of its own; this made it few friends in Germany's well-established *Heer* (regular army). Nor, when it came down to it, was the *Waffen*-SS always a capable army. Though first in line for the latest equipment, its recruits tended to come from less educated farming stock, with officers chosen more for political fervor than hard military competence. The *Waffen*-SS would compensate for this by learning on the job, but in so doing it sustained many casualties that experienced soldiers and leaders of the *Heer* would have avoided. The famous, fanatical determination of mainstream *Waffen*-SS units weighed against their lack of experience. Their daring was fueled by a combination of ideology and the grim reprisal facing any SS man seen to hesitate or retreat in combat.

The SS grew into a vast octopus of terror with tentacles every-where. It ran industries, policed Germany and its occupied territories, operated the sordid concentration and extermination camps, hunted partisans, and fought at the front. With its social precedence over the other German martial arms, an SS title brought preferential treatment and prestige. The SS worked overtime to mold Germans in Hitler's ideal of Germanic culture, cracking down on any expression of dissent or affection for things non-German. Listening to the music of Mendelssohn (a Jewish composer) was enough to run a German afoul of the men in black.

## MEN OF THE SS

At first, SS candidates needed to show impeccable Germanic lineage going back centuries, especially the absence of Jewish forebears. As the war dragged on, the *Waffen*-SS relaxed its standards to admit other Western European recruits. Finally, it resorted to recruiting in Eastern Europe. By 1943, the number of Eastern European recruits approached that of ethnic Germans in service. These units would vary from disastrous (the mutinous Bosnian Muslims of the *Handschar* Division) to very effective (Estonian and Latvian divisions performed quite well). *Waffen*-SS units perpetrated some of the greatest atrocities of the war, from reprisals against the French resistance to the psychotic career of the "Dirlewanger Brigade," a force of convicted criminals led by the brutal Dr. Oskar Dirlewanger, whose swath of rape, sadism, and massacre was so gruesome it sickened most SS generals.

Mainly at Himmler's instigation, the SS replaced Christianity with a bastardized revival of Germanic paganism. Himmler renovated Wewelsburg Castle (near Paderborn in Westphalia, in east-central Germany) as a sort of temple/monastery/retreat where SS men could marry with due pomp and ceremony, reflect upon their Teutonic heritage and birthright according to Nazi ideology, and rest up from the hard work of building and defending the Third Reich. Himmler viewed his SS as a modern order of Germanic knights, heirs to a warrior tradition. In the case of the famous 1st SS Panzer Division *Leibstandarte SS Adolf Hitler*—which had the special duty of guarding the *Führer*—the unit's fierce battle record met those standards. In the case of the traitorous British Free Corps, a platoon-size contingent of POW recruits that loafed in comfort through most of their service, not so much. *Waffen*-SS units ran the gamut between these extremes.

By the end, the *Waffen*-SS served as a fire brigade and counterattack force in Germany's attempts to shore up its defenses against the well-supplied Western Allies and the much more numerous, infuriated Soviets. Many *Waffen*-SS units were encircled and destroyed; a few dissolved, but many fought to the bitter end. The French 33rd SS Grenadier Division "Charlemagne" was one of Berlin's last defenders. Because of aggressive Red Army action, the 33rd SS managed to position just 330 men in Berlin's northwestern suburbs; in the end, only about 30 remained alive.

When the sound of the guns died down and the camps were liberated, many SS men faced death or prison for their wartime careers. Few in Soviet captivity ever saw home again. A good number of war criminals and SS bureaucrats escaped, with all the swag they could carry, to countries that would take them: Argentina, Brazil, Paraguay, and other South American countries, as well as Spain. A few made their way to the Middle East to advise Arab armies facing the rise of an independent Jewish state in Israel. Much postwar Nazi hunting would focus on SS men such as Adolf Eichmann, a key architect of the machinery of genocide, or SS "doctors" such as Josef Mengele who performed inhuman experiments on captives. Perhaps the greatest number had simply given in to their baser instincts, following their leaders into criminality and shame.

Many years after the war, one fact remains: The lightning-bolt runes of the SS provoke apalled reactions second only to those generated by the swastika.

# BRIDGES TOO FAR: GERMAN AND ALLIED AIRBORNE ASSAULTS

*World War II was the first war in which airborne assault paratroops were deployed. Both the Axis and the Allies, however, curtailed their use of offensive airborne actions following two nearly disastrous operations.*

## OPERATION MERCURY

Code-named Operation Mercury, Germany's invasion of Crete began on the morning of May 20, 1941, with history's first massive airborne invasion. According to German battle plans, the airborne troops would concentrate on taking the Maleme airfield in western Crete so subsequent heavy troops could disembark by airplane. However, the plan had problems from the beginning. British intelligence had broken the German Enigma code, and Allied and Greek defenders knew the attack was coming. At the same time, German intelligence grossly underestimated Commonwealth defenders, believing them to number 5,000, and predicted that anti-Royalist Cretans would welcome the Germans as liberators. Although only lightly armed after losing most of their heavy equipment in the evacuation from the Greek mainland, the Allied defenders in fact numbered 40,000 troops, and the Cretans would offer the Germans their first massive resistance from a civilian population.

For Operation Mercury, the Germans deployed 750 glider troops and 10,000 paratroopers, who were joined later by 5,000 airlifted mountain troops and 7,000 seaborne troops. While the German paratroopers should have been well armed, their weapons were dropped in separate canisters rather than strapped to individual soldiers, a serious tactical flaw in their deployment. The German parachute design also used only a single riser connecting the harness to the canopy, making it impossible for paratroopers to guide their descent. Many may have been shot dead in the air by New Zealander and Australian riflemen. Armed with only side weapons and knives when they landed, others were gunned down as they tried to reach their weapons. Many of the gliders were hit by mortar fire within seconds of landing. In the first wave, some units were totally wiped out and most suffered casualty rates of over 50 percent. Paratrooper commander General Kurt Student reportedly contemplated suicide as reports from the field reached headquarters.

A second wave of paratroopers also suffered heavy casualties, as Cretan policemen, police cadets, and civilians joined the battle with unexpected ferocity. One elderly Cretan reportedly beat a German paratrooper to death with a walking stick. Many other Germans were knifed or clubbed to death. The Germans quickly retaliated and began using Cretan civilians as human shields.

The Third Reich seemed to be facing its first ground defeat of the war. But it had a stroke of luck when communication failures led a New Zealand infantry unit at the Maleme airfield to withdraw, leaving the field to the German paratroopers. Reinforcements from the German 5th Mountain Division landed soon after. An Allied counterattack was repulsed, and defense of Crete became doomed as German troops continue to pour in. Over the next several days, 18,000 Commonwealth troops were evacuated from the eastern end of the island. Allied ground forces suffered 3,500 casualties and 17,000 troops captured. The Royal Navy suffered more than 2,000 casualties, as the *Luftwaffe* sank three British cruisers and six destroyers during the assault.

The Germans admitted 6,453 killed, missing, wounded, and captured, but British intelligence estimated that the Germans in fact suffered 16,800 casualties. Hitler was shocked by the losses and banned further offensive airborne operations for the duration of the war, which had a significant impact on the invasion of the Soviet Union just weeks later. The Allies, however, were impressed by the potential of paratroops and started to build their own large airborne divisions.

## OPERATION MARKET GARDEN

While Allied airborne assaults played a large role in the D-Day invasion of Normandy, a number of planned subsequent operations were scrapped as Allied ground forces in France overran intended objectives. In September 1944, the Allies launched what is still the largest air invasion in history, landing 34,876 paratroopers of the U.S. 101st and 82nd Airborne Divisions, the British 1st Airborne, and a Polish airborne brigade behind German lines in Holland. Conceived by General Montgomery, Operation Market Garden intended to capture a series of bridges that would lead Allied troops across the Rhine River, past German lines to—it was hoped—a quick end to the war. But the plan suffered from numerous flaws:

• Success required taking and holding every bridge.

• Landing zones were selected up to 15 miles away from objectives.

• Airborne landings were staggered over two days.

• The plan relied on using a single highway that ran through marshy country, which proved easy for the Germans to defend.

• Unknown to Allied commanders, two SS Panzer divisions were also refitting in the area. Although air reconnaissance and the Dutch underground spotted their presence, the new information was ignored.

Market Garden was launched on September 17. A small force from the 1st Airborne, under the command of Lieutenant Colonel John Frost, quickly took one end of the all-important Rhine bridge at Arnhem, but German defenders prevented taking the other end. Much of the 1st Airborne remained scattered, due in part to the staggered landing schedule and a severe breakdown in radio communications. Units of the 101st Airborne Division eventually captured four of the five bridges it was assigned, but met a strong German defense at the primary objective, the key Nijmegen bridge south of Arnhem.

The German command quickly realized the Allied battle plan and set up new defensive lines, delaying the advance of the British Army XXX Corps, which was supposed to relieve the paratroopers at Arnhem on the third day. In fact, the bridge at Nijmegen was not taken until the end of the third day, and XXX Corps was delayed for another 24 hours by German guns north of the town.

Around Arnhem, scattered units of the 1st Airborne suffered heavy casualties trying to link in a defensive pocket in the nearby town of Oosterbeek. Using the local telephone service in Arnhem to communicate, Frost learned that XXX Corps would not be arriving to relieve his position. Facing point blank attack by German tanks and having run out of ammo, on September 21 paratroopers at the Arnhem bridge pulled back into defensive positions in the town. The Polish 1st Airborne Brigade landed nearby the next day but also failed to reach Arnhem.

Beginning on September 25 and for the next two days, what remained of the British 1st Airborne withdrew across the Neder Rijn river. About 2,200 men escaped, leaving behind 6,000 prisoners and more than 17,000 Allied troops killed, wounded, or missing. German units in Holland successfully blocked the Allied advance in the West until after the Battle of the Bulge in February 1945. Allied airborne troops did not engage in another large-scale air assault for the rest of the war in Europe.

# THE JAPANESE-AMERICAN RELOCATION

*After the attack on Pearl Harbor, America's distrust of anyone with ties to Japan resulted in the internment of more than 100,000 Japanese-Americans. Stripped of most of their belongings, they were confined to camps across the United States for the duration of the war.*

Even before Pearl Harbor, the U.S. government acted against persons suspected of loyalty to the Axis. In 1939, the FBI put together a Custodial Detention Index of citizens and foreigners thought a security risk. In June 1940, a month after the fall of France, Congress passed the Alien Registration Act, which compiled the names, addresses, and fingerprints of millions of "resident aliens," immigrants to the U.S. who were not naturalized citizens.

After the December 7, 1941, attack on Pearl Harbor, military concerns combined with economic interests, prejudice, and fear, resulting in the internment of the West Coast's Japanese. The public was apoplectic over the sneak attack in Hawaii and by Japanese atrocities in the Philippines. Americans widely thought Japan would invade the West Coast; in February 1942, a Japanese sub had briefly shelled the California town of Goleta. "Unless something is done," said California Attorney General Earl Warren, the future U.S. Supreme Court Chief Justice, the Japanese in America "may bring about a repetition of Pearl Harbor."

## PUNISHED FOR THEIR ANCESTRY

In February 1942, President Roosevelt signed Executive Order 9066, authorizing the War Department to designate exclusion zones for "any or all persons." In March 1942, an executive order set up an office that froze the assets of many aliens, prohibiting possible attempts to funnel money to the Axis. The same month, the army imposed a curfew on "all persons of Japanese ancestry" and forbade travel apart from short work commutes.

On May 3, 1942, Lieutenant General John DeWitt ordered every-one of Japanese descent to move to "relocation camps," or intern-ment camps, in the country's interior. DeWitt told Congress and the press, "A Jap's a Jap...a dangerous element. There is no way to determine their loyalty...It makes no difference whether the Jap is a citizen or not."

The orders applied to about 120,000 people; about 62 percent were American citizens. Most of the others were resident Japanese aliens: Asian immigrants were not then allowed naturalization. All were excluded from California and from areas of Washington and Oregon within as much as 150 miles from the coast. Such rules did not apply to Americans of German and Italian descent, though they had a larger population and more eligible voters.

## PRISONERS IN THEIR OWN COUNTRY

From 80,000 to 110,000 Japanese-Americans went first to temporary "assembly centers" before boarding trains or buses to the more per-manent camps. The assembly points were located in fairgrounds and racetracks, the residents often housed in stables. About 17,500 people went straight to the relocation camps. Roughly 10,000 were fortunate to find sponsors and jobs in other parts of America outside the exclu-sion zones, allowing them to move about freely.

Once notices of evacuation were posted in public, internees had a week to ten days to report to the camps. They were allowed to bring with them only the personal effects they could carry. Farms, homes, and businesses had to be auctioned off quickly. "Automo-biles were sold for less than half their worth," according to a his-tory of Wyoming's Heart Mountain camp; "other belongings often went for ten cents on the dollar; pets were given away....Those who stored belongings often discovered, after the war, that those items had been stolen or vandalized." The Farm Security Adminis-tration and Federal Reserve Bank of San Francisco were supposed to guard against unfair purchases, but the agencies almost never intervened. Poor tenant farmers lost rights for tilling their plots. En route to the internment centers, many internees murmured *shikata ga nai*—"it cannot be helped."

The camps were administered by the War Relocation Authority (WRA), headed by the former Agriculture Department director of information, Milton S. Eisenhower, the brother of the supreme commander and a future president of Pennsylvania State and Johns Hopkins universities.

The approximately ten relocation camps were in remote parts of California, Arizona, Arkansas, Wyoming, Idaho, Utah, and Colorado. A few were placed on American Indian reservations. The number of residents in each camp ranged from about 7,300 to 18,700.

The Department of Justice also operated a separate set of 27 camps. These held about 7,000 Japanese in all, including reporters and Buddhist priests. These internees were deemed to be higher security risks. Further, the facilities held 2,264 persons of Japanese descent from Latin America, mostly Peru, possibly for potential prisoner swaps with Tokyo.

Economic interests helped push the internments. After war broke out, the Los Angeles Chamber of Commerce demanded removal of Japanese from California. Austin Anson, head of a Salinas farmer association, claimed, "If all the Japs were removed tomorrow, we'd never miss them . . . because the white farmers can take over and produce everything." Mexican migrants filled many of the open labor slots.

## HEART MOUNTAIN CAMP

Camp conditions were a mix of crowded confinement and all-American bustle. At Heart Mountain, the guard force of 124 soldiers staffed nine guard towers, turning searchlights onto the barbed-wire fences enclosing the encampment. Barracks for the 10,000 internees consisted of 120-by-20-foot buildings that were covered in tarpaper and set out in long blocks. The size of single-room apartments ranged from 20-by-16 feet to 20-by-24. Each unit had one ceiling light, a potbellied stove, and a cot with two blankets.

Construction of the camp touched off an economic boom in nearby Powell and Cody, Wyoming. Yet buildings were shoddy;

residents often repaired windows and floors with tools from the Sears & Roebuck catalog. Open ceilings brought in the conversations of neighbors, according to the *Journal of the West*. There were public latrines and mess halls. Such conditions stripped residents not just of physical comfort, but dignity.

The camp had a hospital and a school, but the WRA fixed the annual salary of Japanese doctors and teachers at $228, a tenth of comparable Anglo salaries in the area. In contrast, internees were able to harvest the crops of local sugar-beet growers for the prevailing wage when the farmers faced a severe labor shortage. Merchants in Cody and Powell forced their city councils to issue visitor's passes for internees.

In spring 1943, a new high school for the camp was finished: It had a machine shop, a library, and a 1,100-seat auditorium for concerts and plays. Its boys and girls basketball teams traveled to other schools for games. The football team lost only one game in two years, to the Casper Mustangs, whose 210-pound fullback shredded the mostly small-statured Japanese-American club. Along with sports, Kubuki theater and the camp's two cinemas and two churches were popular. There were also active Boy and Girl Scout Troops: The former marched its Drum and Bugle Corps outside the barracks on July 4, and both made a hiking trip to Yellowstone National Park.

## CONFLICTS AT THE CAMPS

There was much disorder at some centers, especially at California's Tule Lake, where those deemed security risks were congregated. Many internees refused loyalty tests, and some were pro-Japan; strikes and protests were common. Among all the camps, 5,766 internees renounced their American citizenship, many of whom were first-generation immigrants; 4,724 were repatriated to Japan after the war.

After the draft was reinstated for internees in 1943, scores were indicted at Tule Lake and Heart Mountain for refusing induction. Believing they should not be forced to fight without having full rights of citizenship, most interned males of military age did not volunteer for the armed services. Yet 654 from Heart Mountain signed up; 63 were killed or wounded in combat. Some served in Europe with the very highly decorated Japanese-American 442nd Regiment.

## THE WAR WINDS DOWN

Life in the camps tracked the progress of the war. The camps were set up in spring 1942. At that time, the Imperial Navy was threatening the Pacific and America. In 1944, as it seemed more likely the Allies would eventually subdue Japan, some internees were allowed to return to the Pacific coast.

On December 17, 1944, the White House ended the exclusion zones. By the end of 1945, most internees had left the camps, and the last structures were closed and bulldozed in 1946. Each person released received a train ticket and $25 for the trip home.

Some authorities had opposed the relocations from the start, including FBI Director J. Edgar Hoover. In a memorandum to Attorney General Francis Biddle on charges of Japanese-American disloyalty, Hoover wrote, "Every complaint in this regard has been investigated, but in no case has any information been obtained which would substantiate the allegation."

About half the internees, 54,127, returned to the west coast; 52,798 wound up residing in the interior of the U.S; and 4,724 moved to Japan, according to the book *Japanese-Americans, from Relocation to Redress.*

Many ex-internees paid a steep and lasting financial price for their forced internment. Some estimates peg the value of lost businesses and homes, in today's dollars, at $5 billion. In 1948, Washington began payment of about $38 million in claims compensation. In 1989, the government issued a formal apology for the internment program and paid survivors reparations of $20,000 each, $1.2 billion in all.

Champions of the payments in Congress were Senator Alan Simpson and former internee Representative Norman Mineta. They had met as Boy Scouts at Heart Mountain.

# Fast Facts

- Even some neutrals joined the Waffen-SS: Approximately 1,000 Spaniards, and some 3,000 Swiss and Swedes volunteered.

- The two worst full SS divisions, by all accounts, were "Handschar" and the 21st SS Mountain Division, "Skanderbeg," formed from Albanian Muslims. Handschar mutinied and was forcibly dissolved. As for Skanderbeg, in one of the bitterest ironies of the war, Himmler ordered it disbanded for committing excessive atrocities. However, neither Handschar nor Skanderbeg approached the dreadful record of the 36th SS-Grenadier "Dirlewanger" Division, an ethnically German unit that was responsible for countless atrocities.

- Thanks to recruiting posters, we can see exactly how the Waffen-SS was marketed to particular ethnicities. One in Dutch said, translated: "For your honor and conscience! Against Bolshevism, the Waffen-SS calls you!" An Italian poster displaying an SS man with a bugle said, "For honor and for life—Italian SS Legion!"

- Perhaps the most comically ineffective foreign contingent was the British Free Corps, recruited straight from POW camps. The unit never exceeded 50 men. The Germans did not commit it to frontline battle until Berlin was under attack, at which point the unit deserted en masse.

- On December 2, 1943, a German raid on the shipping terminal at Bari in southern Italy led to the sinking of the USS John Harvey, a U.S. merchant ship. Unknown to most people at the time, the ship was carrying over 100 tons of mustard gas bombs, which had been stored as a method of retaliation in case Germans used chemical weapons on American troops. Of the 800 people hospitalized after the raid, 628 suffered from mustard gas exposure, and 69 deaths were attributed to the gas. The classified cargo was not reported, and the merchant seamen exposed to the toxin didn't receive proper treatment as a result.

# FOREIGN NATIONALS IN THE SS

*By the end of World War II, the* Waffen-SS *had roamed far afield from the stereotypically Aryan, efficient warriors in black.*

Before the war, *Waffen*-SS volunteers needed to prove their German lineage as well as represent the accepted, blond Aryan look. After completing the Scandinavian and French campaigns in 1940, Germany found itself with new territory to garrison, which also opened up new recruiting pools—*Waffen*-SS recruiters were never far behind the conquering *Wehrmacht.*

Foreign nationals as young as 17 were accepted into the SS though, as one might expect, the greatest number were in their early twenties: physically adult yet young enough to be taken in by standard Nazi doctrine about Aryan superiority and the potentially catastrophic nature of Bolshevism. The suggestible nature of these SS recruits also brought with it other qualities that have been typical of young soldiers throughout history: innate respect for authority, largely unquestioning obedience, ideological (if naïve) zeal, and a propensity for physical action, even brutality. Additionally, the SS had lures unique among fighting entities of World War II, including uniforms that were theatrical and intimidating; a real and self-proclaimed tradition of battlefield glory; ornate, almost medieval induction and other rituals; and a supposed racial kinship that encouraged an unusually high level of camaraderie, and the lack of individuality that was desired by the Nazi leadership.

The first foreign recruits were *Volksdeutsche* (ethnic Germans living abroad) or from Germanic-language populations including the Danish, Norwegian, Flemish, and Dutch. Entire *Waffen*-SS divisions were formed from *Volksdeutsche* recruits. Two Dutch, one Flemish, one Walloon, one Scandinavian, and one French division would wear the runes of Himmler's elite SS. With the German conquests and alliances in Eastern Europe came more *Volks-*

*deutsche,* but other non-Germanic ethnic groups were recruited to the ranks of the SS as well. Hungarians, Romanians, Latvians, Estonians, Russians, Ukrainians, and others were accepted as the SS relaxed its standards, realizing it would need more men for the war. In all, more than 900,000 men would serve in the SS: 400,000 Reich Germans, 185,000 *Volksdeutsche,* 137,300 Western Europeans, and at least 200,000 Eastern Europeans and non-Europeans.

Why would any non-German join the *Waffen*-SS? As the pool of volunteers expanded, recruiters focused on potential shared cultural values, prejudices, and vulnerabilities. After Germany invaded the USSR, anti-Bolshevism became the primary appeal, often seasoned with religious overtones reminding the recruit of Soviet atheism. Nationalism worked well; with recent memory of the brutal Soviet takeover in Latvia, for example, 39,000 Latvians volunteered to fight the Soviets. As food became scarcer, some joined because it meant meals. For many it was the ticket out of a miserable POW camp. Some had no choice—they were drafted.

Most *Volksdeutsche* and Western European units performed well in combat. The record of the Eastern European units was mixed; some fought with tenacity, others folded under fire or even mutinied outright. SS leaders went to great lengths to appeal to ethnic pride through unit badges, special uniforms, and other inexpensive touches. The Bosnian 13th SS Mountain Division "Handschar" wore the fez; its chaplains were Muslim imams. A Turkestani brigade recruited from POW camps became the only Waffen-SS unit whose cuffband was green and white (representing Islam) rather than black and white.

After the war, the victorious Allies turned cold eyes upon the survivors of the Waffen-SS, especially the foreign volunteers. Most of those repatriated to the USSR were executed; others stood trial for war crimes in various countries. Some managed to pick up the pieces in their homelands, or elsewhere. Of the survivors, one thing is sure: Few went out of their way to advertise their World War II pasts.

# THE EMPEROR'S SAVAGE SAMURAI

*The widespread German and Soviet atrocities on Europe's eastern front were approximately matched, horror story for horror story, in the Pacific Theater, where the Japanese soldier's ideology and training produced a particularly brutal killing machine.*

The violent ideology of the Imperial Japanese Army soldier was cultivated even before his induction into the Emperor's service. The popular concept of *yamato damashi,* or "spirit of ancient Japan," was a cultural moral code stressing absolute loyalty to the Emperor, as heaven's regent of the Sacred Islands. The combination of this nationalist spirit with Buddhist and Shinto religious beliefs (which preached reincarnation and the Emperor's divinity) produced a warrior's creed expressed as the modern *bushido,* a chivalric code originally applied to the *samurai* class as far back as the twelfth century.

Modern *bushido* indoctrinated Japanese recruits with simple, inflexible precepts: "Honor is everything." "A soldier never surrenders." "Death in the Emperor's service is an honor." Widespread belief in reincarnation made the thought of death more palatable for Japanese conscripts than for many of their Western counterparts, who generally considered death a necessary evil—but one to be avoided by smart tactics.

Part of the brutal nature of the Japanese rifle-company soldier stemmed from tactical doctrines, which favored cold steel when attacking. Because of a relative inferiority of Japanese firearms, Japanese soldiers spent more time than their Allied counterparts on bayonet practice, which encouraged close-in combat with a distinctively personal element of violence.

Another ingredient of a deliberately brutal soldier was physical punishment. The army's absolute code of obedience allowed superiors to beat and otherwise abuse inferiors. Enlisted men and auxiliary troops (such as Koreans in Japanese service) came in for the worst beatings.

After the invasion of China, one former sergeant major recalled:

> In training, we were forced to engage in actual charges in order to kill live humans. They talked about POWs, but in the Japanese Army, any Chinese we caught were called POWs. Didn't matter if they were peasants or what. There were three men tied to stakes, all ready for us. I had applied to be a petty officer, so I got to go first. My squad leader signaled me, shouting, "Forward, forward, thrust!" But it was by no means easy to thrust my bayonet into a living person. I'd never killed anyone before. Still, if I was clumsy at it, it would affect my whole military career. So I showed no mercy or leniency.

Japanese brutality entered its full flower in China, where some 20 million ethnic Chinese died at the hands of the Imperial Japanese Army. As one Japanese officer later conceded:

> The major means of getting intelligence was to extract information by interrogating prisoners. Torture was an unavoidable necessity. Murdering and burying them follows naturally. You do it so you won't be found out. I believed and acted this way because I was convinced of what I was doing. We carried out our duty as instructed by our masters. We did it for the sake of our country. From our filial obligation to our ancestors. On the battlefield, we never really considered the Chinese humans. When you're winning, the losers look really miserable. We concluded that the Yamato race was superior.

When Japan widened the war to the United States and the British Commonwealth, its soldiers treated their occidental "guests of the Emperor" with greater brutality than their German counterparts did. One historian estimated that a Western POW stood a 4 percent chance of dying before the war's end in a German camp, while the same POW had a 30 percent chance of dying of execution, prolonged physical abuse, disease, or malnutrition in Japanese hands. It was a miserable, trickle-down effect of the martial spirit that animated the Emperor's soldiers.

# Timeline

## 1941

**May 10–11**
Heaviest Luftwaffe raid on London occurs, marking the end of Night Blitz

**May 11**
Japan demands cessation of U.S. aid to China

**May 20–June 1**
German airborne troops take Crete in a spectacular but costly air assault

**May 24**
The British battleship *Prince of Wales* and cruiser *Hood* encounter the German battleship *Bismarck* and cruiser *Prinz Eugen* in the Denmark Strait; after a fierce 20-minute gunfight, *Bismarck* sinks the *Hood*

**May 27**
British warships sink *Bismarck*

**June**
Pilots of the American Volunteer Group ("Flying Tigers") arrive in Burma throughout the month

**June 1**
U.S. Coast Guard begins patrols from Greenland

**June 8**
British and Free French forces invade Syria

**June 15–17**
British effort to relieve Tobruk fails

**June 22**
Operation Barbarossa begins; Germans murder their counterparts at the Russian border at Brest-Litovsk, touching off an invasion along the entire 1,800-mile frontier

**June 24**
Germans capture Vilnius and Kaunas in Lithuania

**June 27**
Japan proclaims the Greater East Asia Co-Prosperity Sphere, a front for using the economies of conquered lands to support Imperial Japan

**June 30**
Germans capture the Ukranian city of Lvov

**July 4**
Josip Broz Tito, Yugoslavia's Communist Party leader, calls for armed resistance against the German occupation

**July 7**
U.S. Marines occupy British bases in Iceland, Trinidad, and British Guiana

**July 9**
Germans take Vitebsk, capturing 324,000 Soviets in the Minsk pocket

**July 16**
About 600,000 Russians are trapped when the German Army encircles the Soviet city of Smolensk

**July 19**
U.S. Navy begins escorting convoys to Iceland

**July 26**
The United States and Britain freeze Japanese assets; Hawaii sector put on alert

Filipino Army nationalized under command of General Douglas MacArthur

# THE USS *ARIZONA*

*When the USS Arizona was commissioned on October 17, 1916, no one present at the event would have thought that in just 25 years the venerable ship would become the symbol for America's setback at Pearl Harbor and the incident that sparked America's entry into another World War.*

During World War I, the *Arizona* patrolled waters off the northeastern coast of the United States. The Pennsylvania class battleship burned through oil quickly, and a lack of fuel oil in the British Isles prevented the dreadnought from transiting the Atlantic Ocean. Following the armistice, the *Arizona* served as part of the honor escort that transported President Woodrow Wilson to France, where he attended the Paris Peace Conference.

After the war, *Arizona* was based at San Pedro, California, where she served as the flagship for several battleship divisions. In 1929, the battleship entered the Norfolk Navy Yard. For the next 20 months, crews upgraded her equipment. She received new antiaircraft guns, upgraded armor plating, new boilers, turbines, and tripod masts. The overhauled ship was placed into full commission on March 1, 1931.

With the threat of war looming in 1941, President Roosevelt moved the Pacific Fleet from its base at San Pedro to Pearl Harbor in the territory of Hawaii. The mighty *Arizona* and her sister ships took their places at quays in "battleship row" along the southeastern side of Ford Island.

## DEATH OF A DREADNOUGHT

On November 26, 1941, an attack fleet of Imperial Japanese Navy warships, including six aircraft carriers, departed Japan for the Hawaiian Islands. They arrived undetected at their launch position, some 230 miles north of the island of Oahu, 11 days later.

At 6:00 A.M. the morning of December 7, two waves of fighters, bombers, and torpedo planes launched their attack on the

130 ships of the U.S. Pacific Fleet moored at Pearl Harbor and the other various military facilities on the island of Oahu. The Japanese warplanes descended on the harbor, beginning their devastating attack at 7:55 A.M.

As the alarm sounded throughout the harbor, the men of the *Arizona* quickly manned their battle stations. In a matter of minutes, hundreds of guns from dozens of ships engaged the Japanese planes.

A total of at least seven bombs hit the *Arizona*. One hit the boat deck, another the after turrets, and four more struck mid-ship. At 8:10 A.M. a Japanese Type 97 Attack Bomber dropped a converted armor piercing artillery shell on the *Arizona*. The shell penetrated the decks between the battleship's no. 1 and no. 2 turrets.

The shell ignited the *Arizona's* silk-encased cordite charges and 14-inch shells in the forward magazine. The resulting cataclysmic explosion lifted the 31,000-ton battleship out of the water, showering the surrounding area with bodies and debris. The explosion claimed the lives of 1,177 sailors and marines and remains the largest single loss of life in navy history.

## TRAGEDY LIVES ON IN MEMORY

The cost of raising the *Arizona* was tagged at $2 million. Efforts to retrieve the dead were mounted in the days following the attack and as many as 100 bodies were recovered. But when a diver was killed when his air hose was severed, a decision was made to leave the remaining dead aboard the ship.

In March 1950, then Commander in Chief of the Pacific Fleet Admiral Arthur Radford instituted the raising of the colors over the *Arizona*. In 1958 President Eisenhower signed legislation for the creation of a permanent memorial above the battleship's remains. The USS *Arizona* Memorial was officially dedicated in May 1962. Nowadays, some 4,500 visit the shrine each day. Plans are also underway to rebuild a state-of-the-art museum and interpretive center across from the memorial to replace the deteriorating structure currently in use. The dedication ceremony for the new *Arizona* Memorial Center is scheduled for December 7, 2008.

# JFK AND THE HARD TIMES ON PLUM PUDDING ISLAND

*Long before his days in the White House, John F. Kennedy proved his mettle in the South Pacific. In the early morning of August 2, 1943, Kennedy's PT boat was split in two by the Japanese destroyer, Amagiri. As his crew floated in the shark-infested water, JFK led them in a search for safety and rescue in a famous six-day ordeal.*

## BACK INTO THE WATER

The night had been hellish. After having their boat torn apart by a Japanese destroyer, the surviving crew of the Motor Torpedo Boat PT-109 had assembled on the wreckage of the boat's bow to discuss their options. They had then been led by 26-year-old Lieutenant John F. Kennedy to Plum Pudding Island, a tiny dot of land deemed too small to interest the Japanese. The crew swam for hours, Kennedy towing an immobile Patrick McMahon through the water by clenching the strap of the badly burned man's life jacket in his teeth. They stumbled to shore across the razor-sharp coral, and Kennedy, having swallowed copious amounts of seawater, vomited and collapsed on the beach.

After he recovered, Kennedy announced that he intended to swim the mile and a half into the sea and attempt to contact PT boats on their patrol that evening. Ensign Barney (George) Ross thought the plan was absurd; McMahon thought it was suicidal. Nevertheless, Kennedy was determined to try. At about 6:30 P.M., he slipped back into the water, walking as far as he could on the surrounding reef before swimming out into the deeper channel. Unbeknownst to the survivors, the American fleet had shifted its patrol area miles to the north, and no boats came that night. By 9:00 A.M. the next morning, the men on the island assumed the lieutenant must be dead, only to be proved wrong around noon when he dragged himself back ashore. Despite Kennedy's lack of success, he ordered a skeptical Ensign Ross to make a similar attempt that night. Unfortunately, Ross's effort proved no more effective.

The men exhausted the resources on Plum Pudding by the second day. Driven by a need for more food and the desire to be closer to potential rescuers, Kennedy decided to move the group to another island, Olasana, covered with plenty of coconut trees and located closer to the PT patrol area itself. Again, Kennedy towed McMahon, who by now had difficulty seeing due to scabs forming over his burned eyelids.

## NARU AND ENCOUNTERS WITH THE JAPANESE

The next day, Kennedy and Ross decided to swim to the neighboring island of Naru. Kennedy had no real hope for the effort, but he wanted to remain active to keep up his men's morale. Searching the island, Kennedy and Ross found the wreckage of a small Japanese boat containing a crate filled with crackers and candy, as well as a small dugout canoe with a supply of water. Discussing their windfall, the two men made their way back down to the beach.

As Kennedy and Ross emerged onto the beach, they immediately spotted two other men out on the reef. Convinced that they had encountered the Japanese, they quickly dived back into the bushes. The two strangers in question, Melanesian scouts, Biuku Gasa and Eroni Kumana, were actually in the employ of the Australian military. Convinced that Kennedy and Ross were themselves Japanese, the two natives leapt into their canoe and furiously paddled away, fortunately heading toward Olasana, where the remaining PT survivors were camped. Making contact with the crew, the islanders helpfully offered the information that Naru contained Japanese troops, much to the alarm of the PT crew. Little did they know that one of the "Japanese" Biuku and Eroni referred to was actually their own skipper.

# COCONUTS AND RESCUE

Returning to Olasana in the canoe the next day, Kennedy found Ensign Leonard Thom chatting away with Biuku and Eroni. The scouts were sent off with two messages, one written with the stub of a pencil Thom had somehow managed to keep throughout the entire ordeal; the other was carved into the side of a coconut by Kennedy. The coconut read, "NARU ISL / NATIVE KNOWS POSIT / HE CAN PILOT / 11 ALIVE / NEED SMALL BOAT / KENNEDY." The news quickly made its way back to Lieutenant Arthur Reginald Evans, an Australian coast-watcher near Wana Wana, who had actually seen the wreckage of PT-109 and sent messages to the Americans for several days inquiring about the possibility of survivors. Evans dispatched a larger canoe with supplies. Kennedy made his way back to Wana Wana in the larger canoe, hiding from Japanese air patrols under palm fronds in the bottom of the boat. He met Evans and rendezvoused with a PT-boat patrol bound to pick up his shipwrecked crew, who were rescued on August 8. Except for the two men lost in the initial collision, the crew of PT-109 survived.

Controversy erupted surrounding the loss of PT-109. General MacArthur thought Kennedy should face court-martial, but the official Navy report was much less critical. However, regardless of the circumstances of the loss, John F. Kennedy's determined efforts to save his crew were beyond question. Lieutenant Kennedy was awarded the Navy and Marine Corps Medal for "extremely heroic conduct." Kennedy himself, however, felt as if he hadn't accomplished enough in the war and turned down an offer to return home, instead making a successful effort to obtain command of another boat.

John F. Kennedy eventually rose to a much greater position than that of a junior officer in the South Pacific. He kept the famous coconut on the desk in the Oval Office throughout his presidency. Despite all of his other successes, in 1963 he wrote, "Any man who may be asked in this century what he did to make his life worthwhile, I think can respond with a good deal of pride and satisfaction, 'I served in the United States Navy.'"

# OPERATION PASTORIUS: NAZI SABOTEURS IN NEW YORK

*In the seventeenth century, a group of German immigrants to the New World arrived under the care of their leader, Franz Daniel Pastorius, and founded what would become Germantown, Pennsylvania. Nearly 300 years later, a man claiming to be Franz Daniel Pastorius called the FBI from a hotel room in New York and confessed that he had led a new group of Germans to American shores. This time, however, the recently arrived Germans were saboteurs who had come to America intending to sabotage key industrial targets.*

Recruited and trained by the Nazi *Abwehr* ("Intelligence 2"), eight men reached the United States via submarine in June 1942. Split into two groups of four, they landed on beaches in Long Island, New York, and in northern Florida.

The New York group, led by George Dasch, who had lived in the United States for nearly 20 years before the war, did not fare well. While still on the dark beach, the men were discovered by a U.S. Coast Guard patrolman who doubted that they were the stranded fishermen they claimed to be. According to FBI records, Dasch offered the guardsman a $300 bribe and threatened to kill him unless he "forgot" about the event. Outnumbered on the desolate beach, the guardsman accepted the bribe and then reported the incident to his superiors. When they investigated the site, they discovered discarded German uniforms and bomb-making equipment and saw evidence of a German submarine slipping beneath the waves offshore.

The saboteurs, meanwhile, had escaped to New York City, where Dasch and another man named Ernest Burger checked into a hotel. Soon thereafter, perhaps convinced that the operation was doomed to failure, Dasch resolved to surrender. The FBI, however, had not yet learned of the Long Island incident and thought the man claiming to be Pastorius was playing a joke. Nevertheless, Dasch traveled to the Mayflower hotel in Washington to surrender in person and the FBI, having learned of the landing, immediately took him into custody. The FBI arrested the other saboteurs—the Florida group had made it as far as Chicago and New York.

All eight men were quickly tried and convicted by a secret military court ordered by President Franklin Roosevelt and condoned by the Supreme Court. Six of the men were executed, but at the request of FBI Director J. Edgar Hoover, President Roosevelt commuted Dasch and Burger's sentences to long prison terms in return for their cooperation. Both men were granted clemency by President Truman in 1948 and subsequently deported to Germany.

During their stay, the New York contingent had spent more than $600 on clothing, meals, lodging, and travel. Besides helping the local economy, Operation Pastorius had no effect upon America's war effort, and with the exception of one other occasion in 1944 that ended similarly to Pastorius, no other German agents landed on the shores of the United States during the war.

☆   ☆   ☆

- *Besides spies, Americans worried about "fifth columnists"—Axis sympathizers who lived and worked undetected, often for years, among loyal Americans, awaiting their opportunity to do mischief. Because Japanese-Americans had been interned, the prototypical fifth columnist was a German, or German agent.*

☆   ☆   ☆

- *"Fifth column" comes from a Spanish term, "quinta columna," which surfaced during the Spanish Civil War of 1936–1939. When a pro-Franco general named Emilio Mola advanced on Madrid with four columns of troops in 1936, he bragged that his campaign would be aided by a quinta columna of sympathizers who had been hiding in plain sight. The term gained exposure in 1937, when war correspondent Ernest Hemingway wrote a play,* The Fifth Column.

# CODE BREAKERS CRACK THE ENIGMA

*Oversights in the German code and the Allies' ability to capture working cipher machines gave decrypters at Bletchley Park the edge they needed to decipher Enigma messages.*

Enigma was the code name for a portable cipher machine used by Germany to encrypt and decrypt secret messages. Invented in 1918 by a German engineer named Arthur Scherbius, the machine was initially marketed to businesses as a way of preventing corporate espionage. By 1933, the German Army, Navy, and Air Force were producing their own modified versions of the machine. With hundreds of millions of letter combinations, the German military thought the code was unbreakable.

## HOW DID IT WORK?

Enigma encoded messages by performing sequential substitutions using electrical connections. The machine resembled a typewriter; it had 26 keys—one for each letter of the alphabet.

When a key was depressed, an electrical impulse traveled through a plug board at the front of the machine to a rotor contact inside the machine. The surface of each rotor also contained 26 electrical contacts, again representing letters of the alphabet. Each contact was wired to a key on the keyboard as well as to a contact on the next rotor. An output device illuminated the cipher letter the system created. The rotors were interchangeable, and extra rotors could be added. Enigma also used a device called a reflector, which redirected the electrical impulses back through the machine a second time. The code was exceedingly complex: Enigma could produce a combination of letters "so large that it has no name except $3 \times 10^{114}$."

The Enigma was small enough to be carried into the field, but it required three men to operate: One typed the coded message into the machine, a second recorded the encrypted output one letter at a time, and a third transmitted the result in Morse Code.

## POLAND'S BIG BREAK

In 1932, Poland's intelligence corps received a package from its French counterparts containing Enigma guidelines that had been obtained by a German intelligence clerk named Hans-Thilo Schmidt. Schmidt was later arrested by the Nazis for the theft; he committed suicide in 1942 while in prison for treason.

Using some of Schmidt's information and a commercial version of the Enigma, three of Poland's brightest cryptanalysts successfully recreated the Enigma code and its indicator system in 1933. Though the commercial version was much different from the machines used by the German Army and Navy, Marian Rejewski, Henryk Zygalski, and Jerzy Rozycki deduced the internal wiring of Enigma's rotors. They used advanced mathematics, exploiting the German error of repeating the message setting (a three-letter sequence at the beginning of the transmission). The Poles developed two electromechanical machines that functioned similarly to the machines the Germans were using to decipher messages.

The Germans increased the sophistication of Enigma in 1939. By July of that year, Poland felt its independence threatened. The Polish Cipher Bureau gave its French and British counterparts all of its research in the hopes their teams could crack the new German code. The British had great success.

## BRITAIN'S BEST AND BRIGHTEST

In 1939 the British intelligence community organized its code-breaking operations north of London at an estate called Bletchley Park. The British department operating out of the English manor was referred to as the Government Code and Cipher School.

Staff at Bletchley Park consisted of chess experts, mathematicians, linguists, computer scientists, and even crossword enthusiasts. They made several important discoveries, allowing them to break the Enigma code even when it was altered every two days. Their success was due in part to German methods of coding:

- The reflector ensured that no letter could be coded as itself.

- Because the keyboard contained only letters, all numbers had to be spelled out.

- Military ranks, military terms, and weather reports appeared often, making it easier to decode these words.

- The Germans would not repeat rotor order within a month, and the rotors changed position every two days. This greatly reduced the combinations used in the machines by the end of the month, making it easier to crack those messages.

Allies eventually captured German U-boats and surface ships with intact Enigmas and codebooks, giving code breakers the knowledge they needed to anticipate changes to the code. By 1943, most coded German communications were read routinely.

## TO ACT, OR NOT TO ACT

Intelligence gleaned from decrypted Enigma messages fell under Ultra, the code name used by Britain, and later the United States.

The codes of the *Luftwaffe* were the first broken by Britain's team of cryptologists, and Britain monitored the *Luftwaffe* traffic to learn of planned raids during the Battle of Britain. They also alerted Prime Minister Churchill to the fact that Germany wanted air superiority before launching an invasion of Britain.

Messages intercepted between Rommel and Hitler revealed some of Rommel's planned tactics in Africa, giving the Allies an edge at Alam Halfa.

Cracking the Enigma was perhaps most useful to convoys crossing the Atlantic. As codes were broken and manuals captured, the Allies were able to locate and avoid U-boat patrols.

While the breaking of the Enigma code did not win the war for the Allies, there can be no denying the feat shortened the war, saving many lives in the process.

# THE JEEP

*As Adolf Hitler's Nazi regime scored political and military victories in Europe, American military planners foresaw the need for a lightweight, all-terrain vehicle that could replace the motorcycle as a messenger and reconnaissance vehicle on the battlefield.*

In early 1940, the Army Quartermaster Corps issued a call to manufacturers to produce a prototype all-terrain universal military vehicle. The military gave interested parties just 49 days to complete the task. The Army's Ordnance Technical Committee set out the following specifications for the new vehicle:

- Vehicle weight of less than 1,300 pounds. This specification was deemed unrealistic and later raised to 2,160 pounds.

- Four-wheel drive.

- A wheelbase of 80 inches or less, a tread of 47 inches or less, and a minimum of 6.25 inches of ground clearance.

- An engine that could produce 85 pound-feet of torque.

- A payload capability of 600 pounds.

## VYING FOR THE CONTRACT

While more than 135 companies were invited to participate, the American Bantam Car Company and Willys-Overland were the only two to express an interest in the project. The Ford Motor Company was courted because of its production capabilities, but initially declined the offer to participate.

Bantam was the first to respond to the government's challenge with actual blueprints. The company enlisted the help of Karl Probst, a Detroit area freelance automotive engineer. Probst began work on a prototype on July 17, 1940, and in only two days he had finished the plans for the Bantam model.

Government officials examined Bantam's design, and after receiving the go-ahead, Bantam engineers hand-built their working model in just seven weeks. Company officials delivered the prototype to army officers at Camp Holabird, Maryland, on September 23, 1940. After being subjected to grueling tests over the course of several weeks, the Bantam vehicle, Model BRC-40, was deemed a success in virtually every category.

Despite Willys's failure to submit a prototype by the deadline and the Ford Motor Company's complete lack of interest in the project, designers and engineers from both companies were allowed access to the army's trials of the Bantam-designed vehicle, as well as to Bantam's blueprints. Willys and Ford subsequently built prototypes using many of Bantam's design features. Though both late-arriving manufacturers failed to meet the stated deadline and had problems with their designs—the Willys vehicle was too heavy, while the Ford model had insufficient engine power—army officials allowed the two latecomers to participate in the process. Both companies eventually submitted prototype vehicles for testing.

In March 1941, the military awarded contracts to all three companies to produce 1,500 vehicles each. Four months later, army officials had tested each company's model in the field. Bantam's lack of mass-production facilities and poor financial position led to the army awarding the final contract to Willys. The Willys model also won on the merits of its more powerful engine, having a silhouette lower to the ground, and having a lower production cost per vehicle.

Bantam vehicles, which had already been delivered to the army, were shipped to Britain as the new Willys model was delivered. The Willys vehicles were given to America's Russian allies through the Lend-Lease Act. After losing the contract to Willys, Bantam quit the car business and switched production to torpedo motors, various aircraft parts, and trailers.

In order to meet production requirements, Willys granted the government a nonexclusive license to their design. The move gave the government the right to let other companies manufacture the vehicle, and Ford was quickly awarded a contract to produce the new vehicle based solely on their production facilities.

## WHY WERE THEY CALLED JEEPS?

There is some debate over the origin of the jeep name. One theory is the name came from the army designation "GP," an acronym Ford used to differentiate between vehicles they produced for government and civilian use: The letter "G" stood for government, while the letter "P" signified the size of the wheelbase, which in this case was 80 inches. Others claim the name referred to cartoonist E.C. Segar's cartoon character Eugene the Jeep, Popeye's impish animal friend from the fourth dimension.

The first public reference to the jeep name came in a *Washington Daily News* story, when reporter Katherine Hillyer witnessed a jeep demonstration on the steps of the Capitol. Her story ran with a photo caption, "Jeep Creeps Up Capitol Steps."

## JEEP MAKES ITS MARK

More than 600,000 jeeps were pressed into service in every theater of operation during the war. Journalist Ernie Pyle was quoted as saying the jeep was "as faithful as a dog, as strong as a mule, and as agile as a goat." Jeeps transported every rank of soldier, from privates to four-star generals.

Besides their reconnaissance role, jeeps were also used as ambulances, weapons platforms, and communications and supply vehicles. The jeep was light enough to be packed into C-47 cargo planes and dropped with airborne troops behind enemy lines. The Canadians, British, and Russians also used jeeps in their armed forces.

The first civilian-use Jeep (the name was by now a registered trademark) was produced in 1945. The Willys-Overland CJ-2A was initially marketed as a vehicle for construction workers and farmers. Today, the Chrysler Corporation, which owns the Jeep trademark, has more than 1,000 registrations for the jeep worldwide.

# LOVE THY NEIGHBOR: THE JEWS OF EUROPE FIND HIDDEN SANCTUARY

*When German occupation forces began implementing Hitler's Final Solution in 1942, hundreds of thousands of Jews went into hiding. They would spend the war hidden in attics, behind fake walls, or in holes dug into the ground.*

Many Jews in Europe who survived the war did so with the aid of non-Jews who risked death or deportation to concentration camps for giving aid. Many Jewish children were hidden in plain sight; their parents arranged for them to live in Christian orphanages or with non-Jewish families. For adults, however, passing as a non-Jew required procuring official documents or forgeries, disguising accents and physical appearances, and carrying money or valuables to pay off blackmailers or bribe police.

While the French Vichy regime was complicit in the Holocaust, three quarters of France's Jews survived the war. Many relied on fake papers, ration cards, and the goodwill of neighbors to escape detection while living in larger cities. Led by Huguenot minister André Trocmé and his wife, Magda, 3,000 residents of the village of Le Chambon successfully saved nearly 5,000 Jews from Nazi deportation, hiding them in homes, on farms, and in schools and churches.

## UNDERGROUND AND OUT OF SIGHT

In Poland, where many non-Jews collaborated with the Nazi roundups, 3 million of 3.3 million Jews perished. Those who did not went through gut-wrenching struggles to survive. Michael Shaft, who narrowly escaped the unsuccessful Warsaw Ghetto Uprising of 1943, returned to his native village and knocked on the door of Adam Suchodolski, an acquaintance who had not seen him in years. The Suchodolskis dug a pit below the floor of a granary. They fed Shaft through a narrow crack for almost two years. After the Soviet liberation, Shaft married Suchodolski's daughter, Jadwiga, and the couple emigrated to Israel in 1957. "I come from a very devout Catholic family," Jadwiga Shaft later wrote. "My family and I did what we did because we wished to observe the commandment of 'Thou shalt love thy neighbor as thyself.'"

In another village outside Warsaw, Samuel Glazer and his family of four spent 16 months with as many as 17 other fugitives in a room dug under the floor of Teresa Kozminski's house. The villagers fled when the Germans threatened executions, but Teresa remained for four more weeks until the Russians arrived, caring for the 14 Jews still hiding in her shelter. "The interesting thing about this family," Samuel Glazer remembered, "is that we did not know them before—the whole family was enlisted to help us."

Doctor Nathan Wallach and his wife escaped a Polish labor camp and returned to the town of Lesko, where an acquaintance, Jozef Zwonarz, was caring for their three-year-old daughter. A 45-year-old engineer with a wife and five children, Zwonarz dug a pit beneath his workshop that measured 5 feet by 3.5 feet, and 3 feet deep. There he hid the Wallachs, keeping the secret from his family. The Wallachs spent two years in the pit, then an artillery shell struck the workshop during the Soviet advance. Zwonarz finally told his wife about his charges and hid them in his basement for six weeks until the Red Army arrived. The Wallachs, who had not seen daylight in two years, discovered they could no longer walk and had to crawl to Zwonarz's house. When the Wallachs left after the war, Nathan gave Zwonarz his watch and a $10 bill.

## A SECRET ROOM AND SCHEME
## FOR SURVIVAL

While Holland had a relatively small Jewish population, many Jews had fled to the neutral nation from Germany and other countries as Hitler rose to power. When the deportation of Jews began under Nazi occupation, drugstore owner Bert Bochove and his wife Annie began hiding Jewish friends in the apartment over their pharmacy in the coastal town of Woubrugge. The Bochoves, who built a secret room behind a false wall in the attic, soon offered their hiding place to the Dutch underground and sheltered as many as a dozen Jews at a time. Bert enlisted the local postman to keep the overflow in his living quarters above the post office. In 1944, the Bochoves discovered that a store clerk who was secretly engaged to a German soldier planned to inform Nazi authorities. The Jews were sent to new hiding places; meanwhile, a local doctor posted a "Quarantine, Typhus" sign on the front of the building. The Germans stayed away. Two weeks later their guests returned. The Bochoves continued to shelter Jews until the end of the war.

## A TRAGIC EFFORT

Cornelia ten Boom and her family began hiding Jews in their large, old house in the center of Haarlem, Holland, in 1940, only a hundred yards from the local police station. Her family built a false wall in a second-story bedroom to create a hiding space. A devout Christian, Corrie soon became the center of a network of some 80 Dutch citizens, who helped Jews obtain false identity papers and find safe havens. Some even staged a fake robbery at a local government office to obtain hundreds of ration cards. The ten Booms were arrested in February 1944. Corrie's 84 year-old father died in prison a short time later. Corrie and her sister Betsie were finally sent to the Ravensbruck concentration camp, where Corrie led a prayer group in their barracks. Betsie died of typhus soon after having a vision of a home where survivors of the war would come to be spiritually healed. Somewhat miraculously, Corrie was released by accident just after Christmas that year. A week later, all the women of her age in the camp were killed. After the war, Corrie became a Christian speaker and established the home for war refugees her sister envisioned, after a German woman donated a large property.

Some armed Jewish resistance groups fought the Nazis to save themselves. In Belorussia, a Jewish partisan group attacked the Germans from a hidden camp in the Naliboki forest. Led by the charismatic peasant Tuvia Bielski, they helped rescue others. By the end of the war, more than 1,200 Jews were sheltered in the forest hideout. Many emigrated to Israel, and today the descendants of Bielski's forest camp number more than 30,000.

# WHY THE NAZIS
# FEARED FREEMASONS

*Although Hitler admired its organizational structure, the group
that inspired America's Founding Fathers to enshrine the rights to
life, liberty, and the pursuit of happiness found no favor in Nazi
Germany, and suffered horribly during the war.*

Although most people are familiar with the Nazi persecution of
the Jews, many are not aware that the Freemasons also suffered
in Hitler's Germany. Adolf Hitler's anti-Mason sentiments were no
secret. In *Mein Kampf*, the Nazi dictator had stated that the paci-
fistic philosophy of the Freemasons encouraged a "paralysis of the
national instinct of self-preservation." He believed its members
had succumbed to the Jews, who were using the organization as
a means to spread their alleged agenda of subverting the upper
strata of society.

The reasons Hitler feared the Freemasons and perceived them
as a threat to the Nazis are more complicated. Surely the Nazi
regime could list many prominent Masons among its enemies,
including British Prime Minister Winston Churchill, American
President Franklin Delano Roosevelt, and General John Pershing,
who had directed the American Army against the Germans in the
First World War. But, those figures were not the only reason for
the Nazis' determination to wipe out Freemasonry in Europe.

Hitler was more afraid of the basic tenets of Freemasonry, which
decree that personal political freedom and human dignity are the
rightful foundations of all human society. The Nazis perceived
Masons as a threat because the group defined human freedom in
terms that superseded feelings of nationalism or racial allegiance.
Many Freemasons were known as leading figures of the Enlightenment. Men such as George Washington, Benjamin Franklin,
and Simón Bolívar led revolutions against aristocratic power.
It was natural, then, for a totalitarian regime such as Nazi Ger-

many to want to seek out and destroy the organization. As U.S. Supreme Court Justice Robert H. Jackson, the chief prosecutor at the Nuremburg war crimes trial, observed, "...many persecutions undertaken by every modern dictatorship are those directed against the Free Masons [sic]."

Justice Jackson understood, as did Hitler, that members of such an organization were not likely to cooperate with the oppressive police states necessary for the survival of a dictatorship. As such, Freemasons were regularly put to death by the SS.

☆　☆　☆

• *Five years before Adolf Eichmann rose to a position of power in Nazi Germany and helped implement the Final Solution, he was simply a lowly SS sergeant typing the names of prominent German Freemasons on index cards.*

☆　☆　☆

• *Though he despised the Masons' ideology, Hitler was noted to have admired the Freemasons' use of symbols to evoke ancient rites of power.*

☆　☆　☆

• *After a harried trip from Hamburg, Germany to Havana, Cuba in May 1939, the 937 Jewish refugees aboard the SS St. Louis were denied entry to Cuba upon arrival. Their landing permits were deemed invalid. For 12 days the ship waited in the harbors of Havana and Miami, Florida, yet neither Cuba nor the United States would receive the refugees. The St. Louis had no option but to return to Europe. Fortunately for the passengers, they were not forced back to Germany. Instead they found temporary asylum in Belgium, Britain, France, and Holland.*

☆　☆　☆

• *As late as 1934, Mussolini spoke of Hitler as "a mad little clown."*

# ROSIE THE RIVETER

*World War II was a time of terror and death for millions, but for many others, it brought undreamed-of opportunities.*

For 18-year-old mother Peggy Terry, moving from the Dust Bowl depression of Oklahoma to work at an artillery-shell plant near Paducah, Kentucky, was, "like a journey to the center of the earth." With her hometown economy still staggered, she remembered, "You did good having bus fare to get across town." Suddenly, she was making $32 a week painting the tips of tracer bullets, trading shifts with her mom and sister to take care of the kids. "Before that, we made nothing." Later, at a munitions plant in Michigan, she pulled in $90 a week, a startling sum for a woman who previously couldn't afford a radio.

## THE WAR BRINGS A NEW WORKFORCE

In the 1930s, joblessness had averaged 18 percent a year. Wages and output sunk, while attitudes toward women and work remained traditional. In a 1936 Gallup poll, 82 percent of respondents—including 75 percent of women—thought married women shouldn't work if their husbands had jobs.

Almost overnight, the war buried the Great Depression and attitudes changed. Suddenly, with 16 million men in the armed forces and hundreds of new war plants needing triple shifts, there weren't enough workers. Women streamed into the work world, many for the first time.

The number of working women soared from 11,970,000 in 1940 to 18,610,000 in 1945. A quarter of all married women, an unheard-of proportion, were punching time clocks. By the end of the conflict, women made up 36 percent of the civilian labor force. These figures would decline sharply after V-J Day, but remained above prewar levels, setting the stage for the 1970s explosion of workaday women.

In war factories, pay was good. From 1940 to 1944, average yearly wages for all workers increased from $754 to $1,289. A woman in a munitions factory could readily make $50 a week, an excellent salary for the time. Defense work paid women much better than traditional female employment like retail sales, housecleaning, and restaurant work, where the wages averaged about half as much.

## THE FACE OF THE WORKING WOMAN: ROSIE THE RIVETER

This giant occupational shift was helped along by a War Advertising Council campaign. In 1943, the country's newspapers, radio stations, trade journals, and Hollywood movies sang the praises of women in defense jobs. Hundreds of magazines tucked articles with the patriotic theme into their September 1943 issues.

The campaign's "poster child" was Rosie the Riveter—in fact, several Rosies. The first was conjured up by J. Howard Miller, a graphic artist with Westinghouse. Miller created the famous 1942 poster of a woman in work shirt and bandana, determinedly flexing her right bicep, under the screaming slogan, "We Can Do It!" The model for the poster was a real-life Michigan factory worker, Geraldine Doyle.

But the picture was not yet Rosie. The famous poster became linked to that name the following year, after the hit song "Rosie the Riveter," by Redd Evans and John Jacob Loeb. Its lyrics went:

> *Rosie the Riveter.*
>
> *Keeps a sharp lookout for sabotage,*
>
> *Sitting up there on the fuselage...*
>
> *...Rosie's got a boyfriend, Charlie.*
>
> *Charlie, he's a Marine.*
>
> *Rosie is protecting Charlie,*
>
> *Working overtime on the riveting machine.*

Then, Rosie became a movie star. Actor Walter Pidgeon came across Rose Monroe, an airplane riveter in Michigan's Willow Run assembly plant. She portrayed Rosie the Riveter in a short film that promoted war bonds.

Finally, Rosie was depicted by America's leading commercial artist, Norman Rockwell. On a May 1943 cover of *The Saturday Evening Post*, he painted model Mary Doyle Keefe as a muscular female worker, the name "Rosie" stenciled on her lunchbox, leaning back confidently toward a giant American flag, a huge rivet gun on her lap, work shoes propped on Hitler's *Mein Kampf*. This was the toughest Rosie of all.

Due to the advertising blitz, perhaps two million more women signed up for work.

## OVERCOMING OBSTACLES

Many of the war plants were huge, their social impact tremendous. In Richmond, California, more than 100,000 male and female workers at Ford and Kaiser factories turned out more than 1,500 Liberty and Victory ships, and at a Richmond Ford plant they built some 60,000 tanks and other combat vehicles.

Near sleepy Marietta, Georgia, Bell Aircraft of Buffalo, New York, built a two-million-square-foot factory for constructing P-39s and Bell X-1s. At peak, about 40,000 people worked at the plant, 6,000 of them women. Cobb County's population nearly doubled as workers streamed in from throughout Georgia and other states. Throughout the South and West, such projects set up the postwar Sunbelt boom.

In Alabama, the army built a $40 million factory, the Huntsville Arsenal, which made 27 million units of mustard gas, tear gas, and other chemical warfare agents. Nearby, the $6 million Redstone Arsenal's force of male and female workers churned out 45.2 million grenades, bombs, and artillery shells.

In 1942, some Huntsville officials took a stance against hiring more ladies, as the laboring ability of black women in particular was doubted. An absence of "separate but equal" toilets for whites and blacks was a further concern. At the national level, meantime, a labor expert admonished that, "The employment of millions of untrained workers, including old men, youths, and housewives" will "inevitably result in a material and gradual dilution of labor skills."

## No Rest for Working Moms

For mothers with household and maternal duties on top of their day jobs, the cumulative labor was grueling. This at a time when household conveniences—washing machines, gas stoves, even running water—were far less common than they were just a few years later. Bell Aircraft's Ernestine Slade, a mother of eight, did parts finishing on the night shift. Then "I'd come in from work," she recalled, "do my cleaning, do my laundry, wash the children's clothes, iron whatever, then I would lay down and go to sleep." When the children returned in the afternoon, "I'd get up and do their dinner. Then I'd take another little nap before going to work at night. I'd comb the girls' hair at home for the next day, and I put stocking caps over their heads so their hair would stay nice, and get them ready for bed before I'd leave."

With multiple burdens, female workers had higher rates of absenteeism. The need to juggle work and family led to some plants building nurseries. The Richmond, California, complex provided around-the-clock daycare.

Still, by the end of 1942, 40 percent of the workers on Redstone's factory floor were female, which increased to 62 percent by 1945. By 1944, black women made up over 40 percent of the Arsenal's female employees. Workers recall that, even in the land of Jim Crow, blacks and whites often worked together.

Hourly assembly-line pay for Huntsville men producing mustard gas was $5.76, $4.40 for women engaged in the same work. (Entry-level pay was $5.04/$3.06.) Later, the federal War Labor Board enforced the novel principle of equal pay for equal work.

In many plants, time-honored attitudes among men were tested. At Marietta's Bell aircraft plant, 18-year-old Betty Williams turned her childhood interest in flying into a job supervising a crew of 25, most of them men. "I had three strikes against me," recalled the Indiana-born Williams. "I was a Yankee. I was much younger than they—the men would have a wife and three or four kids; there I would be 18." And the view of such fellows, she explained, was, "You're a woman and you should be home doing the pots and pans and cooking cornbread." Though she had been offered the job because there was a dire shortage of managers, Williams persevered. She served as foreman for the top section of plane wings and met her future husband, who worked on the bottom halves.

Under the pressure of wartime production, the concerns became not race or sex, but the dearth of technical and supervisory skills. Factories made changes to keep up. The Huntsville Arsenal founded a Civilian Training Department to let workers "earn while they learned." It arranged with Auburn University to offer tuition-free courses in chemistry, accounting, engineering, drawing, mechanical and electrical maintenance, and industrial management. The University of Alabama gave a class in chemical lab techniques "for women only, who desire to qualify for jobs in defense laboratories." About a hundred black female students from Alabama University worked for the Redstone Arsenal's assembly line. "From all appearances," wrote a local newspaper, "their work and attendance" offer "an example any of us would do well to follow." Through such means, women trailblazed new professions. At the arsenals, women drove trucks and handled drill presses. Female forklift operators, according to work reports of the day, could "handle 124 pound to 150 pound pallets with the ease and efficiency of old timers."

Moreover, the day jobs could be difficult and dangerous. During the war, three women were killed at Huntsville from work mishaps and two were killed at Redstone. Peggy Terry remembered when a thunderstorm knocked out the lights at her munitions plant, and someone knocked a box of detonators onto the factory floor. "Here we were in the pitch dark," Terry explained. "Somebody was screaming, 'Don't move, anybody!' They were afraid you'd step on the detonator. We were down on our hands and knees crawling out of that building in the storm. If we'd stepped on one...."

Still, for most "Rosies," the war afforded a desirable means to pay the bills, raise children and, for many, their first opportunity to build new careers. Said Marie Owens of the Huntsville Arsenal, whose husband was in combat overseas, "I am interested in carrying on here while the boys do the fighting over there... The harder I work for them here, the sooner they will come home."

# LADY KILLER

*Lyudmila Pavlichenko was the first Soviet citizen ever to be received at the White House. She killed 309 Axis soldiers to gain the honor.*

Her Soviet comrades knew her as the "Death Sniper." German soldiers on the eastern front just knew she was deadly. She is now known as the greatest woman sniper of all time. Lyudmila Pavlichenko earned that title by killing 309 German and Romanian soldiers in less than a year while fighting in the Crimean Peninsula.

## A SHARP-EYED BEAUTY

Born in 1916 in the Ukraine village of Belaya Tserkov, Pavlichenko moved with her parents to Kiev after completing ninth grade. There she joined a shooting club and honed her sharpshooter prowess. After Germany invaded the Soviet Union in June 1941, she left her studies at the University of Kiev to join the fight against the Nazis.

When Pavlichenko told her recruiter that she wanted to join the infantry and carry a rifle, he laughed and asked what she knew about rifles. Pavlichenko coolly responded by showing him her marksmanship certificate. Astounded but not convinced, the recruiter tried to persuade the dark-haired beauty to become a field nurse. But Pavlichenko persisted and eventually joined the 25th Infantry Division, becoming one of 2,000 Soviet women who fought in the war as snipers.

Pavlichenko entered action near Odessa, where in August 1941 she recorded her first two kills while helping to defend a key hill. Over the next two and a half months, using a Mosin-Nagant Russian five-shot, bolt-action rifle, she would record 187 kills.

After the Germans captured Odessa, her unit was sent to Sevastopol. In May 1942, now-Lieutenant Pavlichenko was cited by the Southern Red Army Council for killing 257 German soldiers. Among her eventual confirmed total of 309 kills were 36 Nazi snipers, including one whose kill logbook listed more than 500 victims. Pavlichenko's combat duty ended in June 1942 after she was wounded by mortar fire. By then, she was a hero in her homeland.

## A STAR IS BORN

Recognizing her value to the propaganda effort, the Soviets sent Pavlichenko on a speaking tour of North America in 1942. She became the first Soviet citizen to be received at the White House and enjoyed a hero's welcome when she appeared before the International Student Assembly in Washington, D.C. She later made appearances in various American and Canadian cities, proudly relating her wartime experiences to enthralled audiences. Her American admirers presented her with a Colt semiautomatic pistol, while Canadian fans gave her a Winchester rifle, which is now on display at the Central Museum of the Armed Forces in Moscow. Her celebrity status was cemented when legendary American songwriter Woody Guthrie penned a song about her exploits.

After returning to the Soviet Union, Pavlichenko was kept from action but became a sniper instructor. In 1943, she was awarded the Hero of the Soviet Union, her nation's highest honor. After the war, she remained active in Soviet military circles as a research assistant of the chief headquarters of the Soviet Navy and as a member of the Soviet Committee of the Veterans of War. She died in 1974 at the age of 58.

☆   ☆   ☆

- *Before embarking on a career in the U.S. Army, General George Patton served in a variety of foreign armies—as a Roman legionnaire, a pikeman in the Middle Ages, and a cavalryman with Napoleon's Marshal Murat. At least, that's what he believed. His feeling was reinforced by weeks of relative isolation at Langers, France, in the First World War, as he prepared for the arrival of the newly formed Tank Corps. There he told a fellow officer that he had identified the location of a Roman camp and an ancient theater at Langers without seeing them or being told of their existence—proof in his mind of his past service in Rome's legions.*

# GÖTTERDÄMMERUNG IN THE EAST

*In a war of titanic battles, Stalingrad stands out as a monument of a modern city turned into a vast killing ground. In a battle that ravaged the city, Soviet soldiers and civilians refused to yield to a mighty German Army.*

In early 1942, Germany's panzers were deep in Soviet territory, threatening Moscow and Leningrad to the north. But Hitler's attention was drawn to the south, toward the Caucasus Mountains and the rich oil fields that could keep his war machine driving across Asia Minor, the Suez Canal, and the Middle East. In April, he ordered his armies to move along the Don River. One field force, designated Army Group A, would push south into the Transcaucasus region, while another task force, Army Group B, would move east toward Stalingrad, an industrial city of 600,000 on the west bank of the Volga River.

## THE DRIVE TO STALINGRAD

On June 28, Hitler launched the summer-offensive phase of Operation *Blau* ("Blue"), sending the two army groups deep into Soviet territory. The *Wehrmacht's* initial advance was a smashing success, and the two army units gobbled up huge swaths of Soviet territory.

Confident that he could capture Stalingrad with just the 6th Army, under General Friedrich von Paulus, Hitler detached General Hermann Hoth's 4th Panzer Army from Army Group B and sent it south to join Army Group A. Before long, however, Hitler refocused on Stal-

ingrad as his primary objective, and sent a panzer corps and 4th Panzer's infantry back toward the city.

By the end of July, the 6th Army was a few dozen kilometers west of Stalingrad, with 4th Panzer's tanks advancing on its right. On August 23, the struggle for Stalingrad began.

## INTO THE CITY

The battle opened with a massive *Luftwaffe* air bombardment that killed thousands of civilians and reduced huge sections of the city to rubble. Terrified civilians dug antitank ditches while workers' militias, antiaircraft teams, and the Red Army's defending force, General Vasili Chuikov's 62nd Army, began their slow, stubborn retreat into the city's neighborhoods.

By September 1, Army Group B had reached the Volga on the western side of Stalingrad, and the Red Army could reinforce the hard-pressed city only by sending supplies or men by boat across the broad, vulnerable river. The Germans pushed their way into the city, block by block, using tanks, artillery, and air power to support the advance. In response, local Soviet commanders began using "hugging" tactics, keeping their front lines so close to the German infantry that any *Luftwaffe* attacks or artillery fire called down upon the Red Army would endanger nearby Germans. The Germans referred to the hand-to-hand, house-to-house fighting as *Rattenkrieg,* or "rat war," joking bitterly about capturing an apartment's kitchen but having to fight for the living room.

Through the fall of 1942, Stalingrad consumed thousands of lives as foot soldiers, tanks, and artillery crews struggled through the wreckage of a dying city. Hiding beneath rubble and atop bombed-out apartments, snipers ruled entire neighborhoods; good snipers racked up hundreds of confirmed kills during the bloody siege. Battles raged around factories and buildings—the Red October steel mill, the Stalingrad Tractor Factory, and the Barrikady Gun Factory became the scenes of repeated, violent firefights that sometimes cut down thousands of men. On the ground, as panzers stalled in heaps of rubble, antitank crews descended upon the immobilized giants to knock them out by the score, killing the occupants as they scurried out of their burning armored vehicles.

As the year wore on, both Stalin and Hitler fed fresh troops into the inferno. Stalin shifted Moscow's strategic reserves from the capital area to the south, and General Chuikov obligingly threw these reinforcements into battle as soon as they arrived. Casualties mounted: In one three-day period, the Soviet 187th Rifle Division lost 90 percent of its men. By November, Paulus's 6th Army had taken about 90 percent of the city.

## COUNTERATTACK AND ENCIRCLEMENT

But during November, as Hitler's *Wehrmacht* reached its highwater mark, the weight of the Soviet's numbers began to shift the balance of power. On November 19, an army group under General Nikolai Vatutin, consisting of the 21st and 65th Armies and the 5th Tank Army, came crashing down upon the 3rd Romanian Army, which guarded the German 6th Army's northern flank. The offensive, known as Operation Uranus, shattered the 3rd Romanian after just one day. The following day, a two-army offensive from the south destroyed the Romanian 4th Army south of the Volga. Paulus's 6th Army, under orders from Hitler to maintain its position, was being slowly squeezed in a vice. Within four days, the two Soviet juggernauts linked up west of the city, encircling 250,000 Axis soldiers—most of the 6th Army, a corps from 4th Panzer, and some foreign Axis troops—in a ring of death.

Sixth Army's position was now desperate. It was in danger of starving or running out of ammunition and fuel—any of which would mean death. But Hitler had vowed that the German Army would never leave Stalingrad. When the high command pressed Hitler for permission to withdraw the 6th Army, *Reichsmarschall* Hermann Göring, chief of the *Luftwaffe,* glibly promised Hitler that the air force could supply 6th Army's needs. With that, the fate of the 6th Army was sealed: Trapped along the Volga's banks, it would never leave Stalingrad under arms.

## DEATH OF AN ARMY

Göring's aerial supply effort failed almost from the start. Heavy Soviet antiaircraft emplacements, the Red Air Force, and miserable weather prevented most of the necessary food, fuel, and ammunition from reaching the beleaguered army.

The 6th Army was doomed, though its men did not yet know it. Officers pressed Paulus to defy Hitler and break out, but the ill-fated commander hesitated until his fuel stocks were too low to save himself.

On January 30, it was clear even to Hitler that the 6th Army was beyond hope. He ordered Paulus to fight to the last man, a glorious sacrifice to the heroic Third Reich's conquests, and promoted Paulus to field marshal, noting cynically that no German field marshal had ever surrendered. The ploy did not work, and by February 2, 1943, *Generalfeldmarschall* Paulus led some 91,000 starving, disease-ridden soldiers into captivity. Only 5,000 of these prisoners would live to see their homes again.

The charnel house of Stalingrad cost Hitler and his allies over a quarter million soldiers (some estimates run as high as 850,000, including Axis troops near Stalingrad who were not part of the encirclement), while the Red Army lost close to 1.2 million on all fronts engaged around the city. With more than 40,000 civilians killed in the first week of bombardment, the total number of noncombatant deaths will never be known with precision. But the roughly two million casualty figure gives Stalingrad the sad honor of being the site of one of the bloodiest battles in history.

☆   ☆   ☆

- *At Stalingrad, Lieutenant General Vasily Chuikov insisted on having women operate communications posts—they refused to bug out no matter how dangerous the situation.*

## 1941

**July 28**
Japanese troops land in southern French Indochina

**July 31**
In a memo to SS chief Reinhard Heydrich, Nazi Reichsmarschall Hermann Göring orders the "Final Solution" for Europe's Jews

**August 5**
The United States embargoes raw materials to Japan

**August 8–13**
Heavy Japanese bombing raids on Chungking, China, reduce the city to ruins

**August 12**
Roosevelt and Churchill announce the Atlantic Charter, a promise that the United States will stand with Britain in the fight against German tyranny

**August 20**
German troops reach the outskirts of Leningrad; they will block the last rail supply route to Leningrad on August 30 after occupying the town of Mga

**September 3**
Russian Jews and prisoners of war become the first victims of poison gas at Auschwitz

**September 8**
The German Army encircles Leningrad; the siege of Leningrad will last 900 days

**September 16**
The Russian front at Kiev collapses and some 500,000 Soviets surrender; Kiev will officially fall to the Germans two days later

**September 17**
Japanese launch offensive in Hunan Province

**September 18**
Germans execute Russian troops who surrendered at Kiev; the Soviet death toll in defense of Kiev will top 350,000

**September 27**
United States launches Patrick Henry, first of more than 2,700 so-called Liberty ships, which were relatively inexpensive, quickly constructed merchant ships used to ferry war materiel from the United States to Europe

About 100,000 Japanese are trapped when 11 Chinese divisions cut their escape route, turning the tide in the battle for Changsha, China

**September 28–29**
Germans massacre 33,000 Jews at Babi Yar in the Ukraine

**October 2**
Germans launch Operation Typhoon, the drive into Moscow

**October 12–16**
Germans take 600,000 Soviet prisoners in Bryansk-Vyazma pockets

**October 16**
The "great panic" in Moscow—many civilians flee the city; the government relocates to the eastern city of Kuibyshev

A massive defense perimeter of more than 5,000 miles of trenches is constructed around Moscow by half a million Muscovites—mostly women, children, and old men

# DEFYING DEATH: THE ROSENSTRASSE PROTEST

*While most Germans cowered at the mention of the Gestapo, a group of housewives faced down the feared agents.*

Until early 1943, Jews with Gentile wives had been exempt from deportation to labor and death camps in the East. But during a "final roundup" in late February 1943, Heinrich Himmler's security forces arrested about 1,700 of these Jews and collected them at a welfare center on Rosenstrasse, in the heart of Hitler's capital. From there, the Nazis planned to send them to the camps.

The outraged wives gathered in small groups at the collection center and began to shout to the anonymous SS men inside, "Give us back our husbands!"

Their numbers grew. Around 600 women showed up at first, and by the time the protest was over, up to 6,000 other women had joined the effort. Police scattered the women into the streets, threatening to shoot. SS guards even began setting up machine guns. As a Berlin housewife recalled, "Then, for the first time, we really hollered. Now, we couldn't care less.... Now they're going to shoot in any case.... We yelled, 'Murderer, murderer, murderer, murderer.'"

The Rosenstrasse Protest—and the publicity it attracted—quickly caught the attention of a concerned Joseph Goebbels, Hitler's propaganda minister and the man in charge of maintaining public unity and morale in the Reich's capital. Goebbels noted in his diary, "There have been unpleasant scenes.... The people gathered together in large throngs and even sided with the Jews." After a week of protests, Goebbels ordered the Gestapo to release the 1,7000 Jews with non-Jewish German spouses. As his deputy recalled, Goebbels took this action to "eliminate the protest from the world... so that others didn't begin to do the same." In the end, he never arrested the women who forced the dreaded Gestapo to back down.

# THE SECRET STASH OF THE BOMB PROJECT'S FOREIGN AGENT

*U.S. officials working on the atomic bomb project frantically searched the world for sources of uranium. However, they were unaware that enough nuclear material to make several bombs lay for the taking at a New York City warehouse.*

U.S. Army Colonel Kenneth Nichols was engaged in what he thought was a nearly impossible task. With the war at its height in September 1942, U.S. researchers were beginning work on the Manhattan Project. Yet the United States possessed no uranium, the essential building block for the atomic bomb. The Manhattan Project's chief, Army General Leslie Groves, had ordered Nichols to obtain some of the precious material.

Nichols paid a visit to the New York City office of Edgar Sengier, a Belgian tycoon. Sengier was director of the Union Minière du Haut Katanga, a company that owned the world's most precious uranium mine, located in the Belgian Congo's Katanga province.

Nichols asked Sengier if his company could procure uranium for the U.S. government. He added that he was well aware this was an unusual request that could not be swiftly fulfilled.

Sengier carefully checked Nichols's credentials. Then he replied, "You can have the ore now. It is here in New York, a thousand tons of it. I was waiting for your visit."

As it turned out, Sengier had long been aware, far more than most U.S. officials, of the critical importance of his firm's product. In 1939 as war broke out in Europe, Sengier learned from British and French scientists that it might be possible to devise a superweapon out of processed uranium. In May 1939, he met with Henry Tizard, chief science adviser to the British government. That month, he also consulted with Jean Frédéric Joliot, the cowinner with wife

Irène Joliot-Curie—daughter of Marie Curie—of the Nobel Prize in Chemistry. Joliot had taken out patents on path-breaking work to induce chain reactions in atomic piles using uranium and heavy water (deuterium oxide).

In fact, Sengier negotiated with the French to supply them with 55 tons of uranium ore. When the Germans invaded France in May 1940, Union Minière shipped some eight tons of the promised uranium oxide to Joliot's research team. The material, hidden in French Morocco during five years of German occupation, became the basis for France's postwar nuclear program.

Sengier also sought to aid other nations in the fight against the Nazis. He reestablished his firm's headquarters in the safe harbor of New York and had 1,250 tons of uranium ore shipped there. The consignment cleared customs and was unloaded at Staten Island. It was stored—unguarded and unnoticed for nearly two years—at a warehouse there.

Jesse Johnson, the Atomic Energy Commission's director of raw materials, later remarked, "M. Sengier told members of the State Department and other government officials about the shipment, but the secret of the atomic bomb was so closely guarded that no one with whom he talked recognized the importance of the information."

The shipment was a true mother lode. The only other source of uranium at the time, with a uranium content of only .02 percent, was at distant Great Bear Lake in northern Canada. The Katanga ore, in contrast, was up to 65 percent uranium.

After Colonel Nichols's visit, the army bought and transferred Sengier's stockpile. The ore, said Johnson, supplied "the bulk of the uranium for the [Manhattan Project's] development work and early production of fissionable material for bombs." The army, in the meantime, in one of the war's little-known and most far-reaching operations, acted to exploit the Union Minière's other valuable holdings.

The Katanga mine, Shinkolobwe, had been closed since 1939 because its mineshafts had flooded. The Army Corps of

Engineers sent units to restore the mine, to construct a port on the Congo River, and to renovate an airport in Léopoldville. The United States, with British backing, negotiated a ten-year deal for exclusive rights to the Shinkolobwe uranium with the Belgian government-in-exile. Sengier stayed on to manage the mine, and before the war's end, the army had bought up 12 times Sengier's original hoard—some 30,000 tons.

Sengier was also awarded the Belgian Ordre de la Couronne, the French Légion d'Honneur, and the title of Knight Commander in the Order of the British Empire. Sengierite, a radioactive crystal, is named after him. In 1946, General Groves, in President Truman's presence, presented Sengier with the prestigious Medal for Merit—he was the only non-U.S. citizen to receive the accolade up to that time. Details of the Manhattan Project were still hush-hush, so the citation was cloaked in vague language that lauded the Belgian's "wartime services in the realm of raw materials."

☆　☆　☆

- *What is a depth charge? It looks like a large sledgehammer with an oversized handle, or a trash barrel with a bar sticking out of the side. Sailors would set it to explode at a certain depth, then launch it off the ship's stern. Thanks to water pressure, even a near miss could harm a submarine. Any explosion that impaired a sub's hull integrity could prevent it from diving any deeper for fear of breaking up and could potentially force it to surface. Some U-boats were captured this way.*

☆　☆　☆

- *The* Queen Mary *sailed the Atlantic with as many as 16,000 men aboard throughout the war, free from the U-boat threat. How? One word: speed. At nearly 29 knots, not even a surfaced U-boat at flank speed could catch her.*

☆　☆　☆

- *The number of Russians killed during the war was more than four times the number of Jews killed in concentration camps.*

# COMBAT MEDICS

*Among all the brave men who fought the war, medics and corpsmen stand out for special notice. When a wounded soldier cried out for help, he knew that he would be attended by someone willing to risk his own life to save others.*

## ON-THE-JOB TRAINING

Mere seconds are significant after being wounded, and the U.S. Army instructed all soldiers in the rudimentary care of wounds they might receive. "First aid is self-aid," stated one slogan. All soldiers were issued an individual first-aid kit. On being wounded, they were to sprinkle sulfa powder on the wound, take sulfa tablets, apply a Carlisle bandage, and seek help. But for serious injuries or wounds that were incapacitating, soldiers depended on the care of the medical corps. Trained doctors and surgeons were always in high demand. Civilian physicians and senior medical students could enter the army as commissioned officers and go to work at trauma units and hospitals relatively far from the front lines. But with too few doctors to go around, the bulk of immediate frontline care was the responsibility of the combat medic.

Medics or aidmen were soldiers themselves, having gone through much of the same basic training as their brothers in arms before being given additional training in basic wound care. They were not experienced health care professionals, but they were called on to make immediate life-or-death decisions without a minute's warning. They carried aid kits with more resources than the individual soldier packets, including penicillin and pain-numbing morphine shots—the syringes of which would be pinned to the clothing of the victim after being administered, as a warning to the next medic to avoid overdosing. They also faced a wide range of situations beyond the obvious bullet and burn wounds. Soldiers thrown around in explosions suffered concussions and fractures that protruded from the skin. Gastrointestinal problems and vitamin deficiencies were widespread. Medics in the Pacific had to treat men suffering from malaria and more unusual tropical diseases such as beriberi, which caused some men to lose all feeling in their legs

Medics' duties didn't end there. They had to treat battle fatigue, which was not always viewed sympathetically by a man's fellow soldiers, forcing the medic to play the role of psychologist as well as that of medical doctor. They provided aid to civilians caught up in the war zone, including women and infants. Medics in Europe at the end of the war were some of the first to encounter the horrors of the concentration camps, and tried to treat the victims as best they could. They also treated enemy prisoners of war. The latter group was entitled to care under the articles of war, but rendering aid to them sometimes caused hard feelings among the soldiers who had just been in a firefight with the prisoner.

## MEDIC!

It was in firefights that medics earned their reputation as heroes. When one of his buddies was hit, the medic sprang into action, putting aside his personal fears to perform his duty. Medics were always in the thickest of the fight, since that was where their services were most needed. They crawled out into enemy fire, or even an artillery barrage, to attempt to save a life. A medic's safety depended in part on the theater of war in which he served—the Germans generally respected the symbol of the Red Cross the corpsmen wore and avoided firing on them. One medic even reported he was able to wave at German troops to get them to delay fire while he treated an injured man. The Pacific was a different story, and the medics there felt as if they drew extra Japanese bullets. As a result, many dyed their armbands green to make themselves less visible.

Regardless of geography, medics regularly came under attack, whether intentionally or through the fog of war, and continued their efforts despite the danger. Aidman Thomas Kelly refused to leave his injured buddies when his platoon was driven back by the Germans, crawling on ten separate trips through 300 yards of enemy machine-gun fire, dragging wounded soldiers to safety. Corpsman Robert Bush stayed at a wounded marine's side as the

Japanese overran their position. He killed six of the enemy while managing to hold a life-saving plasma transfusion bag high in one hand, continuing to fight even after he lost his own eye. Navy pharmacist's mate John Harlan Willis performed a similar feat on Iwo Jima, where he picked up and hurled back at the enemy no fewer than eight live grenades that had been thrown at him and his patient, only to lose his life when a ninth one exploded in his hand. All three were awarded the Congressional Medal of Honor for their efforts, as were other medics in the war. Their fellow soldiers knew the medic in their platoon might save their lives one day, and their repeated acts of heroism were a frequent source of awe. As a result, they were singled out for special treatment, their buddies sometimes volunteering to dig a foxhole for them or relieving them of other mundane tasks.

## "THANK GOD FOR THE MEDICS"

Such devotion was made even more difficult by the fact that medics rarely had the satisfaction of seeing a full recovery. Their first priority was saving lives. After providing immediate aid, their patients were evacuated to areas farther behind the lines, given more care, sent farther back, and so forth. The caregivers had little time to do more than ensure that their patient lived long enough to hand them off to the next caregiver before moving on to the next injury.

Despite the hardships it faced, the medical service performed admirably during World War II compared to earlier conflicts. Injured men who received treatment quickly had a very good chance of survival, with mortality rates around 4 percent—half that of World War I. Although one medic claimed that he thought most of the good he did was psychological, making men feel better just by his presence, many soldiers have another opinion. Always ready to put their own life at risk to save others, the combat medic earned the respect and admiration of his buddies and established his reputation as "the soldier's best friend."

# Timeline

## 1941

**October 16**
Hideki Tojo replaces Prince Konoye as Japanese prime minister

**October 30**
Germans besiege Sevastopol, Ukraine

**October 31**
USS *Reuben James* is sunk by a U-boat near Iceland; it's the first U.S. warship sunk during the war

**November 3**
The Japanese high command signs off on Admiral Isoroku Yamamoto's plan to bomb Pearl Harbor

**November 14**
U.S. Marines are evacuated from Tientsin, Shanghai, and Peking in China

**November 17**
Congress repeals key sections of the Neutrality Act, allowing merchant ships to be armed

**November 18**
British launch Operation CRUSADER to relieve Tobruk

**November 26**
U.S. demands Japanese withdrawal from China and Indochina

**November 27**
The U.S government asserts that Japan is likely to attack within a matter of days; the U.S. military is placed on high alert

Italian Army is routed in Gondar, Ethiopia

**November 29**
Finland recaptures its conquered territory from a weakened Soviet Union and restores its previous borders

**December 1**
In a unanimous vote, Japanese leaders officially endorse plans to enter the war against the United States

**December 5**
More than 750,000 German soldiers have been killed or injured in the campaign against Russia; Hitler calls for a break in action

**December 6**
Soviets launch counteroffensive around Moscow; suffering from frostbite, up to 30 percent of the German troops surrounding the city had withdrawn three days earlier

**December 7**
Japanese planes attack U.S. Pacific Fleet at Pearl Harbor, Hawaii

**December 8**
The United States and Britain declare war on Japan

**December 8–16**
Japanese invade Hong Kong, Malaya, the Philippines, the Gilbert Islands, and Borneo

**December 10**
Japanese aircraft sink HMS *Prince of Wales* and *Repulse*

**December 11**
Germany and Italy declare war on the United States

**December 19**
Hitler takes personal command of the German Army

# THE ALLIES' LITTLE GIANT

*During World War II, Canada transformed itself from a junior player in the Allied camp to one of the world's leading military and economic powers.*

On the eve of World War II, Canada was not ready for war. A nation of only 11 million people in 1939, it had a tiny, under-equipped army, an obsolete air force, and a tin-pot navy. Its economy was still in the stranglehold of the Great Depression.

Yet once the war started, Canada quickly mobilized its people and resources. More than one million Canadians would volunteer for service in the armed forces as Canada transformed its military from weakling to juggernaut. Unemployment would virtually disappear as Canada's basket-case economy became an industrial dynamo. By the war's end, Canada would make the fourth largest contribution to the Allied war effort and earn recognition as a major world power.

## A TITAN ON THE HIGH SEAS

At the outbreak of war, the Royal Canadian Navy (RCN) was perhaps the most war-ready branch of Canada's armed forces. That wasn't saying much—the RCN consisted of just over 1,800 officers and sailors and a fleet of 15 ships. But most RCN personnel were well-trained and experienced from prewar exchanges with the British Navy and would form the core of a world-class naval corps.

Canada immediately embarked on a massive shipbuilding program; the country's moribund shipyards increased production tenfold by 1940. The RCN also began a recruitment campaign for men to crew the new ships, which in 1942 was expanded to include women for shore duties so that more men could be freed for ship duty.

In time, the RCN built a "small-ship" fleet of destroyers, corvettes, frigates and minesweepers that became indispensable in the Battle of the Atlantic. Initially limited to defending Canada's Atlantic coast, the RCN played a leading role in protecting Allied convoys crossing the Atlantic and evolved into a killer antisubmarine force. In 1944, RCN vessels were redeployed to the Pacific to fight with the British Pacific fleet.

By the war's end, the RCN ranked as the world's third-largest navy. More than 89,000 men and 6,000 women served in the RCN aboard 471 warships and smaller fighting vessels, most of which were Canadian-built. Approximately 2,000 Canadian sailors died in action.

Just as impressive was the expansion of Canada's merchant navy, which played an equally vital role in keeping the transatlantic lifeline to Britain intact. During the war, Canadian shipyards built some 400 merchant ships. Twelve thousand Canadians served in the merchant navy, which was arguably a more perilous duty than the regular navy: More than 1,600 merchant sailors perished at sea.

## AIR CANADA

In September 1939, the Royal Canadian Air Force (RCAF) was barely an air force. The RCAF had 4,061 personnel, of which only 235 were pilots—fewer than the number of Canadian pilots in the British air force. Only 19 of the RCAF's motley collection of 275 aircraft were suitable for modern warfare.

Given the state of the RCAF, it was decided that Canada's initial contribution to the Allied air war effort would take place on the ground. Canada established and operated the British Commonwealth Air Training Plan (BCATP) which trained 131,553 aircrew personnel in Canada, including 49,507 badly needed pilots. More than 70,000 BCATP graduates were Canadian; others came from Britain, Australia, New Zealand, France, Poland, and Norway. Recognizing the success of the BCATP, U.S. President Franklin Roosevelt praised Canada as "the aerodrome of democracy."

Canada did eventually make a significant contribution in the skies. Aggressive recruitment and a burgeoning Canadian aircraft industry led to a rapid expansion of the RCAF, which counted 86 squadrons at its peak. Canadian fighter squadrons fought in the epic

Battle of Britain and later, Canadian fighter-bombers supported Allied ground offensives in Western Europe. An all-Canadian heavy bomber group participated in the Allies' strategic bombing campaign against Germany, while Canadian maritime patrol bombers fought German submarines. Canadians also flew combat, reconnaissance, and transport missions in Asia and the Pacific. By 1945, Canada boasted the world's fourth-largest air force. Some 232,000 men and 17,000 women served in the RCAF during the war. More than 17,000 Canadian air force members lost their lives.

## ON THE MARCH IN EUROPE

The largest branch of Canada's armed forces in September 1939 was the army. By the end of the month, after calling up reserves, the army numbered 55,500 soldiers. But they were far from ready: They lacked equipment, weapons, uniforms, and boots.

Again, with rapid mobilization of Canadian industry and aggressive recruitment, Canada's army ballooned. By mid-1942, the Canadian Army numbered 400,000 plus men and women in infantry, armored, artillery, and auxiliary units.

The Canadian Army went on the offensive in July 1943 with the invasion of Sicily. The 1st Canadian Infantry Division and 1st Canadian Armored Brigade fought all the way up the Italian peninsula as part of the British 8th Army, engaging in some of the toughest battles of the campaign. The 3rd Canadian Infantry Division and 2nd Canadian Armored Brigade also emerged as formidable fighting forces, commencing with the landing of Canadian troops on Juno Beach on D-Day. Canadians faced and defeated some of the German Army's most fanatical troops as they fought their way through northern France and Belgium. In February 1945, Canadian forces in Italy transferred to northern Europe and a unified 1st Canadian Army, under independent Canadian command, liberated Holland.

Over the course of the war, more than 730,000 men and women enlisted in the Canadian Army. More than 45,000 Canadian soldiers found their final resting places in Europe.

## AN ECONOMIC POWERHOUSE

Once at war, the Canadian government controlled virtually every aspect of the country's economy and mobilized it for war production. During wartime, Canada's economy would recover from the Depression and develop a modern, highly industrialized infrastructure. By the war's end, Canada's economic contribution to the Allied war effort had had as great an impact as its military contribution.

Canada morphed into an industrial powerhouse during the war. It was the world's second-largest producer of military vehicles behind the United States—its production of more than 800,000 trucks outstripped that of the three Axis powers combined. Canada also became a leading aircraft manufacturer, producing more than 16,000 planes of all types. Booming Canadian shipyards, ammunition plants, and textile factories also supplied the Allied war effort.

Canada's agricultural sector experienced unprecedented growth and production levels during the war years. The country's prairie regions produced record wheat harvests, and production of raw materials skyrocketed, especially metals. During the war, Canada accounted for 40 percent of the Allies' aluminum production and a whopping 95 percent of its nickel.

As in the United States, Canada implemented a strict wartime ration program for everyday commodities such as meats, sugar, dairy products, coffee, rubber, and gasoline. More than one million Canadian women entered the workforce to help keep the factories and farms at full production.

## A NEW WORLD POWER

Canada emerged from World War I as a nation; it came out of World War II as major world power. By the end of the war, Canada possessed the world's fourth-largest military and was its third-largest industrial producer.

After the war, Canada willingly descended in rank to a middle power and adopted a quintessentially Canadian role in the world as a "peacekeeper." Most Canadians are justifiably proud of their country's unique identity among the world's nations.

# MASSACRE AT BANGKA ISLAND

*Besides their abhorrent treatment of prisoners of war, one of the worst atrocities committed by Japanese soldiers during World War II took place on a nondescript island in the South Pacific in the early months of the war.*

On December 8, 1941, Japan's Imperial Army invaded the tiny nation of Malaya. The Emperor's soldiers quickly secured the nation's valuable rubber- and tin-production facilities. As enemy troops marched down the peninsula toward the British naval base on the island of Singapore, nurses attached to the 13th Australian General Hospital and their wounded charges were ordered to abandon the hospital and flee.

The escapees commandeered merchant ship SS *Vyner Brooke* (previously owned by the Rajah of Sarawak, Sir Charles Vyner Brooke). Some 330 soldiers, nurses, and civilians hastily boarded the boat and left port on February 12. Conditions aboard the freighter were woefully inadequate.

By mid-February 1942, Japanese military forces had conquered vast tracts of the Pacific including Hong Kong and portions of Siam, Burma, Sarawak, British North Borneo, the Netherlands East Indies, and the Philippine island chain of Luzon down to Mindanao. The ship and its payload of refugees spent one day hiding amongst area islands. On the evening of Friday, February 13, the captain of the *Vyner Brooke* decided to chance a run for freedom. While sailing through the still waters of Bangka Strait in the early afternoon of February 14, the *Vyner Brooke* was attacked by Japanese aircraft. The ship received three direct bomb hits and was raked by machine-gun fire. As water flooded into the hull, the refugees were forced to abandon ship.

The soldiers, nurses, and civilians were subjected to repeated strafing runs from Japanese planes as they abandoned the doomed vessel. The cargo ship slipped beneath the waves, and the unarmed survivors desperately tried to save their own lives and assist the wounded who could not fend for themselves.

By sunrise some 60 soldiers, civilian men, women, and children and 22 members of the Australian Army Nursing Service (AANS) had reached the sandy shore of Radji Beach on Bangka Island. As the nurses tended to the wounded, a small search party was organized and dispatched to a local village in search of food and water. Fearing reprisals, the villagers urged the survivors to surrender to Japanese occupation forces operating in the area.

That evening the ranks on the beach swelled to almost 100 as a large lifeboat came ashore carrying more servicemen. As the group's children became distressed, a fateful decision was made by one of the senior nurses. She suggested all civilian women and children abandon the beach and make their way toward a local village. All agreed, save one civilian woman who decided to stay with her husband.

Shortly after the civilians left, a group of about a dozen Japanese soldiers approached the survivors. Half of the men were split from the group and were ordered to march down the beach. Minutes later the Japanese soldiers returned and ordered the remaining men to head in the same direction. One civilian woman and the 22 Australian nurses were left on the beach.

When the Japanese soldiers reappeared, they sat in front of the nurses and proceeded to clean their rifles and bloodied bayonets. Several nurses surmised all of the men had been executed. The Japanese soldiers then ordered the nurses to stand and proceeded to push them into the surf. The nurses marched abreast into the water, facing the horizon. When the nurses reached waist-deep water, the Japanese soldiers opened fire. Twenty-one nurses and one civilian woman were murdered.

Nurse Vivian Bullwinkel survived the massacre. Wounded, she was spun by the force of the bullet's impact into the water, where she feigned death. After many hours in the surf, she eventually came ashore and hid in the jungle for several days. She came across a British private, Pat Kingsley, who had survived the massacre of soldiers the previous day. The two spent 12 days in hiding before surrendering to the Japanese on February 28.

While Kingsley eventually succumbed to his bayonet wounds, Bullwinkel joined other nurses who had survived the *Vyner Brooke*'s sinking in a prisoner-of-war camp. Bullwinkel hid her wound from her captors, fearing the discovery would bring about her death at the hands of her Japanese masters, who wanted to keep news of the massacre secret.

Bullwinkel worked in the camp's brutal conditions for three and a half years. After the war, she returned to Australia, retired from the AANS, and became a civilian nurse. In 1947 she traveled to Tokyo, where she gave evidence of the massacre at a war-crimes trial.

Bullwinkel raised money for a nurse's memorial located in Melbourne and later became both the President of the College of Nursing Australia, and the patron of the National Service Nurse's Memorial. She died July 3, 2000.

✯    ✯    ✯

- *Of the 65 nurses who boarded the* Vyner Brooke *to escape death on Singapore, only 24 managed to survive the war. Besides the 21 murdered on the beach of Bangka Island, 12 are presumed to have died in the attack on the* Vyner Brooke, *and 8 others perished as POWs.*

✯    ✯    ✯

- *Breakfast of Champions: A Japanese soldiering manual encouraged men to kill any venomous snakes they found and eat the livers raw to strengthen their bodies.*

✯    ✯    ✯

- *The Japanese Army did not award medals for valor—it was assumed and expected.*

## Fast Facts

- Admiral Chester William Nimitz studied diesel engines in Germany before the war and became the leading U.S. authority on submarines. In fact, from November 5, 1930, to April 1, 1931, the USS Holland, a submarine, served as his flagship.

- The U.S. Emergency Maternal and Infant Care Program established free obstetric and prenatal services for military wives during the war.

- Inflation and salary caps essentially prevented American labor unions from fighting for higher wages during the war. Instead, they made progress by securing paid vacations and overtime wages.

- Chinese Generalissimo Chiang Kai-shek was widely criticized for retaining his best troops for use against the Communists after the war instead of deploying them against the invading Japanese.

- Stalin suggested to Roosevelt and Churchill that all Nazi officers be eliminated after the war. Roosevelt thought the Soviet leader was joking; Churchill knew he was not.

- The Nazis paid one of their most successful spies, the valet to the British ambassador in Turkey, in counterfeit currency.

- During the 1942–43 winter, the average Soviet citizen subsisted on about 1,000 calories per day.

- During the war, Allied countries encouraged their citizens to plant "Victory gardens" to provide fruit, vegetables, and herbs. In 1943, Britain boasted more than 1.4 million Victory gardens in yards across the nation.

- In 1940, Brigadier General Benjamin Oliver Davis became the first African-American general in the U.S. Armed Forces.

- The first national European capital captured by the Allies during the war was Rome on June 4, 1944—two days before the Normandy invasion.

# "BOMBER" HARRIS

*Some people may have thought sending 400 bombers on a raid would be enough, but not British Air Chief Marshal Arthur Harris. Under his lead, Allied raids on Germany used twice that number, raining devastation upon cities and turning their streets into infernos.*

Born in 1892, the son of a civil servant stationed in India, Arthur Harris began his work life in British Rhodesia (now Zimbabwe) as a farmer. During the First World War, operating a Sopwith Camel with the Royal Flying Corps, he shot down five hostiles and earned an Air Force Cross. On the home front, he learned that German Zeppelins had bombed England. In France, he viewed aerial raids as a superior alternative to the static horror of trench warfare.

With the fledgling Royal Air Force after the war, Harris bombed native rebels in British India's northwest frontier, near modern Afghanistan. In Iraq, he employed a squadron of refitted cargo biplanes against groups fighting the British occupation. "We cut a hole in the nose and rigged up our own bomb racks," recalled Harris. "I turned those machines into the heaviest and best bombers in the command." He waved off civilian casualties from the raids, reputedly stating, "The only thing the Arab understands is the heavy hand." On returning to Britain, he improved night-bombing techniques, and led the first heavy bomber group. Starting in February 1942, he became Bomber Command's Commander in Chief.

## GERMANY'S OFFENSE PROVOKES BRITAIN'S "BOMBER"

Germany's all-out assault on Poland, France, and the Low Countries during 1939-40 set a terrifying precedent. At the start of the war, the *Luftwaffe* staged a series of raids on Warsaw, Poland's capital city. On September 25, 1939, bombers led by Wolfram von Richthofen, cousin of the First World War's "Red Baron," flew more than a thousand sorties against the city, dropping 572 tons of incendiaries and high explosives. The bombers zeroed in on obvious civilian targets like hospitals, marked by giant red crosses. During the siege, 40,000 residents died; more than half the city was wrecked. Many of the losses, however, were due to artillery bombardment. And numerous aerial bombs missed their targets, sometimes hitting German infantry. But British planners noticed that the Warsaw garrison surrendered the day after the raid.

The following year, during the *Blitzkrieg* in the west, bombing again secured a quick surrender. On May 14, 1940, after invading the Netherlands, a force of 90 German bombers raided the Dutch city of Rotterdam. More than 800 people were killed, and 24,978 homes, 62 schools, and 24 churches were ruined. The Dutch government sued for an armistice the same day.

The following day, the British government abandoned its policy of bombing strictly military targets. That night, British bombers attacked factories and refineries in the Ruhr, Germany's industrial heartland.

Soon after, the *Luftwaffe* launched the aerial Blitz against London and Coventry, which destroyed the latter town's renowned cathedral. During the Blitz's height in October 1940, Churchill stated at a War Cabinet session that Germany's "civilian population around the target areas must be made to feel the weight of the war."

Harris and many others, including Churchill, realized "strategic bombing" would be Britain's best option against Germany. "Pinpoint accuracy" raids had proved to be anything but accurate, and Britain and America were in no way ready to invade Europe. In 1942, Hitler's panzers were gearing up again to knock the Soviet Union out of the war, and Stalin was demanding the Western Allies relieve the pressure.

Harris received powerful support from Frederick Lindemann. The Jewish, German-born Oxford professor of physics was noted for having proved some of Einstein's atomic theories. Along with serving as paymaster general in the war, he was the prime minister's science adviser and friend. In 1942, Lindemann wrote an influential paper advocating the "area bombing" of German cities, industries, and working-class neighborhoods. By displacing German laborers through the widespread destruction of their residences, Lindemann argued, worker output and the German economy would plunge. German morale might also plummet, bringing the war to an early end. Meanwhile, British production lines were replacing ineffective light bombers with masses of potent, four-engine Halifax and Lancaster bombers.

Harris stated, "The Nazis entered this war under the rather childish delusion that they were going to bomb everyone else, and nobody was going to bomb them. At Rotterdam, London, Warsaw, and half a hundred other places, they put their rather naïve theory into operation. They sowed the wind, and now they are going to reap the whirlwind."

## BRITAIN RETALIATES:
## THE RAID ON COLOGNE

The first test case of area bombing was the German cathedral city of Cologne. Previous raids had topped off with about 400 bombers; the Cologne attack of May 30–31, 1942, used 1,047. It was the first of Harris's "thousand bomber raids." The planes were sent in a steady stream aimed at overwhelming the defenders' interlocking radar systems, searchlights, flak batteries, and night fighters. The bombers used technical innovations like metal foil chaff, which when dropped far from the target, showed up on German radar screens as a flock of bombers. Flying at night, the bombers were guided by the novel GEE radio navigation system.

Dubbed Operation Millennium, the attack delivered 1,455 tons of bombs, most of which were incendiaries. No *Feuersturm* (firestorm) ensued. However, aircraft losses—43 planes—were relatively small, and the bombing was judged successful. In Cologne, about 480 people were killed, more than 5,000 were wounded, and 19,000 residences were destroyed or heavily damaged. Sixteen schools and nine hospitals were also destroyed. A quarter of the city's residents fled to other towns.

Future raids, on Pforzheim and other cities, caused far more damage. Cologne itself was bombed again—more than 260 times (although its cathedral, despite blows from 14 bombs, survived).

# DEATH OF A CZECH VILLAGE

*Nazi brutality and depravity in occupied Eastern Europe knew no limits. The liquidation of the Czech village of Lidice by the SS was testament to that reality.*

By September 1941, Czechoslovakia had been under the nightmarish yoke of Nazi occupation longer than any country in Europe aside from Austria. Commencing with the signing of the Munich Pact in September 1938, and the seizure of Prague the following March, the subjugation of the Czechs by the Germans would continue uninterrupted until the final days of the war.

It would also come to be defined by the cold-blooded annihilation of a small Czech village called Lidice.

## INITIALLY SPARED THE WORST

Under the German occupation, Czechoslovakia, as Hitler put it, "ceased to exist." Hitler split the country apart, proclaiming the Czech provinces of Bohemia and Moravia a "protectorate" of Germany and ordering a puppet government in Slovakia to declare its independence.

The occupation arrangement initially imposed on the Czechs was harsh, but nowhere near as oppressive as it was in neighboring Poland. There, overtly sadistic and highly destructive occupation policies brought about mass executions, the uprooting of millions, and the virtual enslavement of the Poles.

The Czechs were spared such upheaval, primarily because the population was highly skilled and was needed to work at local armament and manufacturing plants vital to the German war effort. Everyone in the country was ordered to remain at their jobs—cessation of work was deemed an act of sabotage—and daily life remained relatively normal.

# THE "BUTCHER OF PRAGUE" TAKES OVER

But this more tolerant occupation was not to last. Hitler was never comfortable with a Slavic population living within the German Reich, and as anti-German resistance increased in the Czech territories, he decreed harsher treatment for the Czechs.

September 1941 marked the turning point for the Czechs, when Hitler appointed SS *Obergruppenführer* Reinhard Heydrich as Reich Protector of Bohemia and Moravia. Heydrich, the man who would later draw up the plans for carrying out the Final Solution in Europe, immediately established a reign of terror in the Czech lands. One of his first acts was the summary execution of 340 members of the Czech resistance—thus earning the title, "Butcher of Prague."

Heydrich implemented what he called his "whip and sugar" policy, in which he increased daily food rations for Czech workers with the implied threat that they would be lowered if production faltered or resistance continued. It was a highly effective measure in subduing the Czech people, so much so that the British and the Czech government-in-exile decided that Heydrich had to be eliminated. The Czech exiles knew such an act would bring terrible reprisals on the local population but felt it necessary to give the Czech people hope.

In December, a two-man Czech assassination team was parachuted into the occupied territories. The assassins hid out with Czech partisans until finally carrying out their mission on May 27, 1942, tossing a grenade into Heydrich's open-air Mercedes as it slowed on a hairpin turn on the outskirts of Prague. Badly wounded, Heydrich died in the hospital a week later.

## THE LIQUIDATION OF LIDICE

A vengeful Hitler ordered the execution of 10,000 Czechs as reprisal for Heydrich's death. Within five days, 1,300 innocent Czech civilians were murdered by the SS. The SS and Gestapo launched a massive search for the two Czech agents who assassinated Heydrich, and soon found them and some of their accomplices hiding in a Prague church. One of the agents was killed in the ensuing firefight; the other resisters saved their last bullets for themselves.

The Germans' manhunt also uncovered information that Czech partisans involved in the plot were being sheltered in Lidice, a small coal-mining village west of Prague. In the early hours of June 10, ten truckloads of SS personnel moved in on Lidice. Every house was searched, and residents were herded into the main square. As the day progressed, the village's male inhabitants were imprisoned in barns as they returned from the mines.

The next day, 173 men and boys over the age of 16 were shot in groups of ten along the wall of the village tavern. The last 26 were burned alive in a barn to speed up the process. The 195 women of Lidice were shipped to the Theresienstadt and Ravensbrück concentration camps, where 41 of them perished. Nine of the village's 98 children were sent to Germany for adoption–the rest were sent to the Gneisenau concentration camp in Poland and later to Chelmno, where most died in the camp's mobile gassing vans. Of Lidice's 492 inhabitants, only 143 women and 16 children survived.

After Lidice was cleared, the Germans razed and bulldozed every building in the village. All the rubble was removed, and grain was planted where Lidice once stood in an attempt to remove all traces of its existence.

## LIDICE REBORN

Lidice was destroyed, but the Nazis' attempt to erase its memory failed. News of the atrocity eventually spread, and several villages around the world took the name of Lidice in remembrance. Many Czech girls born shortly afterward were christened with the village's name.

In 1945, the Czechoslovakian government announced plans to rebuild Lidice, and the foundation stone was laid in 1947, only 300 meters from the village's original site. Full reconstruction began in 1948, and many survivors of the Lidice massacre returned to the rebuilt village. Today, a community of about 150 homes stands as a living memorial to the residents of Lidice.

# CITIZEN KANE GOES SOUTH

*Orson Welles didn't fight in the Second World War, but his wartime mission in Brazil stunted his career.*

Brazil began the war as a neutral nation. However, Roosevelt and his advisers recognized that the country would be an ideal supply point for the anticipated African campaign. Though ruled by a Fascist dictator, Brazil sought to curry favor with the United States and declared war on Germany in 1942. But Brazil's ruler, Getúlio Vargas, had reservations about his country's involvement in the war. He also realized Brazil would be the likely landing spot for German forces attempting to establish a base in the Western hemisphere. As a goodwill gesture, Roosevelt chose a personal friend, *Citizen Kane* director Orson Welles, to go to Brazil and film the country's annual Carnival celebration.

As soon as Welles had left the country, RKO began slashing and refilming significant portions of the company's current Welles production, *The Magnificent Ambersons*. Far away in Rio de Janeiro, Welles was powerless to stop the damage. Instead, with characteristic enthusiasm, he began producing three short Brazilian films. When money for the project ran out, Welles took to the jungle with a small camera crew and continued to document the country's indigenous culture. Since Welles remained under contract to RKO, the footage, titled *It's All True,* was taken from the young director and never returned. The film was presumed lost until a month before Welles's death in 1985, when it was discovered in a Paramount studio vault.

Though Welles was in Brazil at the behest of the U.S. government, his absence from the studio and failure to finish *The Magnificent Ambersons* cursed him with a lasting reputation as an irresponsible director incapable of finishing a project. For the rest of his career, he struggled to continue making films outside the powerful studio system. Though he succeeded in producing many brilliant films, his craft was compromised by his constant search for funding.

# THE USO PROVIDES ENTERTAINMENT AND MEMORIES OF HOME

*Why did Hollywood celebrities leave their comfortable lifestyles to entertain soldiers, facing deprivation, disease, enemy bombing, and sometimes death? Maybe the answer lies with what dancer Patty Thomas said of her experience, "Once you entertain these boys and make them happy you know you have to go on and on and on."*

During World War II, approximately 7,000 entertainers joined the United Service Organization (USO), which was established in 1941, to boost the morale of young men and women serving at home and abroad during World War II. The USO provided centers, clubs, and live entertainment, which included Hollywood celebrities. Many celebrities traveled to Europe and the Pacific islands to perform for the troops. Their experiences during the war were forever etched in their minds.

## BOB HOPE: "NO TEARS, PLEASE"

The toughest part of the job for many USO entertainers was visiting wounded GIs in hospitals. It took willpower to keep from shedding tears after seeing the broken bodies of the young men. Bob Hope resolved to remain strong—he didn't want the soldiers to see him or his troupe crying. He wanted them to forget the pain and to enjoy life, even for a little while. He would remind his fellow entertainers, "No tears, please, you can't have tears. You can cry later, but you can't cry in front of them."

## FOR FRANCES LANGFORD, A VISIT TOUCHED HER LIFE FOREVER

During a visit to a military hospital, singer Frances Langford was asked to see a severely wounded soldier. She readily agreed and went to see the young man. While holding her hand and listening to the beautiful starlet sing softly, the soldier looked up, smiled, and then died. The incident was heartbreaking for Langford, who held her tears until she left the room.

## PATTY THOMAS: "DON'T THEY LOVE TAP DANCING?"

During a tour of the Pacific, a USO troupe's PBY Catalina seaplane lost engine power over New Guinea and had to make a forced landing. Patty Thomas worried that her tap shoes would be thrown out and decided to tie them around her neck. Apparently, most of the soldiers, sailors, and airmen saw something else in her besides dancing. "I was a 21-year-old with a 34-24-34 figure with long legs. The tap dancing wasn't exactly what they wanted to hear and see."

## CAROLE LOMBARD: TRAGEDY OF THE PROFANE ANGEL

Film actress Carole Lombard earned the nickname the "Profane Angel" with her bawdy language. She joined the USO shortly after the United States entered the war and went on a bond rally tour. After a rally in her hometown of Fort Wayne, Indiana, she, her mother, and 20 others boarded a TWA DC-3 Skysleeper headed from Indiana to California. As Lombard boarded the plane, she exhorted her fans to "cheer—'V' for Victory!" Outside of Las Vegas, her plane crashed into a mountain, leaving no survivors.

## GLENN MILLER AND HIS ARMY AIR FORCE BAND

Big Band legend Glenn Miller recorded such musical numbers as "Chattanooga Choo-Choo," "In the Mood," "Moonlight Serenade," and "Tuxedo Junction." In 1942, during the peak of his fame, he left his highly successful career to join the U.S. Army. The army placed him in command of the service's band, which he named the Glenn Miller Army Air Force Band. His band toured with the USO in the United States during 1942 and 1943 and transferred to the United Kingdom a year later. After a show on December 15, 1944, he boarded a plane headed for Paris to entertain the troops there. Somewhere over the English Channel, the plane mysteriously disappeared. Miller, along with two passengers and the pilot, was never seen again.

## 1941

**December 20**
Soon-to-be legendary pilots of the U.S. Air Force Flying Tigers engage in their first combat mission, dominating their Japanese counterparts in the skies over Kunming, China

**December 22**
Japanese troops land on Luzon in the Philippines

**December 23**
Japanese take Wake Island, the last American base in the Pacific between Hawaii and the Philippines

**December 24**
U.S. forces on Luzon withdraw to the Bataan Peninsula

**December 25**
Hong Kong falls to the Japanese

## 1942

**January 2**
The Japanese Army occupies the Philippine capital of Manila

**January 3–12**
China emerges victorious in a battle for Changsha in Hunan Province

**January 6**
Britain has its first victory of the war over German troops; the 8th Army routs a division of Rommel's Panzer Corps

**January 9**
Japanese begin offensive on Bataan

**January 12**
Germans start U-boat offensive off the east coast of the United States; a U-boat will sink the *Norness* off the coast of North Carolina's Cape Hatteras two days later

**January 14–16**
Japanese invade Burma

**January 20**
Nazis at the Wannsee Conference in Berlin formalize plans to exterminate the Jews

**January 21**
General Joseph W. Stilwell appointed Chief of Staff to Generalissimo Chiang Kai-shek

**January 30**
In a speech, Hitler asserts that the conflict will end with the "complete annihilation of the Jews," calling them "the most evil universal enemy of all time"

**January 31**
British forces withdraw from Malaya to Singapore

**February 8**
Soviets encircle 90,000 Germans in the Demyansk Pocket

Japanese land on Singapore; they will capture the Tengah airfield, a vital supply link, the following day

**February 11–13**
Unable to return to Brest, France, German cruisers *Schanhorst, Gneisenau,* and *Prinz Eugen* make an audacious escape across the English Channel

**February 13**
Hitler permanently cancels Operation Sealion, the German Invasion of Britain

**February 15**
Singapore surrenders to the Japanese

# THE TANK
# IN WORLD WAR II

*Many people have heard of the mighty Shermans, panzers, and Tigers of the war. But armor alone wasn't enough to win battles.*

While tanks played a part in World War I, they came of age in World War II. Europe abandoned trench warfare, and the tank became a force that had to be dealt with. However, the nations fighting in Europe each had their own ideas of how to use armor most effectively. Here's a look at some of the most pivotal armored battles of the war.

## FRANCE, 1940: GERMANS ATTACK FRENCH AND BRITISH TROOPS

**Tank superiority:** *Britain and France*
**Air superiority:** *Germany*
**Result:** *Decisive German victory*
The Germans' tactics, deployment, and air superiority gave them the superior edge in their conquest of France. The French actually had more and better tanks than Germany, but dispersed them to support the infantry. German attacks showed the value of combined arms as dive-bombers supported the panzers to produce a faster, fiercer assault than the Allies anticipated. Yet it was not all easy going: Very heavily armored Matilda (British) and Char B1 (French) tanks proved tough targets for German infantry and artillery.

## LYBIA/EGYPT, 1940–42: COMMONWEALTH

**Tank superiority:** *Even*
**Air superiority:** *Allied (marginal)*
**Result:** *Seesaw at first, then decisive Allied victory*
Rommel's war in Africa was a low-force-density campaign fought over great distances, which gave tanks lots

of room to maneuver. Italian tanks were inferior, balancing out the better tanks of their German rescuers. Supplies, especially fuel, limited Rommel far more than it did the British and their allies; British tanks, however, were more prone to breakdown. The 1942 Anglo-American landings in Morocco only sped the inevitable: Germany and Italy couldn't get Rommel enough supplies for him to finish off the well-fueled Commonwealth forces.

## BARBAROSSA, 1941–42: GERMANS ATTACK SOVIETS

**Tank superiority:** *Soviet*
**Air superiority:** *German*
**Result:** *Germany scored tactical victories, was ultimately repelled by the Soviets*

Hitler invaded the USSR with a vast army, including plenty of tanks. But panzer crews had trouble facing the speedy, tough T-34s and the near-impregnable KV-1s of the Soviet Union. In open country, audacious panzer tactics allowed the German Army to encircle millions of Soviet soldiers, removing them from the war. The Germans' first real trouble came not from Soviet counterattacks, but from those two historic Russian heroes: General Mud and General Winter. While German forces sliced deep into Russia and the Ukraine, they failed to capture any of their most coveted objectives: Leningrad, Moscow, Stalingrad, or the Caucasus oilfields. With many tanks out of fuel, drivewheel-deep in mud, or unable to start due to the cold, Germany's quality and quantity suddenly didn't mean much.

## OVERLORD, 1944–45: BRITISH AND AMERICANS ATTACK GERMANS

**Tank superiority:** *German (quality), Allied (quantity)*
**Air superiority:** *Allied*
**Result:** *Decisive Allied victory*

Here the Allies met the late-war German tanks (the panzer IVs, Panthers, and Tigers), with their long guns and veteran crews, and

# Tank Variants

**The armored car** Something of an armored dune buggy, this wheeled vehicle's armor was protection only against light weapons; it couldn't take on enemy tanks. Its asset was speed: Armored cars could scout enemy positions, trade a few shots, perhaps shoot up a truck or wagon convoy, then escape. Nearly every armored combatant nation used them, and the concept survives in modern militaries.

**The tank destroyer** This mobile antitank cannon relied on barrel length and caliber to pack a punch. They came in a wide range of styles: turreted and turretless, open-topped and close-topped, and fast or slow. Tank destroyers worked best as defensive weapons to snipe advancing tanks. Years after the war, this role more or less merged with the armored car after the advent of the antitank missile.

**Self-propelled artillery** Artillery towed by horses (still quite common in World War II) or trucks took time to prepare for fire or movement and was vulnerable to shell fragments from enemy counter-battery fire. Self-propelled artillery could move quickly to avoid counter-battery fire; if caught in it, its armor provided some protection—nothing like a tank's, but enough. After the war, most militaries made the transition to self-propelled artillery, though towed artillery did not become obsolete.

**Flail tank** This late-war tank did an outstanding job clearing paths through minefields. Imagine a standard tank with a big rolling pin mounted far out front, parallel to the axles. Dozens of lengths of heavy chain were attached to the rolling pin, which then turned, causing the chains to slap the ground and detonate mines in front of the vehicle. The American and British Sherman flail variants were particularly successful. After the war, the concept shifted to the mineplow "dozer tank," which became a standard feature of major armored forces.

learned that the Sherman didn't measure up tank-for-tank. Still, the Allies overcame German forces in France, in part because the Germans were running out of fuel and air support. With the remnants of the *Luftwaffe* stationed in Germany to defend against bombing raids, Allied fighter and bomber pilots had the leisure to shoot up panzers in France from the air. Both sides had developed handheld antitank weapons (the U.S. bazooka, German *Panzerfaust,* and the British PIAT, for example), which were often a greater asset to the defender (by 1944, the Germans were usually defending). In their last major armored gasp on the Western front, German generals launched the assault the Allies would dub the Battle of the

Bulge. Even with tactical surprise, it succeeded only so long as bad weather hampered Allied airpower.

## SOVIET RESURGENCE 1943–45: SOVIETS ATTACK GERMANS

**Tank superiority:** *Even (quality), Soviet (quantity)*
**Air superiority:** *Mostly Soviet*
**Result:** *Russian tanks enter Berlin*

By now, the Germans had caught up with Soviet tank design but would never produce enough tanks to match Soviet numbers. After Stalingrad, German troops were positioned to delay the Soviets from recapturing land. Soviet tanks paid a high price for the advance, but with Soviet air and numeric tank superiority, German armor was in trouble. The Soviet's vast artillery superiority also factored in. While indirect-fire artillery rarely destroyed a tank outright, it might immobilize it: If armor is trying to withdraw under fire, an immobile tank is a dead tank. Here, as on the Western front, German infantry joined directly in the tank battle with the new *Panzerfaust,* an excellent handheld antitank rocket that took a toll on Soviet tanks from the Ukraine to the Reich Chancellery.

## WARTIME LESSONS

The French campaign proved that tanks should be massed in divisions and corps to create and exploit breakthroughs. North Africa showed that even the greatest armored force dies of thirst for lack of fuel. Barbarossa and Overlord proved that air superiority is key to armor operations, and can enable inferior tank numbers and/or quality to gain victory.

## Tank Lingo

**Spalling** Stuff flying around inside the tank when it gets hit, such as rivets behaving like little bullets. This was one reason welded hulls superseded riveted hulls.

**Buttoned up** When the commander doesn't stick his head out the turret. While he's safer, he can't see the battle situation as well.

**Armor sloping** Sloped armor is harder to penetrate. The physics of this are simple, but it took years for the lesson to find its way into tank designs.

**Hull down** When a tank is partly concealed, such that its enemy can see its turret but not its hull, it's "hull down"—an advantageous defensive position tank commanders actively seek.

**To throw a track** The tracks can slip off a tank, especially on rough terrain or at high speeds.

**Side-skirts** Metal plates welded to the tank's side in hopes of gaining a little more protection. These were often improvised, especially by Germans and Americans, from scavenged scrap metal and pieces of wrecks.

One reason that tanks were so vulnerable to airstrikes was that their top armor was the thinnest. Postwar warfare development has sought to take advantage of the tank's weakness—helicopter gunships fire missiles and strike aircraft carry rockets and cluster bombs designed to hit from above. World War II demonstrated that tank mobility and striking power should be exploited to the fullest—but be sure to bring enough fuel and control the air.

☆　　☆　　☆

- *Panzer is simply German for "tank." The Panther tank that appeared in 1943 was a panzer, so was the Panzer Ib, so was the King Tiger, and so forth.*

☆　　☆　　☆

- *Stuka pilot Hans-Ulrich Rudel destroyed 519 confirmed Soviet tanks, earning the seldom-awarded Knight's Cross of the Iron Cross with Swords, Oak Leaves, and Diamonds.*

## Fast Facts

- *Why didn't the Russian mud and winter affect the Soviet tanks as well? It did cause problems for prewar Soviet tanks, but by winter 1941 the Germans had already shot up or captured many of those. The newer generation had wider track, which were less prone to bog down, and used diesel, which has a higher freezing point than gasoline. Soviet tanks were designed for the Russian environment, and Soviet crews knew what to expect from the Russian mud and winter.*

- *Infantry often rode tanks into battle. The Germans called these "Panzer grenadiers." The advantage of having infantry aboard was that they could see threats to the tank that the crew could not, such as someone lurking to slap an antitank magnetic mine on the hull.*

- *Though they never fought for Czechoslovakia, Czechoslovak tanks were excellent for their time. After the partition of Czechoslovakia, the Germans incorporated hundreds of Czechoslovak tanks into the Wehrmacht. When tank development rendered them out-of-date, the Germans mounted heavy guns, howitzers, and antitank cannons on their chassis to create self-propelled artillery and tank destroyers.*

- *Germany's immense "Elefant" tank destroyer was an immense failure. Lacking machine guns for infantry defense, it snailed along at 12 miles per hour—a wallowing target certain to be flanked.*

- *Wartime German tank photos often show a corrugated hull surface, or Zimmerit coating. This ingenious invention made it harder for infantry men to attach magnetic antitank mines.*

- *For the D-Day invasion of Normandy, British vehicles carried huge spools of coconut-husk matting to unroll on the beach, which helped tanks avoid bogging down in the soft ground.*

- *In 1939, Germany produced only 247 tanks and heavy armored vehicles. In 1943, it produced 13,657—over 3,700 more than during 1939—42 combined.*

# "WILL YOU STARVE THAT THEY BE BETTER FED?"

*In 1944–45, 36 U.S. conscientious objectors volunteered to starve, in hope that lessons learned would save many lives. This is their story.*

### Was it news that starving people lost weight and had health problems?

Surely not. During World War II, millions died of starvation; many others suffered greatly from it. Famines had long been endemic in Southern Asia, and the Soviet Union had known them in 1921 and 1932–33. Yet no one had studied the mechanics of starvation in a controlled, scientific environment.

### How does one get a gig starving people for science?

You need two things, evidently: a major war and a proven track record in nutritional science with the military. Ancel Keys, a professor at the University of Minnesota, was a pioneer in nutritional studies. Early in the war, the U.S. Army contacted him to design a lightweight ration for airborne troops. The K-Ration, named for Keys, proved so compact and nutritious the army ordered well over 100 million throughout the war.

### What kind of people would volunteer to starve?

For religious or idealistic reasons, some draftable men were conscientious objectors (COs): They refused to bear arms. Some COs became medics, but for others, even that was too militaristic. With much work to be done, putting these men in jail would have been wasteful. Instead, the COs became part of the Civilian Public Service (CPS), an organization at the disposal of the U.S. Army.

### Did these CPS people have it soft while everyone else in "The Greatest Generation" was working and fighting?

While some CPS jobs were make-work, many required courage

and dedication. CPS men fought fires as smoke jumpers, worked in insane asylums, manufactured items for the war, and assisted with farming and forestry. They also volunteered for medical experiments: vitamin effects, severe cold, severe heat, extended bed rest, lice infestation, even malaria. Most CPS volunteers believed there was a difference between pacifism and cowardice, and they intended to prove it.

*Even so, these experiments sound rather unpleasant. Was anyone forced into this?*

Hardly. Keys sent out a brochure depicting hungry children that read, "Will you starve that they be better fed?" Four hundred people volunteered—many times more than he needed. Thirty-six were selected, and they actually cheered at the outset of the experiment. This was the heart and soul of their refusal to drop bombs, carry submachine guns, or point battleship cannons: They believed it was better to endure suffering than to kill.

*What kind of doctor would run such an experiment?*

Keys didn't enjoy watching anyone suffer, nor did he make the process worse than necessary—and he did believe it necessary. He doubted anyone could teach starving people democracy; starvation had to be addressed. Though the law imposed few constraints on him, his academic and professional principles governed his actions. During the experiment, he often asked himself, "What am I doing to these men?"

*Then this must have been a very methodical starvation, right?*

Perhaps no one ever starved so scientifically. The doctors first examined and tested nearly every aspect of the subjects' physical and mental health, then regularized their diets on bland but filling fare. On November 19, 1944, the first phase began with a normal, 3,200 calorie-per-day diet. After three months, the starvation phase began: the ration was halved to 1,570 calories per day. The subjects had to walk 22 miles per week, and endured batteries of psychological and medical tests. This phase of starvation lasted six months.

*What do you feed men in order to starve them in a proper scientific manner?*

Keys based meals on typical European famine fare. A sample starvation-phase dinner included 36g of beans, peas, and ham in a soup, 255g of macaroni and cheese, 40g of rutabagas, 100g of potatoes, and 100g of lettuce salad—about 1.17 pounds of food. The men got all the black coffee, water, chewing gum, and cigarettes they wanted. On this diet, they grew weaker, testier, and more apathetic by the day. When they heard that Germany surrendered and Hitler had died, they barely cared.

*Wasn't it hard to keep them from sneaking out and getting a hot dog and fries...with extra ketchup?*

While they had some freedom to move about, they were forbidden to cheat by eating outside food. No man was allowed to go out without a buddy. Four men were prematurely discharged from the test: one for ill health, two for cheating, and one for suspected cheating. In a moment of temporary derangement and frustration, one man cut off three of his fingers with an ax, but begged to remain in the experiment.

*How could the doctors tell who cheated?*

The men's weights were all dropping at roughly the same pace. Anyone who stopped losing weight stood out.

*So how did they look at the end of the starvation period?*

Imagine clean, well-dressed concentration camp survivors. By the end of the starvation phase, the average subject weighed about 115 pounds, down from an average starting weight of 153 pounds. Many had retained water and had bloated shins or ankles. The only man who showed a serious medical side effect (blood in the urine) was discharged for ill health, and he soon recovered.

*By my count, we're nine months in. Was this when they resumed eating normally?*

During recovery, the men kept losing weight at first, as they shed the retained water. Shortly after near-normal rations resumed, the staff psychologist brought Dr. Keys a manifesto from the volunteers, demanding an end to the buddy system. Keys scowled at the psychologist's unseemly amusement. "Don't you see?" answered the psychologist. "It is the ultimate validation of your theories. Hungry people mindlessly follow orders. You feed them enough and right away they demand self-government." Keys gave in.

### What happened after they reached their normal weights?

The primary experiment ended October 20, 1945, not long after Japan's surrender. Twelve volunteers stayed for a fourth phase of "unrestricted recovery." Even on 5,219 calories per day, the men reported many psychological effects: fear that food might be taken away, a tendency to gorge, and feeling hungry even when stuffed.

### But by that time, Dachau, Auschwitz, and the other camps. were already liberated. What good was the experiment?

While the immediate postwar European relief effort had to proceed without Keys's data, the results later supplied a much better understanding of starvation. Neither protein nor vitamin supplements, for example, accelerated recovery from starvation. Recovery was proportionate to the number of calories consumed. Psychologists learned valuable lessons from Keys. Without this experiment, relief efforts today would be less effective.

### Did Dr. Keyes publish his results?

In 1950, Keys published his 1385-page *magnum opus, The Biology of Human Starvation.* It remains the main reference on the subject because it would be very difficult to duplicate.

### Why difficult? How is it hard to starve people? You limit their food and they lose weight while you stand around muttering with a clipboard and calipers and scales.

You'd have to find 36 healthy young people of normal weight willing to give up a year of their lives for no pay while starving away a quarter of their poundage. Yet when interviewed many years later, most of the volunteers said the same thing they would do it again.

- U.S. *wartime handling of conscientious objectors wasn't always so enlightened. Often, the most progressive views came from generals rather than politicians. Dating back to no less a figure than the fire-eating Stonewall Jackson, generals knew that no man could be forced to kill if he absolutely refused. They did not want men on their "rifle strength" who would not shoot to kill: Retaining pacifists in the ranks could hurt morale. So the generals reasoned, it served the army's purpose much better to put the pacifists to work at jobs that freed up able-bodied men willing to kill at need.*

- *Dr. Keys had an interesting uncle: 1920s silent horror film superstar Lon Chaney. Yet while Chaney died of throat cancer before his time, Keys lived to celebrate his hundredth birthday. True to his principles, he refused to attribute his longevity to his dietary advances: he was, he protested, a sample base of one, thus scientifically meaningless.*

- *As important and unique as the experiment was, Keys went on to make other contributions in the field of nutrition. His later research would prove the link between fat consumption and blood cholesterol. If you have ever acted upon concern about either, you've taken Keys's advice.*

- *Anyone who's ever been treated for* anorexia nervosa *can also thank Dr. Keys. In hindsight, the experiment came closer to duplicating anorexia than the conditions of concentration camp survivors. The study teaches doctors that some symptoms result from anorexia itself as a mental health condition, whereas some are merely side effects of hunger. Without treating the hunger, treating the psychology of anorexia is ineffective.*

- *Loss of body fat made Keys's subjects sharply susceptible to chills. Whenever time and weather permitted, the painfully lean men could be found stretched out on the grass, sunning themselves.*

# THE DUBIOUS HEROICS OF ERNEST HEMINGWAY

*Legendary writer Ernest Hemingway was no stranger to war. But his exploits in World War II were atypical, to say the least.*

Ernest Hemingway made his mark writing about war and using his wartime experiences as inspiration for his compelling novels. While he had a tendency to embellish his personal involvement in the fighting, Hemingway took part in some of the major wars of the twentieth century.

During the First World War, Hemingway was an ambulance driver in northern Italy. His experiences there gave him material for his 1929 novel *A Farewell to Arms*.

As a correspondent for the North American Newspaper Alliance in the Spanish Civil War, Hemingway wrote detailed reports about his experiences on the front lines directly in the line of fire. His epic novel *For Whom the Bell Tolls* was promoted as a literary manifestation of his real-life wartime experience in Spain. Truth was, he was seldom close to the action. However, his connections to leftist factions in Spain did attract the attention of J. Edgar Hoover's FBI, who would keep a file on Hemingway.

These dubious battles, as Hemingway expert Kelley Dupuis has called them, helped build the Hemingway myth. The onset of World War II provided Hemingway with new opportunities to further expand the legend.

## HUNTING U-BOATS IN THE CARIBBEAN

Shortly after America's entry into the war, Hemingway volunteered to use his famed fishing boat, *Pilar,* to hunt for German submarines along Cuba's northern coast. The U.S. government had been using Q-ships, which were armed vessels disguised as civilian boats, to lure submarines and attack them with grenades and gunfire. (The plan may have had some merit as German subs often stopped local fishing boats to confiscate their catch and provisions.) Being short of ships for the proposed operation, the government accepted Hemingway's offer to turn *Pilar* into a Q-ship.

While the U.S. government thought the plan credible, Hemingway's third wife, war correspondent Martha Gellhorn, didn't. She mocked the idea as nothing more than a scheme for skirting fuel-rationing regulations so that Hemingway and his buddies could continue fishing and drinking as they pleased.

Maybe Gellhorn was right. Despite regular patrols, including one of 40 days and one sighting of a U-boat, Hemingway and his crew accomplished nothing. The quixotic mission was soon ended by FBI director J. Edgar Hoover, partly because his agency assumed responsibility for counter-espionage in the Caribbean and stopped all Q-ship operations in October 1943, and partly because Hoover had long suspected Hemingway of being a dangerous subversive.

## STORMING ASHORE AT OMAHA BEACH

By June 1944, *Collier's Weekly* had hired Hemingway to work as a war correspondent and sent him to cover the D-Day landings. Hemingway rode aboard an LCVP landing craft as it approached Omaha beach. After disembarking the troops the LCVP turned and headed back to its ship with Hemingway still aboard.

But Hemingway resented that he had been kept back from the action, and with his typical embellishment, he wrote his story as if he had stormed the beach with the troops, even implying that he helped find the designated landing location. He was further insulted upon hearing that Gellhorn, by then more a rival war correspondent than a wife, scooped him by actually making it to shore the next day disguised as a nurse.

## ROLLING WITH THE U.S. ARMY

*Collier's* later assigned Hemingway to accompany units of General George Patton's 3rd Army as it rolled toward Paris. Here his fondness for showboating and military role-playing really showed. At Ville-dieu-les-Poêles, near Paris, Hemingway allegedly threw three grenades into a cellar where SS officers were hiding. He later posed as an unofficial liaison officer at Château de Rambouillet.

Things got stranger still. Hemingway soon assumed the guise of a partisan leader, making flamboyant appearances as commander of a band of irregular French Resistance fighters, later claiming his posse was part of the first vanguard of American troops to liberate Paris. Rivals soon joked that the only thing the hard-drinking Hemingway liberated was the Ritz Hotel.

## EATING CROW TO SAVE HIS BACON

As Dupuis states, Hemingway had by 1944 done such a good job of building his mythical public persona that the world routinely accepted his embellishments as the truth. Inevitably though, his ability to be so convincing got him into serious trouble.

A complaint was filed that his activities during the war violated Geneva Convention rules regarding the conduct of news correspondents in war zones. Brought before a military panel, he had to repudiate all his battlefield feats and deny having taken part in any actual fighting to avoid having his reporter's credentials revoked and being expelled from France.

For a man who spent a lifetime building and promoting his own legend, it must have been an extremely painful and humiliating moment.

✯　　✯　　✯

- *Hemingway's estimates of the number of Germans he personally killed varied from 26 to a gaudy 122.*

✯　　✯　　✯

- *French civilians erroneously assumed that "Papa" was a U.S. officer—a misapprehension that Hemingway did nothing to correct. Top-quality champagne was among his largely undeserved gifts and rewards.*

✯　　✯　　✯

- *Despite the questionable nature of some of Hemingway's claims, his assertions have typically received little attention from his biographers, who prefer instead to focus on his "serious" works and his flamboyant personal life.*

# THE SULLIVAN BROTHERS

*The tragic loss of five brothers who volunteered and served in the South Pacific epitomized America's dedication to winning the war.*

On February 14, 1942, the crew of the light cruiser USS *Juneau* stood tall and proud as their ship was commissioned in a ceremony held at the New York Navy Yard. Members of the commissioning crew included the five Sullivan brothers of Waterloo, Iowa: Albert, Francis, George, Joseph, and Madison.

The brothers, whose motto was "We Stick Together," stipulated as a condition of their enlistment that they be allowed to serve aboard the same ship. Despite accepted navy policy, which discouraged but did not forbid family members from serving together, their request was approved.

After the *Juneau's* Atlantic christening, the cruiser was assigned to the South Pacific. On November 13, 1942, the *Juneau* participated in an intense naval battle near Guadalcanal. One torpedo launched from Japanese submarine I-26 scored a direct hit on *Juneau's* magazine. The resulting explosion cut the cruiser in half. *Juneau* sank within minutes, taking many of the trapped crew to watery deaths.

While dozens of *Juneau's* crew were killed in the initial explosion, approximately 115 sailors survived the attack. All but ten perished in the following days as they awaited rescue. Survivor accounts indicated four of the Sullivan brothers died in the initial explosion, while the fifth, George, survived the attack but died in the water five days later.

The Sullivan brothers were survived by their parents, sister, and one spouse. News of the brothers' deaths was exploited for the war effort. A navy press release dated February 9, 1943, stated that the Sullivans' parents visited "war production plants urging employees to work harder."

President Roosevelt wrote a letter to Mrs. Sullivan after learning her sons were listed as missing in action: ". . .the entire nation shares your sorrow. I offer you the condolence and gratitude of our country. We, who remain to carry on the fight, must maintain the spirit in the knowledge that such sacrifice is not in vain. The Navy Department has informed me of the expressed desire of your sons... to serve on the same ship. I am sure that we all take pride in the knowledge that they fought side by side."

Although an act forbidding family members from serving in the same military unit was proposed after the death of the Sullivan brothers, no such act was ever passed by Congress. In addition, no president has ever issued an executive order forbidding family members from serving in the same unit or on the same ship.

Two U.S. Navy ships were named in honor of the Sullivan brothers: USS *The Sullivans* (DD-537; a destroyer) was commissioned in 1943, while USS *The Sullivans* (DDG-68; a guided missile destroyer) was commissioned in 1997.

☆   ☆   ☆

- *Off Norway in April 1940, the Royal Navy destroyer HMS* Glowworm *encountered the much larger German heavy cruiser* Admiral von Hipper. Glowworm *sustained damage and laid smoke as if to flee; it attempted to hit the* Hipper *with torpedoes from behind the smokescreen, but the attacks failed. Thinking he had no other options, Lieutenant Commander Gerard B. Roope gave the command for the* Glowworm *to ram the cruiser. The crew of* Hipper *didn't realize what was happening until too late, and* Glowworm *tore into the starboard side of the ship. As* Glowworm *backed off, it took more damage and began to sink;* Roope *gave the order to abandon ship. Though damaged, the* Hipper *was still alive, and Captain Helmuth Heye positioned the ship to intercept* Glowworm's *survivors—they spent more than an hour rescuing men. Thirty-one of* Glowworm's *crew of 149 survived. They were taken prisoner aboard the* Hipper, *whose men congratulated them on a fight well done. Captain Heye even recommended Lieutenant Commander Roope, who perished at sea, to receive a Victoria Cross—the only time in history the recognition has been recommended by the enemy.*

# "MISTER" LINDBERGH: FIGHTER PILOT

*Franklin Delano Roosevelt tried to prevent American hero and controversial prewar isolationist Charles Lindbergh from serving in the Army Air Corps. Nonetheless, Lindbergh flew combat missions in the Pacific, and even tagged a kill.*

To many he was "Lucky Lindy," the hero pilot who had flown solo across the Atlantic. To others, he was a jaded recluse who fled his native country for Europe after the intense media attention following the kidnapping and murder of his son. Still others knew him as the man to whom the Nazis awarded the Service Cross of the German Eagle, which Charles Lindbergh received during a visit to Germany in 1938. During that visit, Lindbergh was impressed by the energetic, disciplined drive of the German people and their burgeoning war industry. He returned to the United States convinced that Depression-era America could not stand against Germany. Lindbergh used radio spots to plead his isolationist viewpoint. As a member of the America First Committee, Lindbergh delivered speeches that many considered at best naive and at worst anti-Semitic. Then Japan attacked Pearl Harbor, and whatever ambivalence Americans felt about the war dissipated overnight. Lindbergh also shed his isolationist stance and volunteered to resume his commission in the air corps, but President Roosevelt, whom Lindbergh had publicly chastised, refused the airman's services.

Eventually, Lindbergh was permitted to ply his trade as an adviser and spent the first years of the war test-flying virtually every model of American aircraft used in the conflict. Not content with stateside service, however, Lindbergh managed to be assigned as a technical assistant in the Pacific Theater, where he helped pilots acclimate to Chance Vought's very fast F4U Corsair, "the bent-winged bird," and clandestinely participated in several combat missions.

Lindbergh soon got himself attached to the 475th Fighter Group and its gregarious commander, Colonel Charles MacDonald, who took an immediate liking to Lindbergh and agreed to let him fly combat missions with the "Satan's Angels." In deference to Lindbergh's civilian status, the pilots were ordered to refer to the celebrity pilot as "Mister Lindbergh." During his time with the 475th, Lindbergh used flying techniques he'd first perfected during his cross-Atlantic trip to dramatically increase the fuel efficiency of the group's P-38 Lightnings.

On July 28, 1944, Lindbergh's squadron encountered two Mitsubishi 51 Sonias—armed reconnaissance planes—one of which was piloted by Captain Saburo Shimada, a skilled and experienced flyer. The vastly outnumbered enemy planes managed to slip out of the Americans' sights time after time. In the course of the dogfight, Shimada and Lindbergh wound up racing toward each other head-to-head with guns blazing. Despite the fact that Lindbergh had never fought another aircraft, he bore down on the Sonia and let loose a burst of gunfire that stopped the Sonia's engine. At the last possible moment, Lindbergh veered off, and the stricken enemy plane swept by mere feet from him. This was Lindbergh's only confirmed kill of the war.

On August 1, Lindbergh, MacDonald, and several pilots, bored by routine missions escorting bombers and strafing buildings, used Lindberg's fuel-saving techniques to fly to the far-flung Palau islands in search of enemy aircraft. Lindbergh was nearly killed in the resulting dogfight. Word of the incident spread to the U.S. high command, and MacDonald was disciplined and sent stateside on leave. Lindbergh was also ordered home. Lindbergh later claimed that the reason MacDonald was punished was because the flight to Palau had been deemed impossible, and the Air Corps didn't like being proved wrong.

# Timeline

## 1942

**February 27–March 1**
Allied naval squadron is destroyed in the Battle of Java Sea; Japanese ships are free to roam the South Pacific

**March 1**
U.S. aircraft sink U-656 off Newfoundland; this is the first U.S. success against U-boats

**March 6**
German battleship *Tirpitz* is ordered to attack Convoy PQ 12, beginning the German effort to halt convoys to Soviet Union

**March 8**
Japanese take the Burmese capital, Rangoon, severing the final link between the Allies and the Burma Road to China

**March 11**
General MacArthur leaves the Philippines and heads for Australia; he'll assume his new post as supreme commander of Allied forces in the southwest Pacific Theater on March 17

**March 12**
Netherlands East Indies capitulate to the Japanese

**March 30**
Chinese abandon Toungoo, Burma, and retreat toward Assam, India

**April 1**
Partial convoying instituted along U.S. east coast

**April 7**
The air-raid sirens on Malta sound for the 2,000th time since the beginning of the war

**April 9**
The atrocity that will become known as the Bataan death march begins; 75,000 exhausted and starving American and Filipino troops will march some 65 miles; one third of the captives will perish along the way

**April 18**
Japan is blindsided by a carrier-based bombing raid on Tokyo by 16 B-25B bombers hailing from the USS *Hornet*

**April 21**
Germans relieve the Demyansk pocket

**April 29**
Japanese seize Lashio, Burma, closing the Burma Road

**May 4–8**
The Battle of the Coral Sea is fought exclusively between Japanese aircraft and American aircraft carriers

**May 5**
Corregidor surrenders to the Japanese

**May 8**
Germans launch offensive in the Crimea

Japanese capture Mandalay, Burma

**May 14**
Congress establishes the U.S. Women's Army Auxiliary Corps

**May 20**
U.S. intelligence cryptologists unveil Japan's planned attack on Midway Island and a simultaneous diversionary attack on the Aleutians; the U.S. command responds by deploying a large defensive force to Midway

# THE REAL "MAN WHO NEVER WAS"

*When a drowned corpse washed ashore in Spain holding a briefcase of plans to invade Sardinia and Greece, the Nazis thought they'd made an astounding catch. They couldn't have been more wrong.*

The rough tides slapped against the southern Spanish coast in the spring of 1943, carrying the mangled corpse of a British major who appeared to have drowned after his plane crashed into the sea. The body, one of thousands of military men who had met their end in the Mediterranean waters, floated atop a rubber life jacket as the current drifted toward Huelva, Spain. With a war raging in Tunisia across the sea, a drifting military corpse was not such an unusual event.

But this body was different, and it drew the immediate attention of Spanish authorities sympathetic to German and Italian Fascists. Chained to the corpse was a briefcase filled with dispatches from London to Allied Headquarters in North Africa concerning the upcoming Allied invasions of Sardinia and western Greece. The information was passed on to the Nazis, who accepted their apparent stroke of good luck, and now anticipated an Allied strike on the "soft underbelly of Europe."

Unfortunately for them, the whole affair was a risky, carefully contrived hoax.

## RIGGING THE "TROJAN HORSE"

Operation Mincemeat was conceived by British intelligence agents as a deception to convince the Italians and Germans that the target of the next Allied landings would be somewhere other than Sicily, the true target. To throw the Fascists off the trail, British planners decided to find a suitable corpse—a middle-aged white male—put the corpse in the uniform of a military courier, and float the corpse and documents off the coast of Huelva, Spain, where a local Nazi agent was known to be on good terms with local police.

The idea of planting forged documents on a dead body was not new to the Allies. In August 1942, British agents planted a corpse clutching a fake map of minefields in a blown-up scout car. The map was picked up by German troops and made its way to Rommel's headquarters. He obligingly routed his panzers away from the "minefield" and into a region of soft sand, where they quickly bogged down.

This deception, however, would be much grander. If the planted documents made their way up the intelligence chain, Hitler and Mussolini would be expecting an invasion far from the Sicilian coast that Generals Eisenhower, Patton, and Montgomery had targeted for invasion in July 1943.

## THE MAKING OF A MAJOR

Operation Mincemeat, spearheaded by Lieutenant Commander Ewen Montagu, a British naval intelligence officer, and Charles Cholmondeley of Britain's MI5 intelligence service, found its "host" in early 1943 when a Welshman living in London committed suicide by taking rat poison. The substance produced a chemical pneumonia that could be mistaken for drowning. The two operatives gave the deceased man a new, documented identity: "Major William Martin" of the Royal Marines. They literally kept the "major" on ice while arrangements for his new mission were made. To keep Spanish authorities from conducting an autopsy—which would give away the body's protracted post-mortem condition—the agents decided to make "Major Martin" a Roman Catholic, giving him a silver cross and a St. Christopher medallion. They dressed the body, complete with Royal Marine uniform and trench coat, and gave him identity documents and personal letters (including a swimsuit photo of his "fiancée," an intelligence bureau secretary). With a chain used by bank couriers, they fixed the briefcase to his body.

Martin's documents were carefully prepared to show Allied invasions being planned for Sardinia and Greece (the latter bearing the code name Operation Husky). They also indicated that an Allied deception plan would try to convince Hitler that the invasion would take place in Sicily (the site of the real Operation Husky). With everything in order, the agents carefully placed the corpse into a sealed container—dry ice kept the body "fresh" for the ride out to sea.

The submarine HMS *Seraph* carried "Major Martin" on his final journey. On April 28, the *Seraph* left for the Andalusian coast, and two days later the body of a Royal Marine officer washed ashore. Within days, photographs of the major's documents were on their way to *Abwehr* intelligence agents in Berlin.

## TAKING THE BAIT

*Abwehr,* Hitler, and the German High Command swallowed the story. After the war, British intelligence determined that Martin's documents had been opened and resealed before being returned by the Spanish. The German General Staff, believing the papers to be genuine, had alerted units in the Mediterranean to be ready for an invasion of Sardinia and Greece. They moved one panzer division and air and naval assets off the Peloponnese, and disputed Italian fears of an impending invasion of Sicily.

The Allies captured Sicily in July and August 1943, and after the war, Commander Montagu wrote a bestselling account of Operation Mincemeat titled, *The Man Who Never Was.* The book was made into a film thriller a few years later.

Who was Major William Martin? The original body appears to have been a 34-year-old depressed Welsh alcoholic named Glyndwr Michael, and "Major Martin's" tombstone in Spain bears Michael's name. Historians have debated the identity of "Major Martin," however, theorizing that a "fresher" corpse from a sunken aircraft carrier was substituted closer to the launch date.

Whoever the real "Major Martin" may have been, one thing is certain: He saved thousands of lives, and became a war hero and action movie star in the process—quite an accomplishment for a dead man!

# NIGHT WITCHES ON THE RUSSIAN FRONT

*Marina Raskova and her squadron of tenacious female pilots caused the Germans to lose sleep—and, ultimately, the war.*

In November of 1941, the German Army was within 20 miles of Moscow, Stalingrad was under siege, and more than three million Russians had been taken prisoner. If ever there was a time for Russian heroes, this was it. Into that breech stepped a true hero of the Soviet Union—Marina Raskova. The aviatrix with nerves of steel had won the accolades of the Russian people when she helped her three-woman team complete a cross-Siberian flight in 1938. At the end of the grueling flight, she had bailed out into the frozen tundra when the plane's wings became heavy with ice and there was nothing left to throw out.

Three years later, with the Germans howling at the gates, Raskova was granted permission by Stalin to organize three squadrons for defense of the homeland. These squadrons—the 586th Fighter Aviation Regiment, the 588th Night Bomber Regiment, and the 125th Guards Bomber Aviation Regiment—were composed entirely of women, from the pilots to the mechanics. Although all

> "There is one front and one battle where everyone in the United States—every man, woman, and child—is in action...that front is right here at home...everyone will have the privilege of making whatever self-denial is necessary, not only to supply our fighting men, but to keep the economic structure of our country fortified and secure. Never in the memory of man has there been a war in which the courage, the endurance, and the loyalty of civilians played so vital a part. This great war effort must be carried through to its victorious conclusion by the indomitable will and determination of the people as one great whole."
>
> —President Franklin D. Roosevelt, Fireside Chat 21, April 28, 1942

the units performed laudatory feats, the 588th became famous as the *Nachthexen* (German for "night witches") for their daring and tireless night raids on German command posts and tactical targets.

Raskova's reputation notwithstanding, the female aviators encountered a great deal of prejudice and harassment during their service. For instance, the 588th was provided with antiquated, open-cockpit Po-2 biplanes, which had a top speed of 94 miles per hour (slower than most World War I–era planes) and could carry only two small bombs. Nevertheless, the intrepid women developed techniques that maximized the admittedly few advantages of their outmoded aircraft. The women learned to fly low to the ground (sometimes just above the hedgerows) and to cut their engines before reaching the target. Thus, they would glide over the German soldiers undetected until their ordnance had been delivered. They also learned that the plane's slow speed meant that it could out-turn the German Me-109s, which would stall if they tried to match the Po-2 maneuvers. In fact, many German pilots simply gave up trying to shoot down a Po-2, though they were promised an Iron Cross if they could do so. To penetrate searchlight and antiaircraft emplacements, the Night Witches approached the target in groups of three. Once their planes were spotlighted, the two outside planes would break away and the center plane, left in the gap of darkness, would deliver its payload. Then the planes would regroup and make the run again until each had dropped its ordnance.

The Night Witches endured countless hardships during the war. In some cases the women flew as many as 18 missions a night. During the brutal winter of 1942-1943, the women would often have to lie on the wings of their planes to keep the gale winds and ice from blowing the light craft off the airfield. All told, the 588th completed more than 24,000 combat missions by the end of the war. Marina Raskova was killed in January of 1943 while attempting to make an emergency landing but the squadrons that she formed went on to fight in the very skies above Berlin, bringing victory for the Soviet Union.

# Fast Facts

- During the later years of the war, the Japanese government instructed the nation's fortune-tellers to foresee only good things for individuals who sought their prognostications.

- Tipped off by a German POW, Allied units raced to the Ludendorff Bridge at Remagen, the only undestroyed bridge across the Rhine; they arrived just before Nazi engineers could demolish it. Within 24 hours, on March 7, 1945, 8,000 American troops from the 9th Armored Division had crossed it.

- Iwo Jima proved an effective haven for more than 2,200 damaged U.S. bombers that made emergency landings on the island's airstrip.

- Famed British author H.G. Wells met Stalin before the war and declared him to be the most "candid, fair, and honest" man he had ever met.

- On September 21, 1943, singer Kate Smith raised $40 million worth of war bonds during a marathon 18-hour CBS broadcast.

- In March 1944, Mount Vesuvius erupted at Pompeii and destroyed nearly 90 B-25 bombers in a nearby airfield.

- Many states suspended child labor laws during the war and by 1944, roughly three million 12- to 17-year-olds were being paid for war work, mostly in agriculture or simple manufacturing.

- Norma Jean Baker-Dougherty got her first modeling jobs after a picture of her working at an aircraft factory in Bakersfield, California, was published in Yank. She would later take the name Marilyn Monroe when she moved to Hollywood to pursue acting.

- Frank Sinatra was classified 4-F (unfit for duty) during the war because of his punctured eardrums.

- Betty Grable was the number-one GI pinup girl; Rita Hayworth was a close second.

# AGENT 488:
# CARL JUNG AND THE OSS

*World War II called individuals from all walks of life to duty—
even famous scientists had parts to play. In America, Einstein
wrote Roosevelt to suggest the possibility of an atomic bomb.
In Germany, Wernher von Braun raced to build rockets for his
country. And in Switzerland, Carl Jung used his own talents to
offer the world a glimpse into the psyche of a madman.*

## SERVICES IN DEMAND

In the 1930s, Germany had a reputation as a hotbed of scientific
innovation across a variety of disciplines. The Nazis were quick to
take advantage of much of this research in the form of technologi-
cally advanced weapons, but they did view one particular field with
suspicion: psychology. The most well-known figure in this science
was Sigmund Freud, who was Jewish—and although they were
interested in the topic itself, the Nazis couldn't very well make use
of a Jewish scientist.

One alternative was Carl Jung. He was Swiss, of German extraction, and well respected in the field. Moreover, he had written
about the psychological differences inherent in groups of people,
and anything that supported tribal or racial divisions was of interest to the Nazis. They went so far as to suggest that Jung relocate,
and even discussed arresting him on a visit to Berlin just to keep
him in Germany. He declined the invitation, as he also did with an
offer to migrate to the United States, preferring to remain in touch
with his roots. Unfortunately, the German invitation gave rise to a
rumor that he was a Nazi sympathizer, an accusation he called "an
infamous lie."

His accusers needn't have worried. He "despised politics whole-
heartedly" and had little use for Hitler or any other leader except,
perhaps, as an interesting study in the psychology of power. His
independence may have contributed to a request he received in

October 1939 from Nazi doctors, who asked if he would be willing to examine the *Führer;* Hitler had been behaving erratically, and his personal doctors were worried. Jung turned down the invitation, already convinced that the German leader was at least half crazy. He went on to offer the opinion that both Hitler and the German people were possessed, but his invectives were directed at both sides—he once referred to Roosevelt as the "limping messenger of the apocalypse" and believed that the president had all the makings of a dictator.

## RECRUITING AGENT 488

Regardless of the views he harbored about both leaders, Jung did contribute to the Allied cause. In 1942, American agent Allen Dulles (who would go on to head the CIA) arrived in Berne, Switzerland, which he used as a base to monitor German activity. He enlisted the aid of an American expatriate of some local notoriety, Mary Bancroft, who eventually also became Dulles's lover. Bancroft had been a patient of Jung's, and the two had formed a mutual attachment. Knowing of their association, Dulles began posing questions to the famous psychologist through Bancroft, soliciting his opinion on "a weekly, if not daily basis."

The two eventually met, and Dulles continued to rely on Jung to analyze various events. Jung's responses found their way into Dulles's reports to the OSS, with Jung listed as the source under the code name "Agent 488." Of particular interest was Jung's insight into the personality of the Nazi leaders, especially of Hitler. Dulles urged the OSS to pay particular attention to Jung's analysis of the *Führer,* which included the opinion that Hitler was capable of anything up until the very end, at which point Jung could not "exclude the possibility of suicide in a desperate moment."

The analysis, of course, proved prophetic: Hitler became increasingly debilitated and unstable as the war progressed, eventually taking his own life, trapped in his own bunker. After the conflict, the records detailing Jung's full involvement were strictly classified, but Allen Dulles offered one evaluation: "Nobody will probably ever know how much Professor Jung contributed to the Allied cause during the war."

# ARCHITECTS GO TO WAR

*Two of the world's most prominent architects helped build
German and Japanese working-class villages in the Utah desert.
For good reason, no one ever inhabited the buildings.*

In 1942, with war raging in the Pacific and in Europe, the U.S.
military in conjunction with Standard Oil Company constructed
two villages in the Utah desert. The first was modeled after a
typical Japanese worker's village; the second was designed to the
specifications of German housing for low-wage workers.

The military spared no expense in creating the replica villages.
They hired prominent architects to design the structures. Prison
laborers constructed the edifices in record time. In the case of
the German village, wood was imported from Russia, and the
buildings were hosed down to replicate the wet Prussian weather.
Finally, designers from RKO Picture Studios furnished the buildings in exact detail, from the bedding, linen, and drapes to the
paper wall partitions typical of Japanese interior design and bulky
furniture characteristic of German working families' homes.

When the buildings were finally just right, the army destroyed
them using napalm, gas, anthrax, and incendiary bombs.

Then they rebuilt them and blew them up again...and again.

The site was the Dugway Proving Grounds weapons-testing area
90 miles southwest of Salt Lake City. Created at the request of
President Roosevelt, the program's goal was to measure, as accurately as possible, the potential damage from anticipated massive
aerial bombing campaigns on enemy cities—in particular, the
effects upon the manufacturing segment of the populations. To
further this end, the army staff hired two influential architects
whose unique knowledge of their respective subjects made them
ideal candidates to design mock structures for the tests. Certainly
neither man had ever contemplated designing a structure so that it
could be immediately destroyed.

## ERICH MENDELSOHN

Erich Mendelsohn was a Russian-Polish Jew from Germany who had interrupted his architecture studies to drive a Red Cross ambulance for the Kaiser's army during the First World War. His bold modernist designs marked him as a master of steel and concrete structures that utilized space to create a unique identity for each project. Paramount among his early work is the Einstein Tower, which still stands in Potsdam near Berlin. Persecuted by the Nazis, Mendelsohn moved first to London and then to Palestine. Eventually, Mendelsohn relocated to the United States where he addressed and befriended peers such as Frank Lloyd Wright. Perhaps because of his persecution by the Nazis, Mendelsohn was eager to assist in the design of German worker housing for the Dugway tests. He was particularly useful in the design of the roofs, which would receive the brunt of any bomb damage. When Germany surrendered in May of 1945, Allied raids had eliminated 45 percent of German housing.

## ANTONIN RAYMOND

Antonin Raymond was a native Bohemian who had emigrated to the United States in 1910. In 1916, he worked as an associate in Frank Lloyd Wright's studio Taliesin, in Wisconsin, and aided in the design of the Imperial Hotel in Tokyo. While in Tokyo, Raymond developed a deep fondness for Japanese design—a passion that would last his entire life. Nevertheless, he was amicable when the U.S. Army asked him to design the Japanese village at Dugway. Constructed almost entirely of wood, the mock village burned to the ground after a few tests. Its fate predicted that of real Japanese cities that were bombed during the war. In a single raid upon the paper-and-wood city of Asakua, for instance, 334 B-29 bombers dropped 2,000 tons of napalm and destroyed an unprecedented 265,171 buildings.

✯   ✯   ✯

- *The German-style buildings at Dugway were modeled on "rent barracks"—Germany's most densely packed urban slums.*

# DEFENDING THE HOME FRONT: THE FBI IN WORLD WAR II

*In the late 1930s, the Federal Bureau of Investigation (FBI) held the full confidence of the American public. Its G-men and their boss, the legendary J. Edgar Hoover, were looked on as heroes, and their tireless efforts to bring criminals to justice made them the subject of radio shows and even bubblegum cards. With the outbreak of the war in Europe, they were given an additional new responsibility: defending the United States against an enemy Hoover referred to as "international gangsters."*

## ENEMIES WITHIN

In 1933, J. Edgar Hoover, head of the agency that would become the FBI two years later, was called on to investigate a death threat that had been made against Adolf Hitler. At the close of the 1930s, however, the United States was at least as interested in tracking the activities of the German leader as it was in his well-being. In 1936, President Roosevelt asked Hoover to use his agency to produce a "broad picture" view of Fascist and Communist activities in the United States. Hoover, always extremely concerned with the possible existence of subversives, instructed his agency to proceed to gather information from "all possible sources." Those sources included covert means and illicit wiretaps, since this new function was not public knowledge. However, by 1939, the need for such secrecy disappeared when Roosevelt publicly announced that he was giving the Bureau the responsibility of handling cases of espionage, violation of neutrality laws, and sabotage.

With official sanction in place, the FBI began establishing the range of powers it would use throughout the war:

- The Bureau expanded its domestic surveillance program, asking telegram companies to delay sending messages until the

FBI had time to make copies. Eventually the companies found it easier to simply make the copies themselves and hand them over to the agency.

- The Bureau hunted down draft dodgers.

- At least one agent trained in industrial security was placed in each field office to combat possible saboteurs.

- Special Intelligence Service divisions outside U.S. borders were set up to combat Axis activities in Latin America.

- Double agents were recruited to pass on false information to the country's adversaries for the length of the war.

The FBI also produced and monitored a list of potential Axis sympathizers: the Custodial Detention List. It put the list to use immediately after the attack on Pearl Harbor, overseeing the arrests of 3,846 people. Though his agency participated in those arrests, Hoover was against the more widespread internment of the Japanese-American populace that took place later, considering it an affront to the abilities of his Bureau. In his opinion the FBI had already identified all possible sources of danger, and further detentions were unnecessary.

## PASTORIUS AND MAGPIE

Paranoia about an enemy fifth column, or saboteurs, ran rampant through America, but it was not without basis, as two prominent incidents prove. In June 1942, Germany attempted to strike at America's home front in an action called Operation Pastorius. The Nazi intelligence service had recruited eight English-speaking men who were trained in explosives, chemistry, secret writing, and how to blend into American surroundings. One had even served in the U.S. military. The men were given thousands of dollars, some of which was for bribes, and instructions to destroy targets ranging from power plants to Jewish-owned businesses. They entered the country via U-boats off the coasts of Amagansett, Long Island and Ponte Vedra Beach, Florida, intent on creating havoc. The plot began to unravel when the Coast Guard found traces of the Long Island landing and alerted the FBI. Finally, one of the saboteurs turned himself in to the FBI, leading to the capture of the other seven.

A second operation, code-named Magpie, took place in November 1944 when Germany landed two agents in Maine. The men were charged with observing the 1944 presidential election as well as obtaining any technical information they could find on rocketry or nuclear research. The men were spotted and reported to the FBI by at least two people, one a Boy Scout living up to his promise to do his duty to his country. Again, one of the conspirators turned himself in to the FBI, and the operation was quickly shut down.

The agency made the most of these events from a public relations point of view. The Bureau downplayed the saboteur who turned himself in, and instead gave the public an image of an agency inexorably hunting down Axis spies. Despite the blatant public-relations maneuvering, there was legitimate cause for pride. The FBI left the war years much stronger than it had entered them, having increased its workforce from 700 to 12,000 people in a decade, and the U.S. home front was largely safe from serious attacks during the war.

☆　　☆　　☆

- *Throughout the war, an FBI agent trained in defense-plant security was placed in every Bureau field office.*

☆　　☆　　☆

- *Although the Kremlin instructed the American Communist Party to maintain a neutral stance during the war, the FBI nevertheless monitored domestic Party activity.*

☆　　☆　　☆

- *In the two years following the December 1941 Japanese attack on Pearl Harbor, Hawaii, the number of FBI employees increased from 7,400 to more than 13,000. Many of the newcomers were National Academy graduates who were brought into the fold after accelerated training courses.*

# GERMANY'S SIEGE GUNS: HEAVY GUSTAV AND MIGHTY DORA

*Soviet fortifications protecting the city of Sevastopol crumbled under the onslaught as the world's largest cannon fired its 17-foot-long, 7-ton shells, each capable of penetrating 80 yards of earth and leaving a crater nearly 90 feet across.*

Prior to the outbreak of World War II, the German High Command contracted the Krupp Works, an armaments company, to design a siege gun capable of destroying heavy fortifications, particularly the French Maginot Line. The result was the world's largest railway gun, an approximately 1,300-ton, 800-mm monster with a barrel 107 feet long. It could fire a 7-ton armor-piercing or high-explosive shell to reach targets nearly 24 miles away.

The first model was built in 1939 and successfully tested in 1940, resulting in the order of two operational guns that were christened *Schwere* Gustav ("Heavy Gustav"), named after the chief designer, and Dora, named after the senior engineer's wife. Assembly and transportation of the guns, which could take up to six weeks, required a crew of more than 2,000.

## HEAVY GUSTAV

Heavy Gustav was manufactured too late to be utilized in operations against the Maginot Line, but the German High Command believed it would be useful as a siege gun.

The goliath cannon reached Russia in early spring 1942 for the siege of Sevastopol and was operational by the first week of June. During its 13-day deployment, Gustav fired approximately 48 rounds, hitting four Russian forts and destroying an ammunition dump protected by concrete more than 30 feet thick.

After the siege of Sevastopol, Gustav spent the winter of 1942–

43 near Leningrad. Gustav's last combat use occurred against the Warsaw Uprising in Poland during April and May 1943. During the retreat from Eastern Europe, German troops destroyed Gustav in a forest in southeastern Germany during the spring of 1945.

## MIGHTY DORA

Dora was the sister to Heavy Gustav, but she didn't enjoy the operational success of her brother. Deployed ten miles west of Stalingrad in mid-August 1942, the railway gun was withdrawn a month later to keep it from being captured as the Russians threatened to encircle German forces. There is no evidence that Dora fired a shot during the war. Her remains were found by American troops soon after those of Gustav in 1945.

# AMERICAN WOMEN IN UNIFORM BREAK BARRIERS

*They flew Flying Fortresses from factories to airfields, translated secret radio transmissions from the French underground, and helped build the atomic bomb. American women who joined military auxiliary units during the war shattered many stereotypes, but not without their share of opposition.*

After Pearl Harbor, every branch of military service established auxiliary branches for women to serve, freeing many men to fight abroad. Hundreds of thousand of women served in the Women's Army Auxiliary Corps (WAAC), the Women Accepted for Volunteer Emergency Service (WAVES), the Women's Auxiliary Air Force (WAAF), the Women's Airforce Service Pilots (WASP), the Marine Corps Women's Reserve (MCWR), and the SPARS of the Coast Guard.

## THE NAVY'S FIRST FEMALE OFFICER

In 1942, Mildred H. McAfee became the first female commissioned officer in U.S. Navy history when she was sworn in as a Naval Reserve Lieutenant Commander, serving as the first director of the WAVES. A year later, 27,000 WAVES were in service. While most held clerical positions, WAVES also worked in aviation, the Judge Advocate General's Corps, and intelligence.

## DANGER IN THE SKIES

More than 1,000 women earned their WASP wings, logging over 60 million miles of operational flights. Though their jobs were risky, the WASPs were considered civilian employees and didn't receive military benefits. Piloting aircraft from factories to military bases or towing aerial targets for training, the female pilots freed up experienced male pilots for combat duty. Thirty-eight WASP pilots lost their lives in service. The corps was disbanded in December 1944, after a Congressional bill to give WASPs full military status and benefits failed to win approval.

# SERVING WITH DISTINCTION, OVERSEAS AND AT HOME

Founded on May 14, 1942, the U.S. Army's WAAC was the largest military branch in which women served, with 150,000 enlisting by the end of the war. At first, some U.S. politicians and the American public had difficulty accepting women in army uniform. "Who will then do the cooking, the washing, the mending, the humble homey tasks to which every woman has devoted herself; who will nurture the children?" asked one Congressional opponent of the corps. Even after the WAAC was formed, the women did not earn as much as men, nor did they receive any military benefits until November 1942, when Congress passed a second bill giving the corps full military status. Simultaneously, "Auxiliary" was dropped from the corps's name.

Though many WAACs worked in office support roles, others served as mechanics, weather forecasters, cryptographers, radio operators, mechanics, parachute riggers, bombsight maintenance specialists, intelligence analysts, and control-tower operators. Overseas positions were highly coveted by WAAC personnel. Third Officers Martha Rogers, Mattie Pinette, Ruth Briggs, Alene Drezmal, and Louise Anderson became the first WAACs deployed overseas when they joined General Eisenhower's headquarters in Algiers in 1943. They followed his command until V-E Day two years later. "Their contributions in efficiency, skill, spirit and determination are immeasurable," said Eisenhower of WAACs under his command in 1945.

Despite exemplary service records, gossip and bad publicity severely curtailed WAAC recruitment in 1943. Enlisted men ridiculed the idea that females could be soldiers, and many forbade their wives or girlfriends to join. Rumors of promiscuity were widely reported, but an investigation by the War Department found nearly all of the gossip unsubstantiated. However, an early

WAAC slogan, "Release a Man for Combat," was reconsidered as a bad choice of words and changed to "Replace a Man for Combat." In the Pacific, a theater where many U.S. servicemen had not seen an American woman in 18 months, WAACs were escorted by armed guards and lived inside compounds surrounded by barbed wire. Despite the tribulations, Generals Marshall and Eisenhower remained supportive of the WAAC, and many servicemen who worked with WAACs were impressed with their service.

Several WAACS worked on the Manhattan Project. At the Los Alamos atomic laboratory, Master Sergeant Elizabeth Wilson ran a cyclotron and Jane Heydorn worked as an electronics technician. In Italy, the 6669th Headquarters Platoon of General Mark Clark's 5th Army became one of the most famous WAAC units, often serving within a few miles of the front line. In Great Britain, WAAC stenographer Ruth Blanton worked in army intelligence, translating radio reports from the French underground that specified bridge locations and German-troop strengths in preparation for D-Day. In February 1945, a battalion of 800 African-American WAACs was stationed in Birmingham, England, and later Paris. They were responsible for directing mail to all U.S. personnel in the European Theater. In the Southwestern Pacific, many WAACs who had been sent as clerks and typists were immediately retrained as drivers and mechanics. In the Philippines, WAAC units moved into Manila three days after the city's occupation.

After the war, WAAC director Oveta Culp was awarded the Distinguished Service Medal, the second highest U.S. military decoration. In 1948, the service's new director, Colonel Mary A. Hallaren, became the first commissioned female officer in the U.S. Army. WAACs went on to serve in the Korean and Vietnam wars. The WAAC was disbanded in 1978, and women were integrated into regular units of the U.S. Army.

☆   ☆   ☆

- *Women of the U.S. Navy WAVES didn't shoot Axis soldiers, but they taught the men the fine art of doing so. Many women became naval gunnery instructors.*

# ROLLIN' WITH THE BIG BOYS

*The story of the Allied war effort in World War II is too often told solely from the perspective of the "Big Three." But eventually 55 countries throughout the world, including many small and less prominent nations, joined the Allied cause—earning the right to share in the victory with the great powers.*

Many historical accounts tend to downplay or even ignore the contribution of smaller or less powerful countries to the Allied cause, focusing on the major Allied players: the United States, Great Britain, and the Soviet Union. The fact is, 55 countries of assorted sizes and strengths contributed to the Allied war effort to varying degrees, ranging from providing significant quantities of fighting men and war materiel to merely offering political support. In the end, it all added up to victory.

Here's a brief look at the how some of the smaller Allied countries factored in the win.

## NEW ZEALAND

New Zealand declared war on Germany on September 4, 1939, making it one of the original Allied countries along with Britain, France, Poland, and Australia. Over the course of the war, 140,000 men and women from New Zealand served in army, navy, air force, and auxiliary units in North Africa, Italy, Southeast Asia and the south Pacific. Upright British officers were irked by the New Zealanders' disdain for proper military protocol, but couldn't help but respect the Kiwis' tenacious fighting spirit.

Thousands of Kiwis served in British or New Zealand naval and air force units. The vast majority, however, fought in infantry units as part of the Second New Zealand Expeditionary Force (2NZEF). Some 104,000 New Zealander soldiers fought in some of the war's toughest battles, including Crete, El Alamein, Cassino,

Singapore, and Bougainville. By war's end, New Zealand counted 11,625 killed in action, giving it the grim distinction of having the highest ratio of fatal casualties per capita among all the Commonwealth nations.

New Zealand itself experienced an armed invasion of sorts. More than 100,000 U.S. servicemen were stationed in the country, as it became a prime jump-off point for American operations in the Pacific.

## MOROCCO

Morocco's fierce Goumier mountain fighters, known as Goums, were used as a spearhead raiding force against German alpine defenses in Tunisia and Italy. The Goums were tough, nomadic indigenous people who were highly skilled in traversing nearly impassible mountain terrain. They wore ankle-length striped robes called *djellabas* rather than regulation uniforms and sported long beards and pigtails, which they said provided Allah with handles to carry them to heaven when their time came. They preferred fighting at night and in close quarters using knives, which they wielded with deadly skill. The Goums had a reputation as bloodthirsty fighters, particularly for their tendency to cut off the ears or heads of enemy soldiers. A French officer once asked a Goum going out on patrol to bring him back a German wristwatch—he was later handed the severed forearm of a German soldier with a watch still attached.

Some 12,000 Goums fought in Italy as part of the French Expeditionary Force. Their defining moment came in May 1944 when they unraveled German strongholds in the imposing Aurunci and Lepini mountains that blocked the southern approach to Rome. Their actions forced the Germans to abandon the ranges and opened the way to Rome through the Liri Valley. The Goums pursued the Germans northward through the Italian mountains to Siena before being transferred with the French Expeditionary Force for the invasion of southern France. The Goums continued to fight with effectiveness through the French Alps and into southern Germany.

# MEXICO

Mexico's most notable contribution to the Allied war effort was the Mexican Expeditionary Air Force. Three squadrons of Mexican fighter pilots were trained in the United States, but only one squadron, the 201st Fighter Squadron, saw combat duty. Indeed, it was the only Mexican military unit to see action outside Mexico during the war.

The 201st was commissioned in February 1945 and transferred to the Philippines in April as part of the U.S. Air Force's 58th Fighter Group. Flying P-47 Thunderbolt fighters, the 201st carried out 96 combat missions, primarily in support of American ground troops in Luzon in June and July 1945.

# NEPAL

Some of the most fearsome soldiers to fight on the side of the Allies came from Nepal. The famed Gurkha warriors of the Himalayan highlands had served in the British Indian Army since the 1850s and eagerly answered the call again during World War II. More than 112,000 Gurkha soldiers in 40 battalions fought alongside British and Commonwealth troops in far-flung locations ranging from Italy, North Africa, and the Middle East to Burma, Malaya, and Singapore. British officers commanding the best of the Gurkha battalions considered their units superior to most in the regular British Army.

The Gurkhas earned a reputation among their fellow Allied soldiers for being tough, brave, and extremely likable. They excelled in solo attacks against enemy bunkers and machine-gun nests and seldom lost in hand-to-hand fights. In close encounters, a Gurkha readily traded his rifle for his *kukri,* a boomerang-shape machete with a razor-sharp inner blade. (An unsheathed *kukri* was announced by the battle cry, *"Aayo bir Gorkhali!"*—"The Gurkhas are upon you!") Allied soldiers asking to see the exotic knives would gape in bewilderment when their Gurkha comrades nicked their own fingers with the blade before returning it to its casing: Gurkha tradition dictated that a *kukri* could not be unsheathed without drawing blood.

# THE PHILIPPINES

At the time of the Japanese invasion of the Philippines in December 1941, the regular Philippine Army boasted 100,000 troops. But the vast majority of them were raw recruits who were insufficiently trained, badly under-equipped, and poorly led. Approximately 65,000 Filipino soldiers were taken prisoner by the Japanese during the battle for the Philippines. But most remaining units of the Philippine Army didn't give up the fight. Instead, they melted into the jungles and mountains and formed the backbone of a hardy guerrilla force that incessantly harassed the Japanese during their three-year occupation of the islands.

By the time of MacArthur's return to the Philippines in October 1944, approximately 250,000 Filipino guerillas were actively fighting the Japanese. They provided invaluable reconnaissance and fighting support to American forces throughout the campaign to liberate the Philippines. They also played a major role in one of the most dramatic operations of the campaign—the liberation of the Cabanatuan POW camp.

The Cabanatuan raid was led by the U.S. Army 6th Ranger Battalion, which carried out the main assault against the camp and freed the POWs. But it's highly unlikely that the raid would have succeeded without the vital contribution of several hundred Filipino guerrillas led by former Philippine Army captains Eduardo Joson and Juan Pajota. The guerillas provided key preraid intelligence to the rangers and mobilized support from the local civilians for food and transportation to evacuate sick and wounded POWs. Most importantly, the guerrillas sealed off all routes to the camp and fought off 800 Japanese troops attempting to abort the raid and subsequent evacuation.

☆ ☆ ☆

- *Many of France's finest soldiers were African. Senegalese, Moroccans, Kenyans, Ghanaians, Algerians, Tunisians, and ethnic French colonists served effectively in the French and Free French armies.*

# Fast Facts

- German-born actress Marlene Dietrich ignored a personal order from Hitler asking her to return to Germany in 1937. She was outspoken about her distaste for the Nazi party, and in 1939 she became a U.S. citizen.

- About 12,000 Allied aircraft supported the Normandy invasion.

- When U.S. Marines landed on Guam, they were greeted by a sign that read, "Welcome Marines." The sign had been left by U.S. Navy frogmen who had earlier scouted the area for mines.

- Franklin Delano Roosevelt was elected to a fourth term in 1944 with a narrow 53 percent majority of the popular vote over Thomas Dewey. However, he received 432 electoral votes to Dewey's 99.

- General Douglas MacArthur had to cancel his planned victory parade through Manila in the Philippines because the city had been almost completely destroyed.

- In 1939, the Nazis developed a plane capable of flying from Berlin to New York in about 20 hours. Hitler had his own Focke Wulf Fw 200, Immelmann III, on standby in case he needed to escape to Japan.

- Roughly 1,300 German V-2 rockets were fired at England between September 1944 and March 1945, killing 2,724 people. In that same time, Antwerp, Belgium, was subjected to 1,265 attacks. An article in the March 1945 issue of Time referred to Antwerp as the "City of Sudden Death."

- In 1945, Magda Goebbels gave each of her six children drugged candy to put them to sleep before fatally poisoning them in the Führerbunker.

- On May 5, 1945, 560 Japanese kamikaze attacks were launched against the U.S. fleet supporting the Okinawa invasion.

- Between 1943 and the end of the war, the Broadway musical Oklahoma! gave 43 free performances for servicemen.

# GENERAL GEORGE PATTON: GUTS AND GLORY

*Profane. Pious. Aggressive. Poetic. A tactical genius, but politically inept. More than 60 years after his death, General George S. Patton, Jr., fascinates us like no other American general of the last century.*

Born in southern California in 1880, young George Smith Patton was raised on stories of his ancestors' exploits in the Scottish wars, the American Revolution, and the Civil War. He was a slow learner—he did not learn to read until he was 11 years old, and he may have been an undiagnosed dyslexic—yet his early love of military history laid the foundation for an understanding of war that few people have ever attained.

## RISING THROUGH THE RANKS

Patton graduated from West Point in the middle of his class in 1909, having repeated his first year after failing mathematics. He married into one of Boston's wealthiest families, and spent the next seven years in routine postings learning the basics of cavalry command.

As a junior officer, Patton worked hard to establish himself in the eyes of his superiors through a variety of extracurricular activities. He represented the army on the U.S. Olympic team in 1912 (Patton finished fifth in the first-ever modern pentathlon), he redesigned the cavalry saber in 1913, and he rewrote army swordsmanship doctrine. In 1916 Second Lieutenant Patton persuaded General John J. Pershing to bring him to Mexico as an aide during Pershing's expedition against insurgent leader Pancho Villa. Patton's point-blank gun battle with a band of Villistas made him a momentary hero, and the next year he followed Pershing to France as America entered the Great War.

In France, Patton broke with the cavalry to command a unit of light tanks in the newly formed Tank Corps. He spent six months writing and refining the army's light tank doctrine, in which he always preached the offensive. Patton set forth the tanker's credo in his general orders:

If you are left alone in the midst of the enemy, keep shooting. If your gun is disabled, use your pistols and squash the enemy with your tracks.... As long as one tank is able to move it must go forward. Its presence will save the lives of hundreds of infantry and kill many Germans....

Practicing what he preached, Patton led his battalion in Pershing's St. Mihiel offensive of 1918. In September of that year, Patton (now a temporary lieutenant colonel) took a serious bullet wound through the thigh while leading his tankers in the Meuse-Argonne offensive.

The end of the war threw Patton and the rest of the army into an aimless two-decade drift of boredom, rank reductions, and personnel cuts. The War Department folded his beloved Tank Corps into the infantry, and Patton returned to the cavalry for the next 20 years, where he earned a reputation as an ultra-competitive polo player, a prolific writer on military topics, a tough taskmaster, and the army's most aggressive combat commander. The only problem, as Patton saw it, was that there was no war in which he could put his talents to use.

But as war clouds formed on the European horizon, the awakening army made changes that would put Patton's years of study, writing, and training to use. Patton again left the cavalry to take charge of the 2nd Armored Division of the newly reconstituted Armored Force (nicknamed "Hell on Wheels"). Before long, Patton (now a major general) had established the army's desert training center in California, where tankers began preparing for war in North Africa.

## PUTTING HIS METHODS TO THE TEST

World War II provided an outlet for Patton's martial genius. Serving under the command of his old prewar friend, Lieutenant General Dwight D. Eisenhower, Patton commenced his second war by leading a large landing force in the November 1942 invasion of North Africa. When fighting in the Axis stronghold of Tunisia bogged down after the American defeat at Kasserine Pass, Eisenhower ordered Patton to take charge of the U.S. II Corps, the only all-American combat formation in North Africa. Patton soon led the Americans to a small but impressive victory at El Guettar before turning over command to his deputy, Major General Omar N. Bradley.

Patton left the North African fighting to plan America's participation in the invasion of Sicily, the next major Allied objective. Commanding the U.S. 7th Army alongside the British Army of General Bernard L. Montgomery, Patton's men fought their way ashore and swept over the western half of the island. When Eisenhower's ground commander ordered Montgomery to follow the main highways to Messina, the main Axis base, Patton swept around Montgomery and fought his way along Sicily's north coast in a brilliant series of land and amphibious hops. He beat Monty to Messina, and became a national hero for his leadership.

## A HOT TEMPER AND SHARP TONGUE

Patton's simple yet eloquently profane approach appealed to his enlisted men. "Hold 'em by the nose and kick 'em in the pants," which meant pinning the enemy with heavy fire along its front, and enveloping it with mobile forces from the flank and rear, was his way of explaining his method of fighting. He once declared:

When I want my men to remember something important, to really make it stick, I give it to them double dirty. It may not sound nice to some bunch of little old ladies at an afternoon tea party, but it helps my soldiers to remember. You can't run an army without profanity; and it has to be eloquent profanity. An army without profanity couldn't fight its way out of a piss-soaked paper bag.

In August 1943, as his military reputation reached its zenith, Patton encountered two battle-fatigued soldiers whom he suspected of cowardice. Working himself into a violent, cursing rage, he slapped the enlisted men, violating army regulations and putting Eisenhower under intense pressure to send him home. Eisenhower, however, retained Patton on the condition that he apologize to the men he had offended.

As Allied attention drew toward the French coast, Patton's mouth again got him into trouble. An ill-advised public comment that predicted Anglo-American world domination—at the expense of the Soviet allies—landed him back in the political doghouse. Instead of participating in the major D-Day operations, he led a dummy army to hold German attention near Calais. When he returned to France, he would be working under his old deputy, General Bradley.

## LEADING HIS MEN TO VICTORY

In France, Patton led the U.S. 3rd Army across central France in a dash to the Rhine. As he was about to push through Germany's Siegfried Line, he received word of Hitler's Ardennes Offensive, which had smashed through the U.S. 1st Army to the north. In a legendary feat of arms, Patton pulled three divisions out of a hostile line and led a six-division counterattack against the German flank, smashing Hitler's panzers and destroying Germany's last chance of knocking the western Allies out of the war.

After the German surrender in May 1945, Patton, now a four-star general, spent the next few months as military governor of Bavaria. As a man who was happiest during wartime, he pressed the War Department to continue the fight—correctly predicting that the Soviet Union would become America's deadly postwar foe—and got his superiors into political hot water over his opposition to the Allied de-Nazification policy. Because Patton had outlived his usefulness as a war leader, his old friend Eisenhower reluctantly relieved him as commander of the 3rd Army.

As a young cadet, Patton had written, "I would like to get killed in a great victory and then have my body borne between the ranks of my defeated enemy escorted by my own regiment." He did not get his wish, but he came close. On December 9, 1945, seven months after the war in Europe ended, Patton was paralyzed in a serious automobile accident near Mannheim, Germany. He died of complications 12 days later, and was buried with full military honors in Luxembourg, among the men he led into legend.

# THE POWER OF RADIO

*"To all newspapers and radio stations—all those who reach
the eyes and ears of the American people—I say this: You have
a most grave responsibility to the Nation now and for the
duration of this war."*

—President Roosevelt, Fireside Chat, December 9, 1941

Though most American citizens were thousands of miles from the
front lines, the advent of radio allowed them to experience World
War II in an intimate way. More than 90 percent of American
families owned at least one radio and listened, on average, for
about four hours daily.

## WORLD LEADERS CONNECT WITH THEIR CITIZENS

Allied and Axis leaders used radio to beam messages of hope,
determination, and steadfastness, as well as patriotic messages that
encouraged and spurred citizens to action.

On December 8, 1941, at 12:30 P.M., President Roosevelt
addressed a joint session of Congress and the nation on radio,
requesting that war be declared against Japan. When he spoke,
Roosevelt changed his opening sentence, which was written as "a
date which will live in world history," to the now famous "a date
which will live in infamy."

Roosevelt used radio to deliver State of the Union speeches
and his so-called Fireside Chats to Americans across the nation.
Some of his more famous broadcasts included the December
1940 speech "Arsenal of Democracy," which outlined American
support for Britain, China, and Russia; the January 1941 "Four
Freedoms" speech that made the case for American protection
of basic human rights around the world; the April 1942 speech
that addressed sacrifice and American resolve; and his December
1943 address which hinted at the approaching invasion of France.

British Prime Minister Winston Churchill was one of the war's most powerful orators. Britain had been at war for six months when Churchill broadcast his famous "No Surrender" speech in June 1940. In a rousing discourse, Churchill told his listeners the British would, "Go on to the end. We shall defend our island, whatever the cost may be . . . we shall never surrender."

Churchill won the admiration of his countrymen through his honesty. In one broadcast he acknowledged the British defeat on the beaches of Dunkirk, France, where almost 340,000 British and French soldiers had been evacuated. Churchill used the event to spur his nation to action. "I expect the Battle of Britain is about to begin. Upon this battle depends the survival of . . . our own British life and the continuity of our institutions. Hitler knows that he will have to break us . . . or lose the war. If we can stand up to him, all Europe may be free . . . but if we fail, then the whole world . . . will sink into the abyss of a new Dark Age."

## STATE-SPONSORED PROPAGANDA

Governments around the world were quick to grasp the role radio could play in molding public opinion. All of the war's major combatants organized propaganda and information ministries, and radio became one of the most important tools in their arsenal.

The United States Office of War Information (OWI) was established in June 1942. This federal government agency coordinated the domestic release of war news and operated an overseas branch, which administered a propaganda campaign. The radio arm of the OWI was known as the Voice of America (VOA). VOA began broadcasting news programs about America's war efforts into German occupied countries in February 1942. The U.S. government hoped that by doing so, they could counteract the propaganda being espoused by the Nazis. The department initially used shortwave radios loaned by NBC and CBS.

The American Forces Network was established by the U.S. War Department in 1942 to help counter enemy radio broadcasts, which could often be picked up by servicemen in the field. The first broadcast to American troops occurred on July 4, 1943.

Broadcasts included entertainment shows, newscasts, and sports reports.

The Nazis were masters of propaganda. Joseph Goebbels quickly rose through the ranks of the Nazi party, and in 1933 assumed the title of Reich Minister of Popular Enlightenment and Propaganda.

Goebbels realized the power of radio from the outset. In remarks given at the opening of the German Radio Exhibition in August 1933, the Nazi Propaganda Minister said, "It would not have been possible for us to take power or to use it in the ways we have without the radio."

When the Nazis began their invasion and occupation of neighboring countries, Goebbels kept a European map in his office displaying radio transmitters captured by the Nazis, as well as a world map indicating the global reach of various short-wave transmitters under his control.

To distribute the Nazi's anti-Semitic message, Goebbels ordered production of an inexpensive *Volksempfanger*, or "People's Radio Receiver." By 1939, Germany was second only to the United States in the number of radios owned by citizens.

## THE VOICES OF TREASON

The German and Japanese propaganda machines used several American- and British-born men and women to broadcast their messages of doubt and mistrust to Allied soldiers serving overseas.

William Joyce, an American raised in Ireland, was a senior member of the British Union of Fascists. Facing the prospect of arrest, Joyce fled England for Germany on the eve of the war. In October 1939, Joyce became Germany's main English-speaking radio personality, and although it was illegal for Britons to listen to his broadcasts, Joyce had almost as many listeners as the British Broadcasting Corporation.

Joyce was given the nickname "Lord Haw-Haw" by a London newspaper journalist. He began his broadcasts with the phrase, "Germany calling, Germany calling." He created anxiety amongst the British population with tales of a German Fifth Column operating on the island nation. Joyce was captured shortly after Germany's surrender and was eventually hanged for treason.

The Germans also utilized the talents of Mildred Gillars, a 29-year old aspiring stage actress dubbed "Axis Sally." Gillars broadcast a show called "Home Sweet Home" from Berlin. She conducted interviews with Allied Prisoners of War while disguised as a Red Cross worker, which she then combined with propaganda clips for use on her radio broadcasts.

Gillars was convicted on one count of treason after the war and spent 16 years in prison. The charge was based on just one broadcast—a radio drama titled "Vision of Invasion," which told the story of a mother who dreamt of her dead son, killed when his ship was destroyed during the invasion of France.

The Japanese employed several English-speaking women, collectively nicknamed "Tokyo Rose," to broadcast propaganda messages of cheating wives and girlfriends to servicemen in the Pacific. One of the women, Iva Toguri D'Aquino, was initially cleared of wrongdoing by both the FBI and the Army's Counter Intelligence Corps. When she returned to the United States, gossip columnist Walter Winchell lobbied for her prosecution. D'Aquino was eventually convicted on one count of treason in 1949 and served six years in jail, but was later pardoned by President Gerald Ford.

## A NEW BRAND OF JOURNALISM

As war consumed Europe, Americans were informed of overseas events by daily radio news updates. While newspapers reported current news events, their stories were sometimes delayed for several days before appearing in print. Radio, on the other hand, was immediate: What happened on any given day was in many instances relayed to listening audiences that same day.

In the spring of 1936, a Columbia Broadcasting System (CBS) rookie reporter named Edward R. Murrow moved to London, as Columbia's European news director. Murrow assembled the war's finest ensemble of radio reporters, who subsequently became known as "the Murrow Boys." The small group of men and one woman defined the role of the broadcast correspondent.

Murrow made his first broadcast from Vienna, where he covered Hitler's entry into Austria. Over the course of the war, Murrow and his team transmitted thousands of stories to the CBS studio in New York City, which were then transmitted to affiliated stations.

Murrow and his staff often took risks to bring stories to his listeners. In one instance, Murrow accompanied a British bomber crew on their raid over Berlin. The account, titled "Orchestrated Hell," won the reporter a Peabody Award.

Besides witnessing the bomb runs, Murrow was also given permission to fly on a paratroop drop. As the sound of wind blew in through the open door of the cargo plane, Murrow counted off the men as the soldiers jumped from the plane. He then told the tragic story of two men who plummeted to their deaths when their parachute lines became entangled.

During the D-Day invasion of Normandy, CBS reporter Richard Hottelet flew in a B-26 Marauder along the shores of Utah Beach, while down below him coworker Charles Collingwood used the first portable tape recorder, a 55-pound behemoth, to record events occurring in the landing zone.

One of the war's most riveting broadcasts came after Murrow and Collingwood traveled to the Buchenwald, Germany, concentration camp at war's end. Murrow was traumatized by the experience and broke down in tears. In his broadcast three days later, Murrow told his listeners what he had witnessed, saying, "The tragedy of it simply overwhelmed me." Murrow and his team made the events in Europe real for Americans listening back home, relaying the sights and sounds of a world at war.

Shortly after its invention, radio quickly became the dominant form of home entertainment. Radio was the link to the world, and over the course of the war, the new medium evolved into an effective platform for disseminating news and propaganda.

# GERMAN POWS SIT OUT THE WAR IN THE USA

*World War II was known for the brutal conditions imposed on POWs in most countries. However, many German POWs in the United States had it relatively easy. In fact, some may have been treated better as prisoners in America than they would have been if they remained in the German Army.*

If a German soldier were left with no option but to surrender, he would prefer it to be to the Americans. While more than three million of their comrades disappeared into the Soviet gulag system, nearly 400,000 German POWs were fortunate enough to be shipped to the United States. The first POWs arrived in May 1942, when 33 U-boat crewmen were rescued after the sinking of the U-352 off North Carolina's Outer Banks. Following the defeat of the Afrika Korps, a large number of German POWs arrived in the United States beginning in August 1943. Over the next two years, German prisoners were housed in 47 of the 48 states, though most went to rural areas in the South, Midwest, and West.

## FOR SOME, WAITING OUT THE WAR WASN'T SO BAD

Thousands were sent to Camp Clinton outside Jackson, Mississippi. The camp was unique in that it housed the highest-ranking German officers, including 40 generals and 3 admirals. General Jurgen Von Arnim, who had been Rommel's replacement in North Africa, was among those held in Camp Clinton. But his sentence was hardly punishment—Arnim was given a car and driver. He frequently visited movie theatres in Jackson to enjoy the air-conditioning.

While officers were allowed to forgo labor as part of the Geneva Convention governing POW treatment, prisoners at 3 other Mississippi camps and 15 sub camps worked in cotton fields for much of the year. In Iowa, more than 10,000 German POWs were housed at Camp Algona and 34 sub camps in Iowa, Minnesota, and the Dakotas, providing millions of hours of manpower to farms in the region. Similar regional camp systems were organized across the country.

German POWs were generally astonished at how well they were treated in the U.S., often enjoying a quality of life better than they had in the German military. Though required to work, they earned 80 cents a day, which they used at camp canteens to purchase items such as candy bars and cigarettes. They were housed in tents with wood heaters or rough barracks covered with tarpaper roofs. Rations were plentiful, and most thought the food was good. Camps had their own dentists, doctors, libraries, and newspapers. Prisoners played sports, formed bands, and watched movies for recreation.

## DEFYING CAPTORS

While camps were segregated by branch of service and rank, German POWs maintained their own rigid chains of command. Conflicts sometimes arose between ardent Nazis and other prisoners. In a number of cases, "traitors" to the Fatherland were found murdered. Camp authorities began segregating Nazi fanatics and holding them at special camps in Oklahoma.

Some German prisoners staged elaborate escape attempts. On December 23, 1944, 25 former U-boat crewmen at the Papago Park camp in Arizona escaped through a 178-foot tunnel, hoping to reach Axis sympathizers in Latin America. All were recaptured within six weeks. At Camp Clinton, a 100-foot-long tunnel was discovered ten feet away from completion. In many cases, prisoners simply walked away—a frantic search for 30 POWs who disappeared from another camp in Mississippi found them strolling on the streets of nearby Belzoni. The prisoners told the FBI that they had been bored. A *Luftwaffe* pilot in Mississippi disappeared with the wife of a planter on whose plantation he had been working. The couple was found at a hotel in Nashville and told authorities they planned to steal a plane in New England and fly to Greenland together.

## DEMOCRACY IN PRISON?

In the last year of the war, an ambitious "reeducation" program sponsored by the War Department sent liberal arts professors into more than 500 camps. The professors spoke to the prisoners about the value of U.S.-style democracy and made anti-Communist presentations. Although the program was considered a somewhat laughable failure, most POWs did retain a positive view of America when they returned home. Their experiences in the United States also apparently changed some attitudes. At Camp MacKall in Richmond County, North Carolina, prisoners organized political parties and voted on issues to understand the democratic process. At Camp Butner north of Durham, North Carolina, a local Jewish merchant of a particularly generous nature provided POWs with band equipment. After viewing newsreels on the liberation of Nazi concentration camps, the inmates reportedly burned their army uniforms in outrage.

Tens of thousands of German POWs remained in the United States for over a year after the war ended. President Truman decided to keep them in the United States to alleviate the labor shortage. The POWs often worked in agriculture, as America made the transition from wartime to peacetime farming.

At least one decided to stay after the war. Kurt Rossmeisl walked away from Camp Butner on August 4, 1945, and traveled to Chicago. He lived under the name Frank Ellis, got a job, and joined a local Moose lodge. He finally turned himself in on May 10, 1959, 14 years after the end of the war.

☆　☆　☆

- *German prisoners at Iowa's Camp Algona published a newspaper,* Drahtpost (Wire Post Office), *which was used by POW spokesman Walter Bauer to perpetuate hardcore Nazi ideology. The inaugural issue, dated 1944, featured a drawing of Bauer, signed with a prominent "44" designed to recall the notorious SS runes. Swastikas showed up in the paper, and in other camps, as well.*

# Timeline

## 1942

**May 22–29**
Germans capture 214,000 Soviets near Kharkov, Ukraine

**May 26**
Rommel attacks Gazala Line

**May 29**
Czech partisans attack the automobile carrying Reinhard Heydrich in Prague; Heydrich will die on June 4 from an injury-based infection

**May 30–31**
Cologne, Germany, is devastated in the first RAF raid to employ more than 1,000 bombers

**June 4–7**
The Allies gain a decisive victory at the Battle of Midway, destroying four of Japan's six largest ships; the momentum of the Pacific war shifts in favor of the Allies

**June 10**
The entire Czech village of Lidice is razed in reprisal for the killing of Reinhard Heydrich

**June 18**
Bernard Robinson becomes the first African-American U.S. naval officer when he accepts his commission as an ensign in the reserves

**June 21**
Rommel takes Tobruk, Libya, and pushes east

**June 25**
General Dwight D. Eisenhower is appointed to the post of U.S. Army Chief in Europe

**July 1–30**
First battle of El Alamein halts Rommel's advance

**July 4**
First U.S. Army Air Force (USAAF) raid on occupied Europe: attacks on airfields in Holland

**July 5**
Russia yields the Crimea to Germany

**July 7**
Australians begin campaign on Kokoda Trail in New Guinea

**July 9**
German 6th Army begins drive on Stalingrad

Anne Frank and her family go into hiding in Amsterdam

**July 13**
President Roosevelt approves the creation of the Office of Strategic Services (OSS), the forerunner to the Central Intelligence Agency (CIA)

**July 21**
Japanese land at Gona, New Guinea

**July 23**
The German Army captures some 240,000 Soviet troops at the fall of Rostov, Russia

**July 30**
The U.S. Navy begins a reservist program for women called the Women Appointed for Voluntary Emergency Service (WAVES)

**August 4**
Eisenhower is appointed to command invasion of North Africa

**August 7**
For the first time, the United States seizes control of territory held by Japan when the 1st Marine Division takes Guadalcanal and Tulagi

# V-MAIL

*One of the most common complaints of troops abroad is the separation from loved ones. Messages home today may be delivered with phone calls or e-mail, but during World War II, communication came via letters.*

Sixty years ago, mail was the only connection soldiers had to their loved ones back home. Letters to soldiers were loaded onto boats and shipped off to their destinations, taking up to six weeks to reach their recipients.

The British developed a system called Airgraph, in which letters were microfilmed and reprinted. The system caught the notice of the U.S. Army postal director, who quickly adopted the technique and redubbed it V-Mail. Short for Victory Mail, the system was advertised by the military as a patriotic way to offer someone in the field a "five-minute furlough." Special V-Mail forms combining both stationery and an envelope in a single sheet were available from the post office and from five-and-dime stores across the country. Each form had enough space for a correspondent to write a message of several hundred words. The message was mailed, passed through military censors who blocked out any information deemed inappropriate, and then sent to a processing facility where it was microfilmed onto a reel along with thousands of other letters. The reels were shipped to a printing plant close to their final destination, where the letters were reprinted at ¼ scale and delivered to their recipient in as few as 12 days. Another advantage was that the microfilming process allowed for lost or misdirected mail to be reprinted and delivered, unlike paper mail, which might have been lost forever.

More than a billion pieces of V-Mail were sent between 1942 and 1945. Half of those were from the United States to the military, and half in return. It's difficult to quantify the morale-boosting effect of the program, but for many soldiers, the letters from home meant "the difference between a happy day and a miserable one."

# THE SEABEES

*The official Seabee motto is "We Build. We Fight." The unofficial Seabee motto is "Can Do." While the grunts and flyboys engaged in combat directly with the enemy, the Seabees built and maintained the infrastructure needed to keep the war machine running in every theater of operation during the war.*

After the Japanese attack on Pearl Harbor, civilian laborers in war zones were faced with a potentially dangerous situation. If these workers were attacked, they could not fight back—doing so meant they could be executed on the spot as guerrilla fighters if captured.

On December 28, 1941, Rear Admiral Ben Moreell proposed the formation of a Naval Construction Regiment. The regiment would be a unit of skilled tradesmen with military training. After conferring with the secretary of the navy, a decision was made to give officers of the Civil Engineer Corps command of both officers and enlisted men assigned to the new construction unit.

New recruits received three weeks of basic training, followed by six weeks of advanced military and technical training. More than 11,000 officers joined the Civil Engineer Corps during the war. Almost 8,000 of them served with the navy's new construction battalions. The men eventually became known as Seabees, an acronym for construction battalion.

Seabee battalions comprised four companies of men trained in various construction trades and a headquarters company that consisted of administrative personnel, cooks, doctors, dentists and the like. A typical battalion had about 30 officers and 1,100 men. As larger projects were undertaken, battalions were organized into regiments, two regiments became a brigade, and, when required, two brigades could become a naval construction force.

## FEATS IN THE SOUTH PACIFIC

Though Seabee units served in every theater of operation, the bulk of their work was done in Europe and the South Pacific. In January 1942, the first organized Naval Construction Battalion sailed to the South Pacific island of Bora Bora. Once there, the men battled incessant rain, dysentery, and a multitude of tropical diseases. Despite the horrid conditions, they successfully built a refueling facility, which was later used by American ships and planes during the Battle of the Coral Sea.

Members of the 6th Naval Construction Battalion were the first to work under combat conditions. During their deployment at Guadalcanal, these Seabees were tasked with repairing a large Japanese airfield, which was later named Henderson Airfield. Using both American and captured Japanese construction equipment, the Seabees installed huge sections of interlocking pierced steel Marston matting. The metal sheets provided a solid runway surface for planes to land on and were a necessity in the rain-soaked tropics.

While on Guadalcanal, the Seabees also built a control tower, a runway lighting system, an emergency airfield, a fuel depot, and air-raid shelters. Despite constant enemy air raids and naval bombardments (on two successive nights in October Henderson Field was damaged by more than 1,600 shells fired from Japanese warships), Seabees managed to keep the main airfield in operation.

During the war, the largest concentration of Seabees was at Okinawa. On April 1, 1945, seven Seabee battalions took part in the offensive to capture and rebuild that strategically important island. Commodore Andrew Bisset, a Navy Civil Engineer Corps officer, had under his command some 55,000 Seabees. Facilities built on the island were intended for use during the anticipated invasion of Japan.

Eighty percent of the Navy's construction forces served in the Pacific Theater. Seabees made stops at more than 300 Pacific islands where they built airstrips, ammunition dumps, communication stations, hospitals, water and fuel storage tanks, drainage systems, sewage and water purification facilities, warehouses, piers, electrical generating stations, asphalt plants, and housing for an estimated 1.5 million men.

# OPERATIONS IN EUROPE

The Seabees made their European debut on the sandy beaches of Sicily, where they built pontoon causeways for landing troops. However, their most important contributions in Europe were the Normandy landings; the reopening of the port at Cherbourg, France; and the crossing of the Rhine River. During the D-Day landings, Seabees came ashore as members of demolition units where they helped army engineers destroy German barriers and fortifications. This work was performed under frighteningly precise enemy fire. Seabees also built the Mulberry artificial harbor off the Normandy coast, which allowed thousands of men and tons of materiel to be off-loaded directly onto the beachhead. Within 28 days of D-Day, more than a million Allied soldiers had come ashore using the Seabee-constructed port.

Knowing the Allies needed deepwater ports to supply their men, the Germans destroyed much of the harbor at Cherbourg. Seabees managed to have Cherbourg's port facilities operational just 11 days after the city was liberated.

On March 22, 1945, General George S. Patton called on the services of the Seabees to ferry his troops across the Rhine River. During the challenging, dangerous operation, Seabees built and operated some 300 ferries, which delivered American troops onto German soil.

By war's end, 325,000 men with training in more than 60 skilled trades had fought and built on six continents as members of the Navy's Construction Battalions. The accomplishments and ingenuity of the Seabees proved their unofficial "Can Do" slogan was more than a motto—it was a way of life.

✫　✫　✫

- *The Seabees developed cooks who could put together excellent hot meals just hours after Seabee battalions hit island beaches in the Pacific. A typical dinner put together under pressure might include Yankee pot roast, browned potatoes, snap beans, bread and butter, Bartlett pears, and coffee.*

# Fast Facts

- *The first Seabee hero of the war was Seaman 2nd Class Lawrence "Bucky" Meyer, USNR. While at Henderson Field, Meyer salvaged and repaired a discarded Japanese machine gun. On October 3, 1942, Meyer used the gun to shoot down a Japanese fighter that was strafing the field. Meyer was killed 10 days later, but was posthumously awarded the Silver Star for his downing of the Japanese Zero.*

- *The Seabees who landed on Bora Bora called themselves "Bobcats" after the code name* Bobcat, *which had been given to the island.*

- *To prepare for the invasion of Guadalcanal, Seabees of the 3rd Construction Battalion Detachment landed 500 miles southeast, on the island of Espiritu Santo. In just 20 days, they carved a 6,000-foot airstrip to be used by Allied bombers.*

- *When Americans strung copper telephone line during the occupation of Iran, locals needed very little time to see the profit potential. They stole more than 250 miles of line, most of which was made into jewelry.*

- *When Germans retreated from Naples, they blocked the port with wrecked ships. Undaunted, American engineers built a pier directly atop the wrecks and were soon watching the Liberty ships unload.*

- *D-Day owed its success in part to weather reports from lonely, icy stations in Arctic Greenland and Spitsbergen and Jan Mayen in Norway. The invasion needed to occur on June 5, 6, or 7 to take advantage of the moon and the tides. D-Day was postponed a day due to rain and gale-force winds, which would have been disastrous for the Allies.*

- *Marvin "Muktuk" Marston commanded more than 3,000 native guards along Alaska's Bering Sea coast. They kept vigilant watch, rescued downed fliers, and shot down Japanese firebomb balloons.*

# THE MERCILESS CHICKEN FARMER: HEINRICH HIMMLER

*A one-time chicken farmer who looked like a bland bookkeeper, Heinrich Himmler became arguably the second-most-powerful man in Hitler's regime. He proved to be a shrewd and ruthless opportunist in his rise through the Nazi ranks.*

A bright but unathletic teenager, Heinrich Himmler trained with a Bavarian regiment during World War I, but the conflict ended before he could serve. He went on to study agronomy in his native Munich, then in November 1923 served under Ernst Rohm during Hitler's failed Beer Hall Putsch. Hitler's right-hand man, Rohm commanded the brown-shirted thugs known as the *Sturmabteilung* (SA, or "Storm Troopers").

In 1925, Himmler joined the *Schutzstaffel* Special Squadron (SS), a battalion of the SA that was created to serve as bodyguard for Hitler, but was later used to restrict the power of the Brownshirts. At this time, he also ran a chicken farm—albeit unsuccessfully—at Waltrudering, near Munich. Four years after joining the SS, Himmler, now 29, was appointed *Reichsführer*-SS, rising to full command of its 280 members but still under control of Rohm's SA.

A decorated officer in World War I and one of the first members of the Nazi Party, Rohm became close to Hitler while they were imprisoned together following the failed putsch in Munich. However, by the time Hitler took power in 1933, he saw Rohm as a threat to his own leadership. Coming mostly from the working classes left unemployed by the Great Depression, Rohm's Brownshirts now numbered 2.5 million members and commonly swore loyalty to their own leaders rather than to Adolf Hitler or the Nazi Party. Rohm and his followers advocated a sweeping Socialist revolution, alienating the businessmen who had supported Hitler's rise to power. Rohm also called for the German Army—limited by the treaty of Versailles to 100,000 men—to be absorbed into the much larger SA, infuriating the generals of the *Reichswehr*, whose support Hitler needed to rule. Himmler and other Nazi leaders feared the SA as a dangerous, radical organization, and joined the conservative generals in their dislike of Rohm's overt homosexuality.

Himmler, who once boasted that he would shoot his own mother for Hitler, was blindly loyal to the *Führer*. With Hitler's support, he moved to separate the SS, now numbering 52,000 members, from the SA hierarchy and to create a state security organization, called the *Sicherheitsdienst* (SD), as part of its command. He was promoted to a rank equal to senior SA commanders and introduced black SS uniforms to replace the brown shirts of the SA. Himmler and his deputy Reinhard Heydrich put aside their rivalry with Herman Göring and joined in a plot to consolidate their own power by displacing Rohm and marginalizing the SA.

In 1934 Himmler created a dossier of faked evidence suggesting that Rohm had been paid 12 million marks by France to overthrow Hitler. Hitler refused to believe the report at first, but under pressure from his conservative backers, finally ordered the execution of the SA leadership. He personally arrested Rohm at a hotel near Munich on June 30, 1934, the start of what became known as "The Night of the Long Knives." Hundreds of SA members and others deemed enemies of the new state were arrested or murdered outright. Himmler was told to take care of Rohm, who was being held at a prison in Munich. Under Himmler's orders, on July 2, an SS officer shot and killed Rohm in his jail cell after the SA commander refused to commit suicide with a pistol he had been given.

On July 26, 1934, the SS was made independent of the SA, which continued to exist but in a lesser role than the SS. Over the next decade Himmler worked assiduously at accumulating power. He organized Germany's political police forces into the Gestapo. He led the formation of the military branch of the SS called the SS-*Verfügungstruppe*, later known as the *Waffen*-SS. In 1936, all of Germany's uniformed law enforcement agencies came under Himmler's purview in his new role of chief of the German police, yet operational control of these organizations eluded him until he also became chief of the interior in 1943. By then, as head of the Third Reich's concentration-camp system, Himmler stood as the chief organizer of the Final Solution.

Some historians believe that by 1943, however, Himmler knew that the war was lost and, despite all his supposed devotion to Hitler, began working to secure his position as his *Führer's* heir. Himmler may have been aware of the July 20, 1944, bomb plot and let it go forward so he could succeed Hitler and negotiate a separate peace with the Western Allies. In the final weeks of the war, Himmler attempted to negotiate a peace with Eisenhower without Hitler's knowledge. A furious Hitler stripped him of all titles and power the day before he committed suicide. Disguised as a German sergeant, Himmler was captured by British troops, who soon discovered his identity. Rather than face execution as a war criminal, he committed suicide with a hidden cyanide capsule—the same fate chosen by Herman Göring, his fellow conspirator in The Night of the Long Knives.

☆ ☆ ☆

- *Upon negotiating the 1939 Nazi-Soviet Pact, Hitler insisted on seeing a close-up photo of Stalin to check for "Jewish features."*

☆ ☆ ☆

- *"Lili Marlene" was one of the most popular songs of the war, and it was sung by both Allied and Axis forces. In fact, General Rommel liked the song so much he had it played for his desert troops every night despite Goebbels's orders that it should be banned as subversive material.*

☆ ☆ ☆

- *German forces deployed to Russia had expected the campaign to end by winter0 1941. When temperatures dipped to 40 degrees below zero, the ill-equipped German soldiers stole civilian clothing, including women's underwear and fur boas, to keep warm. The Russian troops derisively referred to these strangely dressed soldiers as "Winter Fritz."*

# Timeline

## 1942

**August 8–9**
Naval Battle of Savo Island, off Guadalcanal

**August 13**
General Sir Bernard L. Montgomery takes command of British 8th Army

**August 19**
The Allied raid on Dieppe, France, amounts to a dismal failure

**August 21**
Marines on Guadalcanal annihilate attacking Japanese forces

**August 23**
Luftwaffe raids kill 40,000 in Stalingrad

**August 23–25**
Naval Battle of the Eastern Solomons

**August 26**
As many as a million German soldiers attack the Red Army at Stalingrad

**August 29**
Japanese drive Australians back along the Kokoda Trail in New Guinea

**August 31–September 2**
Rommel is repulsed at Battle of Alam Halfa

**September 3**
Germans complete isolation of Stalingrad

**September 12–14**
Battle of Bloody Ridge on Guadalcanal; 11,000 U.S. Marines force the 60,000-man Japanese contingent to retreat

**September 20**
German and Soviet troops engage in house-to-house combat through-

out Stalingrad; women and children are evacuated from the city the following day

**September 25**
U.S. Army establishes Manhattan Project to build an atomic bomb

**September 27**
Australians advance along the Kokoda Trail

**October**
For most of the month heavy fighting rages in Stalingrad as Germans continue effort to gain control of the city

**October 3**
Germany successfully launches its first A4 free-flight rocket

**October 7**
U.S. troops advance along Kapa Kapa trail in New Guinea

**October 11**
U.S. forces defeat Japanese in the Battle of Cape Esperance, opening a supply line to Guadalcanal

**October 16**
The supply line to the Burma front is crippled by a cyclone that claims 40,000 lives and devastates southern India

**October 23–24**
Rommel's troops are defeated at the Second Battle of El Alamein

**November 8**
Allied invasion of North Africa (Operation TORCH) begins with landings in Morocco and Algeria; Vichy France announces it will sever diplomatic ties with the United States following the invasion of French North Africa

# THE BEST MOVIES ABOUT WORLD WAR II

*The Second World War has inspired countless retellings on the silver screen. While no list of worthwhile movies about the war could be complete, here are a handful of particularly noteworthy titles.*

*A Bridge Too Far,* 1977. The story of Operation Market Garden, an Allied operation to capture bridges in the occupied Netherlands in 1944. It is one of the more historically accurate Hollywood productions about the war.

*The Bridge on the River Kwai,* 1957. Alec Guinness stars as the officer in charge of a group of British prisoners of war forced to build a railway for the Japanese under brutal jungle conditions. The David Lean production is well-known for its eminently whistled theme song.

*Idi i Smotri (Come and See),* 1985. This shattering Soviet film by director Elem Klimov chronicles the disasters that befall a Russian village that has been invaded by bloodthirsty SS troopers. Audiences squirm because the terror is viewed through the eyes of a young boy who is driven to the brink of madness by what he witnesses.

*Das Boot,* 1981. Regarded as one of the greatest German films of all time, *Das Boot* follows the crew of German submarine U-96 through the course of its mission. The commander of the real U-96 was a consultant on this movie, and the result is a film that immerses the viewer in the tense, claustrophobic world of a U-boat at war.

*The Longest Day,* 1962. A sweeping depiction of the Normandy invasion starring dozens of Hollywood heavyweights, including Robert Mitchum, Richard Burton, Henry Fonda, and John Wayne. More than 20,000 real soldiers were used as extras during filming.

*Mrs. Miniver,* 1942. A sympathetic American depiction of a family in wartime Britain. Winston Churchill reportedly said that the story did more for the war effort than a flotilla of battleships.

*Patton,* 1970. Winner of seven Oscars, this film starring George C. Scott is fascinating both as a psychological study of General George S. Patton and as a war movie.

*Saving Private Ryan,* 1998. Steven Spielberg directed Tom Hanks in this story of a group of eight soldiers putting their own lives at risk to save one man. The D-Day scenes are some of the most gripping ever filmed.

*Schindler's List,* 1993. A staggeringly haunting true story of how one man saved a thousand Jews from the Holocaust. The film won seven Oscars and is consistently ranked among the greatest movies of all time by critics' associations and audiences alike.

*They Were Expendable,* 1945. The John Ford-directed story of American PT boats battling the Japanese in the South Pacific. On hearing the title, a PT-boat sailor had a different recollection of the boats: "It should have been called 'they were useless.'"

*The Thin Red Line,* 1998. This expansive look at the 1942-43 U.S. invasion of Guadalcanal was adapted by director Terence Malick from the highly regarded novel by James Jones. Although often shockingly violent, the film is oddly poetic, as well, encompassing chaos, beauty, unbalanced officers, and ordinary Joes who just want to survive. The solid cast includes Sean Penn, John Cusack, Nick Nolte, Adrien Brody, Jim Caviezel, George Clooney, John Travolta, and Woody Harrelson.

*Tora! Tora! Tora!,* 1970. A retelling of the attack on Pearl Harbor, this film features a look at the events from both an American and a

Japanese perspective. To reflect the two different viewpoints, the film was shot in separate segments by directors from each country.

# FLAMETHROWER!

*Controversial, terrifying, effective: Whether mounted on a tank or carried on an engineer's back, the flamethrower did the job—for those who dared use it.*

### When were these hellish weapons invented?

Combatants have burned one another to death since antiquity, but the modern flamethrower was invented by Germany just before World War I.

### Most Great War weapons improved during World War II. How does one improve a weapon of liquid fire?

The Germans were first to mount flamethrowers on armored vehicles, which could carry more fuel and propellant—and had an easier time getting the weapon into effective range than foot soldiers did. Americans invented napalm (jellied gasoline), which flew more accurately and stuck as it burned.

### How exactly did World War II flamethrowers operate?

A flamethrower consisted of a fuel tank (diesel, gasoline, or a mixture), a compressed propellant (such as butane or nitrogen), and a hose leading to a nozzle with an igniter. Pulling the trigger forced propellant into the fuel tanks, pushing a jet of fuel out of the nozzle. The igniter, of course, set it ablaze as it left the nozzle.

### That sounds almost as scary for the wielder and his comrades as for his enemies.

No one was eager to stand too close to the flamethrower guy, and any flamethrower operator completely unafraid of his weapon was considered insane (or lying). Some *Waffen*-SS troops executed any Allied flamethrower operator they captured. A flamethrower burst is impossible to hide from, and defending troops took suicidal risks in hopes of destroying or escaping it. Anything was better than burning alive.

*Were flamethrowers useful in all combat situations?*

The flamethrower's short range (15–50 yards for portable flame-throwers, about double that for flamethrowing tanks), inherent danger to the operator, and limited fuel always restricted its uses. It was best at neutralizing fortifications like bunkers and pillboxes, where a quick burst of flaming fuel through the firing ports meant a bad day for the occupants. Flamethrowers also worked against troops hidden in caves and other natural fortifications. If the flame reached an ammo pile, the end was quick.

In cases where starting a forest or house fire would give a tactical advantage, the flamethrower was quite efficient. It could even be used in desperation against heavy armor: The best bet was to try igniting the target's gas tank.

*Most of these sound like special weapons situations, normally the province of combat engineers.*

For the most part, only combat engineers and specialized troops carried flamethrowers. In the island-hopping Pacific campaign, however, U.S. Marines bristled with flamethrowers. A 1944 U.S. Marine division at full strength had 17,465 Marines. Fully equipped, they had 153 mortars, 172 bazookas, 48 antitank guns, 48 howitzers,

---

## Creative Flamethrower Tactics

**The Wet Shot**. This meant hosing the fuel into the air without the igniter engaged, creating a mist of fuel, then immediately firing a second inflamed shot which would ignite the mist and create a fireball in the air.

**Hosed Tanks.** On Okinawa, U.S. Army flamethrowing tankers attached long hoses to their tanks' flame nozzles, enabling them to inject flaming napalm into hard-to-reach areas. In one case, an infantry platoon tenaciously sneaked 200 feet of hose up a path before the tankers let the flames rip.

46 tanks—and 267 flamethrowers. Considering the obstinate, suicidal courage of Japanese defenders holed up in many thousands of well-prepared bunkers, caves, and forts, Marine divisions carried more flamethrowers than artillery.

### But no flamethrowing tanks for the Leathernecks?

The U.S. Army supported the Marines with flamethrowing tanks at Okinawa, for example. But the U.S. Marines were fundamentally riflemen, excelling at infantry weapons and tactics. A man could carry a flamethrower places no tank could go. Tanks had a hard time on islands with rough terrain or boggy ground, which were numerous in the Pacific.

### Who made the most use of flamethrowing tanks?

Early on, the Germans; later the British. The *Wehrmacht* had thousands of obsolete prewar tanks, many of them captured, with undersize turrets that could not be fitted with larger guns-but could easily handle a flamethrower. None of the German conversions were resounding successes, but they all gave some useful service. The British Churchill Crocodile was a modified heavy Churchill tank that pulled a fuel trailer and could fire either flame (through a converted machine-gun port) or a standard tank cannon. Between its two main armaments, the Crocodile was very useful against any tough defensive position. Americans and Soviets each built modest numbers of different flamethrowing tank designs and conversions.

### Did any major combatant renounce the flamethrower on humanitarian grounds?

No. Whenever flamethrowers were available, their use was at the discretion of commanders on the spot, who cared about winning at lowest human cost. The old quote "war is hell" was perhaps truest when spoken by a flamethrower nozzle.

# ENSLAVED INSIDE A MOUNTAIN—THE MITTELWERK V-2 ROCKET FACILITY

*V-2 rockets rained random destruction upon England during the final months of the war, but the production of the weapons cost far more human lives than the attacks ever claimed.*

The advances in rocketry during World War II would eventually lead to the Soviet Union's launch of Sputnik in 1957 and the United States reaching the moon 12 years later. The roots of the technology, however, began in Nazi Germany during the darkest days of the Second World War. Few, if any, of those celebrating the conquest of space in the decades that followed thought of the enormous suffering that had made the Space Age a reality.

In the summer of 1943, the V-2 rocket facility at Peenemünde was suffering from increasingly effective Allied bombing raids. To protect their new weapon, the Nazis ordered thousands of Russian, Polish, and French concentration-camp prisoners to enlarge two gypsum mine tunnels in the Harz mountain range near Nordhausen, Germany. Deep inside Kohnstein Mountain, the prisoners bore two enormous parallel S-shaped tunnels that were connected by more than 40 cross tunnels. The facility, which covered more than a million square feet, became known as the Mittelwerk ("Middle Works"). It was used to build the dreaded V-2 rockets.

Nearby, the Nazis opened concentration camp Mittelbau to provide labor. The prisoners were literally worked to death in the harsh underground plant where beatings, exhaustion, malnutrition, and illness were commonplace. Because the rockets were not designed for mass production, each V-2 had to be assembled and tested with custom parts. After several acts of sabotage, regulations required laborers to sign off on their work so that flaws could be traced back to whomever had assembled the rocket. Prisoners still engaged in minor acts of sabotage, such as cold-soldering connections or failing to completely weld components. However, if caught, inmates faced immediate death: They would be hung from cranes in the halls and left for a day or more as a warning to others.

Of the roughly 50,000 detainees working in the Mittelbau complex, approximately half did not survive. For every operational rocket that left the factory, six people had died making it. At least 11,000 of these prisoners were killed in April 1945, when the retreating SS guards obeyed orders to slaughter the prisoners in order to protect the secrets of the Mittelwerk plant. The American 104th Infantry Division and 3rd Armored Division, however, discovered the facility soon after the SS retreat. An intelligence officer was quoted as saying that being in the tunnels was "like being in a magician's cave." Near the "magician's cave," the Americans had already discovered the Dora concentration camp where many of the most horrific scenes of Nazi abuse were documented by film crews. Today, a memorial dedicated to the prisoners who died in the facility is located near the entrance to the tunnels.

☆　☆　☆

- *Some 20 German companies had ties to Mittelwerk and its rockets, including Siemens, AEG, BMW, Junkers, and Heinkel.*

# BEWARE, BALLOON BOMBS!

*In a last-ditch effort to attack America, Japan relied on the wind.*

By late 1944, the United States had cut off much of Japan's supply of food, fuel, and other war materials. Despite a shortage of resources, the Japanese Ninth Research Division laboratory developed a new weapon.

The Japanese knew that a strong wind current swept across the Pacific from Japan to North America (later this current would be called the jet stream). Researchers supposed they could float a large number of missiles on the current to explode over America. They expected Japan could achieve indefensible terror and destruction similar to Germany's buzz bombs and V-1s in Britain.

Military brass called in their engineers and laid out the requirements:

- The missiles' prime purpose would be to burn America's food crops and forests.

- The weapons would need to carry antipersonnel explosives to prevent anyone from interfering with the incendiary devices.

- Originally, targeting major cities was an objective, but it was soon realized the guidance would rely on the whimsy of wind currents.

So began project Fu-go. Planners set about the task. They decided a hydrogen-filled balloon would be the best method of transportation. With rubber in short supply, the engineers created the balloon's skin using thick, impermeable paper called *washi,* made from mulberry trees.

Meteorologists agreed the plan was feasible. The Japanese government evacuated large warehouses on the islands to provide assembly sites for this priority project. Several high schools near the plants were closed, and female students were sent to work gluing paper to create the balloons. In all, about 30,000 soldiers and an equal number of civilians were put to work on the weapon. The product was then sent to northern Honshu, where technicians attached explosives and incendiary devices. The weapons were called *fusen bakudan,* which means "balloon bomb" but has also been translated as "fire balloon."

Engineers refined the mechanisms to ensure the balloons would be carried along the jet stream at an altitude near 30,000 feet. If they slipped below 30,000 feet, a mechanism would release a pair of sandbags, and the balloons would rise. If they got as high as 38,000 feet, a vent was activated to release some hydrogen from the balloons.

Released from northern Honshu, the balloons would take three days to cross the Pacific. With its sandbags spent, a mechanism would drop the bombs and light a fuse that would burn for 84 minutes before detonating a flash bomb that would destroy the balloon. By causing the balloons to self-destruct in midair, the Japanese hoped to add mystery to the source of the fires.

The first balloons were launched November 3, 1944, and one was spotted two days later off the coast of San Pedro, California. They continued to turn up throughout the northwest United States and western Canada, reaching as far east as Farmington, Michigan and south to northern Mexico.

Rather than incite widespread panic, the balloons were largely ineffective and rarely discussed. *Newsweek* ran a report on the weapons in January 1945, and the Office of Censorship issued a notice to the media not to report further incidents.

During January to February 1945, debris showed up as far inland as Arizona and Texas. One bomb exploded near the Boeing plant in Seattle that produced B-29s. Another shorted a high-tension wire, temporarily blacking out one of the Manhattan Project's reactors in Hanford, Washington.

A balloon killed a woman in Helena, Montana, and one in Oregon claimed six lives. On March 5, 1945, a minister's wife and children from the Sunday school were on a fishing trip. They discovered a grounded balloon and tried to move it, but it exploded. After this incident, the media ban was lifted so that people could be warned of the potential danger.

When the balloons arrived, they were indeed a mystery—no one knew where they had come from. Many people feared they could be used to carry biological weapons. Researchers examined some of the balloon bombs that were found unexploded and analyzed the sand in the sandbags. Finding that it was not from America or the mid-Pacific, they eventually isolated its origin as the beaches of northeast Japan.

Troops flew photo reconnaissance missions over the area, and photo interpreters identified two of the three hydrogen plants near Ichinomiya. B-29s were sent to destroy the plants, grinding the balloon-bomb production to a halt.

The Japanese government suspended funding for project Fu-go in April 1945. While Japanese propaganda had declared casualties as high as 10,000, they had no evidence the bombs were actually reaching or exploding in America. In all, of more than 9,000 bombs launched, only about 300 reached the United States.

✮ ✮ ✮

- *Fear of command disloyalty caused Generalissimo Chiang Kai-shek to withhold artillery and motor transport from most of his units, greatly weakening them.*

✮ ✮ ✮

- *The P-40 fighters used by the American Volunteer Group, known as the Flying Tigers, in China were originally meant for the British, who had declined them due to obsolescence.*

✮ ✮ ✮

- *The workhorse C-46s that flew over the Himalayas into China were sometimes loaded by trained elephants, lifting 55-gallon fuel drums with their tusks.*

# MAJOR RICHARD I. BONG: AMERICA'S "ACE OF ACES"

*Calvin Coolidge, wet laundry, and a plane named* Marge *helped create America's highest-scoring ace of all time.*

The scene was a farm on the outskirts of Poplar, Wisconsin. The year was 1928, and the event was the daily flyover by a plane carrying mail to President Calvin Coolidge's summer home in Superior. An eight-year-old boy watched with rapt fascination as the plane passed directly over his house. Even at that tender age, Dick Bong knew he wanted to be a pilot. He grew up a typical American boy of the period—fishing, sports, church, and chores—but he never lost his dream of becoming a pilot. While attending Superior State Teacher's College, Dick became a certified pilot through the government-sponsored Civilian Pilot Training Program and soon afterward joined the Army Air Corps. He never looked back.

Dick Bong's instructors, including future presidential candidate Barry Goldwater, noticed the young man's natural abilities as a pilot. Bong's penchant for antics while stationed at Hamilton Field near San Francisco, however, raised the indignation of his commanding officer, Major General George C. Kenney. He'd been willing to tolerate loops around the Golden Gate Bridge and low-level flights through the city's business district, but reached his breaking point when a lady called the base to complain that one of the pilots had flown so low over her house that all the laundry had blown off her line. Bong was ordered to go to the woman's home and hang whatever laundry needed to be dried.

In October 1942 Bong was assigned to the 9th Fighter Squadron in the Southwest Pacific. He soon began racking up kills in his P-38 Lightning, which he named *Marge* after his fiancée. He developed a unique dogfighting technique in which he would swoop down on enemy planes and engage them at extremely close range. By January 1943, he was an ace (five kills), and on April 2, 1944, he shot down his 27th aircraft, surpassing Eddie Rickenbacker's World War I record. He was sent home on leave but returned in time for the South Pacific campaign, in which his tally reached 40 confirmed kills. Douglas MacArthur personally awarded Bong the Congressional Medal of Honor, claiming that the pilot had "ruled the air from New Guinea to the Philippines." General Kenney pulled Bong out of combat and sent him home with orders to marry Marjorie and start a family. In the meantime, his services promoting war bonds were in constant demand.

At home Bong was a hero. The international press covered his wedding and his accomplishments continued to be celebrated. However, he wanted to be a test pilot. Soon after their wedding, Dick and Marjorie moved to Dayton, Ohio, where new jet aircraft were being tested at Wright Field. On the day that the atomic bomb was dropped on Hiroshima, Dick Bong was tragically killed testing a Lockheed P-80 Shooting Star jet plane. He was just 24 years old.

☆　　☆　　☆

- *Reiko the Riveter? By 1943, Japanese women were encouraged to work in factories and mines. In 1944, the number of working women exceeded ten million, and included the daughter of Premier Tojo Hideki.*

☆　　☆　　☆

- *The invasion of Peleliu, in modern Palau, was among the most costly island captures of the war. U.S. troops killed more than 10,000 Japanese by expending some 15 million rounds of ammunition in a month of combat. The Americans on the island suffered about 7,500 casualties.*

☆　　☆　　☆

- *Japanese camouflage specialists painted U.S. bomber silhouettes on the ground in lime, adding trails to look like smoke. The idea was to lure other bombers to assist the stricken "plane," but it never succeeded.*

# Fast Facts

- *During World War II the Finnish Air Force and the short-lived Latvian Air Force both painted swastika roundels on their aircraft. The fact that Finland ended up a German ally, and that thousands of Latvians joined the Waffen-SS, is coincidental; the swastika on their planes had nothing to do with Nazism.*

- *On August 4, 1942, the Mexican and U.S. governments instituted the Bracero program, which allowed thousands of Mexicans to enter the United States and work on borderland farms left shorthanded during the war years.*

- *Brigadier General Leslie R. Groves, who managed the construction of the Pentagon, went on to oversee the logistics of the Manhattan Project.*

- *The Second World War was the first war in which penicillin was used—it drastically reduced battlefield fatalities.*

- *German scientist Werner Karl Heisenberg claimed to have falsified the uranium calculations necessary for an atomic bomb to prevent the Nazis from producing the weapon before the Allies.*

- *The desperate house-to-house fighting in Stalingrad led the German soldiers to call it a "Rat's War."*

- *In 1943, Vichy France's coerced tribute accounted for roughly 25 percent of Nazi Germany's gross national product.*

- *Dmitri Shostakovich composed his famous Seventh Symphony while in Leningrad during the German siege of the city from 1941 to 1942.*

- *Mohandas Gandhi was jailed for organizing peaceful strikes when the British refused to grant India's independence until after the war. He compared their gesture to offering a "postdated check on a bank that is obviously crashing."*

- *Only two leaders explicitly forbade their generals to retreat during the war: Adolf Hitler and Joseph Stalin.*

# THE JEWISH BRIGADE HELPS LIBERATE EUROPE

*At the end of the war, survivors of the Holocaust and German townspeople were astonished by columns of Jews in British Army uniforms, serving under a Star of David flag.*

Thousands of Palestinian Jews signed up to serve in the British Army at the start of the war. Incorporated into 15 battalions, Palestinian Jews fought in Greece and North Africa. While early calls by Zionist leaders for a Jewish unit under Jewish command were rejected, the idea gained support later in the war with the first reports of the Holocaust. In a telegram to President Roosevelt, Churchill remarked that Jews "have the right to strike at the Germans as a recognizable body."

More than 30,000 Jews fought in the British Army during World War II, with 700 killed in combat. In the summer of 1944, the British Army established a Jewish Brigade comprising 5,000 Jewish volunteers organized into three infantry units, with supporting artillery and service units. Flying the Zionist flag as their standard, the *Chativah Yehudith Lochemeth* ("Jewish Fighting Force") included Jewish refugees from Europe as well as Jews from Palestine, Ethiopia, and Yemen. After training in Egypt, the unit was posted to Italy, and took part in the final northward push of the Italian campaign and helped liberate Bologna.

The unit first encountered survivors of the Holocaust while stationed on occupation duty in Tarvisio. In July 1945, the Jewish Brigade traveled through western Germany en route to its new station in Belgium, flying the Zionist flag down streets where Nazis rallies were once held. In postwar Europe, the unit helped set up Displaced Persons camps for Jewish concentration-camp survivors. The Jewish Brigade was disbanded in the summer of 1946 and many of its members went on to play key roles in the creation of Israel and in its War of Independence.

# FEMALE ESPIONAGE AGENTS: WORKING UNDERCOVER FOR THE ALLIES

*Women played vital roles in conducting acts of sabotage and gathering intelligence. Some paid for their bravery with their lives.*

In Europe in the 1940s, the "invisibility" of women often made them ideal operatives. They could eavesdrop in public or witness encounters with authorities unnoticed. Britain's Special Operations Executive (SOE) realized that female agents could be especially effective in the field.

## HEDGEHOG

When France fell in 1940, Marie-Madeleine Fourcade helped establish a partisan resistance group called Alliance. Headquartered in Vichy, the group became known as "Noah's Ark" after Fourcade gave its members names of animals as their code names. Her own code name was "Hedgehog." The group worked to obtain information about the German armed forces and passed the intelligence on to the SOE. The Alliance was among the first partisan groups organized with the help of the SOE, which supplied the French operatives with shortwave radios and millions of francs dropped by parachute.

Although Fourcade was one of the Alliance's top agents, she was caught four times by the Germans; she escaped or was released each time. Once she was smuggled out of the country in a mail bag. On another occasion, she escaped from prison by squeezing through the bars on the window of her prison cell. While Fourcade's luck held, other members of Noah's Ark were captured in 1944 during a partisan operation aiding the Allied advance in Alsace. They were later executed at the Natzweiler-Struthof concentration camp in France. Fourcade survived the war and wrote a book about her experiences, *Noah's Ark,* published in 1968. She died in a military hospital in Paris in 1989 at age 79.

## LOUISE

Born to a French mother and an English father, Violette Bushell Szabo joined SOE after her husband, a Hungarian serving in the Free French Army, was killed at the Battle of El Alamein. She was given the code name "Louise." Following intensive espionage training, Szabo parachuted into France near Cherbourg on April 5, 1944. On her first mission, she studied the effectiveness of resistance, and subsequently reorganized a resistance network that had been destroyed by the Nazis. She led the group in sabotage raids and radioed reports to the SOE specifying the locations of local factories important to the German war effort. Szabo returned to France on June 7 and immediately coordinated partisans to sabotage communication lines. The Germans captured her three days later, reportedly after she put up fierce resistance with her Sten gun. Szabo was tortured by the SS and sent to Ravensbrück concentration camp, where she was executed on February 5, 1945 at age 23. Three other female members of the SOE were also executed at Ravensbrück: Denise Bloch, Cecily Lefort, and Lilian Rolfe. Szabo became the second woman to be awarded the George Cross (posthumously) and was awarded the Croix de Guerre in 1947.

## PALMACH PARATROOPS

Haviva Reik and Hannah Senesh were Eastern European Jews who joined the SOE to help liberate their homelands. Reik was born in Slovakia and grew up in Banska-Bystrica, in the Carpathian Mountains. Senesh, a diarist, poet, and playwright, was born in Budapest. The daughter of a well-known playwright and journalist, she enjoyed a comfortable, secular life before discovering Judaism as a teenager. Both women immigrated to Palestine in 1939 and joined the Palmach, a paramilitary branch of the Zionist Haganah underground organization. Trained as parachutists, Reik and Senesh were 2 of more than 30 Palestinian Jews dropped behind German lines on secret SOE missions.

In March 1944, Senesh parachuted into Yugoslavia and, with the aid of local partisans, entered Hungary. She was almost immediately identified by an informer and arrested by the Gestapo. "Her behavior before members of the Gestapo and SS was quite remarkable," a comrade later wrote. "She constantly stood up to them, warning them plainly of the bitter fate they would suffer after their defeat." Though brutally tortured, she refused to give up her radio codes. On November 8, she was executed by a firing squad. "Continue the struggle till the end, until the day of liberty comes, the day of victory for our people," were her final written words.

In September 1944, Reik and four other agents parachuted into Slovakia to aid an uprising against the Fascist puppet government installed by the Nazis, and assist the Jews in the passage to Palestine. Back in her native Banska-Bystrica, she aided refugees, helped Jewish children escape to Palestine, and joined resistance groups in rescuing Allied POWs. In October, Nazis occupied the town. A few days later, Haviva and her comrades were captured in their mountain hideout by Ukrainian *Waffen*-SS troops. On November 20, they were executed. The remains of Reik, Senesh, and five other SOE agents were buried in Israel in 1952, in the Israeli National Military Cemetery on Mount Herzl in Jerusalem.

★  ★  ★

• *Romania's contribution to distinguished female agents was Vera Atkins, who worked for the French section of the Special Operations Executive (SOE) as a recruiter, trainer, and facilitator of agents throughout Europe.*

★  ★  ★

• *Following the war, Atkins spent a year questioning former concentration camp guards, who might have held clues to 118 agents who never returned to SOE.*

# A BODYGUARD OF LIES: THE ALLIED D-DAY DECEPTION

*Germany had more than enough muscle behind the guns and forts of the Atlantic Wall to blast any seaborne invasion to rags— but only if that muscle were all brought to bear swiftly in the right place. The Allies planned to make that task as challenging as possible.*

"In wartime, truth is so precious that she should always be attended by a bodyguard of lies."

—Winston Churchill

The Germans expected the Allies to attempt to invade France, but they weren't sure when or how the attack would happen. They knew that the risk of a seaborne Allied invasion increased with the distance sailed. Therefore, Allies would most likely invade as near as possible to British ports to avoid aero-naval interception, remain in range of air cover, and lessen the impact of weather. Royal Air Force fighters had enough range to cover Normandy and the Pas de Calais region just opposite Dover. As the Allies saw it, Calais was the quickest sail, but also the Atlantic Wall's sharpest teeth. Instead, they planned to endure the longer ride to Normandy, where the defenses were less formidable.

Of course, any invasion could fail if the Germans guessed its location in advance. To throw them off, the Allies contrived Operation Bodyguard, a key part of which was Operation Fortitude, a deception plan divided into North and South. Fortitude North's goal was to tie German troops up in Norway to repel a phantom invasion. Fortitude South would try to mislead the Germans about the real invasion's location—and hide that the Allies were planning multiple landings.

Fortitude North faked radio traffic to make the small northern UK garrison sound like a full army preparing to invade Norway.

Thanks to achievements in broadcasting and recording, a single radio truck could simulate the chatter of a divisional headquarters; a signals battalion could simulate an army.

Fortitude South's first job was to convince the Germans that the blow would land near Calais, with possible feints elsewhere. After the troops landed in Normandy, the second phase of Fortitude South would be to maintain the impression that a second, heavier blow was still to come at the Pas de Calais. The planners invented a fictitious army under General Patton: the 1st U.S. Army Group (FUSAG), complete with nonexistent infantry divisions.

Germany depended upon its spies to confirm or contradict what the Allies were really planning. But its intelligence turned out to be unreliable—every German spy reporting from Britain was actually working for the British.

General Dwight D. Eisenhower assumed that if at any point the Germans figured out the plans for the true D-Day invasion, Field Marshal Erwin Rommel would hurl every tank toward the Normandy beaches while the invasion was at sea—perhaps disobeying even Hitler—to prepare a lethal reception. Eisenhower took the possibility seriously enough to prepare two speeches before the invasion: one praising its success, and one taking all blame if it failed.

As it was, D-Day achieved tactical surprise. The Germans had indeed expected the Allies to storm the Pas de Calais sector. Noting that "known" FUSAG elements had not yet been sent into battle, they committed only a portion of the panzer reserve to holding off the Allied forces at Normandy. The rest were withheld to oppose FUSAG's expected second invasion. This gave the Allies those few crucial days needed to reinforce and consolidate the Normandy beachhead. The second invasion came not in June at the Pas de Calais, but on August 15, 1944, in southern France.

FUSAG never fired one rifle shot, yet it helped defeat Germany. The Allies' D-Day deception effort went down as one of the best-executed ruses in military history.

# Fast Facts

- Have you ever looked at a display of U.S. Army World War II divisional shoulder patches and seen the phrase "ghost divisions"? Most ghost divisions were part of the fictitious FUSAG. To aid in the deception, Fortitude South planners designed patches for the nonexistent divisions, ordered tons of them (to fool any listeners in the U.S.), and had a few soldiers wear them in regions where they'd be noticed by Germans.

- Another reason the Germans were prone to assume an assault on the Pas de Calais had little to do with Fortitude South: The very short range of the V-1 and V-2 missiles meant they had to be launched from the Calais area in order to reach England. While they weren't doing major damage, they were taking lives and causing considerable tension among civilians. Surely the Allies would want to capture the launch region as soon as possible to end this headache.

- Harbors influenced German thinking. The Germans assumed the Allies would have to capture a major harbor or their invasion would starve for lack of everything. West of Calais/Boulogne/Dunkirk, the next significant port was Le Havre—which wasn't large enough to support large forces. After that came Cherbourg in Normandy, a very well defended position. The Germans didn't consider that the Allies might create their own ports: the famous "Mulberry" ready-made floating concrete harbors.

- One clever feint involved a British officer who bore a striking resemblance to Field Marshal Montgomery. Lieutenant Clifton James, of the Royal Pay Corps, was assigned to follow Montgomery around for several weeks posing as a reporter—he was actually studying for his acting career. British intelligence knew that the Spanish watched Gibraltar, reporting all they saw to Germany. On May 27, 1944, Lieutenant James dressed up as the full Monty, complete with floppy beret and baton, and flew to Gibraltar with the appropriate aides. But all this amounted to nothing; postwar evidence indicated that the reports were screened out before reaching the German high command.

# THE HEROINE OF AUSCHWITZ

*Human courage did not always wear a soldier's uniform. It was sometimes found in unlikely places: One of the war's bravest fighters labored in the women's workshop of Hitler's most notorious concentration camp.*

Roza Robota was a Polish Jew whose family was gassed in the death chambers of Auschwitz II. Selected as "fit labor," the 21-year-old Robota was put to work in the death camp's clothing-supply section. There she labored for two years, a well-liked, energetic girl who became a natural leader among the female inmates in her section.

Roza was contacted by a member of the Jewish underground in 1943. Rumors had spread of orders to liquidate inmates at a faster rate, before the advancing Soviet Army could uncover evidence of the Nazi Final Solution, and the underground wanted her help.

Robota accepted a dangerous role in the plot. She helped her contacts in the camp's munitions plant to smuggle out black powder in hidden pockets of workers' dresses. When the time was right, male inmates in the camp's underground would rise up, kill as many guards as possible, and blow up the camp's infrastructure while partisans liberated the prisoners.

For weeks, Roza and several women carted out small quantities of explosives in pouches in their dresses. One of the places the stolen powder was hidden was with a *Sonderkommando* unit, a Jewish slave-labor detail charged with hauling bodies out of the gas chambers and operating the camp's crematoria. When the *Sonderkommandos* discovered that they were slated to be disposed of in the ovens they operated, they staged a premature revolt. On October 7, 1944, one crematorium exploded, and the *Sonderkommandos* tried to overpower their guards. Four or five SS guards were killed, and some six hundred inmates rioted before the revolt was put to an end.

A Gestapo team was brought in to investigate, and by torturing inmates, they discovered the source of the powder used to destroy the crematorium. The investigators rounded up and brutally tortured Robota and three of her accomplices. Even after enduring weeks of torture, Roza revealed nothing. Knowing she was about to be hanged, Robota quietly accepted her fate. She smuggled out a final note to her friends: *"Hazak v'amatz,"* meaning, "Be brave and strong."

On January 6, 1945, Roza Robota was taken before assembled munitions workers and hanged for her part in the plot to blow up the death machines. Two weeks later, as the Red Army approached, SS guards blew up the remaining crematoria to keep evidence of their atrocities out of the hands of the Allies. In demolishing the death ovens, the heavily armed SS men committed an act of abject cowardice. By doing the same thing, a frail Jewish girl committed an act of supreme heroism.

☆　　☆　　☆

•*Auschwitz-Birkenau was one of six Nazi extermination camps; the other were Belzec, Chelmno, Majdanek, Sobibor, and Treblinka. All were located in Poland. Concentration camps, as distinct from the extermination camps, were sited throughout Germany and across Occupied Europe.*

☆　　☆　　☆

•*Auschwitz was built near the Polish town of Oswiecim, on dank, marshy ground that had been considered unsuited for development.*

☆　　☆　　☆

•*The first air-reconnaissance photos of the Auschwitz complex were taken, by American aircraft, in April 1944. London and Washington had been aware of the camp's existence as early as 1943. The Allies mounted no concerted bombing against the facility, nor attempted to otherwise liberate it, because the camp was deemed to be of no military value, and thus unsuited for expenditure of Allied resources.*

# FRIENDLY FIRE

*Given the millions of tons of munitions expended in the war, it was inevitable many soldiers fell at the hand of their own forces.*

## AN AMPUTEE'S TRAGIC DOWNING

Recent research indicates that one of Britain's most renowned pilots, Sir Douglas Robert Bader, may have been shot down by friendly fire. In a 1931 crash, the daredevil RAF pilot had lost both his legs, which were amputated at the knees. In his log he wrote, "Crashed slow-rolling near ground. Bad show." Yet he continued to fly, and during the war he commanded squadrons of Spitfires and Hurricanes. A hero of the Battle of Britain, by August 1941 Bader was Britain's fifth-ranking ace, having shot down 22 or 23 German craft. That month, during a raid over France, his plane was shot up. In an attempt to bail, one of his prosthetic legs became trapped. Bader escaped when the leg straps snapped off.

According to RAF records, Bader had been separated from his formation and was flying solo next to the squadron of German fighters. A fellow British pilot claimed to have shot down a German BF-109 whose pilot saved himself by bailing out. Historian Alex Saunders believes the British pilot mistook the Bader's Spitfire for a German craft. Bader later claimed he'd collided with another plane, but he may have fabricated the story to protect his fellow flyer's reputation. A gallant *Luftwaffe* general later allowed an RAF bomber to parachute a replacement prosthetic to the captured commander—who used it to attempt so many escapes he was consigned to a maximum-security stalag. Bader was rescued in the spring of 1945. Upon arriving in Paris, he asked to be able to fly a Spitfire with the RAF for the remainder of the war, but his request was denied.

## The A-Bomb's American Deaths

As might be expected, the terrific explosions set off by the atomic bombs in Japan accounted for collateral deaths. At Hiroshima, 70,000 to 80,000 in the city died from blast effects—including as many as 20 U.S. airmen who were prisoners there, and about 2,000 Japanese-Americans, many of whom had been trapped in Japan by the war. At Nagasaki, seven Dutch POWs died from the bombing; two other prisoners died later from the effects of radiation.

## THE *LUFTWAFFE* VERSUS THE *KRIEGSMARINE*

One of Germany's worst examples of friendly fire occurred at sea, due to miscommunication between air and sea forces.

In early 1940, during Operation *Wikinger,* a German fleet of six destroyers attempted to clear British submarines and fishing boats from the heavily mined Dogger Bank in the North Sea. At the same time, the *Luftwaffe* was conducting a raid on British ships with a force of Heinkel 111 bombers. The two squadrons of ships and planes did not know of each other's operations, although the high command of both the *Kriegsmarine* and *Luftwaffe* did.

On February 19, a Heinkel flew over the flotilla, which consisted of the *Friedrich Eckoldt, Richard Beitzen, Erich Koellner, Theodor Riedel, Max Schulz,* and *Leberecht Maas.* The aircraft didn't recognize the destroyers and failed to signal the ships, which fired on the aircraft. The Heinkel and the other bombers attacked. As many as five bombs struck the *Leberecht Maas,* which broke in two. Later the *Max Schulz* hit a mine—whether it was British or German is unknown—and exploded, its entire crew lost. Thinking it had located a British submarine, the *Theodor Riedel* dropped depth charges, which damaged its own rudder. In the chaos, between 575 and 600 sailors perished.

## THE SECOND BATTLE OF ATLANTA

The fog of war also led to severe "collateral damage" and many fatalities for the light cruiser USS *Atlanta.* Christened in September 1941 by *Gone With the Wind* author Margaret Mitchell, the *Atlanta* supported the offensive on Guadalcanal, escorting ammunition and aircraft transport ships. The *Atlanta,* commanded by Captain Samuel P. Jenkins, was part of a task force that included the cruisers *San Francisco* and *Helena,* as well as destroyers.

In November 1942, Japanese Admiral Yamamoto Isoroku sent a force of two battleships, a cruiser, and six destroyers to bombard Guadalcanal's Henderson Air Field. The *Atlanta*'s force was ordered to protect the cargo ships supplying the Marines on the island.

At the start of the engagement, the *Atlanta* nearly collided with a U.S. destroyer that had steered in the wrong direction. Then it opened fired on the Japanese destroyer *Akatsuki.* Just 1,600 yards separated the ships. One or more torpedoes from the *Akatsuki* struck the *Atlanta*'s engine room, knocking out its power. The cruiser *San Francisco,* with an assist from the *Atlanta,* then sank the *Akatsuki.* Tragedy ensued when, in darkness and general confusion, the *San Francisco* mistook the *Atlanta* for the enemy, riddling it with 19 eight-inch shells. Task-force commander Rear Admiral Norman Scott, who had transferred to the *Atlanta,* was killed with members of his staff. The badly damaged *Atlanta* readied to fire on the *San Francisco,* then realized it was an American ship from its profile.

Some 165 of the *Atlanta*'s 735 crewmen were killed. On November 13, Captain Jenkins ordered the ship abandoned and scuttled.

## THE TOLL AMONG THE HIGHEST-RANKING

Friendly fire claimed all ranks. The highest-ranking American thus killed was Lieutenant General Lesley J. McNair. He was felled in Normandy by bombs from B-17s during Operation Cobra, designed to "soften up" the German lines for a breakout of Allied forces. So close were the entrenched German and American forces that air and artillery attacks often hit the wrong side.

☆　☆　☆

- *The Department of Defense estimates between 15 and 20 percent of U.S. combat deaths—some 21,000—were due to friendly fire.*

# Timeline

## 1942

**November 12–15**
The United States loses 9 ships and the Japanese lose 16 in a ferocious naval battle off the coast of Guadalcanal

**November 18**
Australians reach main Japanese position at Gona-Buna, New Guinea

**November 22**
Some 270,000 German soldiers are surrounded by the Red Army in Stalingrad

**November 25**
The U.S. government selects a site in Los Alamos, New Mexico, to build a lab devoted primarily to developing the atomic bomb

**November 30–31**
Naval battle of Tassafaranga near Guadalcanal

**December 2**
University of Chicago physicists Enrico Fermi and Arthur Compton achieve the first nuclear chain reaction

**December 13**
Rommel withdraws from El Agheila

**December 14**
Despite a massive airlift of supplies, the German 6th Army remains trapped, underequipped, and under siege in Stalingrad; three days prior, Hitler ordered that the army may not retreat from Stalingrad

**December 17**
U.S. XIV Corps begins attack on Mount Austen, Guadalcanal

British begin Arakan offensive in Burma

**December 22–25**
The Allies capture Longstop Hill, Tunisia

## 1943

**January 1**
Americans' annual incomes are capped at $25,000 annual, part of a plan to curb inflation; the law will be repealed within a year

**January 2**
Australian and U.S. troops take Buna, New Guinea

**January 3**
Germans begin withdrawal from Caucasus

**January 12**
U.S. forces move into the Aleutian Islands

**January 14–23**
Allied leadership meets in Casablanca, Morocco, agreeing that they will accept nothing short of unconditional surrender from the Axis

**January 18**
After two and a half years, the siege of Leningrad comes to an end

Jews of the Warsaw Ghetto fight back for the first time

**January 23**
British forces liberate Tripoli, Libya, from Axis occupation

U.S. troops capture Kokumbona and Mount Austen, Japan's last two strongholds on Guadalcanal

**January 27**
First USAAF raid on Germany; target Wilhelmshaven

# HANNA REITSCH: THE REICH'S FAVORITE AVIATRIX

*"My parents had shown me as a child the storks in their quiet and steady flight, the buzzards, circling ever higher in the summer air...when I, too, expressed a longing to fly, they took it for a childish fancy...but, the longing...grew with every bird I saw go flying across the azure summer sky, with every cloud that sailed past me on the wind, till it turned to...a yearning that went with me everywhere."*

—*Hanna Reitsch,* The Sky My Kingdom

Hanna Reitsch was born on March 29, 1912, in Hirschberg, a small town in Lower Silesia that was conceded to Poland after World War II. Reitsch's father was an ophthalmologist, her mother a devout Catholic. When she was just a teenager, Reitsch declared that she wanted to become a flying missionary doctor in Africa. Having been obsessed with flying from an early age, the decision marked her ascent as one of the world's most accomplished pilots.

After completing secondary school, Reitsch enrolled in the Grunau School of Gliding. She quickly outpaced her male rivals and became the first member of her class to pass the introductory flying course. Shocked by her rapid progress, school officials forced Reitsch to retake the exam, which she passed again. Reitsch then completed the next two levels of flight courses before beginning medical studies at the University of Berlin.

## EARLY ACHIEVEMENTS

During the 1930s, Reitsch set many records as a glider pilot. These accomplishments further enhanced her love of flight. In 1931 Reitsch set the women's world record for nonstop glider flying when she remained aloft for 5.5 hours. She extended this record to 11.5 hours in 1933. In 1934 Reitsch set the women's world altitude record when she soared to 2,800 meters.

In the mid-1930s, Reitsch traveled to South America, where she participated in an international study of thermal conditions during flight. She quit medical school after returning to Germany and became a glider test pilot at the German Institute for Glider Research. While at the institute, Reitsch tested the first glider seaplane and naval glider catapults.

Reitsch continued her record-breaking feats through to the rest of the 1930s. In 1936, she set the world's record in nonstop distance flight. In 1937, she became the first German to cross the Alps in a glider. Two years later, she set another world record, this time for the longest point-to-point flight.

## SERVICE IN THE *LUFTWAFFE*

Reitsch's reputation landed her at the forefront of German aviation development. In 1936 she was introduced to Ernst Udet, head of the Technical Branch of the German Ministry of Aviation. Impressed with her work on the development of air brakes in gliders, Udet appointed Reitsch to the position of civilian test pilot in the *Luftwaffe* the following year.

In February 1938, Reitsch became the first person to fly a helicopter inside a building when she piloted the Focke-Achgelis FW-61 in a demonstration inside the *Deutschlandhalle* during the Berlin Motor Show. In the fall of that year, she traveled overseas to the International Air Races at Cleveland, Ohio, where she demonstrated the Habicht aerobatic glider.

Back in Germany, Reitsch participated in the Messerschmitt Me-361 *Gigant* glider program, which sought to develop a glider capable of carrying cargo, troops, and fuel. But tragedy befell the program: A catastrophic crash resulted in the deaths of the glider's tow-plane pilots, the *Gigant*'s crew, and more than 100 troops aboard. Reitsch was not aboard when the glider crashed, but the project ceased following the accident.

Despite the *Gigant* incident, the *Luftwaffe*'s research branch far outpaced its rivals during the war. In 1942, pilots began testing one of the first single-seat rocket-powered interceptors—the Messerschmitt Me-163 *Komet.* Through her contacts, Reitsch managed to test fly the Me-163A prototype and the Me-163B production model. During a test flight in the 163B, the plane's fall-away wheel carriage did not disengage from the airplane after takeoff. After several attempts to dislodge the dolly, Reitsch was forced to land the plane with the carriage still attached. As she brought the jet fighter down, the plane stalled and crashed. Reitsch suffered severe injuries, including several skull and facial fractures.

Reitsch needed five months to recover from her injuries. The Nazi leadership was sufficiently impressed with her devotion to award her a diamond-encrusted Gold Medal for Military Flying and later, the Iron Cross First Class (she was one of only two women to receive this honor during the war). She had previously won the Iron Cross Second Class for her work on a shearing device developed to cut barrage balloon cables.

In 1943 Reitsch participated in Operation *Selbstopfer* ("self-sacrifice"). She test flew a cockpit-added V-1 rocket bomb, which was uncoupled in flight from a Heinkel He 111 bomber. The data Reitsch collected helped the project's engineers develop a stabilization system for the V-1 bombs. Eventually the Germans planned to send pilots on suicide missions, steering the bombs toward Allied production and communication centers, but that idea was abandoned.

## A FINAL ATTEMPT TO SAVE THE *FÜHRER*

On April 25, 1945, Reitsch's longtime friend Field Marshal Robert Ritter von Greim asked Reitsch to accompany him on a flight to see Hitler in Berlin. Hitler had just dismissed *Luftwaffe* head Herman Göring after Göring's attempt to take control of Germany in the war's closing days. The Nazi dictator wanted to appoint Greim as the new commander in chief of the *Luftwaffe.*

The two pilots managed to land a small Fieseler Fi-156C *Storch* on a boulevard near the Brandenburg Gate. In the process, their plane was hit by Russian antiaircraft fire and Greim was seriously wounded in the foot. Reitsch and Greim stayed in the *Führerbunker* for several days, intent on dying alongside Hitler when he refused to fly with them to safety. The Nazi dictator ordered the two to leave the bunker and had an Arado 96 lightweight aircraft delivered from an underground hangar for their use. The two pilots managed to escape. On May 9, Reitsch brought Greim to a hospital in Kitsbuhel, where she was promptly arrested.

Reitsch was interrogated by military-intelligence personnel, who were convinced she had flown Hitler out of Berlin. Reitsch was cleared of war crimes, but spent 15 months in prison.

## NEW RECORDS

Following the war, German citizens were forbidden to fly. A few years later, gliding was permitted, and Reitsch resumed her prewar record-setting ways by taking third place in a Spanish gliding championship and later breaking the women's altitude record (6,848 meters). In 1959, she opened a gliding center in India, and in 1961 she was invited to the White House. In 1962, she opened a glider school in Ghana, Africa, where she lived for four years.

As one of the Third Reich's only female test pilots, Reitsch flew everything the Nazis had in their inventory, from the first functional helicopter to the first jet-powered fighter. She set more than 40 flight records, many of them while flying a glider. A devout follower of National Socialism, Reitsch often wore her Nazi medals after the war. She died of a heart attack in Frankfurt in 1979.

☆　　☆　　☆

•*Hanna Reitsch test-flew the astonishing Messerschmitt Me-163* Komet, *a swept-wing rocket plane with a top speed of 596 mph. A one-seat fighter, the* Komet *had an impractically brief flight time of just 7.5 minutes; pilots had to glide back to base. Limited production of the* Komet *began in 1944, but Germany's diminishing resources prevented the plane from becoming a factor in the war.*

# Fast Facts

- In the Mediterranean, the Royal Navy worried more about Italian frogmen than Italian ships. The intrepid swimmers sank numerous warships and merchant vessels inside supposedly safe harbors.

- Canadians provided most of the force to attack Dieppe, France, in 1942, and paid a stunning price—their casualty rate was 95 percent.

- Greek defenders weren't very impressed with the Italian invaders. One Greek bomber pilot dropped chamber pots on Italian troops after releasing his conventional bomb load.

- The 12-day conquest of Yugoslavia cost Germany only 151 lives. Partisan fighting after the surrender would claim far more.

- As Commonwealth forces prepared to make a stand at ancient Thermopylae in 1941, they held a scheduled soccer game and continued it even when strafed by Stukas.

- One Waterloo, Iowa family, the Sullivans, lost five sons in U.S. Navy service in the Pacific (Madison, 23; Joseph, 24; Francis, 27; George, 28; and Albert, 29). Their sister, Genevieve, promptly took up her fallen brothers' sword: She enlisted in the Navy's Women Accepted for Voluntary Emergency Service (WAVES).

- Nearly everyone could contribute something special to the U.S. war effort. Blind people sorted items by touch; deaf laborers worked in high-noise areas; very short people inspected cramped parts of aircraft.

- An OSS commander advising the Kachin fighters of Burma ordered 500 Springfield muzzle-loaders, which had been left over from the American Civil War, for the men. The Kachins loved the antiquated weapons and found them most useful against Japanese invaders.

- Male civilian internees in Japanese custody at Santo Tom's, Philippines, weighed an average of 112 pounds at liberation.

# WHY DID THE NAZIS KEEP A RECORD OF THE HOLOCAUST?

*The events of World War II were recorded to an extent far beyond that of preceding conflicts. Events were captured in print, photographs, and moving pictures. The most chilling of all was the exhaustive documentation of the Holocaust, much of it created by the very people who committed the crimes.*

Knowledge of the Holocaust stems from many sources, the most compelling of which are the eyewitness testimonies of victims. But there is another source that helps confirm the extermination's unthinkable scale, as well as the fates of individuals. That source is the accounts kept by the Nazis themselves.

Seized by the liberating armies in the last days of the war, the documentation exists in various collections, but the bulk of the records have been under the care of the Red Cross for the last half-century. The files are extensive: millions upon millions of papers covering 16 miles of shelves. Why? Why would a group of people intent on murder risk putting their activities in writing?

The answer may be surprisingly prosaic. In the opinion of Paul Shapiro, director of Holocaust studies at the United States Holocaust Memorial Museum, "They wanted to show they were getting the job done." Many accounts suggest that he may be correct.

## JUST A JOB: "THE BUREAUCRACY OF THE DEVIL"

A stereotypical but not entirely inaccurate image of the prewar German government is one of bureaucracy. Everything was documented, and paper authorizations were generated by the handful for the most mundane of tasks. This attitude extended into the war. The task of running an empire, even a despicable one, is complex, requiring extensive procedures and paper trails. Like many governments, Nazi Germany employed an array of middle managers who wanted to prove their efficiency. The only way an official could show he was performing up to par was to keep records.

Prisoners who were immediately executed had the least documentation, sometimes being reduced to a mere entry in the number of arrivals for the day. Individuals who stayed in the camps longer typically had more extensive records. Because of the sheer number of people involved—some 17 million in all—some startling documents survived, such as the original list of Jews transferred to safety in the factories of Oskar Schindler. Another file contains the records of Anne Frank.

## WHY WORRY?

For most of the war, the Nazis showed little compunction about documenting their activities. In their minds, why should they? To whom would they be accountable? After all, many thought the Third Reich would last a thousand years. In the closing months of the war, there was a slight reversal of this policy, and the commandants of some camps sought to destroy records and eliminate the remaining witnesses as the Allied forces closed in. Fortunately, they were not able to erase the record of their own atrocities.

Private memoirs of the Holocaust also exist. Participants at all levels wrote letters about their experiences, and some SS guards took photographs of the camps and inmates with their personal cameras. Some of the Nazi leadership was also prone to recording daily activities; Joseph Goebbels kept a journal throughout the war, viewing it as a "substitute for the confessional."

Much like Goebbels's diary, the official records of the Holocaust have become the unintentional confession of a Nazi machine that had uncountable crimes for which to answer. The archive exists in Bad Arolsen, Germany, and was opened to the online public in late 2006. Survivors of the camps hope that its presence serves as a counterargument to those who inexplicably deny that the Holocaust ever happened, and as a reminder that humankind must never allow it to happen again.

# Timeline

## 1943

**January 31**
To Hitler's disgust, the German 6th Army in Stalingrad surrenders

**February 8**
The Russians retake Kursk, which had been occupied by the Germans for almost 14 months

**February 9**
The United States declares Guadalcanal secure the day after the last Japanese soldier evacuates the island

**February 10**
Mohandas Gandhi stops eating in protest of Britain's detention of India's independence-seeking Congress Party leader; he vows to consume only diluted fruit juice for the next three weeks

**February 14–25**
Battle of Kasserine Pass, Tunisia

**February 14–April 29**
British "Chindit" expedition into Burma

**February 21–March 15**
German counteroffensive recaptures Kharkov

**March 2**
Battle of the Bismarck Sea

**March 5**
Japanese launch offensive up Yangtze River in China

**March 5–July 10**
Air Battle of the Ruhr

**March 16–19**
Climax of the Battle of the Atlantic; U-boat "wolf packs" sink 22 Allied merchant ships and a convoy escort

**March 26**
Naval Battle of the Komandarski Islands in the Bering Sea

**April 7–16**
Japanese air offensive in the Solomon Islands

**April 12**
The bodies of thousands of Polish Army officers, who had been assassinated by the Soviet secret police, are found in Russia's Katyn Forest

**April 18**
Admiral Yamamoto is shot down and killed over the Solomon Islands

**April 19–May 16**
Warsaw Ghetto uprising

**April 28–30**
German panzer units attack Djebel Bou-Aoukaz, Tunisia, in what will be Germany's last offensive maneuver in North Africa

**May 6–24**
Allies sink 41 U-boats, forcing Germans to withdraw their wolf packs from the North Atlantic

**May 7**
Allies take Tunis, the capital of Tunisia

**May 12**
Axis units in North Africa surrender in Tunisia

**May 13**
As a prelude to the full-scale assault in Sicily, the Allies attack Pantelleria, a small Italian island about 30 miles off the Tunisian coast

**May 14**
British retreat ends Arakan offensive in Burma

# THE RUHR CAMPAIGN

*The region known as "The Armory of the Third Reich" became the site of Germany's greatest defeat.*

Soon after the National Socialists came to power in 1933, Hitler enacted a series of measures to prioritize industrial development in the new regime. At the heart of Germany's industrial revitalization was the densely populated, coal-rich Ruhr Valley. Thus, in the years immediately preceding the Second World War, the Ruhr Valley became rich not only in coal but in factories, railroads, and housing. Nazi war industries such as aviation fuel, synthetic oil, coal, and rubber created jobs and opportunities that had withered during the economic depression Germany had suffered after World War I.

Known for its industrial capabilities, the Ruhr Valley was a priority for Allied strategists from the start of the war. But the Allies were in no position to attack the region in a big way until 1943, when they began gaining supremacy in the skies over cities such as Essen and Cologne. By late summer of that year, many of the larger cities in the area were almost completely destroyed by concentrated raids that claimed thousands of lives. The Nazis continued to repair and operate their factories, however, and evacuated mass numbers of women and children from the increasingly hostile region.

In March 1945, Allied units crossed the Rhine and gained access to the Ruhr Valley. Hitler ordered his commander in the region, Field Marshal Walther Model, to hold the area at all costs. While the bulk of the American, British, and Canadian units deployed north and east in an attempt to beat the Russians to Berlin, the American 9th and 12th Army Groups under the command of Generals Omar Bradley and Courtney Hodges, in conjunction with British forces under the command of Field Marshal Bernard Montgomery, performed a series of actions that completely encircled the remaining German forces in what General Dwight D.

Eisenhower later referred to as "the largest double envelopment in history."

Inside the approximately 3,000-square-mile "Ruhr Pocket," nearly 350,000 German soldiers, 4 million civilians, and vast quantities of materiel were trapped.

Field Marshal Model's armies were left with few options. They lacked the fuel and ammunition to engage in a large battle and had only a few weeks' supply of food. The German general was outmatched and surrounded, and lacked the means to fight his way out of the pocket. However, Model, a fanatical Nazi, refused to surrender so long as he believed that he could keep enemy forces diverted from marching on Berlin. His troops, however, felt differently. Many of the German soldiers in the region were demoralized by years of war; moreover, the war had depleted most units, and young boys and old men had been conscripted to defend the homeland. Most surrendered.

In one of the greatest capitulations in history, the Allies neutralized nearly 320,000 enemy troops in a series of swift actions. The 9th Army advanced 50 miles, captured 47,581 prisoners (including 7 General Officers), seized 120 towns, and cleared 300 square miles of enemy territory in only 11 days. Field Marshal Model chose to commit suicide rather than be captured. In the final days of the battle, disciplined SS troops obeyed horrific orders to kill scores of prisoners and civilians suspected of aiding the Allies.

✯ ✯ ✯

- *The first instance of an all-consuming conflagration as the result of an aerial bombardment occurred in the Ruhr Valley city of Wuppertal in late May 1943. German fire crews were overwhelmed, and most of the city was destroyed.*

✯ ✯ ✯

- *The exodus of women and children, known as the* Kinderlandverschickung, *was the single largest internal migration in history.*

# THOSE DEVILISH HEDGEROWS

*The Allied advance through France's bocage country was nearly a replay of the killing fields of World War I.*

As the sun set on the Normandy coast on June 6, 1944, the war in Europe had taken a turn: The Allies had established a toehold in France. Reinforcements poured ashore, but the march inland slowed to a painful crawl as American, British, and Canadian troops engaged the enemy in terrain aptly suited for the German defenders.

The *bocage* country of Normandy consisted of hundreds of irregular parcels of land used for orchards, grain farming, or cattle grazing. The parcels ranged in size from 10 to 150 acres and were surrounded on all sides by hedgerows: mounds of earth approximately six feet wide and six feet high, atop which grew bramble, rosebushes, small trees, and other dense vegetation. In some areas, trees branches from either side of the road provided a canopy of shade that lasted all hours of the day.

The hedgerows undermined the advantages Allied armor and firepower might have had by providing perfect cover for the German defenders. They hid among the dense undergrowth and ambushed Allied troops. One antitank gun, machine-gun squad, or even a sole sniper could stop the advance of an entire Allied column. The Germans were also able to move men and materiel through the canopied lanes without fear of discovery by Allied fighter planes, which dominated the skies following the invasion.

Allied tanks were at a distinct disadvantage in *bocage* country. The narrow lanes with high embankments impeded the swiveling of tank turrets. Tanks were also vulnerable to enemy fire when they tried to push through the vegetation: While climbing the embankments, drivers exposed the unarmored underbelly of their tanks to German antitank weapons.

Initially, the Allies used explosives to open holes in the hedges. One unit commander calculated a mission covering a mere one-and-a-half miles could encounter some three dozen hedgerows, making the explosives technique impractical from a supply standpoint.

The solution to the terrain problem came from a member of the 2nd Armored Division's 102nd Calvary Reconnaissance Squadron. Sergeant Curtis Culin, a former taxi driver from Chicago, designed and built a hedgerow-cutting device from scrap metal. It was welded to the front of a Sherman tank, allowing it to plough through the brush without exposing its vulnerable underside.

Culin's idea was so successful that the chief of the army's First Ordnance Section was ordered to supply and install as many cutters as possible. Tanks sporting the new tool were affectionately nicknamed "rhino tanks," and by the end of July 1944, 60 percent of the 1st Army's Shermans were fitted with the new steel-pronged cutters. The invention allowed Allied infantry and armor to coordinate their attacks, rout the enemy, and continue their march east toward Paris.

✯　　✯　　✯

- *Because metal was an essential commodity in the United States, the annual Oscars statuettes were made from wood during the war years.*

✯　　✯　　✯

- *Luxembourg was not, as many believed, unarmed. The Grand Ducal defense forces numbered 400 riflemen and a 12-man cavalry troop.*

✯　　✯　　✯

- *As Washington closed its books for the 1943 fiscal year, it was revealed that 93 percent of the federal budget was allocated to national defense spending.*

# "IT'S NOT ILLEGAL IF YOU DON'T GET CAUGHT"

*Americans made many sacrifices during the war, but for some, forgoing sugar, meat, or gasoline was too much. Instead, they turned to the black market.*

> **black market:** *illicit trade in goods or commodities in violation of official regulations.*
>
> Since their country's founding, Americans have generally enjoyed the benefits of a free market economy. During the Second World War, however, the Roosevelt administration realized it would need to control the consumption of many basic goods in order to effectively fight a two-front war.

The World War II-era rationing and price-control system was the brainchild of Wall Street financier Bernard Baruch. He first suggested the scheme in early 1941, arguing that the government should apply rationing vertically (for example, rationing would affect not only automobiles, but also the steel, rubber, and cloth used to make them). To curb inflation, price controls would be needed. Americans would learn to sort through their ration books for items such as gasoline and meat. What Baruch did not take into account, however, was the rise of a vast black market fueled by many ordinary and otherwise law-abiding citizens.

The modern American black market is said to have been born on January 27, 1942. On that day, the Office of Price Administration (OPA) was given authority to enact civilian rationing and price control under Directive No. 1 of the War Production Board. Among the list of items classified as "scarce" were sugar, automobiles, tires, gasoline, and typewriters. Violators could face up to a year in jail and a $5,000 fine, but that was hardly a deterrent. Manufacturers, distributors, retailers, and consumers soon found ways to evade and sometimes profit from the price controls and rationing systems. Consumers learned that with enough money, they could readily find what they wanted—regardless of government regulations. By some estimates consumer industries such as department stores, meat packers, and leather tanners realized profits as high as 1,000 percent during the war.

The subterfuge took many forms: trimming less fat from meat, counterfeiting gas vouchers, processing livestock through unregulated channels, and ignoring rent controls. Counterfeit vouchers, often sold through organized-crime syndicates, were the most common form of black-market exchange. One arrest in Detroit yielded 26,000 counterfeit vouchers that had been sewn into the lining of gang members' coats.

The black market could not have existed, however, if a large number of Americans had not been willing to engage in illegal trade. To most citizens, the transactions seemed so innocuous that they probably never thought twice about the corner gas station owner selling a few extra gallons for a bit more money or their friend the butcher providing them with a larger cut of meat for the same price.

Efforts to enlighten the public did little. In February 1944 Patricia Lochridge wrote an article for *Woman's Home Companion* titled "I Shopped the Black Market." In it, she detailed how homemakers, ministers, bankers, and other average Americans willingly engaged in illegal activity. Realizing the effect of this trade, the OPA launched campaigns that equated purchasing black market meat with doing "business with Hitler." For the most part, however, Americans ignored the pleas of the ineffective bureaucratic agency. In fact, many sympathized with those who were punished for transgressing the price controls.

Many of the items bought through black market channels had their origin in the military, which was where the goods had been funneled. While the penalty for selling goods within the armed services was severe, even rumors of executed transgressors did little to slow the brisk business. In the final months of the war, cigarettes were more valuable abroad than any country's currency. Robert F. Gallagher remembers that while serving as an MP in Belgium, he and his friends often used intermediaries to sell their cigarette rations to locals for a hefty profit. Another common form of profiteering involved the illegal sale of currency. Some soldiers claimed to have made thousands of dollars buying and selling foreign currencies in the confusion and economic depression of postwar Europe. Gallagher: "It's not illegal if you don't get caught."

It is nearly impossible to quantify the amount of black market activity that occurred in the United States during the war. Some have claimed that at the height of the price controls, a majority of the citizens of New York engaged in black market exchanges, and 90 percent of the meat being shipped from San Antonio, Texas, came from black market sources. The black market flourished in part because Americans mistrusted the goods' regulation. Equally important, the OPA was relatively powerless to enforce its controls: Popularly elected officials were reluctant to take measures of which the majority of their constituents would disapprove. Any society that has attempted to overregulate its market has had to increase its security and monitoring forces in kind. The police states engendered by Nazi Germany, Soviet Russia, and scores of Third World dictatorships did exactly that to secure the sanctioned exchange of goods and defend government property. Ironically, it was the war against Fascism and the police states of Nazi Germany and Imperial Japan that gave rise to regulation in America—and to the black market.

☆　　☆　　☆

- *When American pilots signed up for the American Volunteer Group, they were promised a salary of $600 a month. This was more than double what most pilots earned in the U.S. Army Air Corps. By the time the AVG disbanded it had cost the Chinese government $8 million in salaries and equipment. Chennault wrote to Dr. Soong, China's Secretary of the Treasury, his regrets that the group had cost more than originally estimated and received the following reply: "The VG was the soundest investment China ever made."*

# "THE SNAKE WILL SMOKE"—THE CURIOUS HISTORY OF THE BRAZILIAN EXPEDITIONARY FORCE

*The land of Carnival and bossa nova fielded one of the conflict's fiercest fighting units and became the only South American country to fight in the war.*

Brazil's failure to commit troops during the First World War led to a joke: One was more likely to see a snake smoke than to see Brazilians fighting in Europe. But from 1944–1945 the soldiers of the *Força Expedicionária Brasileira* (FEB, "Brazilian Expeditionary Force") were proud to display the insignia patch of a green snake smoking a pipe as they trudged through the mountains of Italy, beating back the Fascist forces and playing a significant role in breaking the so-called Gothic Line defending the Po Valley.

At the outset of the war, Brazil, ruled by dictator Getúlio Vargas, was neutral and maintained strong economic ties with both the United States and Germany. However, Brazil's eventual cooperation was strategically important to the Allies for several reasons:

The northeastern coast of the country was considered the most likely spot for a German invasion of the Western Hemisphere.

The United States needed a base in Brazil from which to supply the African campaign.

German submarines off the South American coast were wreaking havoc on Allied shipping.

After Pearl Harbor, Vargas sensed an opportunity to obtain favorable treatment from the United States and joined the Allied powers. In exchange for a naval and air base at Natal on Brazil's northeast coast, the United States provided technical advice to build the Volta Redonda steel mill. The Natal base proved the perfect springboard for operations in Africa and Italy, and regular patrols soon began to thwart the U-boat menace.

Initially there was no expectation that Brazil would participate in the war. But in a 1943 meeting at Natal, Franklin Roosevelt encouraged Vargas and his government to commit troops; the Brazilians didn't need much convincing.

The country's military commanders wanted to participate in the fighting to avenge German submarine raids in the South Atlantic.

Vargas wished to buy time to build a populist base.

Vargas's opponents within the government believed (rightly, it turned out) that soldiers who fought Fascism abroad would demand democracy at home.

So, while maintaining a domestic force to guard the border with Argentina, the government assembled the FEB. Reaching 25,334 troops at its peak, the FEB was made up of police and all who would volunteer. When no more volunteered, the government conscripted men for the army. The last time Brazilian forces had fought outside their own country's borders had been the 1865-70 war against Paraguay. The regular army was still using surplus equipment supplied by the French after the First World War, including 25-year-old tins of rations.

The FEB was initially slated for action in Africa, but by the time it was ready to deploy, the Germans had been expelled from that continent. Instead, the Brazilian troops were sent to the mountains of Italy, where they suffered in the unfamiliar terrain and cold. Though they operated as an autonomous force, the Brazilians attached themselves willingly to the depleted American IV Corps of 5th Army, in whose service they soon saw heavy combat. In one of the FEB's initial actions it fought seasoned German troops at close range until forced to retreat due to lack of ammunition.

One German officer is said to have exclaimed that the Brazilian troops fought like devils without regard to their own safety. Soon after the FEB's arrival, German propaganda pamphlets and radio broadcasts appeared in Portuguese—a testament to the unit's effectiveness. The FEB's most glorious moment came when, after four months of heavy fighting, it seized the heavily defended summit of Monte Castello. Its heaviest action, however, was during a grueling four-day battle to take the town of Montese, where the FEB suffered 426 casualties in four days of fighting.

Before any battle, the Brazilian troops were heard to say, "The snake will smoke."

✯　✯　✯

- *Not only did the Brazilian forces pick up new weapons and fighting techniques from the Americans, but the rigid caste system of the Brazilian military—in which enlisted men were treated like slaves—began to loosen after prolonged contact with the U.S. military.*

✯　✯　✯

- *The FEB took 20,573 prisoners during its service in Italy, and veterans were always proud that they had shown their enemy respect in defeat. There are many photographs of smiling German prisoners smoking cigarettes with their pleased Brazilian captors.*

✯　✯　✯

- *Brazil was the only nation to field a nonsegregated army during the war. The FEB was made up of men with Japanese, Polish, Russian, African, German, Italian, and Portuguese heritages.*

✯　✯　✯

- *By 1941, the German community in Brazil numbered about 900,000 immigrants and native born. They resisted assimilation, and built a power base in three economically important southern states: Santa Catarina, Rio Grande do Sul, and Paraná. German intelligence counted on wartime cooperation from the region.*

# COMIC BOOK HEROES GO TO WAR

*American comic book heroes fought both on the home front and on the battlefront, doing everything from shaping public opinion to socking the Führer square on the jaw, a sentiment no doubt shared by the troops who followed their adventures ravenously.*

In the late 1930s, American opinion over the turmoil in Europe was split. Many citizens believed in isolationism—why should America solve a European problem? Others were horrified by Japan and Germany's sudden aggression. Popular culture mirrored this division, and comic books were no different.

In 1938, an issue of *Action Comics* featured the colorful new hero Superman uncovering a plot by a dastardly senator bent on getting America involved in a European conflict. Fortunately, Superman was able to keep the United States out of trouble by forcing the sides to overcome their differences.

Other citizens and artists had a different vision, however. In a conscious effort to "take a stand," Jack Kirby and Joe Simon transformed a weakling unfit for military service into a super-soldier through a secret government experiment, and Captain America headed off to Europe to personally confront Hitler a year before the United States entered the war. The authors received threatening letters for their efforts. Kirby and Simon were far from alone in predicting the entry of the United States into the war; Leverett Gleason publications issued a *Daredevil Battles Hitler* comic in 1941, and a prescient November 1941 issue of *National Comics* depicted a fictional attack on Pearl Harbor.

## "THE SENTINELS OF LIBERTY STAND ALONE!"

After the actual attack on Pearl Harbor took place a month later, the isolationist viewpoint all but disappeared, and comic heroes went to war with a vengeance. Captain America served in the army; Wonder Woman became a nurse. In the pages of DC Comics, the Justice Society suspended operations so that all the heroes could join the military. By 1941, Superman himself had reversed his neutralist stance and battled domestic saboteurs or fifth columnists in every issue.

Along with the traditional characters developing a patriotic streak, the war saw the rise of some inarguably pro-American characters. *Startling Comics* introduced Fighting Yank, whose powers came by way of a Revolutionary War ancestor; *National Comics* featured a character called simply Uncle Sam.

Hitler served as the perfect foil for the costumed crusaders: Rather than the authors having to invent a villain, here was a real-life figure bent on world domination, a character as evil as any they could possibly imagine. Heroes such as Daredevil and Sub-Mariner battled the Nazis overseas, but others waged war at home. Since with his powers Superman could easily have ended the war, his creators contrived to keep him home by having Clark Kent fail his military physical. Superman contented himself with battling enemy agents in the United States, at one point even testifying before Congress that American forces were easily powerful enough to triumph without his aid.

## "THE JAPS STARTED THEIR TREACHEROUS ATTACK!"

Publishers began to realize that rather than mirroring common sentiments, their characters could help to shape wartime opinion—not to mention sell a lot of comic books. Superheroes began selling war bonds, organizing scrap metal drives, and offering lessons on how to be a proper American. Along with such positive messages, however, a fair amount of effort went into demonizing the enemy, usually in brutally graphic ways. Germans were depicted as cold, calculating, and ruthless, often sporting monocles or facial scars; Mussolini became a clown. The Japanese were portrayed as bucktoothed ape-men with a predilection for butchering prisoners in stories with titles like "The Slant Eye of Satan" from a *Green Hornet* comic book. Very occasionally, comics admitted the possibility that enemy civilians might be decent people, albeit hopelessly misguided by their leaders, but those portrayals were relatively uncommon.

## SUNSET OF THE GOLDEN AGE

World War II proved to be a gold mine for comic book publishers. The backdrop of the war and identification of superheroes as icons of patriotism helped circulation double from 10 to 20 million issues a month from 1941 to 1944, despite wartime paper shortages. An estimated 44 percent of the armed forces read comics regularly. Men passed the books around until they fell apart, and in 1943 military post exchanges reported that comics outsold *Reader's Digest, Life,* and *The Saturday Evening Post* combined by a 10-1 margin. Following the war, the heroes of the comic pages went on to further encourage the American way of life and fight the Red Scare in the Cold War. But in many ways the World War II era marked their zenith, and fans today remember that time as the Golden Age of Comics.

☆    ☆    ☆

- *Many U.S. athletes were drafted into service during the war, leading some draft rejects to fill positions on professional sports teams. The long-hapless St. Louis Browns, which included a man missing one arm, won their first and only pennant in 1944.*

☆    ☆    ☆

- *Italy's first naval engagement of the war was tragicomic. After the Royal Navy sank the cruiser* Colleoni, *the British hurried to rescue the survivors, but were driven off by Italian aircraft.*

☆    ☆    ☆

- *To explain the Lend-Lease program with Britain to Americans, Roosevelt compared it to lending a garden hose to a neighbor to put out a fire. "I don't say... 'Neighbor, my garden hose cost me $15; you have to pay me for it' ... I want my garden hose back after the fire is over."*

# U.S. NAVY SUBMARINES: THE SILENT SERVICE AT WAR

*The U.S. Navy entered World War II confident in its submarine arm. But when the subs moved in for a kill, they failed again and again. Dozens of Japanese warships and merchant vessels would reach their destinations without ever learning that a U.S. submarine had tried to harm them.*

After the U.S. submarine force's lackluster World War I performance, U.S. Navy (USN) designers were keen to improve on the past. In 1934, they launched the Fleet Boat (F-Boat), a long-range sub with a new diesel engine. Despite Depression constraints, by 1941 these undersea vessels composed nearly four-fifths of the USN submarine arm.

When the Japanese attacked Pearl Harbor, 55 USN submarines in the Pacific were eager to strike back at the Empire.

They would sink very few ships for two agonizing years.

## WHO TESTED THESE THINGS?

Often a U.S Navy sub would fire a spread of several torpedoes without harming the target. The admirals grew livid. The commanders protested that the torpedoes were faulty, but the admirals proclaimed the technology was the most advanced in the world. By January 1, 1943, barely a year into the war, 40 submarine skippers had been relieved of command.

So what was wrong? The navy's sophistocated Mark 14 Torpedo had a magnetic detonator designed to explode on contact with the target's magnetic field; it also had a contact detonator. The problem: As of December 7, 1941, no Mark 14 had yet been test-fired with a live warhead at a real target. At $10,000 per torpedo, destructive tests were considered too expensive during the prewar Depression years. The subs paid the price: No submariner, no matter how brave or devious, could sink even an anchored garbage scow with a bum torpedo.

# WHAT WENT WRONG?

First, through combat and noncombat testing, sub skippers learned that the Mark 14 was running ten feet deeper than its settings—passing well under its targets without exploding. Engineers set the devices to run ten feet shallower, but then the Mark 14s began to explode prematurely!

The designers hadn't considered that magnetic fields vary with many factors, including location on the globe. A magnetic field that is hemispherical in northern waters could flatten out at the equator, which would cause the Mark 14 to explode short of the target. The ideal point of detonation was directly beneath the target ship, breaking the quarry's keel (spine). A side detonation would sink most merchantmen, but against warships this would strike a thick belt of armor. The magnetic detonator would have worked perfectly if all fields were hemispherical at all times in all places and if the torpedo ran deep enough to intercept the field below the keel—but physics was not so kind.

The faulty magnetic detonators were disarmed. Now the torpedoes were hitting but not exploding! In one case, a brave captain deliberately fired 15 torpedoes into one of Japan's largest tankers. Thirteen were duds. Why? Further testing showed the reason: The firing pin was defective.

# REDEMPTION FOR USN SUBS

With an improved firing pin, the Mark 14 worked fine. Navy subs began to put a dent in Japan's battle fleet, sinking 1 battleship, 8 carriers, 11 cruisers, 43 destroyers, and 23 submarines. In 1942, Japan lost barely a million tons of shipping; in 1943, 1.8 million. In 1944, the Allies sank 3.9 million tons of Japanese merchant shipping, plus another 1.7 million in the first half of 1945—U.S. subs sank the majority. A resource-poor island nation, Japan had to import materials by sea or not at all. From 1944 on, U.S. submarines sank Japanese freighters three times faster than Japan could build new ones, and fewer freighters meant fewer raw materials to build replacements. The death of its merchant fleet strangled Japan's war effort.

Even before the torpedo problems were resolved, USN submarines did much for the Allied cause. Subs rescued downed pilots, transported Marine raiders for commando attacks, fetched and delivered secret agents and supplies, spied, and handled many other delicate and risky missions. The vast majority of USN subs fought in the Pacific, as they were far more useful against Japan's surface ships. In the Atlantic and Mediterranean, the major Axis threat was the German U-boat, whose primary hunter was the destroyer.

Fifty-two USN submarines never returned from their missions, with the loss of 3,506 crewmen—about 22 percent of all men serving in the sub force.

☆　　☆　　☆

- *The hard, lightweight steel used in Japanese airplane propellers, collected from aircraft shot down over Pearl Harbor, turned out to be the ideal material for Pearl's navy machinists to fashion into better firing pins.*

☆　　☆　　☆

- *Navy submarines carried no doctors; a pharmacist's mate had to handle medical emergencies. Among many lifesaving accomplishments during the war, navy pharmacist's mates tallied 11 emergency appendectomies.*

☆　　☆　　☆

- *Many navy subs found their targets with aid from the maritime reconnaissance patrols of the navy PBY Catalina flying boats. The PBYs also helped pinpoint Allied pilots downed at sea; submarines, many guided to the right location by patrolling Catalinas, rescued 504 Allied pilots.*

☆　　☆　　☆

- *The most successful submarines in the USN fleet tallied more than 20 sinkings and/or nearly 100,000 tons of shipping. One, USS Flasher, exceeded both milestones.*

# Timeline

## 1943

**May 17**
An RAF raid causes extensive damage to two of Germany's largest dams; more than 1,300 die in the ensuing floods

**May 30**
U.S. troops secure the Aleutian island of Attu from the Japanese almost 20 days after first landing

**June 21–25**
Allies capture New Georgia

**June 22**
First USAAF raid on the German Ruhr in daylight

**June 29–30**
Allies land at Nassau Bay, New Guinea

**June 30**
U.S. troops take Rendova in the Solomon Islands

**July 5–6**
Naval Battle of Kula Gulf in the Solomon Islands

**July 10**
More than 150,000 Allied soldiers land on Sicily, catching the meager Axis defensive force completely by surprise

**July 12**
Some 3,000 tanks clash in the Battle of Kursk, the largest tank battle in world history; the Soviets dominate over the German Panzers

Naval Battle of Kolombangara in the Solomon Islands

**July 22**
U.S. troops capture Palermo, Sicily

**July 25**
Mussolini is ousted in a bloodless coup

**July 27–28**
Some 20,000 German civilians die when an RAF raid on Hamburg ignites a series of deadly firestorms

**July 28**
The United States plans for an invasion of Kiska, unaware that the Japanese have secretly withdrawn from the Aleutian island

**August 1**
USAAF attack on Ploesti oil fields in Romania damages Axis oil refineries

**August 6–7**
Naval Battle of Vella Gulf in the Solomon Islands

**August 12**
Germany withdraws defensive force from Sicily

**August 15**
U.S. and Canadian troops land on Kiska, only to discover it was abandoned weeks earlier

**August 17**
Messina falls; Axis resistance in Sicily ends

**August 23**
Soviets retake Kharkov

**August 28**
End of Japanese resistance on New Georgia in the Solomon Islands

**September 3**
Italy signs a treaty with American officials in Sicily, effectively surrendering to the Allies; the treaty is kept secret for a time to aid Allied operations in Italy.

# TRIUMPHS OF THE CANADIAN ARMY

*The battle that Canada is most remembered for in World War II is its thorough defeat at Dieppe. But Dieppe was the exception rather than the rule for the Canadian Army in World War II. After Dieppe, Canadians fought in some of the most arduous battles in the European Theater—and won almost all of them.*

Ask people to name one battle fought by the Canadian Army during World War II, and their answer will overwhelmingly be "Dieppe." Only a rare few will say "Sicily," "Ortona," "D-Day," "Falaise," or "the Scheldt estuary." Much to the chagrin of Canadians, their country's most notorious defeat in the war has overshadowed its subsequent battlefield triumphs. What if the only World War II battle that the United States was remembered for was its defeat at Bataan? It would unfairly undermine every great victory that American soldiers and marines achieved afterwards.

Here is a look at some notable battles other than Dieppe that were fought by Canadian troops. Not all were victories, but together they demonstrate Canada's crucial contribution to the Allied forces.

## HONG KONG—DECEMBER 1941

Hong Kong was the first battle for Canadian Army soldiers and the only time the Canadian infantry saw action in the Pacific Theater.

At the request of Britain, Canada sent 1,975 troops to Hong Kong in November 1941 to buttress the British garrison. But the men were underequipped and poorly trained. Japan invaded Hong Kong on December 8, 1941, capturing the British colony after 17 days of savage fighting. The Canadians fought valiantly, but were overmatched and overwhelmed. Canada lost 290 troops, and the 1,685 survivors were taken prisoner. Of those, nearly 300 died in captivity.

# THE SICILIAN CAMPAIGN: JULY-AUGUST 1943

Sicily was the Canadian Army's first sustained offensive in the war. It also marked the first of an uninterrupted string of victories for Canadian soldiers in Europe. More than 26,000 troops from the Canadian 1st Infantry Division and 1st Armored Brigade landed with an Allied invasion force of 160,000. The Canadians were embedded in the British 8th Army, which battered its way north along Sicily's east coast to Messina while the U.S. 7th Army drove north through the middle of the island.

Forming the British 8th Army's left flank, the Canadians drove northward between the Americans and British. Through four weeks of the hardest fighting in the Sicilian campaign, Canadian troops punched their way across 150 miles of treacherous mountain terrain, eliminating several heavily fortified enemy positions along the way. Their relentless advance opened the way to the Germans' last line of defense around Mount Etna, which the Americans and British cleared on their way to Messina. In Sicily, the Canadians took more ground than any other British 8th Army division.

## ORTONA—DECEMBER 1943

In November 1943, the Allied armies in Italy moved in to capture North Rome by breaking through the heavily fortified Bernhardt Line, which stretched south of the Eternal City across the Italian peninsula. As the U.S. 5th Army drove north near the Tyrrhenian coast, the British 8th Army marched up the Adriatic coast intending to advance beyond the fortified town of Ortona and swing west toward Rome.

In December, Canadian infantry and armor spearheaded the push to Ortona, into the teeth of fierce German resistance from the 90th Panzer Division. It took two weeks of bloody fighting to advance seven miles to Ortona. Once there, the fighting intensified. Facing the fanatical 1st German Paratroop Division, the Canadians were forced to take Ortona building by building. The battle was soon dubbed "Little Stalingrad" and Canadian soldiers became recognized as the Allies' masters of house-to-house fighting. Eight days later, on December 28, the Canadians secured Ortona.

After Ortona, the newly formed I Canadian Corps joined other Allied divisions and smashed through the Hitler Line in May 1944, destroying the last defensive barrier to Rome. By September, the Canadians punctured the Gothic Line, Germany's last line of defense before the Po Valley. In February 1945, after 19 months in Italy, the 1st Canadian Army transferred to Holland. In April, the I Canadian Corps would join it.

## D-DAY—JUNE 6, 1944

The story of D-Day is well-known, but not always well told. Some accounts of the epic invasion ignore Canada's involvement and blithely designate Canadian soldiers as "British."

In summary, 14,000 Canadian infantry and armored troops of the 3rd Canadian Infantry Division and 2nd Armored Brigade—one of the four invading Allied armies—landed in Normandy. Their assigned beach, Juno, was the second most heavily defended of the six landing beaches, next to Omaha. Despite this, Canadian troops advanced further inland on D-Day than any of the other Allied forces.

## THE FALAISE GAP—JULY–AUGUST 1944

After D-Day, the Allies moved to wrest Normandy from the Germans. By mid-August, the U.S. 1st and 3rd Armies had advanced 85 miles southeast to Le Mans (south of Falaise). The British 2nd Army pushed in the same direction, while the Canadian 1st Army drove south to Falaise. After taking Le Mans, the U.S. 3rd Army turned sharply north to Falaise. Soon, two German armies totaling some 100,000 men were caught in a Canadian-American pincer.

For two weeks the Canadians and Americans pushed to close the Falaise Gap, while the trapped Germans fought desperately to make an eastward escape. On August 21, Canadians and Americans met at Chambois east of Falaise and sealed the gap. Some 50,000 Germans were killed or taken prisoner, and the battle for Normandy was won.

# THE BATTLE FOR THE SCHELDT—
## OCTOBER–NOVEMBER 1944

After Falaise, the 1st Canadian Army moved to clear the French channel ports—gaining some long-sought redemption when it liberated Dieppe on September 1. By the beginning of October, the Canadians reached the Dutch border and linked with British forces that had captured Antwerp. But the low-lying Scheldt estuary, a 60-mile peninsula of three islands that blocked seaward access to Antwerp, remained in German hands, making the great port useless to the Allies. Thus, while the Americans and British stormed into Germany, the Canadians were given the unglamorous but vital task of clearing the Scheldt.

Over the next five weeks, Canadians battled against the well-fortified German defenses in reclaimed lands crisscrossed by a network of dykes and canals. The destruction of the dykes, which was intended to hamper German defenses, left the Canadians vulnerable in flooded, muddy, and wide-open terrain. By November 7, the Canadians had cleared the Scheldt and taken more than 40,000 Germans prisoners at a price of 6,300 dead and wounded. It was Canada's costliest battle in World War II. However, the impressive victory for the Canadian Army made the subsequent Allied advance through Germany possible. Its importance was best stated by U.S. General Dwight Eisenhower: "The end of Nazism was in clear view when the first ship moved unmolested up the Scheldt."

☆ ☆ ☆

- *One submarine carried treasure. As the Allied situation in the Philippines became desperate, USS* Trout *brought $10 million in gold and silver away from the disaster—a major portion of the Filipino national reserves.*

☆ ☆ ☆

- *Dud torpedoes were not only the submarine fleet's problem: The Mark 13 (air-launched) and Mark 15 (destroyer-launched) torpedoes performed just as poorly.*

# RUSSIA'S RUTHLESS HERO

*Georgi Zhukov is generally considered to be the Soviet Union's greatest military commander of World War II. But his successes on the battlefield are tempered by his callous disregard for the lives of the soldiers under his command.*

On June 24, 1945, the Soviet Union held a grand parade in Moscow to officially commemorate the nation's victory over German Fascism in the Great Patriotic War. Leading the victorious procession, riding atop a white Arab charger, was Marshal Georgi Zhukov, commander of the Red Army forces that captured Berlin and national hero to the people of Russia.

Zhukov received deafening applause as he rode by the massive crowds lining the parade route. They hailed him as "our St. George"—the patron saint of Moscow—for leading the successful defense of Moscow in December 1941 and pushing the Germans back from the capital. They praised him for his great counteroffensive in November 1942 that doomed the German 6th Army in Stalingrad and for directing the colossal tank battle at Kursk in July 1943 that permanently turned the tide against the Germans. They cheered for their great liberator who led the Red Army through Poland and Hungary into the heart of Nazi Germany and brought it home again triumphant.

Seemingly forgotten in the moment was that Zhukov achieved these victories by driving the millions of Russian soldiers under his command with such an utter disregard for their lives that those who made it through the war suffered lingering bouts of survivor guilt after reflecting on the appalling number of their comrades who were killed.

## VICTORY AT ANY COST

Zhukov, like most of the Russian military leadership, readily accepted enormous casualties as the price for victory and was willing to resort to brutal methods to motivate subordinates and rank-

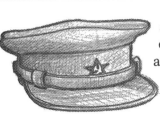

and-file troops. As commander of the defense of Leningrad in 1941, he issued a general order that abandonment of one's post would be treated as a crime against the motherland punishable by death. Later, while commanding the front west of Stalingrad, Zhukov coldly implemented Stalin's infamous and similarly punitive Order No. 227, the so-called "Not One Step Backwards" diktat. There, he organized special tank units that followed the first wave of attacking troops and gunned down any soldiers who wavered or turned back.

Although regarded by many historians as an outstanding military strategist, Zhukov frequently resorted to the traditional Russian bludgeoning tactic of massed frontal assaults. And his assessment of the value of the average soldier could sometimes be blatantly crude and inhumane. "If we come to a minefield, we attack exactly as if it were not there," he once said. "The casualties we get from mines we consider only equal to those we would have gotten from machine guns and artillery if the Germans had chosen to defend the area with strong bodies of troops instead of minefields."

## MASSIVE ASSAULTS, NEEDLESS CASUALTIES

Zhukov was a proponent of the relentless use of massive force against enemy defenses. He regularly employed overwhelming numbers of soldiers, tanks, and artillery in an attack, which tended to inflate casualty rates among Soviet soldiers.

For the Soviet Union's final assault on Berlin in April and May 1945 (which was energized by a competition set up by Stalin among his top commanders), Zhukov massed the greatest concentration of firepower ever assembled—2.5 million troops (by contrast, the Germans invaded the entire Soviet Union with three million soldiers) backed by 6,250 tanks and 41,600 heavy guns.

During the two-week battle for the city, the Soviets suffered an incredible 300,000 casualties, including more than 78,000 killed. Historians consider these losses needlessly high and attribute them to both Zhukov's and Stalin's reckless desire to take Berlin before the Western Allies and the fact that the numerous Soviet armies squeezed into one small area constantly bombarded each other.

## A CARING COMMANDER?

Despite his brutal tactics and the enormous casualties suffered under his command, Zhukov remained immensely popular after the war. Most people viewed Zhukov as a fatherly figure who genuinely cared about the soldiers under his command and understood the hardships they went through. A popular story told of how Zhukov once dressed as a common soldier and stood on a roadside hitchhiking a ride to the front, later reprimanding those officers who didn't stop to pick him up for not caring enough about the average "Ivan."

Tall tale or true account? Who knows? What is known is that Zhukov was, if not loved, then at least admired and respected by the soldiers who fought for him. An oft-repeated saying used by Red Army soldiers during the war probably best summed up their feelings about him: "Where you find Zhukov, you find victory."

- *Roman discipline in the Red Army: On at least one occasion a Soviet officer instilled fortitude in his men through decimation—he summarily executed every tenth soldier.*

- *Where other armies had chaplains, the Soviet Army had political commissars. Two that served with distinction: future premiers Nikita Khrushchev and Leonid Brezhnev.*

- *In a stunning execution of its "scorched earth" strategy, Russia blew up its Dnieper Dam, the largest in the world, on August 20, 1941, to prevent the Germans from benefiting from it.*

- *Of the first five marshals of the Soviet Union, three died in Stalin's prewar purges.*

# THEY GOT IT ON KODACHROME

*"Stevens Irregulars" followed the Allied drive in Normandy and documented some of the war's most major events on color film.*

During his 40-year career in Hollywood, director George Stevens, Sr., worked with such celluloid heroes as Cary Grant, Alan Ladd, and James Dean. He believed that some of his most important work behind the camera, however, was done without a script.

Commisioned as a major in the Army Signal Corps, the Hollywood director and his crew, called "Stevens Irregulars," landed with the U.S. 1st Army on the D-Day beaches. For the next year, they followed Allied troops across Europe. While shooting standard black-and-white film for the Army Motion Picture Unit, Stevens also used 16mm Kodachrome color film for his own "home movies."

## FIRST-HAND ACCOUNTS

Stevens and his crew witnessed the Allied breakout at St.-Lô, the liberation of Paris, the Battle of the Bulge, and the crossing of the Rhine. They also filmed the underground factory at Nordhausen, where slave laborers built the V-1 rockets; the liberation of the Dachau concentration camp; the release of Allied POWs; and the meeting of U.S. and Soviet troops at the Elbe River.

## A DIRECTOR CHANGED

After the war, Stevens went back to California. For decades much of his one-of-a-kind record of the Second World War was never seen. The war, though, seemed to change his style of filmmaking. Known for his light comedies before the war, Stevens turned to more serious dramas, including *The Diary of Anne Frank.*

After Stevens's death in 1975, his son, George Stevens, Jr., discovered his father's World War II archive and later used the unscreened color footage to create the remarkable documentary *D-Day to Berlin,* which won three Emmy Awards in 1994.

# Fast Facts

- As Allied troops surged across Germany in the waning months of the war, some happily helped themselves to citizens' food, jewelry, small arms, artwork, and other personal valuables.

- The Italian CR-42 biplane fighter looked utterly obsolete—until one battled it. While it was slow, underarmored, and lacked radar, its maneuverability caught Spitfire pilots by surprise.

- Denmark was the only European country to cut back on its military after war broke out.

- Prickly Switzerland did not take airspace violations lightly. Swiss fighters shot down 116 intruding aircraft (mostly German) and forced down or interned more than 100 Allied heavy bombers.

- While dictator Francisco Franco of Spain stayed out of World War II, he contributed a division of volunteers to Germany: the highly regarded 250th Infantry "Blue" Division.

- U.S. riflemen often used condoms to keep mud and dirt out of the barrels of their rifles.

- A Soviet soldier's daily vodka ration was 100 grams, or about 3.5 ounces. For a senior lieutenant commanding mortars at Stalingrad, it wasn't nearly enough. "Ivan the Terrible" pirated his dead troops' vodka rations. When a supply clerk reported him to headquarters to cancel the ration, Ivan came unglued. He called upon his batteries, gave them coordinates, and three heavy mortar rounds landed on the supply clerk's warehouse. Headquarters was unsympathetic this time—they told the clerk to just give Ivan his vodka. After all, he had just been given the Order of the Red Star.

- The greatest hero of Paris might be Germany's General von Choltitz, who commanded the defense of the city. Choltitz disregarded Hitler's direct order to destroy the city prior to withdrawal.

# MAGIC TURNS THE TIDE AT MIDWAY

*When U.S. forces faced what seemed to be an invincible Imperial Japan in the aftermath of Pearl Harbor, they had a secret weapon known to only a handful in the U.S. command: Magic.*

The U.S. Navy's Communication Special Unit and the U.S. Army's Signals Intelligence Service had worked together at decrypting secret communication codes used by the Japanese government and military as early as the 1920s. As war loomed in 1939, the Japanese Foreign Office switched to its new Type B Cipher Machine, an electromechanical device that encrypted diplomatic communications. Working under Colonel William Friedman, the Army's chief cryptanalyst, SIS code breakers had difficulty cracking the new machine, code-named Purple for the color of the binders they used to collect its intercepted messages.

After several months of work, U.S. code breakers realized that Purple's design might be based on ordinary telephone switches not commonly used in encryption. They built a duplicate machine without ever having seen one. Friedman's team also shared information with British cryptanalysts, who had already been successful at breaking codes used by the German Enigma machine. SIS code breakers first broke Purple in September 1940, but the process remained slow and the information they gained was usually outdated by the time it was translated.

By 1941, Friedman's team was decrypting increasing amounts of Purple traffic. On December 7, they intercepted a message to the Japanese Embassy in Washington, D.C., ordering its diplomatic staff to inform the United States that Japan was breaking off negotions to avoid war. Translation of the message, however (which did not refer directly to a particular target), did not come in time to warn of the attack on Pearl Harbor.

When the United States entered the war, more people were assigned to the project, and more and more Purple traffic was translated. The program earned the code name Magic.

Six months after Pearl Harbor, Magic provided crucial information that led to U.S. naval victories in the battles of the Coral Sea and Midway. In May 1942, JN-25a (a variation of the JN-25 code) warned of an imminent attack on AF. But where was AF? Washington thought it was the Aleutians; Hawaii guessed Midway. To settle the question, Midway sent a message using Morse code, which the Japanese were sure to read. It said, "Desalinization plant broken. Drinking water supply low." The Hawaii station read the next day's JN-25a output, "AF reports out of water." AF was Midway.

While Admiral Yamamoto had planned a trap at Midway for what remained of the U.S. Pacific fleet, Admiral Nimitz had been warned of the Japanese intentions. He set his own ambush, resulting in the loss of four Japanese carriers. On April 18, 1943, intercepted JN-25 traffic led U.S. Army Air Corps pilots in their shoot down of Admiral Yamamoto's plane over the Solomon Islands.

Historical documents indicate that the Soviets may have independently broken the Purple code and led to Stalin's decision to move Soviet divisions guarding against a Japanese attack in the Far East to Moscow for a decisive counterattack against the Germans in December 1941. The Japanese ambassador in Berlin also used Magic to report at length on German military matters, including the building of Atlantic Wall fortifications. Those messages were intercepted by the Allies and used in planning the D-Day invasion.

Following the defeat of the Nazis, U.S. intelligence officers recovered part of a Purple machine from the wreckage of the Japanese Embassy in Berlin. They discovered that the Japanese had used precisely the same "stepping switch" as the ones used by SIS cryptanalysts in the duplicate Purple machine they had built in 1939. Apparently, all other Purple machines at Japanese embassies and consulates around the world were destroyed at the time of the Japanese surrender.

# EXILES IN HOLLYWOOD

*European cinematic talents found a new home in California and, thanks to Warner Brothers, made one of the best films in movie history.*

Fans of classic American cinema might be surprised to learn that many of their favorite films from the 1930s and '40s benefited from a wave of emigration sparked by the rise of Nazis in Europe. Such leading lights from the period, including Peter Lorre, Marlene Dietrich, Billy Wilder, Jean Renoir, Otto Preminger, and Fritz Lang, had come to Hollywood not only to ply their craft but also to escape Nazi Europe. Many, such as Max Reinhardt, Erich von Stroheim, and Ernst Lubitsch, had been lured to California in the 1920s by the wealth and technical sophistication of the Hollywood system. After the rise of the Nazis, however, some of those who had previously been employed by the European cinematic industry sought safety as well as employment in Hollywood.

## SEARCHING FOR A SAFE HAVEN

The 1938 *Anschluss*, in which Germany annexed Austria, convinced many Europeans that Nazism would not be averted. Then in March 1935, 70,000 Austrians, including many prominent members of Vienna's cinematic community, were arrested and questioned closely about their racial heritage. Following the 1938 *Kristallnacht,* or "Night of Broken Glass," in which Nazis destroyed Jewish property and sent as many as 30,000 to prison camps, the fervor to find a save haven abroad increased. Sadly, the world had not yet recognized the true threat of Nazi Germany, and no country, including the United States, was ready to welcome the flood of Jewish emigrants. Hollywood was no different, and most members of Tinsel Town's artistic community saw the refugees as unwelcome competition.

Proving that money trumped morality, nearly all of the Hollywood studios continued dealings with the Fascist regime until the start of the war. In many cases, studios altered films that might offend the Nazis rather than risk losing the valuable German and Austrian markets. The one exception, Warner Brothers, was headed by the firmly anti-Nazi brothers Harry and Jack Warner, whose family had left Germany at the turn of the century. In 1939, the studio released the highly controversial film *Confessions of a Nazi Spy,* which starred Edward G. Robinson and was allegedly based on accounts by former FBI agent Leon G. Turrou, who had investigated Nazi spies in the United States before the war. As a result, studio head Jack Warner, producer Robert Lord, and many members of the cast and crew received death threats from Fascist organizations operating in the United States.

## A CINEMATIC CLASSIC IS BORN

Although scores of intellectuals and artists who fled Nazi Europe abandoned their artistic talents during their exile in the United States, others prospered and through their efforts changed the course of American cinema. Nowhere is this more apparent than in the enduring Warner Brothers classic film, *Casablanca* (1941). Though much of the film's storyline and setting are complete fantasy (for example, there weren't any Nazis in Casablanca during World War II), the romanticized story of Europeans seeking refuge in the United States featured a cast and crew largely comprised of refugees from Hitler's Europe. In fact, 11 of the 14 names that appear in the film's opening credits are European.

The film's director, Michael Curtiz, had left his native Hungary before the rise of Hitler, and his sensibilities were still deeply rooted in the Viennese cinema where he first made his mark. Technical advisor Robert Aisner had fled France using the same route outlined in the film's opening narration. A few of the film's stars—Conrad Veidt, Peter Lorre, and Paul Henreid—as well as many of the bit players had also fled the Nazis. Veidt, who played the villainous Nazi Major Strasser, was a German refugee who had already garnered critical attention by playing menacing Nazis in other films. Indeed, the vehemently anti-Nazi Veidt reportedly agreed to play Nazi characters only if they were thoroughly detestable. The Hungarian Lorre, who played the short-lived Ugarte in the film, was a refugee from Austria and had starred in fellow refugee Fritz Lang's *M*, which had been filmed while both were still in Germany. Lorre moved to Hollywood after narrowly escaping occupied France. In Hollywood he and Humphrey Bogart became close friends and worked on *The Maltese Falcon* before being cast together in *Casablanca*. Austrian-born Paul Henreid, who played the French resistance leader Victor Laszlo, was a real-life refugee from the Nazis and was extremely critical of the film's numerous plot flaws (for example, why would a man who wanted to remain unnoticed strut around in an all-white suit?) and equally disapproving of Humphrey Bogart's acting abilities.

Other refugees from Hitler's Europe who acted in *Casablanca* include Curtis Bois, who played a pickpocket; Marcel Dalio, cast as a croupier; Helmut Dantine, who played a desperate husband trying to win enough money to purchase freedom for himself and his refugee wife; and S.Z. "Cuddles" Sakall, who played the lovably loose-jowled headwaiter, Carl. The contributions of these and numerous extras, technicians, and crew of European extraction lent *Casablanca* a credibility that has made it one of the most beloved films in movie history.

☆　☆　☆

- *When acclaimed German director Fritz Lang was summoned to the office of Nazi Propaganda Minister Joseph Goebbels in 1933, Lang immediately had a bad feeling. He entered Goebbels's enormous office and stood before the diminutive Nazi, who sat imposingly behind an elevated desk. Lang listened as Goebbels informed him that Hitler was a great fan of such Lang pictures as* Metropolis *and* Spies, *and wanted Lang to be Germany's "official" film director. Lang was promised complete creative freedom—clearly, a lie—and would enjoy all the facilities of the great Ufa film studio as soon as it came under government control. Lang listened and agreed to Goebbels's proposal. As soon as he left, Lang went to his bank, withdrew every mark he had, and prepared to hastily leave the country. By 1935, Lang had directed his first American production, and remained an important Hollywood filmmaker for 20 years.*

# KAMIKAZE!

*As Allied forces decimated Japan's ability to make war, Japan's military leaders took a drastic step, turning their young warriors into human bombs.*

In the early stages of the war, Japan's military machine rolled across the South Pacific unchecked. However, 1942 marked a turning point. Allied forces dealt Japan a series of grievous blows from which they would never recover. America's manufacturing might churned out weapons on an unprecedented scale, yet the industrial output of Japan eventually ground to a halt as conquered countries previously exploited for their raw resources were freed. As fuel, weapons, and spare parts ceased to exist, Japan's military faltered.

## AN UNCONVENTIONAL TACTIC

In October 1944, Vice Admiral Takijiro Onishi, Commander of Japan's 1st Air Fleet, was assigned the mission of assisting Japanese warships with destroying Allied forces gathered in Leyte Gulf for the invasion of the Philippines. The 1st could only muster 40 assorted aircraft for the task. Onishi announced a plan to form a corps of volunteer pilots, to be called the Kamikaze Special Attack Force, whose sole mission was to destroy enemy warships by purposely crashing their planes into them.

In the early morning hours of October 25, 1944, the escort carrier *St. Lo* and her 11 sister ships of Taffy 3, an American naval unit supporting the invasion of the Philippines, engaged a fleet of Japanese warships. After beating back the enemy force, Taffy 3 came under concentrated air attack. One Japanese plane crashed through *St. Lo's* flight deck, igniting her torpedo and bomb magazine. The ensuing explosion rocked St. Lô, and the carrier sank in 30 minutes. Those aboard had no idea they had just been targeted by Japan's newest weapon.

The tactic caught American navy personnel completely by surprise. By the end of October 1944, planes from the special attack force managed to hit a total of 47 American warships, including 7 carriers. Of the ships hit, 5 sank and 35 were either heavily or moderately damaged. Based on the first successes, the *kamikaze* program was expanded, and over the course of the following months, more than 2,000 planes attempted *kamikaze* attacks.

## WHAT'S IN A NAME?

The origin of the word *kamikaze* dates back to the late 13th century, when legendary typhoons destroyed invading fleets of Mongol warriors off the coast of Japan on two separate occasions. The word literally means "divine wind." The western perception of Japan's *kamikaze* pilots differs greatly from those held by most Japanese. Allied propaganda portrayed the Japanese as fanatical, crazed fighters. Hollywood filmmaker Frank Capra referred to the "obedient, fanatical Japanese soldier" in his film *Know Your Enemy: Japan.*

In order to denigrate Japan's *kamikaze* attacks, several misconceptions have been perpetrated during and since the end of the war. Some of the fallacies include the beliefs that Japanese pilots were chained to their cockpits; were flying planes with half-empty fuel tanks; or were given alcohol in order to give them the courage to fly their last mission.

*Kamikaze* pilots were, in fact, young pilots who for the most part volunteered for their missions by way of the glider corps. Many *kamikaze* believed the only way their nation could overcome American military might was to destroy the enemy's capital warships, inflicting large numbers of casualties in the process. The Japanese did not see these men as fanatics. Instead, they believed the *kamikaze* pilots died bravely for their homeland and their families. Many smiled at their comrades before boarding the plane for their final mission.

## NO SURRENDER

*Kamikaze* pilots drew some of their inspiration from a 14th-century Samurai named Kusunoki Masashige, who was charged with protecting Emperor Go-Daigo II. During a decisive battle in 1336, Masashige's force of warriors fought bravely despite facing a numerically superior force. Rather than face the humiliation of surrender, Masashige committed suicide.

Masashige's act of ritualized suicide reinforced the Japanese military's warrior code that placed heavy emphasis on honor, loyalty, and courage. Japan's military class believed there was no greater glory than to die for the emperor. Many of Japan's *kamikaze* pilots accepted the tenet that a glorified death on behalf of then-Emperor Hirohito was, in fact, an honorable way to die.

Most *kamikaze* pilots were under 24 years of age. Many spent their last days in quiet solitude giving away personal belongings, writing final letters home, and if time permitted, toasting their commanding officer with a cup of rice wine.

One 23-year-old pilot wrote, "I have been given a splendid opportunity to die...I shall fall like a blossom from a radiant cherry tree... may [my] death be as sudden and clean as the shattering of crystal."

## HEAVY LOSSES

According to the U.S. Historical Studies Office of the U.S. Air Force, Japan's *kamikaze* exacted a heavy toll. Over the final course of the war, about 2,800 *kamikaze* attackers sunk 34 Navy ships, damaged nearly 370 others, killed 4,900 sailors, and wounded more than 4,800.

Besides piloted airplanes, the Japanese developed several other so-called suicide weapons, including a jet-propelled piloted bomb launched from a bomber, army and navy motorboats packed with explosives, and submarine-launched human guided torpedoes. While all three systems met with limited success, several Allied warships were destroyed or damaged by these weapons.

Today, the Chiran Peace Museum for *Kamikaze* Pilots in Japan is home to a museum that attracts some 500,000 visitors per year.

☆　　☆　　☆

- *The Japanese Army instituted their own program of* kamikaze *pilots, which they called Shinbu, or "military might."*

# Timeline

## 1943

**September 9**
Allies land in Italy in full force; Americans set up a beachhead near Salerno, while the British land on Italy's "heel"

**September 11**
Japanese evacuate Salamaua, New Guinea

**September 12**
German commandos rescue Mussolini in a dramatic raid

**September 13**
Chiang Kai-shek is appointed president of Nationalist China

**September 25**
Soviets recapture Smolensk, Russia

**October**
Throughout the month, Stilwell's Chinese troops advance on the Refugee Trail in Burma

**October 1**
In Italy, U.S. troops enter Naples, British take Foggia

**October 2**
Australians take Finschafen, New Guinea

**October 6**
Soviets move on Baltics

**October 13**
Italy joins the Allies when Premier Pietro Badoglio declares war on Hitler's Germany

**November 2**
The Battle of Empress Augusta Bay erupts when the U.S. Navy attacks a small Japanese fleet attempting to reinforce Bougainville, where the Marines landed the day before

**November 6**
The Soviets retake Kiev; what had been the third-largest Soviet city has been largely reduced to smoldering ruins

**November 18–March 25, 1944**
Air Battle of Berlin

**November 20**
U.S. Marines land on the Gilbert islands of Makin and Tarawa

**November 28**
Roosevelt, Churchill, and Stalin meet face-to-face for the first time in Tehran, Iran

Allies complete their conquest of the island of Tarawa

**December 4**
The Japanese employ poison gas in an attack on Changteh, China

**December 17**
In gratitude for Chinese assistance in the Pacific Theater, President Roosevelt repeals the 1882 Chinese Exclusion Act and sets a quota permitting Chinese immigration to the United States

**December 26**
Battle of North Cape; sinking of *Scharnhorst*

**December 30**
U.S. Marines capture a key airfield at Cape Gloucester on the South Pacific island of New Britain

## 1944

**January 2**
U.S. landing at Saidor, New Guinea

**January 14**
Soviet Leningrad offensive begins

# LAST STAND OF GERMANY'S *VOLKSSTURM*

*In a last-ditch attempt to stem the tide of the advancing Allied armies, Adolf Hitler issued a call to arms. The creation of the Volkssturm, or "People's Storm," was a desperate act that needlessly cost thousands of Germans their lives.*

In the last weeks of the summer of 1944, Germany's Nazi regime found itself fighting a defensive war on two fronts. As American, British, and Canadian forces marched east from the beaches of Normandy, the Russian juggernaut rolled westward, catching the German Army in an ever-tightening vice.

## DESPERATE MEASURES

German manpower losses were mounting at an alarming rate, especially on the eastern front where Hitler's "no retreat" policy cost the lives of tens of thousands of soldiers. So Hitler, on the advice of his personal secretary and Nazi Party Chancellery Chief Martin Bormann, ordered the formation of a nationwide militia. In October 1944, the Nazi dictator issued what can only be described as a desperate decree, drafting all men between the ages of 16 and 60 not already serving in the military into local militia units known as *Volkssturm*.

The order effectively conscripted thousands of men and boys into compulsory, quasi-military service. The units were composed of the elderly, members of the Hitler Youth, and those previously classified as unfit for military service.

Command of the *Volkssturm* fell under the Home Guard, which was controlled in the last two years of the war by SS leader Heinrich Himmler. The decision to place control of the men under Nazi party control, as opposed to the army, ensured the Nazification of the recruits. The Nazi leadership hoped fanatical resistance by self-sacrificing groups of *Volkssturm* fighters would inflict unacceptable casualties on Allied forces and create a stalemate, forcing the Allies to back away from their demands of unconditional surrender.

## A LACK OF ORGANIZATION

The *Volkssturm* operated independently of the German Army until committed to battle. Because of chronic weapon and ammunition shortages, *Volkssturm* members received only rudimentary training, usually at the hands of retired former World War I servicemen. Training focused on the art of close-quarters antitank warfare, as opposed to hit-and-run guerrilla tactics.

There was no standardization when supplying or arming units, and many were issued captured weapons. Some units were armed with the *Mauser* Kar-98k bolt-action 7.92mm rifle, and most *Volkssturm* members were shown how to use the *Panzerfaust,* or "armor fist," recoilless antitank grenade/rocket launcher, which was available in large quantities. This disposable, preloaded weapon fired an explosive charge to maximum range of roughly 100 yards and was capable of penetrating almost eight inches of armor. The *Panzerfaust's* simplistic design allowed the weapon to be mass-produced. During the Battle of Berlin, it was employed by *Volkssturm* units with effective results—the Russians lost an estimated 2,000 armored vehicles during the battle, due in large part to the antitank weapon.

The *Volkssturm* also had no standard uniform. Members were issued an armband marked with the words *"Deutscher Volkssturm"* and *"Wehrmacht."* Wearing such an armband meant captured *Volkssturm* would be treated like regular military combatants under the Geneva Convention and not as partisans, who would be summarily executed.

Group, section, company, and battalion leaders were issued collar tabs featuring from one to four pips to signify rank. Some men went into battle wearing their suit jackets, while others wore whatever military clothing they could cobble together.

# LEVY BREAKDOWN

Conscripts were organized around geographic boundaries and were supposed to be called for duty only in the event enemy forces threatened their hometown or county. The February 1945 issue of *Intelligence Bulletin,* a soft-cover publication compiled by the Military Intelligence Service, indicated the physical area a *Volkssturm* unit was responsible for defending:

**Squad:** one city block

**Platoon:** equivalent to a U.S. precinct

**Company:** equivalent to a Congressional district

**Battalion:** equivalent to a U.S. county

*Volkssturm* personnel were divided into four categories, or levies. Levy IV contained men of limited physical ability. Levy III consisted of 16- to 20-year-olds and fell under the control of the local Hitler Youth organization. Teenagers in this levy were usually moved out of harm's way, although some Hitler Youth units did see action in Berlin. Most recruits fell under the auspices of either levies II or I. Placement in either of these levies was dependent on how valuable the conscript's civilian occupation was to the war effort—the more important the job, the less likely the person would have to fight.

The most extensive use of *Volkssturm* units was during the Battle of Berlin, where hundreds of civilians fought to their deaths rather than surrender and face an unknown fate at the hands of their Russian captors. Berlin and the metropolitan area were ripped by more than 2 million Soviet artillery shells. From an assembled force of 2.5 million Russian infantry, a million took part in the all-out street assault on Berlin. Although close quarters briefly favored the defenders' portable antitank weapons, roughly 152,000 Berliners were killed during the battle for the city. By some accounts, *Volkssturm* fighters comprised nearly half of German forces during the fight for the capital. Total German police and *Volkssturm* casualties during the war numbered 231,000.

# MERRILL'S MARAUDERS

*Brigadier General Frank Merrill led a band of undisciplined troublemakers through northern Burma against one of the Japanese Army's toughest divisions. They would emerge from the Burmese jungles as one of the U.S. Army's most storied units.*

The disastrous Allied retreat from Burma in 1942 was a long and arduous ordeal that was part fighting withdrawal and part death march. Lieutenant General William Slim led the remnants of the British Army in Burma 900 miles north into India, battling Japanese troops, deprivation, and disease the whole way. Only 12,000 of Slim's original 25,000 men crossed the border with him. U.S. Lieutenant General Joseph Stilwell marched a ragged group of 114 stragglers a similar distance to India, traveling mostly by foot.

One of the stragglers who accompanied "Walking Joe" was Major (later Brigadier General) Frank Merrill, who two years later would lead his own band of misfits 800 miles back across northern Burma as the vanguard force that would break Japan's grip on the country.

## A SCHOOLED LEADER

Born in Woodville, Massachusetts, in 1903, Frank Dow Merrill joined the U.S. Army as an underage enlistee, eventually rising to the rank of lieutenant and serving in Haiti and Panama. Initial attempts by Merrill to gain entrance into the U.S. Military Academy were rejected because of his poor eyesight, but he was finally admitted by presidential appointment and graduated from West Point in 1929.

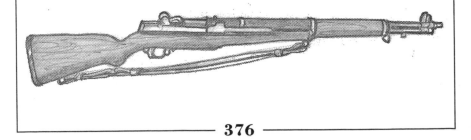

Merrill was subsequently commissioned a cavalry officer and later received a bachelor's degree at Massachusetts Institute of Technology. After a stint as a small arms instructor, he spent three years as an assistant military attaché in Tokyo. In October 1941, he was promoted to major and assigned as a staff officer under General Douglas MacArthur in the Philippines. After Pearl Harbor, Merrill was transferred to Rangoon, Burma, as a liaison officer with the British. He later became General Stilwell's operations officer—just in time to join Stilwell on his walk out of Burma.

## A MOTLEY CREW

In January 1944, Stilwell put Merrill in command of a newly formed unit called the 5307th Composite Unit (Provisional). Its role was to perform long-range operations behind Japanese lines in northern Burma. The objective was to reach the town of Myitkyina near the Chinese border ahead of Stilwell's main force and attempt to reopen the Burma Road to China. Code-named "Galahad," the regiment-sized unit would be the first American combat unit to fight on mainland Asia and would become more famously known as "Merrill's Marauders."

The Marauders were a hardy, rough-and-tumble mix of jungle-fighting veterans from Panama, Guadalcanal, and New Guinea, who answered a call for volunteers for "a dangerous and hazardous mission." Among them were drunks, malcontents, and violent individuals who were no stranger to the stockade. The unit as a whole didn't buy into regular army routine and discipline, and their behavior was unpredictable at best.

There was some trepidation among members of the Allies' Southeast Asia Command about putting Merrill in charge of such a volatile group. He lacked experience in commanding infantry troops. He also had a congenitally weak heart (he collapsed during the retreat to India and had to be carried part of the way), and many questioned if he could handle the strain of guerrilla warfare. But he was optimistic and self-confident, and most important, he knew the Japanese. In the end, he proved to be an excellent choice for leading the mission.

Fighting alongside his men when his heart permitted (other times he was flown to the battles), Merrill led the Marauders across 800 miles of forbidding mountainous terrain and nearly impenetrable jungle in four months. A British officer who witnessed Merrill's command described him as a "cool, clever, and tough fighting man, the type who would never lose his temper or his nerve," and lauded Merrill as a commander who genuinely cared about his men.

The Marauders fought the entire way against the much larger Japanese 18th Division—the same division that had conquered Singapore and Malaya—alternately taking the Japanese head-on or hooking behind them to cut off their communication and supply lines. They spearheaded the way for Stilwell's 23,000 Chinese troops to Myitkyina and capped their remarkable run with the capture of the nearby airfield in May 1944.

## A SPENT FORCE

In a relatively short period of time, Merrill's Marauders became one of the most accomplished American infantry units of the war, and their extraordinary achievements became the stuff of legend. But the horrific conditions endured by the Marauders took their toll. The unit suffered terrible casualties from fighting and disease; by the end of May, only 200 of the original 2,400 combat (non-support) Marauders remained fit for combat. Merrill himself was counted among the casualties after being knocked out of action—but not killed—by two heart attacks and malaria.

In recognition of his admirable leadership of the 5307th, Merrill was promoted to major general and appointed second-in-command of American forces in Burma. He ended the war serving with the American 10th Army in Okinawa and received several decorations, including the Distinguished Service Medal. After the war, Merrill held various senior army staff posts before retiring from the military in 1948. He died in 1955.

# *ICHI-GO:* NIPPON'S LAST GREAT LAND OFFENSIVE

*In 1944, Japan mounted an immense attack on China in an effort to capture a stretch of land and railway lines that would keep supplies flowing to Burma. If successful, they planned to continue the push to India, taking out any British or American troops that stood in their way.*

"I thought I was hallucinating!" recalled Sergeant Hobart Jones as he was flying his B-24 in formation 18,000 feet over the Chinese coastal city of Nanjing. "I happened to be looking over to my left when this Jap fighter... just seemed to drop out of nowhere and form up right behind our left wing.

"The [enemy] pilot and I were staring at each other across a space of maybe 50 feet. The guy had on a fur-trimmed helmet and sported a bushy mustache, and he was grinning! Nobody could take a shot at him because our planes were in each other's line of fire.... My headset erupted with my pilot screaming, 'Step up! Step up!' But the exact instant the other ship moved, the Jap flicked over on his back and got clean away!"

Hobart's bomber was part of the China-based U.S. 14th Air Force. In the summer of 1944, it was targeting Japanese ships, railroad bridges, and vehicles supporting Operation *Ichi-go*, or "one chance in a lifetime." This was a mammoth land offensive that stretched 1,000 miles through the Chinese provinces of Henan, Hunan, and Guangxi. Involving upward of 350,000 troops, *Ichi-go* was Japan's ambitious bid to forge a continuous swath of occupied territory and railway lines from Manchuria and Korea down to Indochina. The plan was to ensure supply routes to its forces in Burma, which aimed to invade India and knock Britain out of the Asian war.

Another objective of the operation was to wipe out the air bases of the U.S. 14th, led by Major General Claire Lee Chennault and his "Flying Tigers," and the U.S. 20th Air Force, also based in China.

They were chewing up Japanese shipping lanes off the Netherlands East Indies and Taiwan (then Formosa). The 20th, through Operation Matterhorn, was even mounting long-distance raids on Japan's mainland. Tokyo's strategists thought the offensive might knock China, where 80 percent of Japan's soldiers were stationed, out of the war and free up troops for other pressing fights. Undersupplied, poorly directed, and badly equipped, China's armies seemed ripe for the taking.

With careful planning, the Imperial Japanese Army, or IJA, assembled 17 divisions, thousands of motorized vehicles, and more than 50,000 horses to haul supplies. Arrayed against it were the forces of Generalissimo Chiang Kai-shek's National Revolutionary Army, or NRA. As in other major pitched battles of the war, Communist Chinese troops under Mao Tse-tung took little part.

## JAPAN STRIKES

The first phase of the attack began April 17 in the province of Henan. In battles near the Yellow River, the 255 tanks of the IJA's 3rd Tank Division, under Lieutenant General Hideo Yamaji, defeated three divisions of the NRA, and on May 25 captured the ancient Chinese capital of Luoyang.

In June, fighting moved south to Hunan province, with the battles of Changsha and Hengyang. The IJA drove toward the city of Changsha, which it had attacked twice before since 1939. Knocking out Chinese artillery on nearby Yuelu Mountain, the Japanese burst through the Nationalist infantry defending the town.

In July the Japanese approached the city of Hengyang. There, the Chinese defenses were firmer. The NRA's 10th Division twice held off several attacking Japanese units. This news, combined with the fall of Saipan on July 7, sparked the fall from power of Japanese Prime Minister Tojo Hideki and his cabinet.

Still, the Japanese pressed the attack against Hengyang, using aerial bombardment against the 12-foot walls the defenders had constructed. A 47-day struggle ensued. The Chinese used interlocking fields of fire to bring the Japanese to a halt. Finally, the Nationalist Chinese ran out of supplies, and the Japanese 58th Division took Hengyang on August 8. A number of American airfields in the region also fell. The IJA fought back incessant Chinese attempts  to take back the city, but its casualties were high, especially among officers, with 910 killed or wounded.

Japan's forces then turned farther south to Guangxi province, near China's Indochinese border. There lay the last swath of unconquered land and railways, as well as cities—Guilin and Liuzhou—that hosted American airbases. The bases had provided the Nationalists with powerful air support, but the Chinese troops were battered from the defense of Hengyang. In October and November, two Japanese armies pushed Chiang's men aside and took Guilin and Liuzhou as well as most of Guangxi.

## MAJOR LOSSES

Along with military losses, Chinese civilian casualties from the fighting and from Japanese reprisals were horrific, approaching nearly 700,000. By year's end, the 14th Air Force had lost 13 of its bases, and Japanese armies in China had linked up with another from Indochina. Tokyo now threatened Chiang's last bastion—his wartime capital of Chongqing in Szechuan province. Japan's success led to the ousting of U.S. General Joseph "Vinegar Joe" Stilwell, commander of the China-Burma-India Theater. Vinegar Joe had fought bitterly with Generalissimo Chiang, who often directed resources to his generals and allied warlords on the basis of loyalty, not performance. With Major General Chennault, the Generalissimo wanted air power diverted from striking Japan to helping China. Chiang also rejected Stilwell's urging to form a pact with the rival Communist Chinese. President Roosevelt, anxious to keep China in the war, replaced Stilwell with Major General Albert Wedemeyer.

## A LOSING BATTLE

Still, the epic-scale *Ichi-go* proved a Pyrrhic victory. The 20th Air Force moved its B-29 Superfortresses to Saipan and handily struck Japan's cities from there. In the meantime, the 14th Air Force, from Chinese bases some 200 miles further inland, targeted the precious rail lines the Japanese had seized. What's more, in its 29 months of wartime operation, the 700 aircraft of the 14th destroyed about 2,900 Japanese planes, around 100 combat ships, almost 5,000 trucks, and more than 800 bridges. American pilots teamed up in their raids with Chinese flyers trained in the United States.

The exertions of *Ichi-go*, along with defeats in the Pacific and in Burma, and relentless U.S. air and submarine campaigns against Japanese shipping, sapped Tokyo's overstretched occupation army. Its remaining air power in China was stripped away to defend the homeland. By 1945, the Japanese Army in the vast land it had hoped to conquer was on the defensive and facing ultimate defeat.

✯   ✯   ✯

- *Historians estimate that about 20 million Chinese soldiers and civilians died during the war; Japanese casualties in China were about 1.1 million.*

✯   ✯   ✯

- *The term* ichi-go *was popularized in 19th-century Japan by writer-philosopher Ii Naosuke. Because* ichi-go *suggests a rare event, Ii interpreted it as a reminder of the fleeting nature of all things. He linked this notion to two Japanese traditions, the artful serving of tea, and* budo, *the way of the warrior.*

# *Fast Facts*

- Not all Soviet soldiers facing Germany came from cold climates, but they all received the golden secret of Red Army cold endurance: the fur hat and greatcoat. The hat trapped nearly all exiting body heat, and the greatcoat doubled as a snow sleeping bag.

- Both men and women served as medics at Stalingrad. They exhibited great courage in defying death to seek and rescue fallen soldiers and civilians.

- The final thrust of the German attack on Moscow in 1941 came within 20 miles of the Kremlin's towers.

- Twenty-three of the pilots serving in the all-female 588th Night Bomber Regiment of the Soviet Air Force, known as the Night Witches, were decorated as Heroines of the Soviet Union, the USSR's equivalent of the Medal of Honor.

- Before Medevac helicopters, there were Po-2 evacuation biplanes in the Soviet Air Force. Creative designers modified the observer's normal position to hold a stretcher.

- After the Dunkirk evacuation, the British were short of everything, rifles included. The home guard armed itself with shotguns, pitchforks, clubs, broom handles, axes, and even golf clubs.

- The Filipino resistance eventually numbered an incredible 250,000 guerrillas, turning their country into one of Imperial Japan's greatest occupation headaches.

- If it were up to Admiral Nimitz, Allied forces would have invaded Formosa (now Taiwan) before the Philippines. However, General MacArthur persuaded leaders that U.S. prestige demanded that the previous U.S. territory take liberation priority.

- Advancing U.S. troops in Germany would phone ahead to the next town and demand capitulation—it often worked!

# THE CAPTURE OF U-505

*The dramatic capture of an intact German submarine provided the Allies with a wealth of intelligence that helped negate the impact of German U-boats prowling the Atlantic.*

During the Battle of the Atlantic, German U-boats sank more than 2,800 Allied ships, while the German Navy lost almost 800 submarines in the process. One German submarine escaped a watery grave and now rests, not under hundreds of feet of water rusting away, but a mere 50 feet below ground in a gallery beneath the streets of Chicago.

## MENACING U-BOATS

As German U-boats plied the waters off the coasts of America and Europe, sinking Allied ships at will, Allied leaders scrambled to find a solution to the problem of marauding U-boats. While the development of convoys reduced the number of merchant ships lost, the tactic was defensive in nature. A convoy's escort could protect a group of cargo ships, but in many cases enemy submarines were able to escape after launching their initial attack.

In 1943 the Allies developed a new strategy to confront the U-boat menace-hunter-killer groups composed of one escort aircraft carrier and several destroyer escorts that would proactively search for German prey. Captain Daniel V. Gallery, USN, was commanding officer of one such hunter-killer force: Task Group 22.3, comprised of the escort carrier USS *Guadalcanal* and five destroyer escorts, including USS *Pillsbury,* USS *Jenks,* USS *Pope,* USS *Flaherty,* and USS *Chatelain.*

## TARGET: U-505

The year 1944 had been a particularly successful one for Gallery. Under his leadership, the *Guadalcanal* participated in actions that resulted in the destruction of the U-544, U-515, and U-68. The U-505, a Type IX-C German submarine, was responsible for sinking eight Allied ships totaling 47,000 tons. The U-boat patrolled the coast of West Africa, the Panama Canal, and Trinidad looking for prey. In June 1944, the sub left her pen in Lorient, France, on an 80-day patrol in the Gulf of Guinea.

On May 15, 1944, TG 22.3 set sail from Norfolk, Virginia, to the Canary Islands. In his official report detailing U-505's—capture to Admiral Ingersoll, Commander in Chief of the U.S. Atlantic Fleet, Gallery said the task group sailed "with the avowed intention of capturing an enemy submarine." Indeed, U-505 had been tracked by U.S. antisubmarine command since March 1944.

After two weeks of fruitless searching, the task force set sail to Casablanca for refueling. Minutes after setting course for port, *Chatelain's* commander reported "possible sound contact." After a brief 15-minute battle, which included hedgehog and depth-charge attacks as well as .50-caliber, 20-mm, and 40-mm gunfire, U-505 was on the surface with most of her crew in the water.

While men from the *Chatelain* and *Jenks* rescued survivors, a nine-man boarding party led by Lieutenant (junior grade) Albert David from the *Pillsbury* quickly took control of the stricken sub. German sailors had attempted to scuttle their boat by opening a pipe called a sea strainer. Motor Machinist Mate 1st Class Zenon Lukosius searched for, recovered, and resecured the cover, pre-venting further flooding.

## PRICELESS PICKINGS

The capture of U-505 was an intelligence coup that resulted in the acquiring of two complete M4 Enigma encoding machines, codebooks, notebooks containing decrypted messages, and several acoustic torpedoes. The captured material gave Allied crypt-analysts insight into the German Navy's coordinate code, which indicated the precise locations of German submarines. The breaking of this code afforded Allied commanders the opportunity to send submarine hunter groups to specific areas. Convoys could also now be rerouted from areas where German subs were known to be operating. The captured material saved the American intelligence community countless hours of computing work, while the German G7E (T5) acoustic torpedoes were the first to fall into Allied hands.

## RESTING SPOT

U-505—was eventually towed to Bermuda, where it was scrutinized by experts from the Office of Naval Intelligence. The sub's crew was transferred to a POW camp in Louisiana, where they were kept in isolation to keep news of the submarine's capture secret. Because the crewmen were not allowed to send letters home, some families assumed their men were dead.

Captain Gallery successfully campaigned to have U-505 donated to the Chicago Museum of Science and Technology, and in September 1954, the sub was relocated from the Navy Yard in Portsmouth, Virginia, to the museum. In April 2004, the submarine was refurbished and relocated to an underground, climate-controlled, 35,000-square-foot exhibit.

Gallery received the Distinguished Service Medal for his actions and retired from the Navy in 1960 with the rank of Rear Admiral. Lieutenant David received the Medal of Honor, Radioman 2nd Class Stanley Wdowiak and Torpedoman's Mate 3rd Class Arthur Knispel each received the Navy Cross, while the entire crew of Task Group 22.3 received the Presidential Unit Citation.

# THE PORT CHICAGO MUTINY

*Enlisted munitions workers who survived a deadly blast at Port Chicago later refused to go back to work. Their stand led to the largest mass mutiny trial in U.S. naval history.*

The night of July 17, 1944, was quiet and calm in the small town of Port Chicago, northeast of San Francisco. The evening serenity gave no hint of the catastrophe about to befall the nearby Port Chicago Naval Munitions Base that night, where 1,400 munitions handlers, all of whom were black navy-enlisted men, were carrying out their highly dangerous work loading munitions ships headed for the Pacific.

## A DEVASTATING BLAST

At 10:18 P.M., two explosions seconds apart ripped the loading pier, where two ships, the SS *E.A. Bryan* and the SS *Quinault Victory*, were being filled with more than 4,600 tons of ammunition and explosives. The massive blast was heard 200 miles away and a fireball rising more than two miles lit the night sky. The pier and two ships were obliterated and huge chunks of smoldering metal and unexploded bombs were propelled thousands of feet in all directions, including onto Port Chicago. Equivalent to a five-kiloton detonation, the explosion would become the worst stateside military disaster of World War II.

The blast killed 320 people, instantly incinerating the entire on-duty crews of the two ships, as well as 202 munitions workers. Another 390 military personnel and civilians were injured, including 233 workers. Incredibly, the disaster would account for 15 percent of all deaths suffered by black servicemen in the war.

## A DISASTER WAITING TO HAPPEN

Shortly after the disaster, the Naval Court of Inquiry held hearings to determine the cause of the explosion. Testimony from blast survivors, ordnance experts, base personnel, and eyewitnesses revealed numerous unsafe munitions handling practices and working conditions, many stemming from the U.S. Navy's segregationist policies.

The black servicemen at Port Chicago had volunteered for service hoping to be assigned to a ship or combat. Instead, and despite training as full seamen, they were barred by the navy from combat duty and were relegated to mainly unchallenging noncombatant tasks. Furthermore, *only* blacks were assigned to the highly dangerous munitions work.

Disheartened by their assignment, the men also suffered abject working conditions. They were inadequately trained for the job, and the equipment they used was in poor shape. Besides the constant fear of an explosion, the servicemen's stress was exacerbated by the physically exhausting labor. Workers toiled 24 hours a day, seven days a week in eight-hour shifts, often maneuvering ammunition and explosives by hand. Worse still, the white officers commanding the work divisions pushed the men hard, hoping to win bets on whose division could load the most ammunition in the least amount of time. Moreover, the officers callously ignored the grievances brought to their attention by the enlistees.

The hearings failed to determine an official cause of the explosions. The officers were acquitted of any responsibility—their actions of gambling with the lives of their men were viewed as healthy competition. Blame for the accident was attributed to the perceived carelessness of the dead seamen.

## THE MUTINY AND ITS AFTERMATH

Within weeks of the disaster, those who survived the explosions, still in shock and mourning and hoping for other duties, were assigned back to munitions handling. On August 9, more than 300 men were ordered out onto the loading pier of the Mare Island Naval Ammunition Depot. Most refused out of fear of another explosion, citing poor training and the same unsafe conditions present at Port Chicago. The Port Chicago Mutiny had begun.

In its wake, 258 men were arrested and incarcerated for three days in a barge moored to the pier. Under threat of being charged with mutiny, which was punishable by death during wartime, the men were offered the chance to return to work. Fifty men still refused and were subsequently charged. Three hundred twenty-eight men returned to work; of that number, 208 were later court-martialed.

On October 24, after a trial marked by racial tension, all 50 "mutineers" were found guilty. Sentences were passed ranging in length from 8 to 15 years hard labor, and all 50 men were dishonorably discharged. The other 208 servicemen facing lesser charges received bad-conduct discharges and three months' loss of pay. (The NAACP took up the case after the convictions; Thurgood Marshall was chief counsel.)

## STILL SEEKING REDEMPTION

The mutiny, however, became a catalyst for change. Shortly after, the navy introduced new munitions training and handling procedures and announced that whites would begin working at munitions depots. In 1945, the navy was completely desegregated.

In January 1946, the Port Chicago 50, as the convicted men became known, were released under a presidential clemency order. Still, none had their convictions overturned, and all were denied navy veterans benefits. In a further insult, a proposed award of $5,000 to their families was reduced by Congress to $3,000 because they were black.

Family and advocates of the 50 convicted servicemen long sought not only redemption but also recognition for their bravery in their willingness to fight and die for their country and their important contribution to the war effort. Both have been slow to come, but come they have.

In 1992, the Port Chicago Naval Magazine National Memorial was dedicated in memory of those killed and injured in the Port Chicago explosion. And in 1999, President Bill Clinton granted a full pardon to Freddie Meeks, one of the last remaining survivors of the Port Chicago 50.

# THE DARING EXPLOITS OF HITLER'S FAVORITE COMMANDO

*An unremarkable engineering student who came to be considered the "most dangerous man in Europe" during the war went on to consult for other undercover militant groups.*

Otto Skorzeny's military career took him to more than a dozen countries on three continents. He had personal access to Adolf Hitler, who credited him with nothing less than "saving the Third Reich." President Eisenhower thought Skorzeny was the most dangerous man in Europe. Skorzeny even got away with dressing down the most feared Nazi of all, Heinrich Himmler, telling him to his face that he was useless.

## SHADOW SOLDIER

When war broke out in 1939, Skorzeny volunteered for the *Luftwaffe,* but at 31 was deemed too old for flight training. He transferred to the *Waffen*-SS and served on the eastern front until he suffered a head wound from Russian artillery. Reassigned back to Berlin for desk duty, he was summoned to headquarters in April 1943. Hitler was reorganizing the feared Nazi intelligence machine, which included the creation of a special commando unit tasked with handling missions that the regular military was too "squeamish" to handle. Skorzeny was offered the job based on a recommendation from Ernst Kaltenbrunner, Reinhard Heydrich's successor as head of RSHA intelligence. With no prior clandestine experience, he decided to borrow ideas from the best source of the time—captured British manuals. He soon put together a crack commando outfit and was the man directly responsible for some of the most fascinating operations of the war.

# THE MUSSOLINI RESCUE

On July 26, 1943, Skorzeny, along with a number of other officers, received a summons to attend a meeting with Hitler. Evaluating the men before him, the *Führer* dismissed everyone but Skorzeny and informed him of the arrest of Benito Mussolini by King Vittorio Emanuele III. Hitler told Skorzeny he believed that the loss of Il Duce could lead to Italy deserting its alliance with Germany, and therefore, Skorzeny must free Mussolini from captivity. The commando units departed the next day for Italy and spent weeks trying to determine where Mussolini was being kept, finally locating him in the isolated mountaintop resort of Gran Sasso.

The resort was accessible only by a single railroad line and was so heavily guarded that there was no question of using it for an approach. So Skorzeny settled on a bold plan, landing gliders under cover of darkness in a small boulder-strewn clearing on the mountaintop. Kidnapping an Italian general at gunpoint and forcing him to accompany the commandos in an attempt to keep the troops guarding Mussolini calm, the scar-faced Skorzeny rescued the dictator and took off again without firing a shot. The operation made headlines around the world and was considered so significant that the U.S. Army Historical Division asked Skorzeny himself to provide an account of the action after the war.

## HITLER'S FAVORITE COMMANDO

The Mussolini episode was only one of Skorzeny's several encounters with wartime leaders. In September 1944, Hitler learned that Miklós Horthy, the Regent of Hungary, was attempting to negotiate a separate peace with the Soviets. The *Führer* dispatched Skorzeny to deal with the problem.

Skorzeny's solution combined finesse with violence. Disguising himself as a civilian, he located the regent's adult son, Milos Horthy. Leading his commandos in a raging gun battle with the younger Horthy's guards, Skorzeny took the man captive and personally ordered that Milos be rolled up inside a carpet and driven away. Stuffing the Hungarian into a plane bound for Vienna, the Nazis used his life as a bargaining chip in a telephone call with his father. The crying regent—his peace plan now in tatters—quickly agreed to abandon his overtures of peace.

## THE BATTLE OF THE BULGE

One of Skorzeny's last wartime exploits came during the opening stages of the Battle of the Bulge, Hitler's December 1944 last-ditch attempt to stave off ultimate defeat. In a personal meeting with Hitler, Skorzeny was given the task of capturing key bridges needed for the German offensive as well as sowing general discord among the Allied troops, a task which he carried out to perfection. Using captured American uniforms and jeeps, his commandos penetrated deep behind Allied lines, removing road signs and minefield markers, destroying supplies, and, on one occasion, giving false directions to an American regiment that promptly spent three days wandering around lost.

As news of German infiltrators began to run through Allied forces, paranoia struck all the way to the top of the U.S. command. There was speculation that Skorzeny intended to assassinate Eisenhower—a charge Skorzeny denied to his death—but the possibility was taken seriously enough that Ike's guards kept him a virtual prisoner inside his own headquarters during the week of Christmas. Another rumor was that one German infiltrator was posing as British Field Marshall Bernard Montgomery. American troops were on such an edge that when the real Montgomery approached a checkpoint, they shot out his tires and forced him into a bunker, holding him at gunpoint until his identity was confirmed.

## POSTWAR LEGACY

After surrendering to the Allies and being acquitted of war-crime charges following the conflict, the former commando's services were successfully sought by both the Americans and Soviets seeking to expand their spy organizations. Skorzeny's first loyalty, however, remained to his wartime acquaintances. Using contacts and funds he managed to conceal during the collapse of the Reich, Skorzeny set up financial and travel networks to assist his former associates in escaping Nazi hunters by relocating them to Spain or South America. Skorzeny was reputedly even able to use secret letters between Mussolini and Winston Churchill that he had stolen during the Gran Sasso operation to blackmail the British leader into releasing war criminals.

However, Skorzeny was financially as well as ideologically motivated, and his talents were also sought by such groups as Juan Peron's Argentinean secret police, the Irish Republican Army, and Al Fatah and the PLO under Yasser Arafat—all of whom employed him as a consultant and adopted the shadow tactics of kidnapping and deception developed by Skorzeny during the war. Those methods continue to prove as difficult to combat in the world today as they did six decades ago.

Skorzeny died of cancer in 1975, still unrepentant. Confronted about his role in the war, Skorzeny forcefully stated, "I am proud to have served my country and my *Führer.*"

☆   ☆   ☆

- *The Skorzeny commando unit had a rival, the Brandenburgers (named for a region around Berlin), who operated at the pleasure of* Abwehr *intelligence chief Admiral William Canaris. By the fall of 1942 the group existed at division size, and saw action across the Eastern Front before being eclipsed by the Skorzeny group, and reorganized as elite infantry.*

☆   ☆   ☆

- *Germany fielded other commando groups as needed. The Nightingale battalion was formed shortly before Germany's June 1941 offensive against the Soviet Union. It entered the Ukraine a day before the invasion, and made preliminary entry into the city of Lvov. When confronted by NKVD (Soviet secret police), the Nightingales successfully claimed to be Soviets who had been posing as German soldiers in German-occupied Poland.*

# Timeline

## 1944

**January 17**
Fighting ceases on New Britain as U.S. forces capture the island from the Japanese

**January 22**
Allied forces land at Anzio on the coast south of Rome and launch a surprise attack on Germans in south-central Italy

**January 29**
The United States' assault on the Marshall Islands begins

**February 2**
Soviet troops enter Estonia

**February 4**
Japanese launch Ha-Go offensive in Burma

**February 5**
British launch a second "Chindit" expedition in Burma

**February 15–18**
Allies attack the historic Monte Cassino abbey in Italy in an effort to root out the Germans from their hilltop post

**February 17**
Soviets destroy Korsun pocket in the Ukraine

Americans occupy the Eniwetok Atoll in the Marshall Islands

**February 20–27**
"Big Week" bombing raids on German fighter and ball-bearing plants

**February 23**
Allies launch attacks in the Marianas islands of Guam, Saipan, Tinian, and Rota

**March 4**
Soviets open spring offensive in the Ukraine

**March 6–8**
First USAAF heavy bomber raids on Berlin

**March 8**
Japanese launch U-Go offensive into Assam, India

**March 29–July 8**
Battle of Imphal-Kohima: Japanese repulsed from India

**March 30–31**
U.S. aircraft from 11 carriers attack Palau Island

**March 31**
Japanese Admiral Koga, commander of the Japanese Imperial Navy, is presumed dead after his plane disappears over the Philippines

**April 2**
Ukrainian troops invade Romania and plan to recapture the oil-rich nation for the Allies

**April 10**
Soviets recapture Odessa, an important port on the Black Sea

**April 11**
The RAF destroys the Gestapo's headquarters in the Hague in the Netherlands

**April 17**
Soviets take Ternopol, Ukraine

Japan initiates a campaign, code-named *Ichi-Go*, against American and Chinese positions in China's Honan Province

# HALF FISH AND HALF NUTS: FROGMEN OF WORLD WAR II

*Before there were Navy SEALs, there were Underwater Demolition Teams—squads that specialized in scouting and clearing underwater obstacles for troops landing on beaches in Europe and the Pacific.*

**Frogman:** A swimmer provided with breathing apparatus and other equipment to execute underwater maneuvers, especially military maneuvers.

## FROM BOATMEN TO SWIMMERS

More amphibious assaults occurred during the Second World War than in any conflict prior or any since. Attacking a fortified enemy beach from the sea, however, is a high-risk operation. The disastrous landing at Gallipoli during the First World War had proven that to succeed, an attacking force needed to have thorough knowledge of the terrain as well as an opportunity to disable enemy obstacles before storming the beach. The U.S. Navy now had to consider planning an invasion of France and an island-hopping campaign in the Pacific. This led to the creation of the Scouts and Raiders unit in the summer of 1942. These special units would scout enemy beaches and destroy obstacles before the landings. Recruits were put through a rigorous training program designed to weed out weaker members.

Initially the group's objective was to destroy enemy obstacles using specially designed explosives. The men were trained to use rubber boats to work the shallows near the beach. It was assumed that the Scouts and Raiders would spend all their time in the boats and, as such, each soldier wore full Navy fatigues, a life jacket, and a steel helmet. Their training placed very little emphasis on swimming. All of that changed during the days leading up to the invasion of the South Pacific Island of Kwajalein atoll during the Marshall Islands campaign in early 1944.

Lewis Luehrs and Bill Acheson, two members of the Scouts and Raiders, sat in a small rubber boat bobbing in the waves beyond the coral reef surrounding Kwajalein. They had a problem.

Their mission: to get as close to the beach as possible and note any Japanese defense obstacles that would impede the imminent landing by the 5th Amphibious Force. The 5th's commander, Admiral Turner, was apprehensive about the operation and had ordered the daylight reconnaissance mission by the Scouts and Raiders—though the unit was accustomed to working under the cover of darkness. Daylight or not, Luehrs and Acheson could not proceed farther than the reef without being detected, but they were still too far out to accurately observe the Japanese defenses. Cognizant of the importance of their mission, the two men stripped down to their underwear and swam to the beach.

They found beach gun embankment locations and a submerged log wall. Underwater reconnaissance was born.

Training of Underwater Demolition Teams (UDTs) began in earnest in February 1944, and after April, UDT operations became a priority facet of atoll landing operations. UDT members, swimming without lifelines and clad only in trunks, masks, and flippers, were nicknamed the "Naked Warriors," and were fondly described by landing crews as "half fish and half nuts."

The group's opinion was so respected by the end of the war that when 23-year-old UDT member Don Lumsden suggested a change in the invasion plan for the landings on Borneo, General Douglas MacArthur promptly implemented the suggestion without question. Thirty-four operations UDTs would eventually clear safe paths in every major Pacific landing, including Eniwetok, Saipan, Guam, Tinian, Peleliu, Leyte, and Iwo Jima.

## NORMANDY

The Allied invasion of France remains the single largest amphibious assault in history. It was rife with challenges: The Germans had studded the beach with explosive-tipped steel posts, and the surf was littered with large steel barricades. The elite members of the Navy's UDT were to arrive in the second wave after the enemy gun emplacements and bunkers had been cleared by tanks and troop carriers from the first wave. This would allow the subsequent waves to move unimpeded and secure the beachhead. A strong tide on the day of the landing, however, pushed many of the UDT units ahead of the first wave, and the team was at the mercy of German machine guns and mortars before they could reach the beach. At Utah beach, at least 23 were killed and 60 wounded out of a force of 175 men. Those who reached the shallows were able to destroy some of the obstacles with explosives. In the confusion, some American soldiers from the first wave took shelter behind obstacles that were rigged to detonate. Enemy fire, however, forced the soldiers to abandon their dangerous cover before it exploded.

## UDT WARFARE AT ITS PEAK—OKINAWA

The most extensive use of UDTs occurred at Okinawa. On March 29, 1945, three days before the scheduled main assault, 1,000 UDT swimmers were dropped by landing craft 500 yards from shore. Each swimmer was covered in silver camouflage paint and carried a reel of fishing line knotted at 25-yard intervals, a length of sounding line with an attached lead weight, a stylus, and a sheet of Plexiglas wrapped around their forearms. Under the cover of naval bombardment, they set out to scout out the reefs and defenses guarding the Okinawa beachheads.

Upon reaching the reef, each swimmer, working in concert with the others, began by tying one end of the fishing line to the seaward edge of the reef. They then swam across the reef toward the shore, unwinding the reel and stopping every 25 yards when a knot appeared to take a sounding with the lead weight. Each time, the swimmers would use the stylus to write down their measurements on the Plexiglas sheet, along with the location of safe channels and information of other obstacles or defenses.

For the duration of their scouting mission, the swimmers faced the risk of being hit by errant American cover fire or gunfire by the Japanese, as well as hypothermia and cramping. Within an hour,

## The Italian *Decima Flottiglia*

Of the major powers, Italy was by far the most advanced in the effective use of underwater warfare at the onset of the war. In the 1930s, Italian sport fishermen began using an adapted industrial rebreather to assist in their dives; the military soon adopted the setup. Italian Army Majors Teseo Tesei and Elios Toschi also developed a human torpedo called *siluri a lenta corsa* ("slow running torpedoes"), which allowed two divers to drive to an enemy ship, attach a limpet mine from the front of the torpedo, and motor away—all the while under water and undetected. Junio Valerio Borghese organized the first units to combine frogmen with human torpedoes in 1939. This evolved into the *Decima Flottiglia*, which was soon divided into two units, one whose men swam away from their targets and one in which human torpedoes were used to escape. The *Decima Flottiglia* was composed of only the most zealous and capable soldiers. During the course of the war, these units destroyed over 72,000 tons of Allied warships and more than 130,000 tons of merchant ships.

The *Decima Flottiglia*'s most innovative tactic developed during its raids on ships in the Strait of Gibralter. The frogmen used the docked Italian freighter *Olterra* as a covert base and conducted operations from it throughout the war. It was not until Italy's surrender in September 1943 that the British learned that the interior of the *Olterra* had been altered to allow human torpedoes to exit below the water line. The ship was later dubbed the "Floating Trojan Horse of Gibralter."

Fiercely loyal Fascists to the end, the *Decima Flottiglia* refused to join in the Italian surrender and fled to the German-backed Socialist state in the north. Cut off from access to the ocean, the group became known for their merciless killings of partisans and other acts of cruelty that rivaled those of the SS.

the reef was scoped, and the UDTs returned. They reported no mines, but did discover hundreds of poles threaded with barbed wire. The next day, the swimmers headed for the reef again, this time armed with small explosive charges. After setting the timed fuses, the UDTs witnessed a thunderous chain explosion that cleared a safe assault path to the beaches.

More UDT operations followed after Okinawa, but never again on such a scale. UDTs were later used during the Korean War before being reorganized as the SEALs in 1962.

# A WING AND A PRAYER

*Thousands of World War II's aviators spent their days in small wooden boxes, didn't use parachutes, and couldn't fire a gun—yet managed to save hundreds of lives.*

By 1939, the era of the homing pigeon was mostly history. Radio technology had improved over the Great War era, when war pigeons were in their heyday, making the winged messengers a thing of the past. But for men on a hot battlefield or partisans operating behind enemy lines, sometimes getting a message back to headquarters wasn't so simple. On such occasions, a humble carrier pigeon was a unit's best friend.

## ALLIED BIRDS

Great Britain used carrier pigeons, also known as homing pigeons, more than any other military. An estimated quarter million of His Majesty's feathered subjects flew in service from 1939 to 1945. The U.K.'s RAF, Civil Defense, and Home Guard made good use of pigeons, and even the home front did its part to support England's littlest wingmen: Pigeon racing was prohibited, birds of prey were hunted along the English coasts, and pigeon corn was rationed.

Homing pigeons were employed in a variety of jobs. RAF bombers and reconnaissance aircraft were equipped with pigeons so that if a plane had made an emergency landing, the birds could alert headquarters and a rescue could be launched. They were also extremely useful for sending secret messages to London. In occupied France, for example, resistance fighters regularly sent homing pigeons from the French coast to London with messages describing the dispositions of German units stationed along potential Allied landing zones.

The U.S. Pigeon Service, a branch of the Signal Corps, assigned more than 3,100 officers and men to manage some 54,000 pigeons during World War II. About a dozen pigeon companies were activated, and most were deployed overseas in all theaters.

## AXIS BIRDS

Germany, had used carrier pigeons for many years. According to MI5, Britain's secret service agency, SS *Führer* Heinrich Himmler, a pigeon aficionado, made a "pet" project of air-dropping carrier pigeons to German spies stationed in England. One declassified MI5 report noted that two clandestine German birds had been captured, commenting wryly, "Both birds are now prisoners of war working hard at breeding English pigeons."

## HIGH-FLYING HEROES

One British pigeon, named Scotch-Lass, was dropped into the Netherlands with a secret agent and arrived, wounded, back in London bearing 38 microfilm images. Another, a hen named Mary, was wounded several times during her five-year career before being killed in action. The pigeon White Vision flew more than 60 miles across churning waters near Scotland to deliver a distress message from a downed PBY flying boat in October 1943.

One Italian campaign veteran, a cock named G.I. Joe, flew 20 miles from the town of Colvi Vecchia, which British troops had occupied ahead of schedule, to U.S. bomber headquarters. The bird arrived in time to halt a planned bombing run on the city that would have brought down friendly fire on the Brits. The 5th Army's commander, Lieutenant General Mark Clark, estimated that G.I. Joe saved the lives of as many as 1,000 men. The bird was awarded the U.K.'s highest honor for a war animal—the Dickin Medal of Gallantry, nicknamed the "Animal's Victoria Cross."

Of course, pigeons were susceptible to the kinds of hazards every bird faces. For example, pigeon "10601" of the Royal Canadian Air Force, deployed from Allied submarines, accomplished many missions but was eventually brought down by a bird of prey. To neutralize the German spy threat, MI5 actually set up a falcon program to catch eastbound pigeons in one high-threat area.

But through winds, hostile fire, and even the occasional enemy barn owl, these feathered messengers made tangible contributions to the war efforts on both sides.

# FROM ALLIES TO ANTAGONISTS

*As the war against Germany drew to a close, the United States, Britain, and the Soviet Union held meetings intended to establish a peaceful new order in postwar Europe. Though they reached some agreements, ultimately they ended up setting the stage for the Cold War.*

## THE MOSCOW CONFERENCE— OCTOBER 1944

The Grand Alliance convened in Moscow for a conference that would change the nature of inter-Allied diplomacy. British Prime Minister Winston Churchill and Soviet General Secretary Joseph Stalin were present, while the American Ambassador to the Soviet Union, Averell Harriman, filled in for U.S. President Franklin Roosevelt.

Previously, Allied meetings had focused on strategies for hastening an end to the war. At Moscow, the issue of the postwar European order was raised for the first time. Roosevelt's absence offered a chance for Churchill and Stalin to confer alone. The result was the famous "Percentages Agreement" for dividing control of the Balkans among the Allies.

Churchill handed Stalin a handwritten note that proposed Soviet control over 90 percent of Romania and 75 percent of Bulgaria. Britain and the United States were allocated 90 percent control over Greece. Yugoslavia and Hungary were to be split 50-50. Stalin purportedly looked at the note briefly, then marked a blue check on it. Subsequent negotiations between British and Soviet foreign ministers bumped up the Soviet Union's share in Bulgaria and Hungary to 80 percent.

Churchill's production of the note contradicts his later claim that he thought the Moscow discussions would focus on the Soviet

Union's entry into the war against Japan. Churchill also knew Roosevelt would be appalled by such a ploy for power and suggested to Stalin that they keep their agreement secret until he could think of a diplomatic way of telling the president about it.

There has been much debate about the significance of the agreement. Churchill claimed it "saved" Greece from Communist control, while detractors condemned him for giving impetus to Stalin's grab of Eastern Europe. Others have argued that the agreement had little impact since control of Eastern Europe eventually followed the Italian precedent: Whoever liberated the country, occupied it.

## THE YALTA CONFERENCE—FEBRUARY 1945

With Germany's defeat nearing, the Allies met again in Yalta, in the Soviet Union. This time Roosevelt, although ailing, made sure to attend.

The future of postwar Germany was one of two key items on the agenda. On this issue, the Allies agreed to divide Germany and Austria into four zones of occupation administered by the Allied Control Commission. France would serve as the fourth occupying power.

The other major item of discussion at Yalta was the Soviet Union's participation in the war against Japan. Turning the tables on Churchill, Roosevelt met alone with Stalin to discuss Japan. He secured Stalin's promise to declare war on Japan, but had to concede to Stalin's demand for control over Mongolia and the annexation of the Kurile Islands from Japan. The two agreed to keep these concessions secret from Churchill, and Roosevelt suddenly found himself playing the same big-power politics game for which he'd admonished the British leader.

A new issue arose at Yalta that would cause the first cracks in the Grand Alliance—the future of Poland. Stalin agreed to reorganize the Soviet-established Provisional Polish Government into a more broadly representative Polish Provisional Government of National Unity and to hold democratic elections. But the Western

Allies knew Stalin held all the cards in Red Army-occupied Poland, and there was little they could do to prevent him from leaving Yalta with Poland in his pocket.

## THE GERMAN SURRENDER

As the German defeat became imminent, the Western Allies received armistice overtures from various Nazi leaders. Hermann Göring tried, through a Swedish intermediary, to negotiate a separate surrender to the British and Americans. Later, Heinrich Himmler offered a bizarre proposal through the Swedish Red Cross: All forces under his command in the west would surrender, while those in the east would continue fighting and later join the Western powers in their impending war against the Soviets.

On April 29, Waffen-SS General Karl Wolff surrendered all German forces in Italy to the Americans after weeks of secret negotiations. On May 4, British Field Marshal Bernard Montgomery accepted the surrender of all German forces in Holland, northwest Germany and Denmark. Mindful of their pact not to negotiate a separate surrender with Germany, the Western Allies informed the Soviets of all German surrender talks. But the paranoid Stalin, suspicious of the fact that German armies in the west were readily surrendering while those in the east continued to fight, remained wary of British and American intentions right up until the signing of the final surrender documents.

On May 6, General Alfred Jodl, representing the German government now headed by Grand Admiral Karl Dönitz, contacted American General Dwight Eisenhower to negotiate a final surrender of Germany. Eisenhower told Jodl there would be no negotiations—Germany's surrender was to be unconditional, and the Soviets were to be involved in the process. On May 7, Jodl signed the document for the unconditional surrender of all German land, sea, and air forces, wherever they may be. The surrender was to come into effect at 11:01 P.M. Central European Time on May 8.

But as a sign of the widening gulf between the Western Allies and the Soviets, there was disagreement as to when Victory-in-Europe Day would officially be proclaimed. Stalin wanted it postponed

# V-E Day: A Day of Mixed Emotions

The formal announcement of V-E Day on May 8, 1945, sparked spontaneous celebrations in many European and North American cities, towns, and villages. Perhaps because the war had gone on for so long, or maybe because unofficial word of the German surrender had broken in the west the day before, it seemed to take a little while for the news to sink in.

But once it did, wild and joyous mayhem erupted in the streets. "The day was like any other," recalled Eva Loewenstein, a 20-year-old German refugee living in London, who on that day went with her mother to the cinema. "While we were watching the world changed—coming out of the cinema we were confronted by a crowd of thousands cheering and chanting, and waving the Union Jack, and roaming through the streets and squares; and there was not a taxi to be had to take us home."

Once it got going, it kept going. Dorothy Wallbridge remembers the V-E Day celebrations in the small English town of Shamley: "The village hall was packed. The band played. We danced and sang, no one seemed tired. I remember...there was a loud bang in the porch, there was a lot of startled yells and screams, when they realized someone had let off a firecracker they had pinched from the Home Guard. No one was angry at the prank; there was a roar of laughter, as we had all jumped a foot in the air, by then even the band had recovered and we carried on singing and dancing till about 1 A.M. We still had to turn up for work in the morning."

For many people, the excitement of V-E Day was tempered by the fact that the war with Japan continued. For the millions of servicemen who were still fighting in Asia and the Pacific, as well as for their families who were waiting for them to come home, V-E Day was just another day.

Those sentiments were perhaps best expressed by a young newspaper journalist and Pacific veteran who described the reaction to V-E Day in San Francisco. "San Francisco took V-E Day in stride," reported future U.S. President John F. Kennedy. "This city overlooks the Pacific and to the people here 'the war' has always been the war against the Japanese. The servicemen who crowd the streets have taken it calmly too. The war in the Pacific is the only war that most of them have ever know[n]—and when you have just come home from long months of fighting and are returning to the war zone in a few days, it is difficult to become excited about 'the end of the war.' V-Day for them is a long way off."

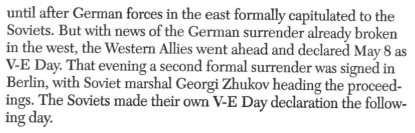

until after German forces in the east formally capitulated to the Soviets. But with news of the German surrender already broken in the west, the Western Allies went ahead and declared May 8 as V-E Day. That evening a second formal surrender was signed in Berlin, with Soviet marshal Georgi Zhukov heading the proceedings. The Soviets made their own V-E Day declaration the following day.

## THE POTSDAM CONFERENCE—JULY 1945

The last "Big Three" conference saw a changing of the guard for the Western Allies. Clement Attlee replaced Churchill mid-conference after the latter's defeat in the general election for prime minister. The recently deceased Roosevelt was replaced by President Harry Truman.

Truman brought with him a giant ace in the hole—the atomic bomb. Although the Western Allies no longer still wanted the Soviets in the war against Japan, Stalin's bargaining power was weakened, and the Western Allies were less acquiescent to Soviet demands. But Stalin still had one trump card left—the millions of Soviet troops in Eastern Europe.

The conference resulted in contentious but fruitful bargaining:

The Allies issued the Potsdam Declaration, which called for Japan's unconditional surrender.

A Council of Foreign Ministers was formed to negotiate peace treaties with Germany's former allies.

The Polish-German border would be moved westward to the Oder and Niesse rivers.

A process for the denazification and demilitarization of Germany was established, as was a formula for reparations to the Soviets.

Nazi leaders would be tried for war crimes.

Poland, however, remained a prickly issue. The Polish Provisional Government of National Unity was formally established, and commitments to free elections were reaffirmed. But no timetable was set for elections—which effectively doomed the Poles to Soviet domination.

## DESCENT INTO COLD WAR

By the end of Potsdam, it was clear that the Western Allies and the Soviet Union had very different ideas on how postwar Europe should look. It was also evident that the mutual acrimony and suspicion that had developed through ten months of contentious negotiations would prevent them from concluding a definitive peace treaty. Stalin's reneging on his promise to hold elections in Poland and share power in Eastern Europe ended any hope of that.

Instead, Europe descended into the Cold War, which would last nearly half a century. Perhaps the saddest consequence was that half the continent was denied the benefits of the highly progressive and successful Marshall Plan. The United States offered Marshall Plan aid to all of Europe, but Stalin, by then openly hostile to the West, rejected the offer as a plot to undermine Soviet power and refused to allow the eastern countries under his control to participate in the program.

As a result, Western Europe was reborn through postwar economic redevelopment and the spin-off revitalization of its political and social institutions. Eastern Europe, in contrast, settled into a long period of economic stagnation and social decay from which it is still trying to recover.

☆　　☆　　☆

- *Allied leaders met in conference nine times between 1941 and 1945. Besides those discussed above, these were **Placentia Bay** (Newfoundland: Atlantic Charter); **Arcadia** (Washington: long-term Anglo-American strategy); **Casablanca** (Morocco: discussion of a second front in Europe for relief of Russia); **Trident/ Quadrant** (Washington/Quebec: D-Day planning, bombing of Germany, Pacific campaign, A-bomb program); **Cairo/Tehran** (Egypt/Iran: D-Day, UN charter, Soviet war against Japan); and **Bretton Woods/Dumbarton Oaks** (New Hampshire/ Washington: postwar reconstruction, structure of UN).*

# A MIGHTY ENTERPRISE

*The USS* Enterprise *had a humble wartime start, but went on to launch the Doolittle raid on Tokyo, serve as flagship in the pivotal battle of Midway, set a record for continuous combat, survive multiple* kamikaze *attacks—and emerge as the most decorated ship of the war.*

Odd for a great fighting ship, the USS *Enterprise* was financed in part by a public-welfare program. In summer 1933, at the worst of the Great Depression, President Roosevelt signed New Deal legislation that authorized $40 million for the construction of two new carriers. As part of this program for defense and jobs, the keels of *Enterprise* and sister ship the USS *Yorktown* were laid the following year at Newport News, Virginia. In 1936, the *Enterprise* was christened as the seventh U.S. ship to bear that name. Her skipper, Captain Charles Pownall, started a lasting precedent of keeping the ship in the highest readiness.

## A NEAR MISS AT PEARL

On December 7, 1941, the *Enterprise* was supposed to be in Pearl Harbor. For weeks the more than 800-foot-long aircraft carrier had been ferrying planes and pilots to Guam and Wake Island as part of a buildup to counter possible Japanese aggression. Stalled by rough weather, the *Enterprise's* return was delayed. That fateful morning, she was still about 150 miles west of Pearl Harbor. Her radio operators listened in horror as *Enterprise* flyer Manuel Gonzales tried to land at Fort Island's naval air station. "Please don't shoot! ... This is an American plane!" he screamed. Then he was heard telling air crewman Leo Kozelek to bail out. Both died.

The 19,800-ton ship spent the next two days searching futilely for the retreating Imperial fleet in the waters southwest of Hawaii. When the *Enterprise* slipped into Pearl Harbor at sunset on December 8, surviving sailors called out, "Where in hell were you?" and "Get the hell out of here or they'll nail you too!" Under the wavering light of still-smoldering ships, the crew frantically took on fuel and, by dawn, returned to the protection of the open ocean.

## 1942

With the war's start, the *Enterprise* began a remarkable 20-month run of critical objectives. In April 1942 it served as Vice Admiral William "Bull" Halsey's command ship on a daring mission. Accompanied by the carrier USS *Hornet, Enterprise* steamed within 700 miles of Japan. The *Hornet* launched Lieutenant Colonel James Doolittle's 16 medium B-25Bs for their surprise raids on Tokyo, Osaka, Kobe, Nagoya, and Yokohama.

On June 4-6, the *Enterprise, Hornet,* and *Yorktown* were the carriers in the Pacific war's turning point, the Battle of Midway. During it, the "Big E" served as flagship for fleet commander Vice Admiral Raymond Spruance. The carrier's air group commander, Wade McClusky, according to Admiral Chester Nimitz, "decided the fate of our carrier task force and our forces at Midway." While scouting

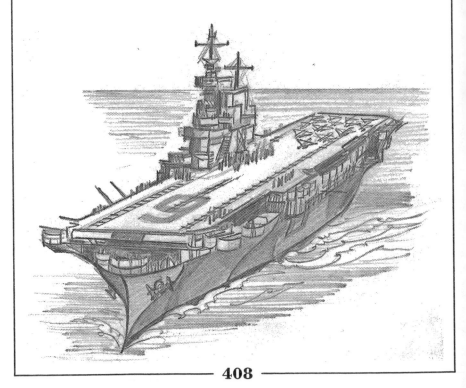

for the Japanese, McClusky later explained, a "stroke of luck met our eyes. Both enemy carriers had their decks full of planes which had just returned from the attack on Midway." Caught by surprise, the Japanese carriers *Kaga* and *Akagi* were sunk, along with flattops *Hiryu* and *Sorya*, shortening Japanese Fleet Admiral Isoroku Yamamoto's post-Pearl Harbor dream of "a year to run wild."

In October, the *Enterprise* and *Hornet*, with the support of one battleship and six cruisers, went against Japan's four carriers, eight cruisers, and four battleships in the Battle of Santa Cruz. The U.S. forces killed 400 enemy aircrew members and lost 44 of their own crew. In November, during the Naval Battle of Guadalcanal, the *Enterprise* was instrumental in thwarting the Japanese effort to reinforce Imperial forces on Guadalcanal, leading to the Marines' successful defense of that vital island.

From October 26 through December, as its five fellow carriers had been sunk or damaged, the *Enterprise* was the only U.S. carrier operating in the Pacific. Its hangar boasted a sign, "*Enterprise* vs. Japan."

The ship's *Yorktown*-class design was key to its considerable success. Capable of 32.5 knots and more maneuverable than its predecessors the USS *Saratoga* and *Lexington,* the *Enterprise* could dodge enemy attacks. If a torpedo or bomb did strike, its hundreds of watertight compartments limited the damage. It was fuel-efficient, an important attribute given its fuel capacity was over 1.5 million gallons of oil.

## 1943

In the midst of other missions, the "Galloping Ghost" was accorded the first Presidential Unit Citation given an aircraft carrier in May 1943. In July, the ship returned to the States, berthing at the Bremerton, Washington, navy yard. The weary crew took 30-day shore leaves while the *Enterprise* underwent major repair and retrofitting. "Engineers, welders, steamfitters, metalworkers, and mechanists of Bremerton Navy Yard swarmed over the ship," according to the USS *Enterprise* CV-6 Association, installing 90 new and replacement radar-controlled 20- and 40-mm Bofors antiaircraft guns, a protective torpedo "blister" around most of the hull, and a wider, longer flight deck.

## 1944

The revamped *Enterprise* left the States on November 19, not to return for 560 days. In January 1944, the Big E's aircraft bombed the Marshall Islands. In February, while raiding Truk, Japan's major base in the mid-Pacific, the *Enterprise* set a new mark for the quantity of bombs delivered in one day. In June during the invasion of the Marianas Islands, it assailed Japan's carriers in the Battle of the Philippine Sea, ending the Imperial fleet's ability to use carrier planes effectively. *Enterprise* narrowly avoided serious harm during the battle when a torpedo exploded in its churning wake.

After wide-ranging raids on Japanese bases in the Philippines and Formosa (now Taiwan), in December it was back to dry-dock at Pearl Harbor. There the ship was transformed into a night carrier. Deck lighting was installed, maintenance crews were carefully retrained, and radars were placed on the larger planes. It became the first flattop to conduct 24/7 warfare, including regular night missions. But those missions were "sheer terror," recalled crewman Joe Hranek. "I was never sure where we were until [a returning pilot] cut the engine and the deck lights suddenly appeared."

## 1945

In 1945, even as the war seemed won, *Enterprise* underwent its most dangerous missions. The carriers *Saratoga* and USS *Independence* joined its Night Air Group 90. The *Enterprise* attacked Japanese aerodromes, ports, and radar stations in Indochina and South China and, on February 16–17, Tokyo. Two days later it supported the Marines' invasion of Iwo Jima. There, the Big E spent 174 straight hours in combat, setting the record for continuous air-sea combat. After a storm forced a respite, the ship conducted operations for seven more consecutive days.

The carrier's run of luck began to dry up in March during raids on air bases in the Japanese home islands of Shikoku and Kyushu, part of the run-up to the invasion of Okinawa. On March 20, while under attack by Japanese bombers, two 5-inch shells from an escort ship missed the planes—and hit the *Enterprise,* igniting 40- and 20-mm shells, killing seven. After ten days of repairs, the carrier steamed to Okinawa, where in April two kamikaze planes missed it by yards but exploded close enough to wrench its hull, wounding 18. After three weeks of repairs, it again bombed Kyushu.

During the war, 1 of every 14 *kamikazes* hit their targets. On May 14, one finally penetrated the wall of lead thrown up by the escorts, the fighters on combat air patrol, and the carrier's own radar-controlled guns. The plane crashed into the deck next to the forward elevator and threw the 30,000-pound lift 133 yards into the air. Twelve were killed, 72 wounded. The "Galloping Ghost" kept fighting until May 16, then sailed across the Pacific to Bremerton for its last overhaul. The war ended while it was in dry-dock.

The *Enterprise,* stated Secretary of the Navy James Forrestal, was "the one ship that most nearly symbolizes the history of the U.S. Navy in World War II."

✯　✯　✯

- *Ship commanders kept detailed logs, action reports, and damage reports. On October 26, 1942, during the Battle of Santa Cruz, the* Enterprise *came under attack by carrier-based Japanese aircraft, and suffered damage that would not have been reported by American media. Damage was particularly serious at compartment A-306-L of Third Deck Forward, where a bomb that had already scarred a portion of Flight Deck Forward detonated, demolishing staterooms and Repair II locker. Forty sailors at the repair and battle-dressing stations were killed.*

# THE BEDFORD BOYS

*When the residents of a sleepy Virginia town awoke one fine June morning, little did they realize that many of their lives had been impacted by events that had unfolded on a French beach the night before.*

On June 6, 1944, Allied forces launched their assault on Hitler's Fortress Europe along five beaches on France's Normandy coast. The bloodiest of the five was Omaha in the American sector. Some 1,465 Americans lost their lives that morning, including a group of young men from Bedford, Virginia, a small town nestled in the Blue Ridge Mountains.

The 29th Infantry Division's 116th Regiment, Company A, was composed of men from the Virginia National Guard, including 35 volunteers from Bedford. Many had joined the Guard to escape the effects of the Great Depression. After being posted overseas in late 1942, the 116th was the first unit within the 29th to complete its amphibious-assault training at Slapton Sands in southern England.

On D-Day, the soldiers of Company A were tasked with securing an exit on the Dog Green portion of Omaha Beach near the French town of Vierville-sur-Mer. Their boats were among the first seven landing craft that sped toward the beach. As their small boats pitched in rough seas and manuevered around hidden water obstacles, the men came under German artillery, mortar, and machine-gun fire from fortifications along the shore.

Several landing craft were destroyed before they came within reach of the shore, their cargo of men tossed into the surf where many drowned. Other soldiers were cut down by gunfire as the ramps on their boats opened.

Nineteen Bedford boys died within the first 15 minutes of the invasion. Three more Bedford soldiers died later that evening, while two others perished before the war was over. Company A suffered 90 percent casualties on D-Day and ceased to be a fighting unit.

On July 17 telegrams began arriving at the Western Union booth in Bedford's drugstore. All of the death notices started with the same somber sentence: "The Secretary of War desires me to express his deep regrets that your son...." " A deep sense of sorrow descended on the town as the reality of the situation hit home—almost everyone knew someone that had been killed.

While no military records exist that indicate the number of casualties in relation to the locations where the men lived, the widely held belief is that Bedford County (population 3,200) lost more men on D-Day, per capita, than any other locality in the United States.

In 1996 Congress recognized Bedford's tragic D-Day losses by naming the town as the site for the National D-Day Memorial. The monument, which was dedicated by President George W. Bush on June 6, 2001, recognizes those who participated in the D-Day landings, as well as the soldiers from Bedford.

"Upon this town fell the heaviest share of American losses."

—President George W. Bush, speaking at the dedication of the D-Day Memorial in Bedford, Virginia, June 6, 2001

☆　☆　☆

- *An American soldier who was wounded on the "Bedford beach" was tended to by a Navy medic who wore dry, spotless coveralls. No one else recalled seeing the medic, but if he was a figment of the GI's imagination, who took care of the soldier's wounds?*

☆　☆　☆

- *As the sun set on the Dog Green portion of Omaha beach, only 18 of the 230 men of Company A were unhurt. Most who still lived huddled against a seawall, exhausted and in shock.*

# BAT BOMBS AWAY!

*Small, winged, nocturnal, furry, and explosive. These critters were supposed to help end the war but succeeded only in destroying an American airplane hangar and a general's car.*

World War II inspired innovation and invention as scientists and engineers from the major powers strove to develop weapons that would provide a winning edge. Many of these innovations are well-known—jet engines and rockets in Germany, for instance. However, those that did not work so well are scarcely remembered.

In the early days of the war, an American dental surgeon from Irwin, Pennsylvania, named Lytle S. Adams conceived an idea while on vacation in the American southwest. He proposed that the United States develop a method for attaching incendiary bombs to bats and releasing thousands of the flying mammals over Japan. Under Adams's logic, the bats would roost in wooden buildings and explode, causing fires that would spread out of control. On paper, Adams's idea held merit—a typical bat can carry 175 percent of its body weight, and since the Japanese populace would not detect the roosting bats, the fires could spread unchecked.

In the weeks following America's entry into the war, thousands of citizens sent ideas for new weapons to the White House, and the bat-bomb proposal was one of the very few that went into development. Approved by President Roosevelt, it eventually consumed a modest $2 million of taxpayers' money.

By March 1943 a team consisting of Dr. Adams and two chemists (one from Harvard, the other from UCLA) had scoured the caves of the southwest in search of the perfect bat species for the project. Although the mastiff bat was larger and the mule-eared bat more common, the team settled on the Mexican free-tailed bat, because it could carry the requisite weight and was available in large numbers (in fact, one colony of free-tailed bats near Bandera, Texas, numbered some 20 to 30 million animals)

Months of testing followed. The creatures were tricked into hibernation with ice, then a small explosive device was surgically attached by a string. The procedure was delicate and required lifting the bats' fragile skin, which was liable to tear if done incorrectly. The prepared bats were then loaded into cardboard cartons, which were parachuted from aircraft and opened at a preset altitude. There were numerous complications, however. Many of the containers did not open or the bats did not wake up and plummeted to their deaths. Still, the bats did succeed in burning down a mock Japanese village. On the other hand, they managed to start a fire in an airplane hangar that also destroyed a visiting general's car. Perhaps for this reason in June 1943, after more than 6,000 bats had been used in tests, the army handed the project to the navy. It was renamed Project X-Ray.

The navy eventually handed off the project to the Marine Corps, which determined that the bat bombs were capable of causing tenfold the number of fires as the standard incendiary bombs being used at the time. However, when Fleet Admiral Ernest J. King learned that the bats would not be ready for deployment until mid-1945, he called off the project. Dr. Lytle Adams was bitter about the cancellation of his novel idea. He maintained that the bat bombs could have caused widespread damage and panic without the loss of life that resulted from the use of the atomic bomb.

☆     ☆     ☆

- *Dr. Adams and his associates visited 1,000 caves and 3,000 mines as they searched for the most appropriate species of bat. Time was short, so whenever the group wasn't exploring a site, it moved in an automobile convoy to the next location. As the cars rolled, team members slept in shifts.*

☆     ☆     ☆

- *Bats were captured by three nets, each about three feet in diameter, that were mounted on 10-foot poles and passed back and forth across the entrances to bat roosts.*

# UNCOMMON VALOR: THE BATTLE OF IWO JIMA

*Tens of thousands of American and Japenese soliders died as the United States attempted to secure the volcanic island of Iwo Jima.*

"The Battle of Iwo Jima has been won. Among the Americans serving on Iwo, uncommon valor was a common virtue." Fleet Admiral Chester W. Nimitz spoke those immortal words during the final days of what became the bloodiest battle in Marine Corps history, in which 6,821 Marines paid the ultimate sacrifice in service to their nation.

What possessed the Japanese military to defend a barren, sulfuric, volcanic island of eight square miles that ultimately ended with the deaths of almost the entire garrison of some 20,000 men? Why did the 36-day battle between February and March 1945 result in more than 28,000 American casualties?

Iwo Jima held important strategic value to both the Americans and Japanese, due to its three airfields and its location approximately 600 miles from mainland Japan. Under Japanese control, the island  could be used for intercepting Amercan long-range bombers on their way to and from bombing missions on Japan. In American hands, the airfields would be ideal as emergency landing strips for B-29 Superfortress bombers and as an advance air base to provide fighter cover for the bombers.

## JAPANESE PREPARATIONS

After the American seizure of the Marshall Islands in February 1944 and the invasion of Saipan in June of that year, the Japanese

High Command realized the need to strengthen their forces in the Bonin-Volcano Island chain, which was comprised of Chichi Jima, Haha Jima, and Iwo Jima. Emphasis was placed on Iwo Jima because it was the only island suitable for building an airstrip.

In order to prepare for the impending attack, Japanese forces under the command of Lieutenant General Kuribayashi Tadamichi built an elaborate fortification system. Artillery emplacements, ammunition storage, and living quarters were located inside caves connected by a series of tunnels so deep that they were virtually impervious to air and naval bombardment. Blockhouses were built with concrete walls as much as four feet thick, along with pillboxes and individual fighting positions called spider holes.

From their well-camouflaged positions, the island's defenders could deliver a deadly hail of gunfire with their artillery pieces, antiaircraft guns, tanks, and other weaponry. Kuribayashi hoped to inflict so many casualties that the Americans would be forced to leave the island. To reinforce this strategy, the Japanese commander ordered every man to kill ten Marines before dying himself.

## BLACK SAND AND BLOOD

From their safe underground positions, the Japanese watched as an American naval force consisting of nearly 500 ships appeared on the morning of February 16. For the next three days, the defenders endured an air and sea preparatory bombardment as American forces attempted to destroy visible installations and gun positions.

Shortly after 9:00 A.M. on February 19, Marines of the 4th and 5th Divisions hit the beaches and instantly encountered the soft, black, volcanic sand. Movement was difficult for the heavily laden men, each carrying 100 pounds of equipment. Corporal Edward Hartman, a rifleman with the 4th Marine Division, testified, "The sand was so soft it was like trying to run in loose coffee grounds." It also became apparent that the sand permeated everything—weapons, vehicles, food, and uniforms. Landing craft became bogged down in the sand and were swamped by violent surf, wrecking

## Gridiron Heroes of Iwo Jima

During World War II, professional sports figures routinely volunteered to serve in the armed forces. In World War II, more than 600 National Football League players served in uniform, and 21 players, coaches, and officials were killed. Two players, Jack Lummus and Howard "Smiley" Johnson, lost their lives during the Battle of Iwo Jima.

### First Lieutenant Jack Lummus

Jack Lummus played one year as a defensive lineman for the New York Giants before enlisting in the Marine Corps Reserve in January 1942. Advancing on enemy positions on March 8, 1945, Lummus destroyed several enemy emplacements before stepping on a land mine. He was rushed to a field hospital where he told the physician attending him, "Well, Doc, it looks like the Giants have lost a good end." He died later that day on an operating table and was buried at the 5th Marine Division Cemetery on Iwo Jima.

After the war, his remains were returned to his hometown of Ennis, Texas. On Memorial Day 1946, his mother was presented with her son's Congressional Medal of Honor.

### Captain Howard "Smiley" Johnson

An orphan, Howard "Smiley" Johnson grew up poor in New Providence, Tenessee, and attended Clarksville High School before entering the University of Georgia in 1936. Johnson earned a spot on the Green Bay Packers as a guard and played 22 games for the team during the 1940 and 1941 seasons before enlisting in the Marine Corps shortly after the attack on Pearl Harbor. "Smiley" Johnson slogged ashore on Iwo Jima as part of the initial amphibious landing on the morning of February 19, 1945. Later that day, while returning to his command post, an enemy artillery shell exploded nearby and he was mortally wounded. For his actions on Iwo Jima, "Smiley" Johnson was awarded the Silver Star Medal.

equipment and ammunition. Many tanks that were needed by the advancing infantry stripped their tracks as they tried to make turns in the soil. Infantry weapons frequently jammed as the sand fouled the inner mechanisms of pistols, rifles, and machine guns.

Advancing from the beaches, the Americans initially encountered little resistance. However, as the Marines moved forward, and when supporting naval gunfire subsided, the Japanese unleashed a heavy barrage of mortar fire. The Marines, trying to find protective cover from the hellish enemy gunfire, sought craters blasted by naval gunfire or aerial bombs since it was impossible to dig protective foxholes in the soft sand and hard bedrock below it. The men hugging the ground that morning realized that the pre-invasion softening of Iwo Jima had failed to reduce the enemy's ability to wage strong opposition to the marine landing.

During preliminary shore bombardment, American ships fired more than 40,000 rounds of ammunition ranging from 16-inch armor-piercing shells to 20-mm ammunition. Despite the massive number of explosives fired, only a direct hit from one of the battleships' 16-inch guns could destroy a concrete blockhouse or enemy artillery hidden in the caves. The Marine command had wanted ten days for attack; instead the navy gave them three. The burden of destroying the fortifications fell to the Marine infantry, or grunts, who used flamethrowers, demolitions, 75-mm field artillery, and antitank weapons that were fired at point-blank range. The infantry paid a heavy price for the failure to destroy Japanese positions. By the end of the first day, the Americans had advanced only 500 yards yet suffered some 2,420 casualties.

## ADVANCE TO VICTORY

Bloodied but not defeated, the Marines gained a foothold on Iwo Jima by the dawn of February 20. Mount Suribachi and Airfield No. 1 had been isolated, and the southern perimeter of Airfield No. 2 had been breached by the invasion force. Japanese soldiers continued to pour artillery and mortar fire onto the crowded landing beaches for several days, until they were destroyed by naval gunfire, air strikes, and the pure tenacity of the Marines.

Three days after landing, the American flag was raised atop Mount Suribachi, but fighting continued for a month. General Kuribayashi's strategy of inflicting as many casualties upon the enemy as possible was proving to be successful, as hundreds of Americans were wounded or killed each day. But Kuribayashi's hope of the enemy fleeing the island began to crumble as the Marines continued their advance, and the general's desperate hold on Iwo Jima began to weaken.

Fanning out to the north and south, the Marines slowly moved forward a yard at a time while the Japanese made sure their enemy paid heavily in blood. The Marine 3rd Division captured Airfield No. 2 in the center of the island seven days after the landing and Airfield No. 3 in the north on March 3. Five days later the island was declared secured, and by March 11, Japanese forces had been driven to the northern edge of Iwo Jima. Organized resistance ended on the March 16, when the 3rd Marine Division crushed the only remaining opposition at Cushman's Pocket in the north. Bypassed pockets of Japanese continued to resist until March 26, when a small band attacked a Marine and Army bivouac area, but they were quickly defeated.

## IWO JIMA: ISLAND AIRFIELD

The main American objective of using Iwo Jima's airfields as an advanced airfield and an emergency-landing site was realized on February 26, 1945, during the height of battle. Stinson OY single-engine observation planes of Marine Observation Squadron (VMO) 4 landed on Airfield No. 1, and the first B-29 heavy bomber made an emergency landing on March 4. By the end of March, 36 Superfortresses had used the emergency facilities on the island, possibly saving the lives of almost 400 men who might have been forced to ditch their crippled aircraft at sea.

The rationale for invading Iwo Jima is still debated among historians. Was it worth 28,000 American casualties in order to save an unknown number of bomber crews? In the end, approximately 2,400 ten-man B-29 bombers made emergency landings at Iwo Jima. It's unknown how many might have been lost if not for the island. Furthermore, the Americans acquired an air base 600 miles closer to Japan, which provided a means of fighter escort over Japan, possibly saving additional bombers and crews. But if military planners had foreseen the wounding and deaths of so many men, would the invasion have occurred?

The debate continues.

# CODE NAME "DIANE"

*During stints for both British and U.S. intelligence, Virginia Hall so excelled at her duties that she became a marked woman by the Gestapo and ultimately was awarded the U.S. Distinguished Service Cross.*

"The woman who limps is one of the most dangerous Allied agents in France," proclaimed Gestapo wanted posters, showing a young brunette American. "We must find and destroy her." So dangerous was Virginia Hall's position that even her wooden leg was given a code name, "Cuthbert." Escaping France by crossing the Pyrenees on foot in November 1942, Hall cabled London that "Cuthbert is giving me trouble, but I can cope." Misunderstanding that Cuthbert was another agent, a Special Operations Executive (SOE) officer cabled back, "If Cuthbert is giving you trouble have him eliminated."

Born in Baltimore, educated at Radcliffe and Barnard colleges, and fluent in French and German, Hall had aspired to a Foreign Service career and worked at the U.S. Embassy in Warsaw in 1931. Her hopes were dashed a year later when she accidentally shot herself during a hunting trip in Turkey and her left leg was amputated. In Paris at the outbreak of World War II, Hall volunteered for the French Ambulance Service Unit. When France fell to Germans in June 1940, Hall trekked to London and volunteered for British intelligence.

During 15 months of SOE service, Hall was instrumental in Britain's effort to aid the French resistance. Working from Vichy, she posed as an American journalist while securing safe houses, setting up parachute drop zones, and helping rescue downed Allied airmen. After the United States entered the war, Hall went underground. Her position became untenable when German troops occupied Vichy following Rommel's defeat in North Africa and she barely escaped to Spain.

Back in Britain, Hall volunteered for the U.S. Office of Strategic Services (OSS) and trained in Morse code and wireless radio operation. Unable to parachute because of her leg, she landed in Brittany by British patrol boat prior to the D-Day invasion. Code-named "Diane," she contacted the French Resistance in central France and helped prepare attacks supporting the Normandy landings.

Still hunted by the Gestapo, Hall adopted an elaborate disguise as a French milkmaid, layering her fit physique with heavy woolen skirts that hid her limp. Peddling goat cheese in city markets, she listened in on the conversations of German soldiers to learn the disposition of their units. Hall helped train three battalions of partisan fighters that waged a guerrilla campaign against the Germans and continued sending a valuable stream of intelligence until Allied troops reached her position in September 1944.

After the war, President Truman awarded Hall the Distinguished Service Cross, though she turned down a public presentation to protect her cover for future intelligence assignments. In 1951, she joined the CIA as an intelligence analyst and retired in 1966. She died in Rockville, Maryland, in 1982.

☆　☆　☆

- *On May 2, 1944, schoolteacher and crossword-puzzle creator Leonard Dawe attracted the attention of the Allies when one of his puzzles, published in the* London Daily Telegraph, *contained the word "Utah." Subsequent puzzles included the words "Omaha," "Mulberry," "Neptune," and "Overlord," leading Allied security to suspect Dawe was leaking intelligence about the planned invasion.*

☆　☆　☆

- *The famous U.S. bazooka antitank weapon fired a 60-mm projectile. Germany's counterpart, the less common* Panzerschreck, *packed an 88-mm wallop, but had a much shorter effective range.*

# ROLAND FREISLER: NAZI GERMANY'S KANGAROO JUDGE

*An accused person standing trial before Nazi Party member and most-feared judge Roland Freisler had little chance of being found anything but guilty.*

"If you have nothing to say for yourself then kindly keep your mouth shut!" Judge Roland Freisler yelled at a defendant before handing down a death sentence. One of the most notorious members of Nazi Germany, Freisler often berated and humiliated those unfortunate enough to stand before him in the *Volksgerichtshof,* or People's Court. His acts within the courtroom earned him the nicknames "Raving Roland" and the "Hanging Judge." He was judge, prosecutor, and jury of a kangaroo court where the rights of the accused were ignored and guilty verdicts were generally a foregone conclusion.

Freisler began practicing law after serving in World War I, and became a member of the Nazi Party in 1925. As he rose through the country's judicial system, he became known for his superior speaking skills, his absolute mastery of legal texts, and his strict adherence to Nazi philosophy. Those characteristics combined with his record earned him the title of the most feared judge in Germany.

## "GUILTY!"

Freisler is most famous for presiding over the trials of German conspirators involved in the July 1944 plot to assassinate Hitler. During the trial, in which nearly all of the conspirators were condemned to execution, he often screamed at and belittled the defendants. For example, he refused to allow the conspirators to use belts or suspenders during the court proceedings, causing their trousers to fall down. When the trousers fell, the entire court broke out in laughter. None of the individuals who stood before him had the chance to defend themselves. The verdict was always the same—guilty.

The last individual to stand trial before Raving Roland was Fabian von Schlabrendorff, a German officer who planted a bomb that failed to detonate on Hitler's personal aircraft. On February 3, 1945, Schlabrendorff stood in front of the judge attempting to defend himself, when an air-raid siren sounded and everyone in the courthouse evacuated to nearby bomb shelters. Dedicated to a fault, Freisler went back to the courthouse to retrieve important court documents when an Allied bomb scored a direct hit. The Hanging Judge was found crushed under a pile of masonry clutching the Schlabrendorff file.

## TRIUMPH OF THE DEFENDANT

The unexpected death of Freisler was a reprieve for the man who had been standing trial for treason. In a twist of fate, Schlabrendorff survived the war and, like the man who had held his life in his hands, became a judge. However, unlike Freisler, who used his position to victimize individuals, Schlabrendorff served on the Constitutional Court of West Germany, protecting human rights.

☆　　☆　　☆

- *Ironically, as a judge, Freisler was considered a civil servant under federal law. Therefore, his widow continued to collect his pension benefits from the German government for years after his death.*

☆　　☆　　☆

- *On one prewar visit to the United States, Winston Churchill asked his wealthy friend Bernard Baruch to let him "play" the stock market. When the closing bell rang, Winston was a bankrupt man—except that Baruch had ordered an aide to buy what Churchill sold and sell what Churchill bought, saving his friend from ruin.*

# "FAKE" GIs AT THE BATTLE OF THE BULGE

*An elite German unit led by "Scarface" Otto Skorzeny choreographed an elaborate scheme that put undercover Germans behind Allied lines.*

In the early stages of the Battle of the Bulge, word spread like wildfire through U.S. forces that Germans dressed as GIs had infiltrated their lines. On December 17, 1944, an alarmed General Patton informed General Eisenhower of "Krauts speaking perfect English . . . raising hell, cutting wires, turning road signs around, spooking whole divisions, and shoving a bulge into our defenses."

Disruption by the elite German unit, *Panzerbrigade 15*, was considerable. In one instance, phony American soldiers directed the 3,000 men of an army regiment in the wrong direction. Members of the "Trojan Horse brigade" also stopped U.S. troops from blowing up a key bridge on the river Amblève. Meanwhile, truck drivers stopped cold at fake signs planted by the commandos to indicate that roads were mined. Several GIs suspected of being closet Germans were mistakenly shot.

Thousands of MPs threw up roadblocks to ferret out infiltrators, bringing some operations to a crawl. An MP put Brigadier General Bruce Clarke, the hero of St. Vith, under custody, telling him, "I was told to look out for a Kraut posing as a one-star general." All through the Ardennes, soldiers nervously interrogated each other: "Who's married to Betty Grable? Who's Minnie Mouse?"

## GRIEF CAUSED BY *GREIF*

All this resulted from Operation *Greif,* a top-secret mission dreamed up by Hitler that sent a brigade of German commandos in U.S. uniforms and riding in American vehicles behind enemy lines in the beginning hours of the Battle of the Bulge. The *Führer* was inspired by an American attack on Aachen, Germany, where a trio of captured German tanks had scored a splashy victory.

The order was to sow confusion and seize strategic bridges over the Meuse. The commander of the operation was 36-year-old *Waffen*-SS Major Otto Skorzeny, already a special-operations legend. At an SS-run training camp, Skorzeny's 3,000 recruits were trained extensively in American mores over five weeks. Soldiers took lessons in American slang and were drilled to march like GIs. They learned that "cowboys" did indeed "shoot from the hip" and practiced firing submachine guns that way. To refine their talents, the most skilled imitators were slipped into prisoner-of-war camps.

Unfortunately for Skorzeny, out of 600 men who were supposed to pass as Americans, only about a dozen were fluent in English; just 400 members had rudimentary English. If questioned by a real U.S. soldier, they were told to reply, "Sorry!" and scamper away. These men, Skorzeny later wrote, "could never dupe an American—not even a deaf one!"

With Germany sorely short of war materiel, the equipment assembled for such an important operation was meager. American uniforms were in short supply, so summer issues with POW markings were employed. Skorzeny wanted sufficient vehicles to outfit a full panzer brigade. He ended up with two American tanks and two American armored cars, although considerably more jeeps and trucks. More of his heavy equipment, like assault guns and Panther tanks, were German weapons painted as American ones.

## MASS CONFUSION

Still, Operation *Greif* went ahead. And partly because of Skorzeny's reputation as "the most dangerous man in Europe," the panic spread by his disguised troopers reached the staff of General Eisenhower. Three captured *Panzerbrigade* 15 members lied during interrogation that their mission was to kidnap or assassinate Eisenhower. Intelligence officers, aware that "Scarface" Skorzeny was leading the operation, believed them. So the U.S. general abandoned his headquarters villa near Paris, and an Eisenhower "double" was driven in an open car around Paris, inviting assassination. After several days, a fed-up Ike informed his secretary, "Hell's fire. I'm going for a walk. If anyone wants to shoot me he can go right ahead!"

American troops learned many ways to tell a "real" GI from a "fake" one. By regulation and inclination, real GIs rode two to a Jeep; fake GIs were readily spotted because they rode in groups of four. Americans in mechanized units referred to themselves as a "troop." When German commandos riding in captured self-propelled guns ran into a U.S. tank division and referred to their unit as a "company," the Americans opened fire, killing the Germans. Some 18 captured commandos were shot as spies.

Those fake GIs who did get through suffered their own share of confusion. Some Germans were captured at fuel depots after asking for "petrol" instead of gas. After capturing an American, one German "MP" was stunned to find his captive was a fellow commando in disguise. The infiltrators wore distinctively colored scarves and placed yellow triangles on their transport, but such identifiers were often not enough to make the imposters recognizable to their comrades.

Overall, however, Operation *Greif* was a failure. *Panzerbrigade* 15 never reached the Meuse in force. Skorzeny quickly gave up hope of his vehicles achieving a major breakthrough and ordered them to operate as a regular mechanized unit. Only a fraction of his force penetrated American lines.

## THE LEGEND LIVES ON

Much of Skorzeny's career also lay in the future, shrouded in mystery. In a war crimes trial, he was charged with having his men impersonate enemy soldiers but was acquitted when a British officer testified that Allied commandos had done the same. Skorzeny then staged a daring prison escape, fleeing to Franco's Spain. He likely played a major role in running Odessa, the shadowy organization that helped former Nazis flee Germany. He was an advisor to Argentina's fascist leader, Juan Peron, and may have had an affair with Peron's wife, Eva. He advised young Palestinians, such as Yasser Arafat, in organizing resistance to Israel, yet may have been on the payroll of Israel's secret service, the Mossad. For years, when a noteworthy assassination or abduction took place, Hitler's favorite commando would deny it, stating, "I'm a retired kidnapper."

# Fast Facts

- In Yugoslavia, Mihailović's Chetniks sometimes collaborated with German and Italian occupiers, fighting first the Ustaše and then the Partisans. Mihailović was no quisling at heart; he knew that Axis reprisals were monstrous—on the scale of dozens to one—and he didn't want innocent people butchered for minor military gain. Tito, on the other hand, was an active fighter and a constant thorn in the Axis's side. In hindsight, this helps show why Tito was able to hold Yugoslavs together after the war. Of all the power bases in wartime Yugoslavia, only his welcomed Yugoslavs of all ethnicities and faiths. Only his upheld the fighting sentiment that had led Yugoslavs to cheer the regency's fall to begin with. That sense of solidarity carried on after the war.

- Mihailović and Tito did meet early in the occupation to try working out their differences. It didn't go well. The Chetniks were fond of a plum brandy called slivovitz, and Mihailović served Tito a cup of the heated and sweetened alcohol under the guise of tea. Tito took a big gulp and spewed it all over his fancy uniform, much to Mihailović's amusement.

- Given the deeds of the Ustaše, well might Pavelić flee for his life after the war. His attitude toward Serbs was ethnic cleansing at its worst: "Kill one-third, convert one-third to Catholicism, and expel the other third." He set up concentration camps to confine and murder most of the same groups Hitler confined in the Nazi camps, plus Serbs. The Ustaše regime drove many Croats right to Tito's partisans. The Ustaše was entirely dependent on German and Italian armed support, which waned as both occupying powers lost patience with Pavelić.

- Not that Tito's hands were clean, especially after the war. The lowest death estimates of the Bleiburg massacres, in which supposed or assumed Ustaše-sympathetic Croatian refugees were slaughtered by Partisans, begin at 30,000 and range into six figures; the true number will likely never be known.

- Yugoslavia simply means "South Slavia" in Serbo-Croatian.

# INSIDE THE M3 TANK

*Despite several design flaws, M3 tanks did their best to rival Germany's panzers before being replaced by M4s in the latter part of the war.*

When World War II began in September 1939, German tank technology and armored doctrine were far superior to anything the Allies had developed to that point. When Germany's panzers, mechanized infantry, and dive-bombing planes rolled the French and British armies back to the shores of the English Channel in a matter of mere weeks, American military planners were put on notice that any future wars would be fought in a manner and with weapons not previously experienced.

While the Germans adhered to the doctrine of unified tank formations with a mix of armament, American strategists of the day expected tanks would be used only in conjunction with mobile infantry. Based on their limited World War I experiences, U.S. Army commanders believed tanks would take a secondary, supporting role to infantry units, which they incorrectly assumed would again dominate the fields of battle.

Germany's so-called *Blitzkrieg* tactics served as a wake-up call to American military planners. In July 1940 the War Department authorized the design and development of a new medium-class tank. The resulting M3 was eventually sold to Great Britain and Russia through the Lend-Lease program.

The M3 was designed as a stopgap measure. The new tank was built to counter the superior armor found on German tanks, and to that end was well armed. It packed a 75-mm gun, which was on par with anything the Germans produced at the time, and could fire both armor piercing and high-explosive (HE) rounds.

A small turret with a high-velocity 37-mm gun and coaxial .30-caliber machine gun were mounted atop the M3's hull. A small cupola on top of this turret held a second .30-caliber machine gun, while two additional .30-caliber machine guns were mounted in a fixed position on the front left side of the hull.

## DESIGN FLAWS

Because of time and production constraints, the major drawback of the M3's main gun was that it was not turret mounted. The desire to get the tank into production in the shortest possible amount of time precluded the design of a rotating turret big enough to house the new gun. As the U.S. Army had not yet developed a turret capable of holding a large caliber gun, the M3's 75-mm gun was instead mounted in an ungainly fashion in a sponson in the right front side of the tank's hull. This archaic design feature was a throwback to the first tank designs of World War I and restricted the gun's range of movement to a mere 15 degrees to each side.

Another shortcoming was the tank's ungainly height. It stood a whopping 10-feet 4-inches tall, making the vehicle a prime target on any battlefield. Having the 75-mm gun located midpoint on the tank's vertical frame meant the top half of the M3 would be exposed to enemy gunners before the M3's crew could fire on their target.

Instead of being welded, the M3's steel components were riveted together. A hit on an M3 by an enemy shell could pop rivets out of place, which might then ricochet around the inside of the tank, wounding or killing crewmen. Later variants were produced with welded components.

The M3 also suffered from poor off-road performance. Tanks sold to Russia were often referred to by their crews as the "grave for six brothers," and Russian tankers complained of continual track failure. The combination rubber-metal tracks had a tendency to burn out during the heat of battle, causing the tracks to collapse and the tank to become immobilized.

# M3 IN BATTLE

M3s were first used by the British in North Africa. On May 26–27, 1942, 167 of these tanks took part in the Battle of the Gazala Line, which pitted elements of the British 8th Army Division against an offensive launched by General Erwin Rommel's *Afrika Korps*. The M3 performed admirably and was more than a match for the German's Panzer III and IV tanks. By the end of the battle, the British, sporting their new American-made tanks, had cost Rommel almost one-third of his panzers.

In North Africa, British crews used the M3's 75-mm HE rounds with great effect against the enemy's 88-mm antiaircraft gun, which the Germans had ingeniously converted into an antitank gun. The use of HE rounds enabled the British to shell German antitank positions while remaining outside the effective range of the German guns.

As the war progressed, the M3 was quickly outclassed. The introduction of the German Panther and Tiger tanks rendered the M3 obsolete, and the tank was withdrawn from service in every theater of operation, save one—the China-Burma-India frontier, where the British employed the tank until the end of the war. While M3 variants continued to operate in Europe as tank recovery vehicles or howitzer gun platforms, the M4 (the famed "Sherman") effectively replaced the M3 as the Allies' main battle tank by mid-1943.

☆ ☆ ☆

- *The first M3s were assigned a crew of seven including: commander, 37-mm gunner, 37-mm loader, 75-mm gunner, 75-mm loader, radio operator, driver.*

☆ ☆ ☆

- *The British referred to the M3 as the "General Lee," named after General Robert E. Lee. The modified M3 minus the machine-gun cupola mounted above the 37-mm gun turret was referred to as the "General Grant," for Ulysses S. Grant.*

# FROM ILLUSTRIOUS TO INDEFATIGABLE

*Royal Navy carriers turned the tide of the war in the Atlantic and the Pacific.*

In November 1940 the HMS *Illustrious,* called "Lusty" by her crew, became the first aircraft carrier in naval history to launch a solely airborne strike against an enemy fleet, sinking one Italian battleship and heavily damaging two others. The surprise attack on the port of Taranto became the model for the Japanese attack on Pearl Harbor.

The *Illustrious* and her three sister ships, *Victorious, Formidable,* and *Indomitable,* accumulated one of the most heralded combat records in the history of the Royal Navy. Although limited in the number of aircraft they could carry compared to U.S. carriers, the armored flight decks of the *Illustrious*-class carriers made the ships less vulnerable to battle damage. Joined by the *Implacable* and *Indefatigable* (subsequent ships with a modified design), the six aircraft carriers served in nearly every theater of the war while surviving dive bombers and torpedo bombers in the Mediterranean and *kamikaze* attacks in the Pacific.

The carriers won battle flags in the Allied campaigns in North Africa and Sicily, on Arctic convoy duty, on hunts in the North Atlantic for the German battleships *Bismarck* and *Tirpitz,* and in the Allied landings at Madagascar. Several spent time at Norfolk Navy Yard in Virginia for repair of battle damage. In 1941, the *Formidable* was repaired at Norfolk after being hit by bomb off Malta; the *Indomitable* was there twice in 1943 after a bomb went through her deck off Malta and after being torpedoed during the invasion of Sicily.

As the tide of battle turned in Europe, the carriers were redeployed to the Pacific. During eight months in 1944, the *Formidable, Illustrious, Implacable, Indomitable,* and *Indefatigable* launched strike after strike against Japanese forces in Indonesia. As part of Admiral Nimitz's 5th Fleet, the *Illustrious, Victorious, Indefatigable,* and *Indomitable* covered the landings at Okinawa in May 1945. All four ships were struck by *kamikaze* attacks, with the *Illustrious* and *Victorious* hit by two each. The *Formidable* suffered several strikes, including a suicide plane that crashed at such a steep dive that it left a ten-foot-wide dent in the *Formidable's* flight deck. Eight crew members were killed, and 47 were wounded. Miraculously, within eight hours the *Formidable's* deck was repaired and aircraft were landing again.

After V-E Day, several of the carriers served as transports to bring troops home. The *Victorious* also repatriated prisoners of war and in 1946 brought Australian war brides of British serviceman to their new lives in Great Britain. Over the next decade, as the Royal Navy converted to jet aircraft, the *Illustrious*-class carriers were decommissioned due to wartime damage or after brief stints as training ships. After extensive reconstruction, the *Victorious* served until 1968, when she was decommissioned and sold for scrap.

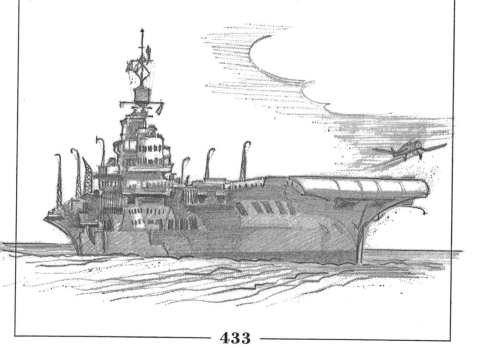

# "THE GOOD NAZI"

*Albert Speer was a Hitler favorite who ran the German armament plants that exploited millions of slave workers. Yet he escaped the noose at Nuremberg and later basked in a favorable public image.*

November 20, 1945, marked the commencement of the landmark Nuremberg trial, in which the most prominent surviving political, military, and economic figures from the Nazi regime stood collectively accused of conspiring to wage war and of committing crimes against peace, crimes against humanity, and war crimes. Of the 21 defendants who took to the prisoner's dock that day, one of them, Albert Speer, seemed from the very outset not to belong.

Speer served as the Minister of Armaments and War Production in the Nazi government, which was responsible for the armament plants where millions of slave workers from the occupied territories toiled and died. As Hitler's chief urban architect, he was a favored member of the Nazi party inner circle. Yet many observers of the Nuremberg tribunal questioned if Speer should even be there.

Speer readily provided detailed answers to interrogators' questions about German weapons and production and the country's economic performance and strategies. He impressed his captors with his candor and intelligence. He was unlike other senior Nazis in Allied custody, who tended to be obstinate, boorish, and defiant. As a result, he was held separately from the other prisoners and for a while was freed. His later arrest and indictment for war crimes surprised many.

## A UNIQUE STRATEGY

Speer's chosen strategy was to set himself apart from his co-defendants. The crux of this strategy was his willing acceptance from the outset of the collective responsibility of the defendants for the crimes of which they were accused. Speer calculatedly portrayed himself as an apolitical technocrat who was a cog in the machine—not one of the operators—and unaware of the atrocities perpetrated by the Nazis.

While many of the others, particularly Hermann Göring, defended their Führer, Speer strove to distance himself from Hitler. Speer also refused to acquiesce to Göring's united-defense approach, as the others did. He resented the domineering role Göring assumed over the rest of the defendants and refused to let him dictate the course of his defense as the others had.

While Speer worked to set himself apart, the court tended to treat him differently from the others. Perhaps it was because he was closer in social strata to those trying him than most of his codefendants; maybe it was because they found his gambit convincing. Whatever the case, Speer had to endure much less rigorous cross-examinations than the other defendants did.

In the end, Speer, the man who excelled in keeping the armaments plants churning with slave labor, escaped the hangman's noose, receiving instead a 20-year prison sentence. The man who supplied the labor for Speer's plants, Fritz Sauckel, was executed.

## POSITIVE PUBLIC IMAGE

Speer's portrayal of himself at Nuremberg as a Nazi leader like no other, who had no knowledge of the Holocaust despite being part of the regime's inner circle, resonated beyond the Nuremberg courtroom. For decades afterward, Speer was viewed by the public as "The Good Nazi" who was rightly spared the death penalty. Capitalizing on this favorable image after his release from Spandau prison in 1966, Speer became a two-time best-selling author. In his autobiography he continued to portray himself as a blameless bureaucrat who remained unaware of Nazi atrocities by adopting a "hear no evil, see no evil" attitude to what happening around him. He lived in London as a semi-celebrity until his death in 1981.

Despite this, the questions remain: Did Speer honestly come to see the criminal nature of Nazi policies and practices (if not his own)? Were his subsequent expressions of remorse genuine? Or was his professed culpability of the Nazi regime at Nuremberg merely a manipulative declaration designed to save his neck?

# HERMANN GÖRING'S KARINHALL

*Adolf Hitler had the Berghof, his luxurious chalet located in the Bavarian Alps. Not to be outdone, Hermann Göring had Karinhall, an opulent country estate and hunting lodge that came to symbolize the self-indulgence of Nazi Germany's No. 2 man.*

In October 1933, the Prussian Department of State granted to Hermann Göring, as a gift for his personal use, an old hunting lodge located in the Schorfheide forest approximately 65 kilometers northeast of Berlin. Almost immediately, Göring embarked on a constant reconstruction, expansion, and renovation plan that would transform the modest lodge into the opulent Karinhall, a 120-hectare country estate and hunting retreat. Reflecting the pompous and extravagant manner of the Third Reich's No. 2 man, Göring spared no expense in creating a sumptuous mansion, built to satisfy his particular senses of taste and self-importance.

## DEDICATED TO HIS BELOVED

Karinhall was built by Göring as a tribute to his first wife, Swedish noblewoman Karin von Kantzow, who died in 1931. One of the first new structures built at the site was a large mausoleum that served as a hallowed resting place for Karin. Her remains were interned at the estate in 1934 after her gravesite in Sweden was vandalized.

Wanting only the best for the place dedicated to Karin's memory, Göring commissioned renowned German architect Werner March to design Karinhall. March was best known for his design of Berlin Olympic Stadium, the showpiece edifice of the 1936 Olympic Games.

Karinhall was large and lavish. It featured a great main hall with four long wings and built-in stages extending beside and behind it. The estate also had a large inner courtyard adorned with statues and lush gardens as well as several ancillary buildings. Other amenities included two casinos, a tennis court, and a shooting range. The main hall was a testimony to Göring's personal ego. Its 50-meter corridor displayed many paintings, tapestries, and other art treasures stolen from museums throughout occupied Europe. It had a heavy oak bar with an inscribed plaque proclaiming: "To his Prussian Prime Minster Hermann Göring, who leads the fate of Prussia with strong hand."

The hall's numerous showrooms were decked out with more stolen art and hunting trophies, including one that featured dozens of mounted antlers surrounding a large framed photo of Göring wearing the official uniform of Reich Master of the Hunt.

It is not known exactly how much money Göring spent on Karinhall, although Prussian state tax records show a 1944 insured value of 15 million Reichsmarks (in 1944, about $6 million, U.S.). What is known is that Göring had even grander designs for the place. In 1944, plans were drawn for the construction of a new wing housing a luxurious art museum, which would offer the public a glimpse of Göring's looted art treasures.

## VIP GROUNDS

Göring firmly believed that problems could be more easily solved and deals better made in the realm of the hunt and the comfort of the fireplace than at the cold negotiating table. As such, Karinhall hosted many meetings of Nazi party and government bigwigs. High-level political, economic, and military planning occurred there as well, including Germany's 1940 air assault against Britain.

Göring also entertained foreign dignitaries at Karinhall, often taking his guests on hunting trips in the Schorfheide. Benito Mussolini and his foreign minister Count Ciano, British foreign minister Lord Halifax, British ambassador Neville Henderson, and U.S. undersecretary of state Sumner Welles all visited the elite estate.

As the war went on and the fortunes of Göring and Germany began to turn, Göring retreated more frequently to the tranquility of Karinhall. Although he felt comfortable there, it was evident that he never felt completely secure. Fearful of Allied air attack,

# Plundered Art on Display at Karinhall

Throughout the war, Nazi leaders engaged in a systematic plunder of Europe's great works of art. Hundreds of thousands of artworks were stolen, confiscated, or "purchased" from private owners, museums, churches, and public buildings throughout the occupied territories.

An Allied postwar inventory showed Göring to possess more than 1,375 paintings, 250 sculptures, 108 tapestries, and 175 objects of art—a collection estimated in 1950 to value about $162 million, U.S.

A better part of Göring's collection was displayed or kept at Karinhall. Ironically, the Karinhall collection, which featured Renaissance painting, Dutch and Flemish old masters, and the court art of 18th-century France, revealed Göring's personal taste to be very much in contrast with the official preferences espoused by the Nazi government.

Here is a look at some of the more notable pieces of the Göring collection once available for view at Karinhall.

- *Portrait of the Artist's Sister*—Rembrandt, c.1632. One of five works by Rembrandt displayed in Karinhall.

- *Sunflowers*—Vincent Van Gogh, c.1888. Displayed along with other Van Gogh works, *Bridge at Arles,* and a drawing of a landscape.

- *Mary Magdalene* (also known as *La Belle Allemande)*—Gregor Erhart, c.1500. Limewood sculpture taken from the Louvre in Paris.

- Nine Flemish tapestries depicting hunting scenes. Six were works by Daniels Eggermans, woven in the mid 17th century. The other three were woven by Frans van der Borght and date back to the mid 18th century. All were "lent" to Karinhall by the Museum of Art History in Vienna and remain missing.

- *Venus and Amor*—Lucas Cranach the Elder, 1531. One of 19 works of the German Renaissance artist that Göring owned.

- *Pretty Polish Girl*—Jean-Antoine Watteau, early 18th century. Stolen from Poland.

- *Young Girl with Chinese Figure*—Jean-Honore Fragonard, 18th century. Confiscated from the private Rothschild collection in France.

- *Infanta Margarita*—Diego Velazquez, c.1656. Purchased in the Netherlands.

Göring had camouflage nets erected around the property to thwart air reconnaissance. Searchlight towers and flak guns were also installed nearby.

Most telling, however, was the presence of deep underground bomb shelters at the estate, allegedly built a year before Göring's fateful boast that no enemy plane would ever penetrate German airspace. Allied bombers did take a toll on Germany, of course, and even Karinhall was a potential target.

## A RUINED RETREAT

As the war neared its end, Göring moved to ensure that neither Karinhall nor the art treasures within it fell into enemy hands. In January 1945 his art collection was relocated by train to Berchtesgaden for storage and hiding. In April, as the Red Army approached Berlin, Göring ordered Karinhall to be completely destroyed. Most of the art was eventually recovered.

Today, little is left of Karinhall, although there are a few remains at the site that testify to its existence. A granite road marker bearing the estate's name still sits near the former front entrance along with two large stone gate posts. Beyond that are a few crumbling foundation walls, broken cellars, and remnants of the swimming pool.

In the end, Karinhall's ruin, like that of its pompous owner, was to be inglorious and complete.

✮ ✮ ✮

- *One reason the swastika became so universal may lie in a basket. Many natural basketweaving patterns result in endless swastikas, and it's hard to find a culture without some heritage of this useful craft.*

✮ ✮ ✮

- *The concentrated bombing of the Ruhr Valley killed more than 15,000 people, including many foreign slave laborers working in the region's manufacturing plants.*

# Timeline

## 1944

**May 12**
German forces in the Crimea surrender

**May 13**
The Allies finally break through the German Gustav Line, the western segment of the Winter Line, and begin their march forward into the Liri Valley in Italy

**May 18**
Allies finally capture the ruined hilltop of the Monte Cassino monastery in Italy

**May 18–20**
U.S. forces seize Wadke Island, New Guinea, giving them a base for the planned invasion of the Philippines

**June 4**
Allied troops enter Rome, one day after Hitler orders his armies to withdraw; though there is sporadic fighting, the city is spared for the most part

**June 6**
D-Day: Allies land in Normandy in the culmination of Operation OVERLORD

**June 13**
Germans fire first V-1 rocket bomb against Britain

**June 15**
Operating out of Chinese bases, the first B-29 raid on Japan targets a steel plant in Kyushu

U.S. forces land on Saipan

**June 19–20**
The Battle of the Philippine Sea deals a blow to the Japanese naval and air fleet; it will later be called the "Great Marianas Turkey Shoot"

**June 20**
Soviets take Viipuri, Finland

**June 22**
Soviets launch Operation Bagration, main summer offensive

President Roosevelt signs the GI Bill of Rights

**June 27**
U.S. troops liberate Cherbourg, France

**July 3**
Soviets liberate Minsk, Belarus

**July 9**
U.S. troops take the island of Saipan, virtually eliminating the 30,000 Japanese troops occupying the island

**July 17**
Two ammunition-laden ships explode at Port Chicago, California, killing 322 people

**July 18**
Hideki Tojo resigns as Japanese Prime Minister

U.S. troops capture Saint-Lô, France

**July 20**
A member of Hitler's inner circle attempts to assassinate him; Claus von Stauffenberg succeeds in killing four others, but the Fürher survives

**July 21**
U.S. Marine and Army divisions retake the island of Guam

# THE PLOT TO KILL HITLER

*A failed assassination plot resulted in the execution or imprisonment of "conspirators," many of whom were not even involved in the attempt.*

Although the assassination attempt on Hitler's life on July 20, 1944, was not the first against the Nazi leader, the consequences of the failed coup were far reaching. The Gestapo used the attempt as justification for the murder or incarceration of thousands of dissenters who had no connection to the plot. Meanwhile, the failed plan pushed Hitler into a form of self-exile at his Prussian headquarters and his mountain retreat near the village of Berchtesgaden. And the German military, which supported the dictator and brought him great victories at the start of the war, was never again trusted by Hitler.

## A MARKED MAN

Several plans to kill Hitler had been developed as early as 1938, but were aborted when German Army leaders wavered. Various attempts on Hitler's life were then made in 1943. In one instance, a bomb disguised as a bottle of brandy was brought aboard Hitler's private airplane, but the explosives failed to detonate. One week later, a colonel planned to blow up both Hitler and himself with bombs carried in each pocket of his overcoat. He changed his mind when Hitler left a weapons exhibit in Berlin early. A third attempt involved a captain who planned to detonate a hand grenade while embracing the Führer. This plot failed when the event Hitler was scheduled to attend was canceled.

As the fortunes of war turned against Germany in mid 1943, army plotters became convinced Hitler had to be assassinated in order for peace to be negotiated with the western Allies, a move they felt would also prevent a Russian invasion of Germany. The most important part of the coup fell to a conspirator who was both a colonel and a count—Claus von Stauffenberg. He was a staff officer whose bloodlines descended from a Prussian general in the

Napoleonic War and the former chamberlain to the last king of Wurttemberg.

In August 1943, Stauffenberg met Henning von Tresckow, an officer with Army Group Central who'd had a hand in organizing two of the previous attempts on Hitler's life. Although he had been an early supporter of Hitler's National Socialist movement, Stauffenberg became disenchanted with the regime after the debacle at Stalingrad that saw tens of thousands of German soldiers killed or captured.

In April 1943, Stauffenberg was critically wounded in North Africa when struck by bullets from a strafing plane. The attack cost the career soldier the sight in his left eye, part of his right arm, and two fingers on his left hand. While recuperating in a hospital, he decided to take an active role in the conspiracy to kill Hitler.

## OPERATION *VALKYRIE*

In September 1943, co-conspirator Ludwig Beck, the former chief of the Army General Staff, asked Stauffenberg to formulate plans for the seizure of power. The plan, code-named Operation *Valkyrie,* called for Reserve Army units to arrest Nazi leaders and sympathizers, and seize control of key government institutions and media outlets once Hitler had been assassinated.

By July 1944, Stauffenberg had recovered sufficiently from his wounds to be appointed chief of staff to the General of the Reserve Army. The position gave him access to Hitler's military meetings, including one scheduled for mid July at Hitler's so-called "Wolf's Lair"—Rastenburg in East Prussia.

On July 20, 1944, Stauffenberg flew to Rastenburg carrying a briefcase filled with British-made plastic explosives. After a brief meeting with the Supreme Commander of the Armed Forces (OKW), Chief Field Marshal Wilhelm Keitel, Stauffenberg excused himself for several minutes, at which time he armed the bomb. The explosives were set to detonate in 10 minutes.

Stauffenberg accompanied Keitel into the meeting, which had just started as the men arrived. Stauffenberg managed to place himself one position down from Hitler at the large rectangular oak table that dominated the conference room. He placed his briefcase on the floor against one of two thick supports, which ran down the width of the table. As the military men listened to a Russian Front situation report, Stauffenberg slipped out of the room.

## FOILED AGAIN

In a move that would have fateful consequences, an officer attending the meeting accidentally kicked and knocked over the briefcase while leaning over the table to get a better look at a map. The officer bent over, picked up and then moved the briefcase to the other side of the oak support beam, away from Hitler.

When the bomb detonated at 12:42 P.M., the explosion caused the building's roof to collapse and the windows to shatter. As flame and smoke rose from the demolished mass of rubble, Stauffenberg stepped into his car, bluffed his way through two checkpoints, and boarded his airplane for the three-hour journey to Berlin, confident he had killed Hitler.

Four people died in the blast, but Hitler was not one of them. The Nazi dictator was thrown across the room by the force of the explosion but managed to stagger out of the rubble with help from Keitel. Although he was far from dead, the dictator suffered ruptured eardrums, burns to his legs, a severely bruised right arm, and singed hair.

One of Stauffenberg's coconspirators, General Fellgiebel, witnessed Hitler leaving the conference room and immediately phoned his contact in Berlin with news of the failed attempt. The situation became even more confusing when Stauffenberg phoned after landing at the Berlin airport to say Hitler was dead.

Believing the assassination attempt was successful, others involved in the plot began carrying out their assigned roles. As Keitel began contacting key members of the military to alert them of the assassination attempt, several of the less resolute conspirators faltered and changed sides. When Berlin radio announced Hitler would address the nation that evening, the final bloody chapter of Operation *Valkyrie* began.

# PAYBACK TIME

Stauffenberg was quickly arrested at the Benderblock, the head-quarters of the Reserve Army. In the ensuing confusion he tried to escape and was wounded in the act. Shortly after midnight, Stauffenberg and three other conspirators were taken to a court-yard and executed.

The Gestapo immediately began rounding up suspects. More than 5,000 people were eventually arrested. Those who survived the brutal interrogation were given show trials before the SS-controlled People's Court and its bullying judge, Roland Freisler. Under SS Chief Himmler's new "blood laws," the families of the conspirators were also punished. Eight of the co-conspirators were hung from meat hooks at Berlin's Plotzensee prison (the executions were filmed for Hitler's benefit). An estimated 100 to 200 people implicated in the plot were either executed, or in the case of Field Marshal Erwin Rommel, committed or were "allowed" to commit suicide.

As many of the conspirators belonged to the German Army's officer ranks, Hitler never again trusted his generals, and punished them by lavishing favor on the ranks of the *Waffen*-SS. The failed results of the assassination had further implications for the army, whose members were now forced to recite a pledge of loyalty to the *Führer* and use the stiff-armed Nazi salute.

☆ ☆ ☆

• *In addition to a national ban on dancing, Mussolini banned beauty contests in Italy as immoral and banned the Marx Brothers' comedy* Duck Soup *because he perceived it as a direct attack on his character.*

☆ ☆ ☆

• *The Volkswagen was born a Porsche. Famous engineer Ferdinand Porsche designed Hitler's beetle-like "people's car" before war broke out. The basic shape had been sketched at a restaurant by Hitler in 1932.*

# THE ORIGINAL QUISLING

*When a leader's name becomes a synonym for "traitor," history isn't gentle. Yet in the end, the real Vidkun Quisling was hardly Norway's most sinister traitor; he was first and foremost a Norwegian nationalist with a deep loathing of Bolshevism.*

Vidkun Quisling was a pastor's son from southern Norway, just west of Christiania (later Oslo). In 1911 Cadet Quisling graduated with distinction from the Norwegian War Academy. His service in the USSR representing British interests earned him a prized decoration: the rank of Commander in the Order of the British Empire.

During his stint in eastern Europe, Quisling did genuine good deeds, such as helping battle famine. However, by the time he finally returned to Norway, he was stunned to find that his Russian service counted as something of a career sabbatical. Quisling's sense of entitlement would not allow him to buck up and work harder to make up lost ground, and thus his military career was permanently derailed and the embittered man soon entered politics.

A close look at Bolshevism in action had bumped Quisling's politics hard rightward—too far for Norwegians, who wanted to hear less "Nordic greatness" and more practical solutions to Norway's real problems. Always politically tone deaf, Quisling kept shifting, and by 1931 he sounded eerily like Hitler. In 1933 he appointed himself Fører (leader) of the new *Nasjonal Samling* (NS), a nationalist, Fascist party.

The more Quisling said, the less Norway liked it. By 1940, the NS was a fringe party with only a few thousand members and zero power. Quisling began plotting treason in earnest in 1939 with senior Nazis, hoping to keep the British out while securing Norway the maximum possible independence under German protection. Top Nazi opinion was divided on Quisling: Ribbentrop thought him useless, while Rosenberg rather liked him. Quisling did the most effective politicking of his career convincing Hitler to support him.

When German troops invaded Norway, Quisling hurried to proclaim himself Norway's premier—an announcement the Germans might have accepted had he secured Norwegian passivity. It took them only five days to realize that Quisling commanded neither respect nor fear. *Reichskommissar* Josef Terboven, Hitler's next choice to govern Norway, shunted the upstart to a powerless post.

Quisling hovered on the edges of German authority, and in 1942, his patience paid off: Terboven reappointed him premier in hopes of diluting Norwegian resistance. It didn't help, but Quisling would remain Germany's Norwegian figurehead throughout the war—even while working against Germany's interests behind its back. He envisioned a Fascist Norway, allied with Germany but maintaining its own borders and military so that Norway would not become just another German *Gau* (district). He constantly lobbied Berlin to recall Terboven and grant Norway greater autonomy.

On May 8, 1945, the German occupiers surrendered to the Norwegian resistance. Terboven blew himself up; Quisling was arrested the next day. On October 24, 1945, a firing squad executed the former Fører for high treason. To this day, his name symbolizes sordid betrayal.

☆   ☆   ☆

- *On January 9, 1940, a German officer carrying plans for the invasion of the Low Countries and France mistakenly landed in Belgium. Fortunately for Hitler, the Allies who intercepted the plans didn't believe what they were reading.*

☆   ☆   ☆

- *On September 12, 1942, a U-boat sank* Laconia, *a British liner traveling near Ascension Island in the South Atlantic. To the horror of the U-boat crew, some 1,500 Italian POWs were among the victims.*

# Fast Facts

- *Traitor, yes; idiot, no. Quisling was so good at mathematics that one of his proofs was still in use in Norwegian textbooks long after the war. In addition to his outstanding grades at the War Academy, he was well educated in history and spoke fluent Russian. This nimbleness of mind, coupled with an opportunistic streak a mile wide, made Quisling the ideal cat's paw.*

- *After the Nazi conquest, not even outlawing every other political party in Norway could get Norwegians excited about the NS. At its wartime peak only 1.5 percent of the population belonged— and most of those were forced to join in order to gain or keep jobs.*

- *To the extent Quisling—essentially little more than a puppet— could justly be called a head of state, he was the last foreign head of state to meet with Hitler. The Fører flew into Berlin for the visit in January 1945.*

- *On one visit to Hitler, Quisling ended up inadvertently helping the Allies. Resistance members cleverly used a wheel on his aircraft to smuggle information on the German V-2 surface-to-surface missile to Norway, whence it was sent to London via Sweden.*

- *Terboven got far more use out of his Minister of Police, Jonas Lie, who obeyed Nazi orders with zealous, ruthless precision. In addition to helping Terboven police Norway, Lie organized the Norwegian SS with himself as* Standartenfører *(colonel), and served with it in Russia. Lie, not Quisling, was the true homegrown power in Nazi-occupied Norway. Lie also would surely have been shot in Akershus, but like Terboven and other Nazi leaders, he committed suicide first. Only 25 Norwegian collaborators were executed; more than 18,000 were sentenced to prison.*

- *The collaborator Jonas Lie should not be confused with the famous novelist Jonas Lie (1833–1908), nor the painter (1880– 1940) of the same name.*

# THE GREAT MARIANAS TURKEY SHOOT

*When Operation A-Go, part of the Battle of the Philippine Sea, went awry, Japan was faced with a major depletion of aircraft and aircraft carriers.*

When British colonists first landed on the North American continent, they encountered a strange, slow-witted bird that proved to be easy and enjoyable to hunt: the humble, unsightly but thoroughly American turkey. That was long before Americans flew F6F Grumman Hellcats in a dogfight over the Marianas islands, but on June 19, 1944, a young pilot from the carrier *Lexington* couldn't contain his enthusiasm at seeing so many Japanese fighters falling from the sky. "Hell," he yelled over the radio, "this is like an old time turkey shoot!"

Thus the violent and unusually significant battle became known as "The Great Marianas Turkey Shoot," and it ended Japan's seaborne airpower for the remainder of the war. The engagement was part of the larger Battle of the Philippine Sea, which ranks among the most one-sided victories in the history of recorded warfare. It was also the largest and last major battle between aircraft carrier groups.

## OPERATION A-GO—NO

The battle began as Operation A-Go—a last-ditch effort by the Japanese Imperial Navy to check American sea power in the Pacific. Admiral Ozawa Jisaburo hoped to use the advantage of land-based aircraft in the Caroline Islands, plus the element of surprise, to strike at the American carrier force under Admiral Raymond Spruance covering the Marine landings in the South Pacific. In effect, Operation A-Go was designed to bring about a "reverse Battle of Midway," where a smaller American force—thanks to a combination of luck, surprise, and daring—had emerged victorious.

From the start things began to go wrong for the Japanese. The Americans struck at the Marianas, where far fewer planes were available to support the Japanese operation. U.S. forces also learned of Ozawa's whereabouts before the Japanese commander could engage in battle.

In a decision that still sparks controversy today, Admiral Spruance chose not to direct his carriers toward the Japanese battle group but opted to remain on post guarding the landings. His air commander, Vice Admiral Marc A. Mitscher, among others, protested that Spruance was missing a golden opportunity to eliminate the Japanese force. Moreover, the Japanese would be able to attack the next morning and the American forces would not be in a position to launch a first strike. Spruance reasoned, however, that it would be easier to let the Japanese come to his forces, where the full brunt of the fleet's aircraft could be deployed in high concentration. What's more, Spruance feared that the Japanese carriers were a ruse to draw him away and expose the U.S. Marines on Saipan and Guam to sea-based attack.

✯　✯　✯

"This operation has an immense bearing on the fate of the Empire."

—Admiral Ozawa, Japanese Navy

"If we were doing something so important that we were attracting the enemy to us, we could afford to let him come—and take care of him when he arrived."

—Admiral Spruance, U.S. Navy

✯　✯　✯

Undeterred, Ozawa launched a first strike at dawn on June 19. American planes had been engaging island-based aircraft all morning, but they were called back to the carriers when the fleet's radar detected Ozawa's first wave of attackers. Mitscher's carriers launched all available aircraft, and a savage dogfight ensued in which more than 40 Japanese planes were destroyed at the loss of a single American fighter. The second, larger wave was intercepted 60 miles from the carriers, and 97 of the 109 Japanese aircraft never returned. A third assault was turned back as well. Half of the fourth and final wave failed to find the American ships and was destroyed as it attempted to land on the island of Rota for fuel. The other half suffered heavy losses and failed to score any hits on American ships. In one day's fighting the Americans destroyed 315 Japanese aircraft while suffering only 29 losses.

Meanwhile, Ozawa's flagship carrier, the *Taiho,* had come under attack by the American submarine *Albacore.* A Japanese pilot crashed his plane into one of the torpedoes, diverting it, but another found its mark and by the end of the day the ship was gone. Another Japanese carrier, *Shokaku,* a veteran of Pearl, met a similar fate from torpedoes launched by the submarine *Cavalla.*

## THE FLEET CARRIES ON

Despite the day's heavy losses, Ozawa decided to continue his attack on June 20. During the night the American fleet steamed westward in order to launch an assault the following day. Their searches yielded nothing until late afternoon, when an American plane spotted the Japanese fleet. Knowing that his planes would have to return in darkness, Mitscher decided to press his advantage, and in 11 minutes the carriers had launched 216 aircraft. In the resulting battle the Japanese lost another carrier and several smaller ships. At the end of the day Ozawa had only 35 operational aircraft remaining.

The returning Americans were forced to make dangerous night landings. Despite the risk of submarine attack, Mitscher illuminated all the ships in the fleet and destroyers fired flares throughout the landing process. Eighty planes crashed or ditched in the sea but with remarkably low loss of life. That night Ozawa received orders to retire, and the "Turkey Shoot" was over.

The tallies are staggering: By the end of the engagement's second day, the Japanese had lost more than 600 aircraft and three aircraft carriers while American losses were limited to 123 aircraft, most of which crashed during the night landings. After the Battle of the Philippine Sea, the Japanese carriers were strategically reduced to acting as decoys in future operations.

# Timeline

## 1944

**July 24**
The Red Army liberates the Majdanek concentration camp near Lublin, Poland; for much of the world, it is their first look at the horror of the Nazi "Final Solution"

**July 27**
Soviets take Lvov, liberate western Ukraine

**August 1**
With the Soviet Army on the outskirts of Warsaw, Polish resistance activity moves into high gear

U.S. forces secure Tinian

**August 3**
Stilwell's troops take Myitkyina, Burma

**August 15**
Allies land in southern France

Audie Murphy, the most decorated soldier in American history, wipes out a force of Germans who had shot and killed his friend

**August 19**
Paris Resistance rises against Germans

**August 20**
Romania effectively switches sides, turning against the Germans as the Red Army soldiers march through the country

**August 21**
The Falaise pocket is closed; Germans are defeated in western France

**August 25**
Allies liberate Paris

**August 26**
Bulgaria announces it is pulling out of the war and will no longer tolerate German offensive maneuvers from its soil

Germany begins withdrawing troops from Greece

**August 30**
Soviets occupy Romanian capital of Bucharest and the oil fields of Ploesti

**September 3**
British free Belgian capital of Brussels from Nazi occupation

Japanese capture USAAF air base at Lingling, China

**September 8**
First V-2 rocket strikes London

**September 9–14**
U.S. carrier planes sink 59 Japanese ships in the Philippines

**September 12**
Allies breach German Gothic line in Italy

**September 15–October 14**
U.S. forces take Peleliu

**September 17–26**
Operation MARKET GARDEN; Allied airborne attack to seize Rhine Bridge at Arnhem fails

**October 2**
After two months of fighting, Germans crush the Polish resistance in Warsaw

Allies break through the Siegfried Line (a defensive line along Germany's western border) near Aachen

# WHO BETRAYED ANNE FRANK?

*Anne Frank and her family thwarted Nazis for two years, hiding in Amsterdam. They might have remained hidden and waited out the war, but someone blew their cover.*

Annelies Marie Frank was born in Frankfurt am Main, Germany, on June 12, 1929. Perhaps the most well-known victim of the Holocaust, she was one of approximately 1.5 million Jewish children killed by the Nazis. Her diary chronicling her experience in Amsterdam was discovered in the Franks' secret hiding place by friends of the family and first published in 1947. Translated into more than 60 languages, *Anne Frank: The Diary of a Young Girl* has sold 30 million copies and is one of the most read books in the world.

The diary was given to Anne on her 13th birthday, just weeks before she went into hiding. Her father, Otto Frank, moved his family and four friends into a secret annex of rooms above his office at 263 Prinsengracht, near a canal in central Amsterdam, on July 6, 1942. They relied on trustworthy business associates, employees, and friends, who risked their own lives to help them. Anne poignantly wrote her thoughts, yearnings, and descriptions of life in the secret annex in her diary, revealing a vibrant, intelligent young woman struggling to retain her ideals in the most dire of circumstances.

On August 4, 1944, four or five Dutch Nazi collaborators under the command of an Austrian Nazi police investigator entered the building and arrested the Franks and their friends. The family was deported to Auschwitz, where they were separated and sent to different camps. Anne and her sister, Margot, were sent to Bergen-Belsen, where they both died of typhus a few weeks before liberation. Anne was 15 years old. Otto Frank was the only member of the group to survive the war.

Dutch police, Nazi hunters, and historians have attempted to identify the person who betrayed the Franks. Searching for clues, the Netherlands Institute for War Documentation (NIWD) has examined records on Dutch collaboration with the Nazis, the letters of Otto Frank, and police transcripts dating from the 1940s. The arresting Nazi officer was also questioned after the war by Nazi hunter Simon Wiesenthal, but he could not identify who informed on the Franks. For decades suspicion centered on Willem Van Maaren, who worked in the warehouse attached to the Franks' hiding place, but two police investigations found no evidence against him.

Two recent theories have been offered about who betrayed the Franks. British author Carol Anne Lee believes it was Anton Ahlers, a business associate of Otto's who was a petty thief and member of the Dutch Nazi movement. Lee argues that Ahlers informed the Nazis to collect the bounty paid to Dutch civilians who exposed Jews. She suggests he may have split the reward with Maarten Kuiper, a friend of Ahlers who was one of the Dutch Nazi collaborators who raided the secret annex. Ahlers was jailed for collaboration with the Nazis after the war, and members of his own family, including his son, have said they believe he was guilty of informing on the Franks.

Austrian writer Melissa Müller believes that a cleaning lady, Lena Hartog, who also worked in the warehouse, reported the Franks because she feared that if they were discovered, her husband, an employee of Otto Frank, would be deported for aiding Jews.

The NIWD has studied the arguments of both writers and examined the evidence supporting their theories. Noting that all the principals involved in the case are no longer living, it concluded that neither theory could be proved.

☆　　☆　　☆

- *The house at 263 Prinsengracht and its secret annex were turned into a museum in 1960. Almost a million people visit the site each year.*

# THE FIRE BOMBING OF DRESDEN

*The Allied raid on Dresden was well calculated to inflict as much damage and as many casualties as possible. This cultural center of Germany was demolished—a step many believe went too far.*

Four waves of bombers hit Dresden, Germany, over three days and nights from February 13 to 15, 1945. The raiders dropped a mix of ordnance upon the city. The first wave used a greater proportion of higher explosives to damage buildings, exposing wood and other flammable matter. Follow-up incendiaries stoked a firestorm and high explosives hindered firefighters. The conflagration at Dresden reached temperatures of 2,700 degrees Fahrenheit, pushing a mass of superheated air above the town, causing gale-force winds to rush in, sucking people along with them.

Survivor Lothar Metzger recalled, "Burning people ran to and fro, [there were] burnt coaches filled with civilian refugees, dead rescuers and soldiers ... and fire everywhere, and all the time the hot wind of the firestorm threw people back into the burning houses they were trying to escape." Some tried taking refuge in the Old Market's historic fountain, but were broiled alive when the heat boiled the water away. Said survivor Margaret Freyer, "I saw people one after the other simply seem to let themselves drop to the ground. Today I know that these unfortunate people were the victims of lack of oxygen. They fainted and then burnt to cinders."

British after-action reports stated half the city's buildings were destroyed or severely damaged. A Dresden police report listed a toll of 647 shops, 31 hotels, 18 cinemas, 11 churches, 5 cultural buildings, 39 schools, 10 civilian hospitals, and 19 military hospitals, as well as 136 badly damaged factories and a ruined German Army headquarters. The U.S. Army Air Force reported that Dresden's "railway bridges over the Elbe River—vital to incoming and outgoing traffic—were rendered unusable for many weeks." Based on German burial records and the number of bodies found after the war, approximately 25,000 were killed in the attack.

## WHY DRESDEN?

Some seeking a culprit for the Dresden raid point to Royal Air Force Air Chief Marshal Arthur "Bomber" Harris. However, plans for the attack originated from the highest levels.

On January 15, 1945, General Eisenhower's Deputy Supreme Commander, Sir Arthur Tedder of the RAF, met with Stalin in Moscow. The men discussed the danger of Germany's shifting hundreds of thousands of troops east to fight the Soviet armies. Tedder suggested using the Allied air effort to bomb strategic sites to hamper German communications and impede their organization.

Later, on January 26, Chief of the Air Staff Sir Charles Portal noted "a severe blitz will [also] cause confusion in the evacuation" of German troops "from the East." That same day, Churchill asked whether "large cities in east Germany should not now be considered especially attractive targets." By January 31, Tedder prioritized bombing the rail centers of "Berlin, Leipzig, Dresden, and associated cities where heavy attack will...hamper movement of reinforcements from other fronts."

Stalin met with Churchill and Roosevelt at Yalta on February 4–11. During the conference, General Aleksei Antonov, Deputy Chief of the Russian General Staff, requested that Western "air action on communications hinder the enemy from carrying out the shifting of his troops to the East...In particular, to paralyze the junctions of Berlin and Leipzig." The Western Allies pointed out to the Russians that "the structure of the Berlin-Leipzig-Dresden railway complex...required that Dresden, as well as Berlin and Leipzig, be bombed." Otherwise, the Germans could have rerouted rail traffic from the other cities through Dresden. The Allies and the Soviet Union were firmly in agreement to devastate Dresden.

## STEEPED IN CONTROVERSY

Unlike other saturation bombings, Dresden was controversial from the start. Associated Press reporter Alan Cowan characterized the raid as a "terror bombing." The town harbored some 200,000 refugees, a fact that made some planners uneasy. British Labor

Member of Parliament Richard Rapier Stokes condemned it in the House of Commons. Nazi Propaganda Minister Joseph Goebbels even elicited some sympathy in neutral countries with press coverage of the aftermath, perhaps by inflating the death tally to about 200,000. (After the war, some sources claimed 500,000 dead.) While Germany's production of war materials increased well into 1944, the bombings did not have the decisive effect on German output and morale that its chief advocates hoped. Some argue, however, that the bombings did help end the war. The raids diverted major resources of the German economy into antiaircraft production and greatly weakened the *Luftwaffe,* which lost masses of planes and pilots in its effort to protect Germany's cities. Eventually the bombings also shut down German transportation and communication systems, and destroyed many industrial plants.

Contrary to the assertions of sources eager to issue a blanket condemnation of the raid, the city of Dresden was an arms-manufacturing center. It contained the Zeiss-Ikon optical goods plant as well as factories for making such things as radar parts, bomber engines, and fighter cockpits. However, by 1945, many of its factories had been moved to the suburbs, outside the raid's target area.

On March 28, Churchill, who had strongly backed the raid, wrote: "It seems to me that the moment has come when the question of bombing of German cities simply for the sake of increasing the terror, though under other pretexts, should be reviewed. Otherwise we shall come into control of an utterly ruined land... I feel the need for more precise concentration upon military objectives..."

After the war, Dresden became part of Communist East Germany, which claimed such bombings were meant to destroy the parts of Germany falling under Moscow's orbit. Some, like historian Jörg Friedrich, characterize the fire bombing of Dresden as a war crime—an unneeded act of mass destruction against a defenseless city, taking place near the end of a conflict whose outcome was no longer in doubt.

Dresden has taken on a special importance, especially among intellectuals, partly because of its cultural cachet. It was, and is—due to painstaking postwar reconstruction—the home of such treasures as the Dresden State Opera House and the *Frauenkirche* cathedral. The tragedy of those killed has been commemorated in symphonies, films, and books, such as *Slaughterhouse Five* by Kurt Vonnegut, an American imprisoned in Dresden after his capture in the Battle of the Bulge.

## Fire Bombing Tactics Put into Perspective

The raid on Dresden occurred within about a month of Germany's massive offensive in the West, the Battle of the Bulge. To Allied war planners, that battle seemed to prove the war was still far from over, and called for the sternest actions against a still-dangerous foe.

The Dresden bombing was not without precedent, either; offensive air tactics had been evolving through the war. Japan shocked the world in the 1930s with its aerial attacks on Chinese cities. In Poland in September 1939 and Holland in May 1940, the *Luftwaffe* deliberately targeted civilian neighborhoods to force the surrender of those countries—a tactic that proved extremely successful.

In autumn 1940, during the Blitz, the Germans tried to bomb Great Britain into submission, but ultimately failed. Once the British built up a large force of long-range bombers, they sought to turn the tables. The British and Americans were intent on area-wide attacks because the precision bombings attempted earlier had brought disappointing results.

Despite the attention since accorded Dresden, other saturation bombings caused far more fatalities and destruction. The fire bombing of Hamburg in July 1943 killed some 50,000, and displaced a million people. Hit by continual raids, Berlin was turned to rubble. Just ten days after the Dresden bombing, a raid on the much smaller city of Pforzheim caused proportionally many more deaths. The Tokyo fire bombing of March 9–10, less than a month after Dresden, killed some 100,000 and incinerated 16 square miles of a city built largely of paper and wood. The atomic bombing of Hiroshima in August 1945 killed more than 90,000, and destroyed about 90 percent of the city's structures.

Seen in this context, Dresden appears less of a unique event, and more a part of its destructive time.

# WINTER SHOCK: THE BATTLE OF THE BULGE

*In the closing days of 1944, the Allies were anticipating a swift fall of Germany. Instead, Hitler launched a surprise counteroffensive as a last-ditch measure to thwart the Allied advance.*

For weeks the observation battalion of U.S. VIII Corps, the undermanned unit defending the strategic Ardennes Forest, knew something was afoot. Aiming sophisticated microphones at the *Schnee Eifel,* a wooded, German-occupied ridge near the Belgian-German border, analysts picked up the telltale sounds of tracked vehicles and artillery moving into position. The German Army had launched its invasions of France in 1914 and 1940 from this place, and it was gearing up for another attack.

The Allied high command, however, turned a deaf ear. Still elated from its swift liberation of France that summer, top generals in December 1944 were convinced Germany had no punch left. Along 70 miles of Ardennes front, they'd placed just four U.S. infantry divisions and one armored—two of the infantry were green, the others chewed up from previous battles.

Area commanders were focused on dealing with an outbreak of trench foot, triggered by the constant wetness and chill. They ordered a cutback in active reconnaissance by foot soldiers, which led to a sharp drop in prisoner grabs and local intelligence. Some VIII Corps intelligence officers employed their spotter planes for hunting wild boar. Most Allied craft were grounded by the bad weather.

## HITLER'S BOLD MOVE

Under the cloak of late autumn's snow and mist, the Germans had secretly marshaled two panzer armies. Their forces bristled with 420 tanks and assault guns, and 1,900 artillery pieces. Still, despite its ten panzer divisions, the German infantry was undermanned. *Volks-grenadier* units staffed with youths and overage men filled the gap.

Hitler slipped from his Wolf's Lair in East Prussia to the Eagle's Nest in Bavaria to direct the operation, code-named *Unternehmen Wacht am Rhein* ("Operation Guard of the Rhine"). He told his staff, "I have made a momentous decision: I shall go over to the offensive."

His scheme foresaw the panzers rolling through the rugged Ardennes and, after seizing bridges over the River Meuse, driving north 60 miles to take Antwerp, the Allies' only close supply port. With the British and American armies cut off, the *Wehrmacht* could proceed east to deal with the Soviet Army nearing Germany's other frontier.

German Chief of OKW Operations General Alfred Jodl recalled the assault took place "in the West because the Russians had so many troops that, even if we had succeeded in destroying 30 divisions, it would have made no difference. On the other hand, if we destroyed 30 divisions in the West," the Western Allies would be staggered.

Given Germany's weakened state, however, the ambitious operation was a huge gamble, and Hitler's commanders knew it. General Josef "Sepp" Dietrich, chief of the 6th SS Panzer Army, was a fanatic Nazi. But even he noted sarcastically, "All Hitler wants me to do is to cross a river, capture Brussels, and then go on and take Antwerp. And all this...when the snow is waist deep."

A huge obstacle was petrol, in such scarce supply that horses hauled it to the front. Panzer crews were told to fill their tanks with captured stocks of American gasoline.

Yet playing to the Germans' advantage, for once, was the Allies' ULTRA intercepts of decrypted radio messages. In preparation for the offensive, the *Wehrmacht* imposed a strict wireless blackout. Further, it conducted a phantom buildup near Düsseldorf, moving in flak guns and artificially increasing wireless traffic there, gulling Allied intelligence. In occupied France, the German command had communicated by radio, which was open to interception. But it had now retreated to Germany, where messages were relayed by secure telephone and telegraph.

# GERMANY LAUNCHES ITS ATTACK

At 0530 December 16, the 1,900 artillery pieces slipped secretly into the Ardennes were unleashed on surprised American troops. In the center, near the *Schnee Eifel,* the 5th Panzer Army cut off two regiments of the rookie 106th Division, forcing their surrender. At least 7,000 Americans were lost in the battle.

From the start, confusion reigned for both sides in the heavy mists. Americans stranded in the woods tried to hook up with their units, but bumped into German ones. The Germans were disoriented by the rugged region's fog-draped welter of roads. Lieutenant Colonel Joachim Peiper's *Kampfgruppe,* or armored battle group, was the spear point of the 6th Panzer Army. Troops in it came across an American truck column, mistook it for one of their own, and rode together unknowing before a firefight finally broke out.

German commandos disguised in American uniforms spread panic behind U.S. lines, causing huge traffic jams at hastily thrown-up checkpoints. Bad weather gridlocked the German columns, worsening their dire shortage of gas. The operation's secrecy, meanwhile, had prevented German officers from drawing up lines of attack and routes of supply, sowing further chaos.

In Operation *Stösser* 1,200 *Fallschirmjägeren* parachuters were dropped at night in a snowstorm, with instructions to seize key crossroads. Blown by gusts over a wide area, the paratroops couldn't join up to take their objective. But the wide dispersal made the Americans think an entire division of elite troops, perhaps 20,000 men, had landed behind their lines.

## TIED UP AT THE BULGE

After the initial shock, U.S. troops stiffened, spoiling the Nazi's timetable. In the north, the 1st and 3rd Battalions of the rookie 99th Infantry Division, with units from the battered 2nd Division, were outnumbered five to one. Yet they were ordered to hold the vital Elsenborn Ridge for weeks against repeated attacks.

The German infantry bogged down trying to take critical roads. After failing to trap the U.S. divisions, Peiper's *Kampfgruppe,* with its hundreds of motorized vehicles, tried forcing its way to the Meuse. It was harried by teams of U.S. engineers, who torched gasoline dumps as they retreated. Then the *Kampfgruppe* was blocked on December 18 by a stout defense at the town of Stavelot. Peiper's 1st SS Panzer Regiment raced for a bridge on the river Amblève at Trois-Ponts, but American troops blew it up. Peiper later tried crossing at another town, but engineers blew up the span as his tankers approached. On December 19, a U.S. counterthrust trapped the *Kampfgruppe*, forcing Peiper to retreat while abandoning his heavy equipment.

During these battles, a group of Reiper's 1st SS Panzer Regiment captured a U.S. artillery observation unit near the town of Malmédy. The *Waffen* (Fighting) SS men then massacred 84 of the captives. Enraged Allied troops began shooting SS prisoners in retaliation.

On December 19, Eisenhower and his generals huddled in a Verdun bunker. The press was reporting the 30-mile German salient as a dangerous bulge in the Allied lines. But Ike, aware his foe was more vulnerable outside his lair, was upbeat: "The present situation is to be regarded as one of opportunity and not of disaster," he pronounced. "There will be only cheerful faces at this table." Patton responded, "Hell, let's have the guts to let the bastards go all the way to Paris. Then, we'll really cut 'em off and chew 'em up." The head of the Third Army added he could have his troops counterattack in 40 hours. No one believed Patton, but he'd already issued orders to attack.

## DEFENSE OF BASTOGNE

In the center of the Bulge, the towns of St. Vith and Bastogne straddled key crossroads. General Troy Houston Middleton, head of the VIII Corps, ordered a fighting retreat to slow the advancing juggernaut.

The Americans improvised, combining disparate units into coherent defenses. The terrain favored the defense, as the forests and ridges channeled the panzers onto narrow roads. Parts of two U.S armored and two infantry divisions held St. Vith until December

21—four days after the Germans had planned to take it. Under General Bruce Clarke, the Americans then fell back to prepared positions, slowed the 5th Panzer Army for two more days, and fell back to a river.

These events bought time for parts of the 9th and 10th Armored Divisions, and the 101st Division of paratroopers trucked in from Rheims to beat the Germans to Bastogne, setting up an epic defense. Still, by December 21, American forces at Bastogne were surrounded and badly outgunned by the 17th Panzer Corps. They had almost no medicine. Artillery teams were almost out of shells: Gunners were instructed to fire only at large groups of tanks.

The German commander had an ultimatum delivered to the 101st's acting chief, General Anthony McAuliffe. It read, "There is only one possibility to save the encircled USA troops from total annihilation; that is the honorable surrender of the town... German Artillery are ready to annihilate USA troops... all the serious civilian losses caused by this would not correspond with the well-known American humanity."

McAuliffe scoffed ("Nuts," according to those present, but he may have used another four-letter word). In his formal written reply, he did employ "Nuts," which stumped the German commander as well as the French-speaking Belgians. The battle continued.

The panzer corps erred, however, by methodically attacking one point after another instead of using its superior numbers to rush the town. Assistant division commander Brigadier General Gerald Higgins, a veteran infantryman, shuttled about his best foot soldiers, the 327th Glider Regiment and the 502nd Parachute Regiment, to meet the assaults of the *Panzergrenadiers*. McAuliffe, the 101st's artillery commander, massed 130 cannons from 11 battalions against the mechanized attacks. The German's charges were repulsed, and they falsely concluded their enemy had plenty of ammunition.

It helped that the United States fielded elite troops, such as those in Easy Company of the 101st's 506th Parachute Regiment, depicted in the book and TV series *Band of Brothers*. With no armor and little morphine for the injured, the brethren dug out trenches in the frozen earth, withstood the terror of shells bursting in the forest canopy, and held their ground.

The Americans also helped themselves by obeying orders too slowly. Early on, the army group's headquarters ordered VIII Corps to evacuate Bastogne, but the paratroops hesitated after realizing they'd withdraw smack into the Panzer Lehr Division sweeping around the town.

Behind the scenes, Eisenhower acted decisively. Along with backing Patton's counterthrust, he had Field Marshal Bernhard Montgomery take command of the U.S. armies in the Bulge's north. Monty scraped together personnel to guard the Meuse bridges. Ike ordered up 250,000 reinforcements, many from England, and let 4,500 African-American troops, previously barred from combat, volunteer for the infantry. In contrast, the German commander in the West, Field Marshal Gerd von Rundstedt, spent much of the battle drinking cognac and perusing novels. Certain the plan was doomed, he turned over the reins to Field Marshal Walther Model.

## CLEAR SKIES TURN THE TIDE OF THE ARDENNES

Clear weather arrived on December 23. Waves of theretofore-grounded P-47 Thunderbolt fighters took off and strafed German columns and depots. Major General Frederic von Mellenthin of the 9th Panzer Division commented, "I witnessed the uninterrupted air attacks on our traffic routes and supply dumps. Not a single German plane was in the air, and innumerable vehicles were shot up and their blackened wrecks littered the roads."

At Bastogne, C-47s air-dropped 1,400 crates of supplies. The medical crisis eased when a team of doctors arrived suddenly by glider. The German units that had bypassed the town were gunned to a halt by the U.S. 2nd Armored Division and roving fighter-bombers.

In the north, Sepp Dietrich's fuel-starved panzers were stemmed well short of the Meuse. Manteuffel, chief of the other panzer army, recommended Hitler call off the offensive. *Der Führer* refused.

After swinging north, marching through snowstorms, Patton's men approached Bastogne. By Christmas his 4th Armored Division was within five miles of a linkup. The next day, the commander of its 37th Tank Battalion, Lieutenant Colonel Creighton Abrams, ignored orders to assault a stoutly defended town and raced through a lightly defended one, reaching Bastogne. After the war Abrams became Army Chief of Staff; the army's main battle tank is named for him.

Hitler desperately played a last card. On New Year's Day 1945, the *Luftwaffe* launched Operation *Bodenplatte,* a sneak attack by hundreds of aircraft on Allied airfields in Holland and Belgium. Four hundred sixty-five Allied planes were damaged or wrecked. But the secrecy of the attack proved a two-edged sword for the Germans. Its air force lost 277 precious craft—171 to flak, and much of that from Nazi gunners. Kept in the dark about the raids, they downed many of their own bombers. The *Luftwaffe* was spent.

Patton's tanks advanced northeastward from Bastogne, while the more cautious Montgomery moved southeast, both pinching the center of the Bulge. On January 7 Hitler conceded to pull out his troops. They left, abandoning most of the irreplaceable panzers, fuel holds empty.

The human losses for the Allied victory and German debacle were similar. The official toll of U.S. casualties was 80,987; the German, 84,834.

☆   ☆   ☆

- *Five days after the Battle of the Bulge, the Red Army launched its great winter offensive against Germany. No longer possessing a strategic reserve, the* Wehrmacht *was on life support. The attack carried the Soviets to 40 miles from Berlin.*

# Timeline

## 1944

**October 6–December 12**
Battle of Huertgen Forest in Germany

**October 12**
First B-29 lands in the Marianas Islands

**October 14**
German General Erwin "Desert Fox" Rommel, suspected to have collaborated with the July 20 conspirators, swallows poison after being told by Hitler's henchmen that unless he commits suicide, the Nazis will detain his wife and son

British liberate Athens, Greece

**October 20**
Soviets and Yugoslavian partisans liberate Belgrade, Yugoslavia

U.S. forces invade Leyte in the Philippines

**October 21**
Aachen becomes the first German city to fall to the Allies

**October 23–26**
Battle of Leyte Gulf; Japanese fleet is crippled

**October 25**
Soviets capture Kirkenes, Norway

**October 28**
The first of the soon-to-be legendary Japanese kamikaze pilots crashes his plane into the deck of the USS *Denver*

**November 3**
The Japanese launch hydrogen balloon bombs; only about 300 of them will reach North America

**November 7**
Roosevelt is elected to a fourth term

**November 10**
Japanese capture air bases at Liuchow and Kweilin in China

**November 23**
Allied troops capture Strasbourg, France

**November 24**
The United States launches its first B-29 raid on Japan from the Mariana island of Saipan

**December 3**
Civil war between pro- and anti-communist factions breaks out in Greece

**December 8**
American forces launch an offensive against Japanese positions on Iwo Jima; they will spend two months softening defenses before a ground assault

**December 16**
Germans launch Ardennes offensive; Battle of the Bulge begins

**December 26**
Patton's troops relieve Bastogne, Belgium

Soviets encircle Budapest, Hungary

**December 31**
The Battle of Leyte ends, clearing the city of Japanese forces

## 1945

**January 15**
Commercial shipping resumes in the English Channel for the first time in nearly five years

# THE ROCKET SCIENTIST

*Through an unlikely turn of events, the scientist in charge of developing the Nazi's V-2 rocket would help the Americans reach the moon.*

Born in 1912, Wernher Magnus Maximilian Freiherr von Braun had a pedigree of greatness. His father Baron Magnus von Braun was the minister of agriculture under the Weimar Republic, and his mother was descended from Swedish and German aristocrats. At age 12, inspired by Fritz von Opel's land speed records, he took a "rocket-propelled" trip after lighting six large skyrockets fitted onto a wagon. "The wagon careened crazily about," Braun recalled, "trailing a tail of fire like a comet." The propellants made a thunderous noise; alarmed police briefly put Braun under custody.

## FROM SKYROCKETS TO THE VENGEANCE WEAPON

Inspired by scientist Hermann Oberth's landmark 1923 work *The Rocket Into Interplanetary Space,* in 1930 Braun attended Berlin's Charlottenburg Institute, where he worked with Oberth on liquid-fueled rockets. As Nazi Germany rearmed in the 1930s and banned research on civilian rockets, Braun began work conducting missile tests for the *Wehrmacht*'s Ordnance Corps. He formed a long-term friendship with an artillery captain, Walter Dornberger, who arranged funding for Braun's doctorate. Braun and Dornberger went on to work at Peenemünde, as technical and military directors. Along the way Braun joined the Nazi Party. He later stated, "My refusal [to join] ...would have meant abandon[ing] the work of my life."

Braun's team designed the A-4 ballistic missile, renamed by Josef Goebbels as the *Vergeltungswaffe 2*, the "Vengeance Weapon 2," or V-2. (The shorter-range V-1 "buzz bomb" was designed by engineer Robert Lusser under *Luftwaffe* supervision.) The designer of the V-2 engine was Walter Thiel, who was killed during a 1943 British air raid on Peenemünde.

The 46-foot-long, ethanol-and-water-fueled missile could hurl its 2,800-pound warhead some 200 miles. Its highest recorded altitude was 117 miles, making it the first craft to reach outer space. But its guidance system was inaccurate: Chances were about even that it would come within 10 miles of a target. Ironically, Braun regarded the V-2 primarily as a device for space travel, and was briefly imprisoned by the Gestapo in 1944 for his presumed disinterest in weaponry.

## DEATH FROM THE SKIES

Hurtling down from an altitude of 60 miles at supersonic speeds no fighter could catch, the V-2 struck without warning. "The V-2 was a truly remarkable machine for its time," recalled Braun. From September 1944 to March 1945, 3,172 V-2s were successfully launched: 1,610 hit the vital port of Antwerp; 1,358 hit London. In one incident, 567 people died after a V-2 landed in a Belgian movie house. The attacks on the British capital killed 2,754 and wounded 6,523. The Nazis relied on the weapons even when impractical: 11 V-2s were fired toward the Remagen bridge while Patton's troops poured over the Rhine into Germany.

The British incessantly bombed fixed sites for launching the missiles, so the V-2s were fired instead from mobile launchers, the equipment and fuel borne by a caravan of 30 trucks. It took two hours to set up the rocket, launch the V-2, and repack the equipment and crew.

The German missile program also successfully tested a "rocket U-boat," which fired V-2s from a submarine-towed platform. Had the method been developed sooner, Germany may have used the subs to launch rockets from off the U.S. coastline. German scientists worked on chemical weapons agents for the V-2. Braun's technicians also adapted the V-2 into the *Wasserfall,* perhaps the first antiaircraft missile.

## CREATED IN DEPLORABLE CONDITIONS

Much of this ordnance was built with slave labor. The V-2's chief assembly plants, called *Mittelwerk,* were in the Harz Mountains near the town of Nordhausen. There, Russian, Polish, and French inmates from the nearby Dora concentration camp dug out an underground factory from an old mine. The V-2's top engineer, Arthur Rudolph, helped arrange for the transfer of the inmates, after SS General Hans Kammler, an engineer who had built Auschwitz, came up with the idea of using slave labor for rockets. (Decades later Rudolph fled the United States after the Justice Department accused him of war crimes.)

Braun visited the *Mittelwerk* plant often enough to know, he later admitted, that many laborers died from brutal treatment and wretched conditions. Perhaps 15,000 perished. One eyewitness noted, "You could see piles of prisoners every day who had not survived the workload and had been tortured to death by the vindictive guards...But Professor Wernher von Braun just walked past them, so close that he almost touched the bodies." At the time Braun remarked, "It is hellish. My spontaneous reaction was to talk to one of the SS guards, only to be told with unmistakable harshness that I should mind my own business, or find myself in the same striped fatigues!...I realized that any attempt of reasoning on humane grounds would be utterly futile."

## A NEW LIFE FOR THE NAZI SCIENTIST

As the war ground to a close, Braun again faced the SS. In spring

1945, Soviet troops closed to 100 miles of Peenemünde. Most of the V-2 staff decided to surrender to the Western Allies, but in the meantime the SS was ordered to liquidate the rocket engineers and burn their records. With forged documents, Braun and 500 of his staff put together dozens of train cars, as well as about 1,000 automobiles and trucks, and headed toward advancing American troops. At the end of the journey, Braun's brother Magnus button-holed a GI: "My name is Magnus von Braun. My brother invented the V-2. We want to surrender." The Americans took Braun and his staff into custody, recovered their hidden records, and seized hundreds of freightloads of V-2 components.

Under Operation Paperclip, Braun, his team, their families, caches of scientific records, and enough V-2 components for 100 missiles, were brought to America. Since their Nazi associations would have barred many from visas, the scheme was hush-hush. Stationed at Fort Bliss, Texas, they called themselves "Prisoners of Peace." At the White Sands Proving Grounds in New Mexico, they continued their missile work; progress was rapid. By October 24, 1945, one of their reconstituted V-2s snapped photos from space.

Thereafter, Braun was transformed into an honored, naturalized American citizen, and fulfilled his boyhood dreams. He married his German sweetheart and had three children. In 1950 his group moved to Huntsville, Alabama, and designed the army's Jupiter ballistic missile, which later launched the first U.S. satellite. He made television programs with Walt Disney that argued for manned space flight. In 1960, in the wake of Sputnik, he was made head of the NASA team that built the Saturn V rocket, which ferried Americans to the moon. He retired in 1972 when NASA opted for the earthbound space shuttle instead of a piloted mission to Mars.

☆    ☆    ☆

- *The V-2 program roughly equaled the Manhattan Project in expense, costing about $2 billion in 1944 (equivalent to $22.2 billion in 2005), about as much as it would cost to manufacture 48,000 panzers.*

# Timeline

## 1945

**January 16**
Hitler moves his residence and base of operations to the underground bunker at Berlin's Reich Chancellery

**January 17**
Soviet troops take Warsaw, Poland

**January 19**
The Soviets occupy the Polish cities of Tarnow, Lódź, and Kraków

**January 26**
The Soviet Army liberates Auschwitz

**January 28**
German Ardennes salient is eliminated; Battle of the Bulge ends

For the first time in nearly three years, supplies reach China over the Burma Road, which is newly reopened and renamed in honor of General Stilwell

**February 3**
U.S. forces reach the Philippine capital, Manila

**February 4–9**
The Big Three meet for the Yalta Conference

**February 13–14**
The Allies unleash a devastating attack on Dresden in a bombing raid that triggers intense firestorms

**February 19**
U.S. Marines storm the Japanese-held island of Iwo Jima

**February 21**
The Americans recapture the Philippine province of Bataan

**February 23**
The U.S. Marines capture Iwo Jima's

Mount Suribachi

**February 25**
First incendiary bombing raid on Tokyo

**March 2**
The Allies secure Corregidor

**March 3**
U.S. forces take Manila

**March 5**
Allied troops march on Cologne, Germany

**March 7**
U.S. 1st Army seizes the Remagen bridge over the Rhine

U.S. and Chinese troops take Lashio, Burma

**March 9**
The deadliest air raid of the Pacific war claims the lives of some 83,000 Japanese civilians when the Allies attack Tokyo with incendiary bombs

**March 20**
British troops capture Mandalay, Burma

**March 27**
The last V-2 rocket strikes Britain

**March 29**
American troops occupy the German heartland city of Frankfurt Mannheim

**March 30**
Soviets take Danzig, Poland

**April 1**
U.S. troops invade Okinawa

More than 300,000 German soldiers are entrapped as the U.S. Army closes ranks around the Ruhr region

# THE MANHATTAN PROJECT'S ODD COUPLE

*In the world of creative tension, perhaps no more unlikely pair ever collaborated on a project to change world history.*

Brigadier General Leslie R. Groves was the Manhattan Project's military leader. Tall, impatient, and bombastic, the general tapped J. Robert Oppenheimer, a brilliant physics theoretician, to head the scientific team building the bomb. Oppenheimer, a wiry, intellectual Communist supporter, was a security risk and an odd fit for a military project, but he threw himself into his work and assembled a brilliant group of scientists—including Enrico Fermi, Edward Teller, Hans Bethe, and Richard Feynman—at the Los Alamos laboratory not far from his ranch in New Mexico.

Groves ran roughshod over the intellectually gifted group. Needing the atomic bomb to be completed as quickly as possible, he (and the FBI) kept a close eye on Oppenheimer. As an example of Groves's whip-cracking approach, he promised his scientists on Christmas Eve 1944, "If this weapon fizzles, each of you can look forward to a lifetime of testifying before congressional investigating committees."

Personality differences led to an intense personal feud between Groves and Oppenheimer, but their sense of duty kept their personal feelings from affecting the breakneck pace of the project.

As Paul Tibbets, pilot of the *Enola Gay,* recalled his impressions of the two men years later:

[Oppenheimer's] a young, brilliant person. And he's a chain smoker and he drinks cocktails. And he hates fat men. And General Leslie Groves, he's a fat man, and he hates people who smoke and drink. The two of them are the first, original odd couple.

However, this "original odd couple" managed to get past their personal differences long enough to change history.

# THE TRAGIC LOSS OF THE USS *INDIANAPOLIS*

*Two weeks after unloading a top-secret cargo of uranium and components for the atomic bomb, the crew of the USS* Indianapolis *went through a hellish ordeal.*

From the time Charles Butler McVay III took command of the USS *Indianapolis* in November 1944, the cruiser and her crew had served honorably in the Pacific. The *Indianapolis* had participated in the invasion of Iwo Jima, and during the bombardment of Okinawa, gun crews aboard the heavy cruiser downed at least seven enemy planes.

On July 16, 1945, the ship partook in a mission that would change the world—she sailed from California to the Pacific island of Tinian carrying the material for the first atomic bomb. After delivering the top-secret cargo, the *Indianapolis* sailed to Guam. From there the cruiser was ordered to join the battleship USS *Idaho* in the Philippines in preparation for the planned invasion of Japan.

## NIGHTMARE AT SEA

Unbeknownst to McVay, USS *Underhill* had been sunk by a Japanese submarine in the area he was set to sail through on his way to the Philippines. Naval Intelligence knew an enemy submarine was in the area, but this information was not passed on to McVay.

Since the *Indianapolis* was not equipped with antisubmarine equipment, McVay requested a destroyer escort between Guam and the Philippines. Despite the fact the Naval routing officer in Guam knew of the potential submarine threat lurking in McVay's path, that officer denied McVay a destroyer escort.

The *Indianapolis* set sail for Leyte on July 26, 1945. McVay was ordered to "zigzag at his discretion." Zigzagging was a naval maneuver used to decrease the chances that an enemy would land a successful torpedo attack. Under heavy cloud cover and limited visibility, at about 11:00 P.M. on July 29, McVay gave orders to cease zigzagging. The Captain then retired to his cabin.

Shortly after midnight, Hashimoto Mochitsura, Commander of the Japanese submarine I-58, spotted the lone American cruiser. Hashimoto maneuvered his submarine into position unchallenged and launched a spread of six torpedoes. One blew the bow off the cruiser, while the second struck starboard, igniting a fuel tank and magazine.

The night sky lit up with explosions that ripped the *Indianapolis* in two. The explosions knocked out the ship's electrical and communication systems, and the call to abandon ship was passed through the ranks by word of mouth. The *Indianapolis* sank within 15 minutes of the attack.

## FIGHT FOR SURVIVAL

Of the 1,196 sailors aboard, approximately 300 were killed in the attack. The remaining 900 abandoned the *Indianapolis* as she slipped beneath the waves. The men clung to pieces of wreckage, or tread water in their kapok life jackets awaiting rescue. They would spend five days clinging to life at sea before help arrived.

Due to a series of miscommunications at Leyte, no one reported that the *Indianapolis* was overdue. As life went on as normal at the Philippine naval base, the crew of the *Indianapolis* began a hellish fight for survival.

Hundreds of wounded men endured dehydration, exposure to the tropical sun and saltwater, and mental exhaustion. Most terrifying of all, sharks attacked the sailors at sunrise the following morning. Single men and whole groups of wounded sailors were helplessly dragged under the waves and killed.

Shortly before noon on the fourth day, the remaining survivors were accidentally spotted by pilot Lieutenant (junior grade) Wilbur Gwinn. Gwinn was flying his PV-1 Ventura bomber on a routine antisubmarine patrol when he spotted an oil slick and men in the water. After radioing his base, a PBY rescue plane, piloted by Lieutenant R. Adrian Marks, was dispatched to the area.

Seeing the soldiers struggle against the sharks, Marks immediately landed his plane in the water and began taking on survivors. Marks and his crew rescued 56 men and when his fuselage was full, more men were lashed to the wings of his aircraft. The destroyer USS *Cecil Doyle* diverted to the scene of the disaster and arrived in the area several hours after the PBY. Marks and his men then transferred survivors and the bodies of the dead to the destroyer. Of the 900 men that survived the submarine attack, only 317 were rescued.

## WHO WAS TO BLAME?

Captain McVay faced a hastily convened court of inquiry. Secretary of the Navy James Forrestal and Chief of Naval Operations Admiral Ernest King directed that court-martial proceedings be held against McVay. The captain was charged with "failing to issue orders to abandon ship" and "hazarding his vessel by failing to zigzag in good weather."

Captain McVay was denied his first choice of defense counsel. He was provided with a lawyer, Captain John P. Cody, who had no trial experience and had only four days to prepare his case. While the first charge was dismissed, McVay was found guilty on the second charge of failing to zigzag, despite testimonies from both a decorated U.S. submarine commander and the commander of the Japanese sub that sank the *Indianapolis,* who stated that zigzagging would not have saved the cruiser from attack.

The conviction might have ended McVay's navy career, but in 1946, Admiral Nimitz convinced the secretary of the navy to remit McVay's sentence and restore him to duty. McVay retired in 1949 with the rank of Rear Admiral.

Believing an injustice had been committed, former crew lobbied Congress to pass a joint resolution that declared, "Captain McVay's record should now reflect that he is exonerated for the loss of the *Indianapolis* and the lives of the men who died." President Clinton signed the legislation on October 30, 2000, and while the act did not clear the conviction from McVay's record, many former crewmen believed they had at least partially righted a wrong that had occurred some 50 years before.

# Fast Facts

- During the German occupation of France, German troops used the Maginot Line as handy storage for spare parts.

- Many Maginot Line casements and other structures were auctioned to the public in the 1970s.

- In the 1930s, British negotiators had given up the right to use Irish ports in wartime. Churchill bemoaned this decision—launching escort ships from Cork or Galway would have added hundreds of miles to their range. He even hinted that Britain would consider invading the Republic from Northern Ireland—the Six Counties whose British control many Irish still resented. The day after Pearl Harbor, Churchill sent Taoiseach (Prime Minister) Eamon de Valera a simple message: "Now is your chance. Now or never! A nation once again. I will meet you wherever you wish." However, de Valera never replied to the message.

- In 1942, with Japan's war gains at their height, the Japanese Literature Patriotic Association organized the first Greater East Asian Writers Conference.

- Blimps might not sound warlike, but the U.S. Navy knew otherwise. The K-class blimps, built by Goodyear, fought in the Battle of the Atlantic by flying above convoys to help escorts detect U-boats. No convoy protected by a blimp ever lost a ship to a U-boat.

- In 1945 the U.S. federal budget was $100 billion; in 1939 it had been $9 billion.

- On April 16, 1941, German youth Joseph Ratzinger turned 14 and, by law, was forced to join the Hitler Youth. Ratzinger would become Pope Benedict XVI in 2005.

- Many U.S. athletes were drafted into service during the war, leading some draft rejects to fill positions on professional sports teams. The long-hapless St. Louis Browns, which included a man missing one arm, won their first and only pennant in 1944.

# AUDIE MURPHY

*A striking thing about Audie Murphy, the most decorated American soldier of the war, was that his whole life was a series of battles. From a dirt-poor childhood to infantryman heroism in Europe to tumultuous personal struggles after the conflict, Murphy seemed ever in a desperate fight.*

Born in Hunt County, Texas, in 1924, Audie Murphy was the seventh of Emmett and Josie Murphy's 12 children. Tragedy struck the family early on. When Murphy was just 12, his father left. Four years later, his mother died. "Getting food for our stomachs and clothes for our backs," Murphy recalled, "was an ever-present problem." Three of his siblings went to an orphanage. Audie Murphy worked picking cotton, and to feed his family, he became an expert at shooting rabbits with a .22-caliber rifle. When the family gathered, he listened raptly to his uncles telling tales of valor during the Great War.

## FROM COOK TO COMBAT HERO

When war broke out, Murphy jumped at a chance to join the Marine Corps. But it rejected him. And no wonder—at 18, he was all of 5 feet 5 inches and 112 pounds. He enlisted in the regular army, which, after he swooned during a close-order drill, tried to make him a cook. "To reach for the stars," wrote Murphy, "and end up stirring a pot of C rations. I swore I would take the guardhouse first."

His ceaseless demands to see combat finally paid off in 1943. Murphy was sent to North Africa, then to the ferocious battle of Anzio in Italy, as part of Company B, 1st Battalion, 15th Infantry Regiment, 3rd Infantry Division.

His upbringing and outlook made him a natural soldier and combat leader. In battle, he preached that a "calm fury" was the best tactic. Under fire, he noted, "Things seem to slow down for me." He shrugged off malaria and a wound in the hip from a sniper's round. By the time his unit invaded southern France in August 1944, he'd earned his first medals and been field-promoted to second lieutenant, a rank he accepted only when assured he could stay with his unit.

In one battle, after taking out several machine-gun nests, he lost his best buddy when Germans feigning surrender shot his comrade down. In a fury, he killed the attackers, then turned their machine gun against other strong points. He was awarded the Distinguished Service Cross, the military's second-highest honor.

Murphy's greatest feat occurred on January 26, 1945, during bitterly cold fighting along the German border. His company of 18 was attacked by 6 Tiger tanks and more than 200 infantry. As his men fell back, Murphy jumped onto an abandoned tank destroyer whose gasoline was expected to blow any second. He grabbed its .50-caliber machine gun and sprayed bullets toward the Germans while radioing in artillery on himself.

"50 [yards] over!" he shouted on the field phone.

"50 over?" came the reply. "That's your own position."

"[Keep it coming!]," shouted Murphy.

After single-handedly breaking the attack and killing scores of Germans, he led the counterattack. His actions that day earned him the Medal of Honor. For other feats he was awarded two Silver Stars, two Bronze Stars, three Purple Hearts, the Legion of Merit, and two Croix de Guerre. Of his 37 medals, he sardonically noted soldiers ended up with a "Wooden Cross."

## HAUNTED BY WAR

When Germany surrendered, Murphy's men celebrated wildly, but he was desolate. Murphy wrote, "Like a horror film running back-

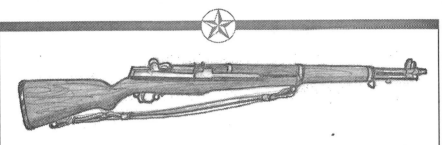

wards, images of the war flicker through my brain. The tank in the snow with smoldering bodies...." Thereafter his psyche was stuck in the war. He exhibited the classic symptoms of post-traumatic stress syndrome, then called "shell shock." He wrote, "We have been so intent on death that we have forgotten life."

At home, after welcomes befitting an Achilles, he was wracked with nightmares. Murphy went to bed armed, sometimes waking up to fire his revolver at the wall. He'd twitch violently and freeze up. Insomnia led to a sleeping pill addiction. His first wife, actress Wanda Hendrix, divorced him. She said he once drew a gun on her. He married again, and with his second wife he had two sons, Terry and James.

Murphy fought his "demons" and helped others with theirs. Ahead of his time, he became an advocate of aid to veterans returning home with mental health woes. He also bought a house for his sister and found care for his three orphaned siblings.

## ON TO THE SILVER SCREEN

After the war, Murphy worked as a rancher and horse breeder. He also wrote country and western songs, some of which were recorded by Roy Clark and Dean Martin. But Murphy channeled most of his pent-up energy into acting. He moved to Hollywood at the suggestion of James Cagney. Training as an actor, he spent penniless years there, bedding on the floor of a friend's gym.

His fortunes changed in 1949 with the publication of his self-penned (with friend Dave McClure) best seller *To Hell and Back*, a terse, savagely honest account of his combat experience. Six years later, the book became a movie of the same name, starring none other than

Audie Murphy as himself. The Universal movie grossed $10 million, a record that wasn't broken until *Jaws*.

Best at playing soldiers or outlaws, Murphy also impressed critics in John Huston's *The Red Badge of Courage*. He made a total of 44 films, most of which were Westerns. For his work on the big screen, Murphy was awarded a star on the Hollywood Walk of Fame.

On Memorial Day weekend in 1971, he died at 46 in a plane crash. The craft was manned by an unqualified pilot and had run into dense fog. Murphy was buried at Arlington National Cemetery. Today it's the second most-visited site at Arlington after JFK's grave.

★　　★　　★

- *Late in life, Audie Murphy was once accused of manhandling and firing a gun at a dog trainer who'd reportedly mistreated a friend. When a reporter asked, "Audie, did you shoot at that guy?" the ultimate war hero replied, "If I had, do you think I would have missed?"*

★　　★　　★

- *After the war, Audie's longing for comradeship, and his comfort with rules and regulations, were manifested in his membership in fraternal organizations: He was a 32nd degree Mason, and as a Shriner he ascended to Knight Commander and Master of the Royal Secret.*

★　　★　　★

- *At a Hollywood party in the 1950s, hulking actor Lawrence Tierney grew loud, rowdy, and verbally abusive. He was notoriously quick with his fists, and now he was spoiling for a fight. Audie Murphy was at the party, too. He approached Tierney and quietly suggested that Tierney go home. The bigger man looked down at the slightly built Murphy, turned on his heel, and left. Tierney said later that Audie's eyes revealed a complete lack of fear. Tierney left, he confessed, to save himself a beating.*

# Timeline

## 1945

**April 6**
Japanese begin mass kamikaze attacks on Okinawa

**April 6–7**
Battle of East China Sea; Allied planes sink the battleship *Yamato*

**April 11**
The Allies liberate the Buchenwald concentration camp

**April 12**
Roosevelt dies after suffering a sudden stroke; Harry S. Truman becomes president

**April 18**
Germans in the Ruhr pocket surrender, the Allies take 325,000 prisoners

**April 23**
Soviet forces storm Berlin and engage in street-to-street fighting

**April 24**
Himmler tries to negotiate a separate peace with the British and Americans, but they reject his offer

**April 28**
Italian partisans kill Mussolini and his mistress Clara Petacci

**April 29**
Hitler and Eva Braun exchange wedding vows in the underground Berlin bunker

**April 30**
Hitler and Braun commit suicide by biting cyanide capsules, as do Joseph and Magda Goebbels after murdering their six children

Allies capture Munich and liberate the Dachau concentration camp

**May 1**
Australians land at Tarakan, off Borneo

**May 2**
German forces in Italy surrender

**May 3**
British forces capture Rangoon in Burma

**May 5**
Germans surrender in north Germany, Holland, and Denmark

**May 7**
Germans sign unconditional surrender to the Allies at Reims, France

**May 8**
V-E Day: War in Europe officially ends

**May 11**
Australians take Wewak, New Guinea

**May 23**
Heinrich Himmler commits suicide while in British custody

**May 27**
U.S. forces capture Naha, capital of Okinawa

**June 10**
Australian troops land in Brunei Bay, Borneo

**June 19**
British forces invade Thailand

**June 22**
U.S. forces secure Okinawa, ending the bloodiest battle of the Pacific war

**July 1**
Australian troops land at Balikpapan, Borneo

# *FÜHRERBUNKER*: THE LAST DAYS OF THE THIRD REICH

*With the Thousand-Year Reich fleeing, dying, and collapsing on top of him, Hitler had no intention of facing Soviet justice. But did he escape justice after all?*

## BERLIN 1945: THE SITUATION

In January 1945, Adolf Hitler moved into a 30-room underground complex in the Berlin *Reichskanzlei* (Reich Chancellery) garden. This *Führerbunker* was designed and built with the spendthrift abandon of anything intended for the *Führer*. It was about 25 feet below ground level, with 12-foot concrete walls sheltering Hitler, Eva Braun, the eight members of the Goebbels family, and various guards, specialists, secretaries, and functionaries. On March 13, 1945, Hitler left the *Reichskanzlei* alive for the last time to visit the nearby Oder front. His pasty, frail countenance was a shell of his once-animated manner. By then, few sights could shock *Wehrmacht* and SS officers—this was one.

By April 1, 1945, what remained of Nazi Germany stretched from the Baltic Sea to Czechoslovakia, between the Elbe and Oder rivers. Its *Kriegsmarine* mostly rested on the ocean floor. Its *Luftwaffe* had few planes and little fuel. Its social systems were disintegrating. Once Nazi Germany had measured strength in divisions and armies; now a "division" might mean a remnant *Waffen-SS* company, a teenage battalion of the ill-armed *Volkssturm*, a platoon of clerks issued pistols, or the survivors of a Ukrainian police detachment. Germans in East Prussia were learning firsthand that Red Army occupation meant robbery and rape, with death the penalty for resistance.

Hitler no longer broadcasted nor made public appearances. He limped, dragging his left leg. His left hand trembled so badly he had to clasp it in his right. Years of combined stress and paranoia, quack injections varying from vitamins to methamphetamine, and

## Hitler's Death, a Hoax?

Rumors of Hitler's survival persisted for years. The charred corpse was a double; he had offspring; he was living in South America, keeping that old Nazi spirit alive. Some of the wilder tales were fueled by Soviet propaganda.

They were false. In 1993 the Russian government opened the old Soviet files. We now know beyond any reasonable doubt what happened.

The NKVD (Russian intelligence) investigation began the moment Soviet troops overran the *Führerbunker*. They exhumed the Hitler and Goebbels bodies, bringing in close acquaintances for positive I.D.; for example, Eva and Adolf's former dentist and his assistant both recognized their own professional handiwork. The original announcement had been correct: Adolf Hitler had died April 30, 1945. After sending Hitler's jaw back to Moscow for safekeeping, the NKVD secretly reburied the other remains at a military base near Magdeburg, German Democratic Republic (East Germany).

In 1970, the Soviet military prepared to transfer the Magdeburg base to East German control. The KGB (successor to the NKVD) dared not leave the Nazi remains. On April 4, 1970, the KGB exhumed the fragmentary remains of Adolf and Eva Hitler and the Goebbels family. Hitler's skull was identified, and the bullet-holed portion was sent to Moscow. The next day, the KGB incinerated the rest of the remains, crushed them to dust and dumped it in a nearby river.

Therefore, of Eva Braun and the Goebbels family nothing at all remains. Of Hitler, today only his jaw and a skull fragment exist in Russian custody.

the 1944 assassin's bomb had eroded Adolf Hitler. Nearing 56, he looked, walked, and behaved as if suffering from Parkinson's disease. Sometimes he limped about uncomprehending; other times he ordered nonexistent formations into battle, or ranted about treason.

## HITLER TURNS 56

On April 20, Adolf Hitler celebrated his 56th birthday. Most remaining senior Nazis attended, as did Eva Braun and her brother-in-law Hermann Fegelein of the SS Cavalry. The Anglo-Americans rattled the walls with a birthday spanking: their next-to-last massive bombing raid on Berlin. Zhukov's 3rd Shock Army gave Hitler "a pinch to grow an inch" with the first Soviet artillery shelling of Berlin's suburbs. In his last film appearance, Hitler went out to the *Reichskanzlei* garden to praise some Hitler Youth defenders.

The exodus began the next day. Hitler began to speak of suicide, weeping openly and screaming about betrayals. *Luftwaffe* commander Hermann Göring, oscillating between lucidity and drug-soaked apathy, entrained with his loot for *Berchtesgaden*. He then messaged the *Führer* asking to take over the Reich; Hitler ordered the presumptuous *Reichsmarschall* stripped of all titles and arrested. Armaments Minister Albert Speer, no fool, left while he could. Heinrich Himmler, chief of the SS, went to north Germany and opened secret talks with the Allies. When this was reported by radio on April 28, Hitler sacked the *Reichsführer*-SS as he had Göring. Eva Braun maintained a sort of sad serenity through it all.

Once Soviet troops surrounded Berlin, entry and exit became problematic. General Ritter von Greim, heir apparent to *Luftwaffe* command, flew in with Hanna Reitsch. They offered to remain with Hitler, but he ordered them to fly out and make sure Himmler did not become *Führer*. They flew north in a light plane dodging Soviet flak bursts. Hermann Fegelein was captured trying to sneak out of Berlin in civilian clothing; he was shot for desertion. Soon Soviet artillery began landing around the *Reichskanzlei* as their troops tightened the ring toward the city center.

## WEDDING BELLS (WELL, EXPLOSIONS ...)

On April 29, Adolf Hitler rewarded Eva Braun with the title no other woman ever held relative to him: *Frau* Hitler. Hitler wore his Nazi uniform; Eva wore black silk taffeta. Goebbels summoned civil servant Walter Wagner to perform the nuptials, in Nazi uniform with *Volkssturm* armband. The actual ceremony was short, with Goebbels and *Reichsleiter* Martin Bormann signing as witnesses. For the first (and probably only) time, Eva signed her new name to the marriage document: "Eva B [for Braun] Hitler, geb. [née] Braun." Hitler promptly went into a side room to dictate his will to Traudl Junge, one of the two remaining secretaries.

## HITLERDÄMMERUNG

The next day, April 30, 1945, Adolf Hitler obtained cyanide capsules from a *Reichskanzlei* doctor. He ordered one tested on his beloved German Shepherd Blondi in the garden; her floppy-pawed puppies, favorite playmates of the Goebbels children, soon joined their dam in death. Hitler ordered Otto Günsche, his personal SS adjutant, to burn his and Eva's bodies after death. The *Führer* had a last lunch with his dietitian and secretaries, then traded farewells with Goebbels, Bormann, and the remaining generals.

Eva took cyanide around 3:00 P.M.; Hitler fired a Walther PPK semiautomatic pistol into his brain. Günsche got help to carry bodies up to a bomb crater, soused them with fuel, and set them afire. Oily smoke rose from the funeral pyre of Adolf and Eva Hitler. The men buried the charred corpses beneath the abundant rubble.

Thereafter, the bunker's remnant population escaped (or tried), committed suicide, or surrendered to Soviet forces. On May 1, 1945, Goebbels insisted that his family must die; the children, he said, would be marked as the "children of Goebbels." A doctor helped Magda inject her five daughters and one son with morphine, then poisoned them to add six more innocent children to the war's terrible toll. Next, husband and wife chewed cyanide capsules, with an SS officer firing two pistol shots to ensure the result. SS men cremated the Goebbels family with gasoline near the Hitler burial crater. Bormann died attempting to escape Berlin. Gestapo chief Heinrich Müller vanished; no one knows whether he survived—or where. Traudl Junge survived, as did Otto Günsche. *Grossadmiral* Karl Dönitz became *Führer*, in accordance with Hitler's wishes, and surrendered the Third Reich on May 8, 1945.

☆ ☆ ☆

- *By 1945 Hitler could not have read these words. His eyes had grown so bad that all his reports had to be prepared on special* Führer *typewriters, which used a typeface triple the normal size.*

- *The NKVD even dug up Blondi and one puppy, and compiled "Documents Concerning the Dogs in the* Führer's *Bunker"— complete to postmortem exams on the unfortunate canines, which were conducted after the animals were burned in fuel.*

☆　☆　☆

- *The law required Wagner to ask if both Adolf and Eva were Aryan, and if either had a family history of disease.*

☆　☆　☆

- *Somehow, the* Führerbunker *was built without suitable military communications facilities. As the Red Army tightened the clamps on Berlin, German intelligence officers picked up the Berlin phone book and phoned random people in various suburbs, asking if they had seen any Russians. Sometimes the answer came in profane Russian phrases, which fairly well answered the question of the area's occupation.*

☆　☆　☆

- *The NKVD and its intelligence/counterintelligence functions changed names, shifted responsibilities and whatnot during and immediately after the war. MVD, MGB, Smersh (Smyert Shpionen, "Death to Spies"), and the KGB are all part of the sea of names. To avoid confusion, the two best-known names— "NKVD" and "KGB"—are used here, though either may be technically inaccurate depending on the timing of a given event. Whatever the name, Russian intelligence was feared across Europe.*

☆　☆　☆

- *Contrary to most accounts, Joseph Goebbels did not have a "club foot." He had suffered from a bone marrow affliction as a child; the surgery shortened and weakened his left leg. He wore orthopedic correctives most of his life, and witnesses brought by the NKVD to identify the Goebbels's corpses immediately spotted the brace and special shoe.*

# ENDURING MYSTERY: HOW DID HERMANN GÖRING CHEAT THE HANGMAN?

*On October 15, 1946, former Reichsmarschall Göring was to hang for war crimes. He did not hang; he poisoned himself. What went wrong?*

Early Hitler supporter Hermann Göring had commanded the *Luftwaffe* throughout World War II. Following the war, he was sentenced to hang for his involvement. Expecting he might attempt suicide before the sentence could be carried out, a U.S. military policeman (MP) peered into his cell every 30 seconds.

Two hours before hanging time, Göring's MP watcher found him in convulsions. The MP hurried to get the key, but he couldn't outrun a bitten cyanide capsule. Göring left a note explaining how he'd done it (supposedly without assistance). The official inquest corroborated the note and blamed no one. Case closed?

Not quite. Some believe he had help.

## WAS THE SS INVOLVED?

In 1951, former SS officer Erich von dem Bach-Zelewski came forward with a confession: He claimed he had slipped Göring the toxin hidden in a bar of soap, under cover of a handshake. However, Zelewski had given a damning Nuremberg testimony against Göring—why help him? While Zelewski escaped prosecution at Nuremberg in exchange for the testimony, in 1951 he was facing prosecution for prewar crimes, and may have confessed hoping for leniency. Historians doubt Zelewski, who died in prison in 1972.

## WHAT ABOUT GÖRING'S GUARDS?

A 1984 book hung the deed on Jack "Tex" Wheelis, a U.S. Army officer who had befriended Göring while serving on his guard detail. Wheelis's son, a judge, believed that his father passed the *Reichsmarschall* the toxin; so did some who served with Wheelis. Göring, who had counted among his titles Reich Master of the Hunt, did strike up a friendship with Wheelis, a Texas country boy and avid hunter. However, Wheelis never admitted the act, and there's no direct evidence implicating him.

In 2005, another former U.S. soldier took responsibility. Herbert Lee Stivers, a 19-year-old guard at Nuremberg in 1946, said a young German woman flirted with him and convinced him to smuggle items to Göring—including a pill-loaded pen. Stivers claimed that he had confessed to clear his conscience. Many believe him. Like other theories, his is plausible—and like those, unproven.

### WAS SOMEONE ELSE INVOLVED?

Could a German prison employee have smuggled the poison? Or did some other unknown American take the truth to the grave? Could Göring truly have sneaked it in himself? We don't know. We do know two things:

1. Only one theory is true.

2. Hermann Göring swore, with confidence, never to hang—and kept this final oath.

☆   ☆   ☆

• *The suicide created a media feeding frenzy. Some reporters had already filed their stories, stating how all the condemned were hanged—but of course, Göring did not hang.*

☆   ☆   ☆

• *Except for the dying part, prison did Göring a lot of good. He entered the jail a paracodeine addict, so obese he couldn't remove his own boots, and suffering from heart trouble. His jailers weaned him off the drugs and put him on a diet. He died a much healthier man, though one doubts it was much consolation.*

# Timeline

## 1945

**July 4**
Allied occupation of Berlin officially begins

**July 5**
General MacArthur announces that forces under his command have succeeded in liberating the Philippines from Japan

**July 16**
First atomic bomb explosion is successful at Alamagordo, New Mexico

**July 17–August 2**
The Potsdam Conference results in an agreement on postwar division of Germany and the necessity of Japan's unconditional surrender

**July 25**
Allied leaders issue a statement from Potsdam that Japanese will face "utter destruction" if they do not surrender unconditionally; Tokyo will reject the ultimatum within the week

**July 26**
Churchill steps down after losing general elections; Clement Atlee will become prime minister the following day

**August 6**
The United States drops an atomic bomb on Hiroshima, Japan, killing as many as 80,000 civilians

**August 8**
The Soviet Union declares war on Japan

**August 9**
Allied bombers take airfields on Honshu

More than 30,000 die as the United States drops a second atomic bomb on Nagasaki, Japan

Soviet troops invade Manchuria

**August 15**
The Allies celebrate V-J Day as Emperor Hirohito broadcasts a message to the Japanese people that he has agreed to unconditional surrender

**August 21**
Truman orders an end to the Lend-Lease aid program

**August 28**
U.S. Army and Marine forces arrive on the Japanese home islands to begin military occupation

**September 2**
Japanese officials formally surrender to the Allies aboard the USS *Missouri* in Tokyo Bay

**September 8**
MacArthur arrives in Tokyo to assume control of the occupation

**September 9**
Some one million Japanese surrender to General Chiang Kai-shek in Nanjing, China

**October 24**
The United Nations charter is ratified by its five permanent members: the United States, Britain, France, China, and the Soviet Union

**November 20**
The Nuremberg Trials open; for the next ten months a tribunal of Allied jurists will pass judgment on scores of Nazi war criminals

# FUGITIVE NAZIS IN SOUTH AMERICA

*Nazi leaders were sentenced to death after the war, but a few managed to escape the grip of Nuremberg and sneak into South America.*

In July 1972, an old man complaining of intense abdominal pain checked himself into a hospital in Sao Paulo, Brazil. The admitting physician noted that the man, obviously a foreigner, looked much older than the 46 years listed on his identity card but accepted the excuse that the date was misprinted. The man had an intestinal blockage: He had a nervous habit of chewing the ends of his walrus mustache, and over the years the bits of hair had accumulated in his digestive tract. The man had good reason to be nervous. He was Josef Mengele, a Nazi war criminal, who had been hiding in South America since the end of the Second World War.

After the war, many Nazi war criminals escaped to start new lives in nonextraditing countries like Argentina, Brazil, Uruguay, Chile, and Paraguay. They lived in constant danger of discovery, though in several cases, friendly dictatorships turned a blind eye in exchange for services. Many were found and kidnapped by the Israeli *Mossad,* tried, and sentenced for their crimes. Some, including Mengele, the cruel concentration camp doctor, eluded capture until their deaths. Mengele died by accidental drowning in 1979.

South America was a welcome refuge from the net of international justice that swept Europe at the end of the war. Several of the countries had enjoyed friendly prewar relations with the Reich— Argentina, in particular, was sympathetic to the plight of the fugitive Nazi war criminals. Many Nazis found positions in Argentina's Fascist government, controlled by Juan Perón. His wife, Evita, later traveled to Europe, ostensibly on a goodwill tour. However, she was actually raising funds for the safe passage of war criminals.

In Argentina, Uruguay, Chile, Bolivia, and Paraguay, scores of Nazis found familiar traditions of elitism and militarism. Perhaps most importantly, corruption in those countries made it easy to obtain false identification papers through bribery.

## NAZIS WHO SLIPPED OVERSEAS

- **Walter Rauff** invented the Auschwitz "death trucks" that killed more than half a million prisoners. Rauff was arrested in Santiago, Chile, in 1963, but the Chilean authorities released him after three months in jail. Many believe that Rauff designed the concentration camps where Chilean political prisoners were killed under the Pinochet regime.

- **Paul Schäfer** served in the Hitler Youth. Years later, he was arrested for pedophile activities while working at an orphanage in postwar Germany. Schaefer fled to Chile where he established a bizarre settlement known as *Colonia Dignida,* in which abuse, torture, and drugs were used to control cult followers. The adults were taught to call Schaefer "The *Führer*"; the colony's children called him "Uncle." Schaefer sexually abused hundreds of children in the decades that followed. The colony prospered economically and, despite information from escaped members, it remained in operation until 1993 when Schaeffer went into hiding. He managed to escape justice until 2006 when he was sentenced to 20 years in prison.

- **Klaus Barbie,** the notorious "Butcher of Lyon," became a counterintelligence officer for the U.S. military which helped him to flee to Bolivia soon after the war. In 1971, he assisted in a military coup that brought the brutal General Hugo Banzar to power. Barbie went on to head the South American cocaine ring called Amadeus that generated funds for political activity friendly to U.S. interests in the region. When a more moderate government came to power in 1983, Barbie was deported to France, where he was tried and convicted of war crimes. He died of cancer after spending four years in prison.

## NUEVA GERMANIA

German colonists had settled in South America long before the start of the Second World War. One of the more outlandish attempts occurred in the late-nineteenth century when Elisabeth Nietzsche-Forster and her husband Bernhard Forster led a group of 14 families to Paraguay. They founded a utopian village dedicated to anti-Semitism and an "authentic rebirth of racial feeling." They called their remote settlement Nueva Germania. Within two years, many of the colonists had died of disease, Bernhard drank himself to death, and Elisabeth returned to Europe where she successfully worked to have her husband's writings adopted as the favorite philosophy of the Nazi Party. After the Second World War, many fugitive Nazis were rumored to have sheltered in Nueva Germania, including Josef Mengele.

## SUBMARINES FULL OF NAZI GOLD

Despite evidence suggesting that Hitler's secretary, Martin Bormann, died in the streets of Berlin in 1945, rumors persist about his escape to South America. According to the same accounts, Bormann witnessed his *Führer's* suicide and then followed prearranged orders to escape to Argentina, where he had been transporting large amounts of Reich gold and money using submarines. In the final days of the war, go the stories, Bormann and dozens of other Nazi officials left Germany in ten submarines, five of which arrived safely in Argentina. Waiting for them was a friendly government and the stolen wealth of Europe, safely deposited by the Peróns in Swiss bank accounts. Some estimates place the accumulated wealth at $800 million.

✳   ✳   ✳

- *Bariloche, a village in western Argentina, is notorious as a postwar haven for fugitive Nazis. SS captain Erich Priebke lived happily in the town until his arrest the late 1990s for the 1944 massacre of 335 Italian civilians. Some other fugitive Nazis who called Bariloche home include Joseph Schwammberger, excommandant of the Polish ghetto at Przemysl; Hans Ulrich Rudel, onetime head of the Luftwaffe; Frederich Lantschner, former Nazi governor of the Tyrol region of Austria; even Auschwitz death doctor Josef Mengele, who took his driver's test (twice) in Bariloche in the 1940s.*

# THE ALLIES' FINAL SOLUTION

*Hitler's Thousand Year Reich ended in Nuremberg, a Bavarian town that once played host to great propaganda rallies that symbolized the beginning of the Nazi era. But instead of a stadium filled with chanting, saluting followers of National Socialism, the final verdict on Hitler's regime was issued by a solemn panel of robed justices who sentenced the Führer's top lieutenants to confinement and death.*

## PROSECUTING THE CRIME OF WAR

The idea of trying Nazi leaders—rather than shooting, exiling, or paroling them—had been stirring within the Roosevelt Administration since the fall of 1944, when Colonel Murray Bernays, an officer in the War Department's Special Project Branch, proposed treating German war crimes as a criminal conspiracy. In their February 1945 summit at Yalta, Roosevelt, Stalin, and Churchill agreed to put Nazi ringleaders on trial at the conclusion of the war.

On May 2, six days before the German surrender, Truman appointed U.S. Supreme Court Justice Robert Jackson as chief U.S. prosecutor for Nazi war crimes. Beginning in late June, Jackson held a series of meetings with prosecutors from Allied nations to select the site of the tribunals and the procedures to be used. Over Soviet objections, the courthouse selected was the Nuremberg's Palace of Justice, and on August 8, 1945, the Allies signed an agreement in London to allow prosecution of Hitler's top henchmen to proceed under an eight-judge International Military Tribunal.

From a collection of hundreds of Nazis and German leaders, the prosecution grouped defendants into several categories: senior Nazi leaders, medical doctors, Nazi judges, *Einsatzgruppen* (mobile paramilitary groups charged with the actual killing), and heads of German ministries. The Allies broke their case into separate trials for each of these groups. The first tribunal—the major-figures trial—began on November 20, 1945, and set the stage for the world's first close-up look at the men who plunged the world into darkness and destruction.

## THE MANY FACES OF EVIL

The defendants were an assortment of villains who, to the surprise of many observers, were mostly ordinary-looking fellows—family men who seemed more likely to hold jobs as accountants and corporate board members, rather than monsters responsible for the deaths of millions of innocent people. Only a few looked like they might be capable of running an industrial killing machine.

The major figures included two dozen of Hitler's top civilian and military leaders. Those most closely associated with the Nazi atrocities included:

- **Hermann Göring,** Hitler's second-in-command and head of the *Luftwaffe*. Göring had presided over Germany's internal plan to confiscate Jewish property, looted valuable art and other treasures from across Europe, and mused in 1941 about Germany's need to kill or condemn to starvation some 20 million Eastern Europeans during the invasion of Russia, to make room for German expansion.

- **Hans Frank,** governor-general of occupied Poland who earned the nickname "Jew Butcher of Krakow." He encouraged the execution of Jews on sight, deported slaves to Germany, and implemented a policy of reprisal shootings against Polish civilians in retaliation for partisan killings of German soldiers.

- **Ernst Kaltenbrunner,** head of Germany's security apparatus that included the Gestapo, the SD, and the Criminal Police. Kaltenbrunner had ordered prisoners in Dachau and other concentration camps to be liquidated before the camps could be liberated by the Allies, and was primarily responsible for the implementation of Hitler's Final Solution to the "Jewish Problem."

- **Alfred Rosenberg,** Hitler's minister for the eastern occupied territories and the top Nazi ideologue. Rosenberg set slave-labor quotas for Reich ministries, crafted policies for the Germanization of occupied territories, and segregated Jews into ghettos that facilitated their liquidation by Kaltenbrunner's groups.

- **Wilhelm Frick,** a lawyer by trade who, as Minister of the Interior, signed the Nuremberg Laws suppressing Jews and implementing the Nazi goal of "racial purity."

- **Fritz Sauckel,** Germany's minister of slave labor, responsible for the conscription of more than five million slaves for Nazi projects.

- **Arthur Seyss-Inquart,** Germany's minister of the occupied Netherlands. Under his rule, some 40,000 Dutch citizens were killed as hostages and another 50,000 died of starvation. The industrious governor helped eliminate over half the Dutch Jewish population.

- **Joachim von Ribbentrop,** Hitler's foreign minister. Ribbentrop helped speed the deportation of Jews to death camps in the east and participated in planning the invasions of Poland and Russia.

- **Rudolf Hess,** Nazi Party functionary and Hitler's deputy. Hess ran the party machinery until 1941, when he flew to London in a quixotic attempt to broker an end to the war.

- **Wilhelm Keitel,** the German High Command's chief of staff. Keitel planned the invasions of Czechoslovakia, Poland, and the Low Countries, and signed orders authorizing nighttime arrests of Resistance members and the killing of captured enemy commandos.

- **Alfred Jodl,** chief of operations for the German High Command, who planned the German invasions of the Netherlands, Belgium, Norway, Poland, Greece, and Yugoslavia.

Other major defendants included Admiral Karl Dönitz, who succeeded Hitler and negotiated the surrender to the Allies; Albert Speer, minister of armaments; and Julius Streicher, editor of the Nazi newspaper *Der Stürmer* and one of Hitler's most violently anti-Semitic propagandists. Another leader, Hitler's secretary, Martin Bormann, was not apprehended but was tried in absentia. (His remains were found in Berlin years later.)

## EVIDENCE OF GUILT

The Allied prosecutors built their case around a conspiracy implemented by Nazi and German organizations, including the Nazi Party, German civilian ministries (such as the Gestapo and Labor Ministry), paramilitary ministries (such as the SS and SA), and the *Wehrmacht* high command.

The prosecutors relied heavily upon documentary evidence—chilling because of its coldly impersonal records of the deaths of millions—but also used grisly physical evidence to demonstrate the human cost of the Nazi crimes. Tattooed human skin from Buchenwald—used to make lampshades and other household furnishings for the camp's commandant—riveted the attention of the justices and onlookers, as did grotesque items such as the preserved shrunken head of an executed Pole used as a paperweight by one death camp commandant. In addition, films and photographs taken by Allied liberators were given a human voice by the tearful testimony of witnesses to mass executions and inhuman brutalities of concentration camps and racial ghettos. *Eisatzgruppen* leaders and death camp commandants confirmed the eyewitness accounts; they were open about their methods of rounding up and executing men, women, and children by the thousands. The evidence brought many onlookers—and even some of the defendants—to tears, while other defendants simply looked away, or appeared bored with graphic evidence of their labors. After a day of watching ghastly footage of stacked bodies being bulldozed into mass graves while skeletal survivors stared at the cadavers, Göring quipped in his cell that evening, "It was such a good afternoon, too, then they showed that awful film and just spoiled everything."

## DEFENDING INHUMANITY

The defendants tried to exonerate themselves in different ways. The pompous Göring harangued the courtroom with statements deflecting his guilt and defending certain Nazi policies. Albert

Speer willingly (some say *cleverly*) accepted a major degree of guilt for his part in Nazi atrocities. Others, such as Generals Keitel and Jodl, insisted that they were simply following orders as soldiers were bound to do—notwithstanding that the Allies explicitly refused to allow "following orders" as a defense to crimes against humanity.

## THE FINAL VERDICT

On October 1, 1946, the International Military Tribunal rendered its verdicts. Eleven of the twenty-one principal defendants, including Göring, Kaltenbrunner, Keitel, and Rosenberg, were sentenced to hang. Three others were acquitted, and the rest were sentenced to long prison terms. All appeals were rejected 12 days later, and on October 16, ten of the eleven condemned men dropped through the gallows into their final judgment. (Göring, one of the most culpable Nazis, cheated the hangman by swallowing a smuggled cyanide pill hours before his scheduled execution.)

The Nuremberg Trials continued with 11 subsequent trials of lesser-known defendants. Fourteen members of German killing units and seven Nazi doctors were sentenced to death, and many other members of German ministries and military groups received varying sentences. Appeals continued through 1951, bringing an end to the immediate Allied problem of how to use civilized means to punish the architects of some of the century's worst crimes.

☆ ☆ ☆

• *During Nuremberg prisoner interviews with* Der Stürmer *publisher Julius Streicher in 1946, U.S. Army psychiatrist Leon Goldensohn was struck by Streicher's obsessive preoccupation with the Jews. Although Streicher had little formal education, he assured Goldensohn that he was an expert on all aspects of Jewry—so much so, in fact, that he claimed he knew Goldensohn was Jewish the moment the psychiatrist walked into his cell. While he spoke, Streicher repeatedly squinted, looked at his nails, and licked his lips. He had no rational explanations for his opinions.*

# Timeline

## 1946

**January 1**
Emperor Hirohito tells his subjects that contrary to belief, he is not a divine being

**January 24**
The International Atomic Energy Commission is established to help regulate emerging nuclear weapons technology

**October 1**
High-ranking Nazi officials, including Hermann Göring, Hans Frank, Joachim von Ribbentrop, and Arthur Seyss-Inquart, are sentenced to hang; Göring will escape the fate by taking his own life shortly before his scheduled execution

**March 5**
Winston Churchill proclaims that an "Iron Curtain" of Communist despotism divides Eastern Europe from Western Europe

**April 10**
War crimes trials of high-ranking Japanese begin in Tokyo

## 1947

**June 5**
U.S Secretary of State George Marshall announces a sweeping plan for economic support and rebuilding of Europe; the program will become known as the Marshall Plan

**June 14**
The Auschwitz-Birkenau Memorial and Museum opens its first permanent exhibition on the seventh anniversary of the arrival of the Nazi camp's first prisoners

**July 4**
The United States grants independence to the Philippines

## 1948

**April 3**
The Marshall Plan is signed into law by President Truman

**May 14**
Britain's mandate to govern Palestine expires; Palestine is divided into the state of Israel and the kingdom of Jordan

## 1949

**April 4**
The United States, Canada, and several Western European nations form the North Atlantic Treaty Organization (NATO)

**October 1**
In a victory for China's Communist Party, Mao Tse-tung proclaims the People's Republic of China

## 1951

**September 8**
Forty-nine nations sign the Japanese Peace Treaty in San Francisco, officially ending World War II and reestablishing Japanese sovereignty

**October 19**
President Truman signs an act formally ending World War II in the Atlantic Theater

**October 26-27**
Election victory for Britain's Conservative Party brings Winston Churchill, 77 years old, back as prime minister

# PUSHING THE NUCLEAR BUTTON

*Truman's "decision was one of noninterference—basically a decision not to upset the existing plan."*
—General Leslie R. Groves on President Harry Truman's decision to drop an atomic bomb on Japan

Prior to taking office as president in April 1945, Truman knew nothing of the Manhattan Project. He had served only 83 days as vice president, during which his time with Roosevelt was limited. The bomb had never been mentioned to him, nor had many of Roosevelt's intentions about foreign policy. Truman had a lot to catch up on. He worked with Roosevelt's trusted military, scientific, diplomatic, and political advisers to learn in days what had taken years of planning and research.

## OPTION A: INVASION

As early as 1943, the United States had begun to make plans for invading Japan. When Germany surrendered in the spring of 1945, attention shifted to subduing the Japanese home islands, which were defended by some two million soldiers. The plan for invasion was called Operation Downfall. The first stage, Operation Olympic, would require roughly 767,000 Allied soldiers to invade Kyushu, Japan's large southern island, on November 1, 1945. Olympic would be followed by Operation Coronet in March 1946, an invasion of Honshu, Japan's largest island, which would require some 28 divisions.

Truman worried that Operation Downfall would result in "an Okinawa from one end of Japan to the other." He later claimed that the United States might sustain as many as one million casualties—to say nothing of the loss of Japanese lives. Meanwhile, Japan would continue the fight with its army of three million men stationed throughout China, destroying thousands of Chinese, Japanese, and Soviet lives on Asia's mainland.

## OPTION B: STAY THE COURSE

On the other hand, Truman considered that perhaps more of the same could force Japan to surrender. Firebombing of Japanese cities by American B-29s had leveled many of Japan's major cities with a force far greater than the estimated power of the atomic bomb. Air and sea power might work. But despite the repeated raids, so far Japan had remained defiant.

## OPTION C: RELY ON RUSSIA

If the Soviet Union entered the war against Japan, Truman felt that Emperor Hirohito might persuade his cabinet warmongers that unconditional surrender was preferable to conventional destruction by the two emerging superpowers. However, discussions at the Potsdam Conference in July had revealed disagreements and tensions between the Big Three over control of Europe and policy with Japan.

## OPTION D: DROP THE BOMB

Political and moral considerations weighed heavily on the decision to use atomic weapons. Influential scientists petitioned Truman not to use the atomic bomb, predicting erosion of U.S. moral authority if it became the first nation to unleash nuclear destruction. Conversely, more than $2 billion had already been spent developing the weapons, and the momentum for using them was in place. Some hoped the bombs' power could be used as a demonstration against Japan. Yet with only two live bombs in stock in July 1945 and with the technology still uncertain, the risk of a dud or the loss of one operational bomb was judged too great for the demonstration approach. The plan for a drop proceeded.

The United States, Britain, and China issued an ultimatum to Japan on July 26, 1945, demanding unconditional surrender under threat of "prompt and utter destruction." In the end, Japan remained outwardly unmoved by the Allied ultimatum, and Truman refused to alter existing plans to use the atomic bomb. He knew that using the bomb would end the lives of many Japanese citizens. But not using it would condemn many more citizens—of many countries—to more traditional deaths.

# THE CLOAK-AND-DAGGER AGENCY

*Spies, psychologists, paratroopers, partisans—the Office of Strategic Services had them all. Together they devised elaborate plans to trick and foil their foes.*

For most of its history, the U.S. government gathered intelligence—in an uncoordinated, albeit often effective, way—through the War, State, and Justice departments. That ended in 1941–42, under the pressures of global conflict, with the formation of the Office of Strategic Services (OSS). The OSS collected strategic intelligence; it also conducted espionage and special military ops.

The organization was led by William J. "Wild Bill" Donovan. A standout Columbia University football player (whence his nickname), he won the Medal of Honor in the First World War as a battalion commander in New York's "Fighting 69th" Infantry division. During Prohibition, he participated in the Justice Department's crackdown on bootlegging, becoming an expert in clandestine means of smuggling liquor. Donovan also spent time as a lawyer on Wall Street and earned the trust of President Roosevelt, who made him a major general.

By 1944, about 13,000 people were working for Wild Bill. Most of them held formal military ranks, usually in the army. OSS agents were often Ivy League graduates who were versed in foreign languages. They were hardy and adventurous.

Seven thousand five hundred agents were stationed overseas throughout Europe, the Middle East, most of Asia, and even in French Indochina to help Ho Chi Minh fight the Japanese occupiers. The OSS was shut out of Latin America, however, as that turf was guarded by the FBI and its bulldog chief J. Edgar Hoover.

Despite an international focus, the OSS's early missions, approved by Roosevelt, were domestic break-ins of the pro-Axis embassies of Vichy France and Fascist Spain in Washington, D.C. An under-world safecracker was imported from New York City to help.

## COVERT OPS IN EUROPE

The OSS was most active in Europe. Allen Welsh Dulles, who worked out of the U.S. legation in Bern, Switzerland, was the most notable operative there. His post was popularly known as "Hitler's Doorstep."

Dulles cultivated agents from France's prewar intelligence apparatus to spy on German troop movements. He made contact with *Wehrmacht* officers involved in the July 1944 attempt to assassinate Hitler (the men had helped prove their allegience by passing on data about the V-2 rocket). Still, Washington ordered Dulles not to cut any deals with the plotters. He was also case officer for super-spy Fritz Kolbe, an anti-Nazi courier in the German Foreign Ministry, who handed the OSS more than 2,500 mimeographed documents. The papers contained revelations on the Messerschmitt jet fighter and where the Germans expected the D-Day landings to be. Kolbe also played a role in fingering the notorious Axis spy "Cicero," working in the home of Britain's ambassador to Turkey.

"My aim," Kolbe wrote, "was to help shorten the war for my unfortunate countrymen, and to help concentration-camp inmates avoid further suffering."

In Switzerland, near the end of the war, Dulles pulled off two more coups. In Operation Sunrise, he headed secret negotiations with SS General Karl Wolff for the surrender of the large German forces in Italy several weeks before Germany's surrender. He also cut a deal, based on a tip from Kolbe, with Major General Reinhardt Gehlen, the chief of German intelligence on the Eastern Front. In exchange for lenient treatment of Gehlen and his colleagues, some of them Nazis, Gehlen handed over a buried cache of microfilm on Soviet military doctrine.

Another OSS leader in Europe was William J. Casey, head of its London office of Special Intelligence. His job, as the Allies advanced to the German border in 1944–45, was to plant agents in Germany who would scout out military and industrial sites. Since too few American spies could pass as Germans, Casey used Germans—he recruited willing POWs and supplied them with fake IDs and custom-made clothes. About 200 such agents were slipped in, from Bremen to Stuttgart. Many of the agents collected useful intelligence, though 36 were captured or killed.

The most famous OSS unit in Europe was the "Jedburghs." These were three-man teams who parachuted into France to disrupt German transport and communications after the Normandy invasion. There were 95 teams, each consisting of an OSS officer, a British officer, and a Free French radioman. One Jedburgh trio was Team Bruce, commanded by Major William Colby, code name "Berkshire." His squad hooked up with the French Resistance outside Paris. Together they blocked roads and tore up railroad tracks used by German reinforcements trying to stop Patton. Other Jedburghs directed Allied bombers for crushing strikes on the *Panzer Lehr* division before it reached the Normandy front. The price was stiff: In France, 22 of the 285 special operatives were killed.

## STOKING RESISTANCE IN BURMA

In Asia, the most notable OSS success was in Burma, now Myanmar. That country was occupied by a major Japanese force with only small Allied units—U.S. Major General Frank Merrill's "Marauders" and British Major General Orde Wingate's "Chindits"—fighting back. But the occupiers had a major disadvantage—their brutality. After witnessing the Japanese slaughter hordes of Kachins, the indigenous fighters were ripe to rebel. OSS strategist Millard Preston Goodfellow formulated a plan to stoke a revolt through OSS operatives, dubbed Detachment 101. Burma theater commander General Joseph "Vinegar Joe" Stilwell grudgingly signed off on the scheme after handpicking the unit's commander, a tough, burly army captain, Carl Eifler.

Across a 600-mile front, the 120-man unit signed up 11,000 villagers, training and providing them arms. Shrugging off dengue fever, storms dropping 12 inches of rain, and temperatures rising above

120 degrees, Eifler's army spotted Japanese jungle outposts for U.S. 10th Air Force bombers. They also picked up downed pilots from General Claire Chennault's "Flying Tigers" carrying war materials to China.

Phantoms of the forest, the Kachins and their OSS advisors terrified their foes with sneak attacks, taking body parts as trophies. In three years of vicious fighting, the kill ratio of Allied to Japanese dead reached incredible proportions. Perhaps 5,400 Japanese died, while 338 Kachins and 27 Americans were lost in combat.

A skeptical Stillwell once asked a Kachin commander, "How can you be so sure of your numbers [of slain Japanese]?" The OSS-trained soldier dumped a sack on the general's desk.

"Just count the ears," he replied, "and divide by two."

## WHOSE SIDE ARE YOU ON?

The OSS had weaknesses, especially internal security. The agency was riddled with foreign spies—not from the Axis, but the Soviet Union. The Venona files of intercepted Soviet cables, confirmed by Stalin-era archives, show that at least six OSS officers were in Moscow's employ. The highest-ranking double agent was Duncan Lee, a descendant of Confederate Robert E. Lee and confidential assistant to Wild Bill himself.

Lee informed the Kremlin of D-Day preparations and OSS operations in China, where Mao's moles penetrated the agency's training camps. A chief OSS researcher, Maurice Halperin—Soviet code name "Hare"—handed Moscow U.S. diplomatic cables on Yugoslavia, Greece, and Poland, all battlegrounds in the coming Cold War.

## PSYCHOLOGY AND WAR

In addition to espionage and commando strikes, the OSS built a reputation for quirky, artistic endeavors. Its Morale Operations Branch jump-started the new field of psychological warfare. German-born American star Marlene Dietrich was recruited to record songs radioed to homesick German troops.

In Operation Sauerkraut, agents—mostly disaffected German POWs—were slipped through lines in Italy to distribute fake leaflets and rumors aimed at busting Nazi psyches. Near Bologna they passed around phony stories, for example: "Himmler found a *Doppelganger* ('double') for Hitler and presented that man as Hitler himself. The Führer has disappeared; it is possible he is dead, seriously ill, or that he fled to some foreign country like Switzerland or Argentina."

The operatives even stopped at public houses to drop off ersatz toilet paper with text that read, "Comrades! Stop this s***! We do not fight for Germany but only for Hitler. They want us to hold out until the last bullet. However, we need the last bullets to free Germany from this SS-s***. Enough!"

Some of the same expert forgers from Operation Sauerkraut worked on Operation Cornflakes. It created replicas of German postage stamps, altered to show Hitler's face in the form of a skull. The risks the Allies took to "deliver" mail carrying the stamps were astounding. Aircraft bombed German trains that included postal cars, then dropped bags of fake letters onto the wreckage. Rescuers assumed the bags had been on the trains, and routed the tampered missives, by the tens of thousands, into the German postal system.

Even in the bloodiest war of all, spying could be fun.

## A Career Like No Other

Of all OSS employees, perhaps the best-known was Julia McWilliams, a senior clerk in Wild Bill's office. Intensely sociable, and 6-foot-2, Julia "was a tomboy who loved competing with boys in hiking, hunting, and playing golf." In 1944, she was assigned to Kandy, Ceylon (now Sri Lanka), to handle the top-secret papers for the invasion of Malaya.

In 1945, Julia and future husband Paul, an OSS graphic artist, transferred to China, where she clerked for agency dealings with Chiang Kai-shek and Mao Tse-tung. She grew fascinated with the spicy cuisines of Szechuan. After the war, Julia married Paul, last name Child, and became a world-famous chef.

# INDEX

# AUTHOR CREDITS

✭ ✭ ✭

**Illustrations:** Daisy de Puthod

**Fact-checkers:** Joe Bator, Regina Montgomery, Katrina O'Brien, Marilyn Perlberg, Richard Sauers, Ph.D.

**Contributing writers:** Robert Bullington, Alan C. Carey, William W. David, Jonathan W. Jordan, J. K. Kelley, Bill Leary, David Lesjak, Bill Martin, Ed Moser, Bill Sasser

**Robert Bullington** earned his master's in English from the University of Virginia and currently makes his home in Richmond, where he spends his time writing, raising a family, and performing with Nettwerk Recording Artists the Hackensaw Boys.

**Alan C. Carey** began his professional writing career in 1999 and is the author of several books on World War II aviation-related topics. In addition to writing, Mr. Carey conducts research services for individuals, the media, and businesses who seek information regarding U.S. Navy and Marine Corps aviation. He currently resides in Round Rock, Texas, with his wife and two daughters.

**William W. David** lives in Jacksonville, Florida. He is an IT professional by day and writes in his spare time. He hopes that someday the order of the two activities will be reversed.

**Jonathan W. Jordan** is the author of numerous articles on military history and the books *Lone Star Navy: Texas, the Fight for the Gulf of Mexico* and *The Shaping of the American West.* He is currently researching a book on the American high command in World War II.

**J. K. Kelley** has a B.A. in history from the University of Washington in Seattle. He resides in the sagebrush of eastern Washington with his wife, Deb, and his parrot, Alex.

**Bill Leary** was employed in management positions with AT&T before retiring to write books and magazine articles. Having served in the Pacific during WWII as a Japanese translator, his experiences furnish background for many of his publications.

**David Lesjak** has been interested in military history since he was a teenager. He collects war-related Disney items and has written one book on the topic. Visit his blog for more info: *toonsatwar.blogspot.com.*

**Bill Martin** is a freelance writer whose diverse portfolio of work includes creative, media, and business writing. He holds a B.A. in history and political science from the University of Toronto and lives in Toronto with his wife, Marianna, and three daughters, Samantha, Paige, and Erica.

**Ed Moser** is a former presidential speechwriter and writer for *The Tonight Show.* He also authored *The Politically Correct Guide to American History.* He currently works as an editorial consultant in IT and biotech.

**Bill Sasser** is a freelance writer and journalist based in New Orleans. He writes for *Salon.com* and *The Christian Science Monitor,* among other publications.

"Life Amid the Falling Bombs: Survival Stories from the Blitz" is excerpted from *WW2 People's War,* an online archive of wartime recollections gathered by the BBC. The stories in the archive were contributed by members of the public. The views expressed are theirs, and copyright rests with them. Texts from these stories may not be reproduced without prior permission from the BBC. The stories included here, and many others, can be found at *bbc.co.uk/ww2peopleswar.*

"V-E Day: A Day of Mixed Emotions" contains excerpts from *The Day the War Ended: May 8, 1945—Victory in Europe* by Martin Gilbert. The copyright rests with Gilbert and has been reprinted with permission from Henry Holt and Company.

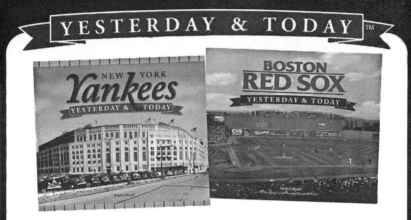

# Hope you enjoyed this Armchair Reader™

You'll find the rest of this year's crop quite exciting.
Please look for these titles wherever books are sold.

**ARMCHAIR**
**• READER™ •**

## Grand Slam Baseball

## Civil War

## The Extraordinary Book of Lists

## The Amazing Book of History

## The Book of Incredible Information

## Coming attractions

Armchair Reader™ The Colossal Reader
Armchair Reader™ Weird, Scary & Unusual

Visit us at *www.armchairreader.com*
to learn all about our other great books from
West Side Publishing, or just to let us know
what your thoughts are about our books.
We love to hear from all our readers.

WEST
SIDE
PUBLISHING